Stagnation, retrograde change or positive progress?

Vignettes from the journey of the OBC communities in the process of change in India

Stagnation, retrograde change or positive progress?

Vignettes from the journey of the OBC communities in the process of change in India

Edited by
H.S. Verma
Nadeem Hasnain

Under the auspices of
Centre for Social Action and Development
Lucknow

SERIALS PUBLICATIONS
NEW DELHI

First Published - 2006

ISBN : 81-8387-010-4

Published by

SERIALS PUBLICATIONS
4830/24, Ansari Road, Darya Ganj
New Delhi-110002 (India)
Phone : 91-11-23245225
Fax : 91-11-23272135
E-mail: serials@satyam.net.in,
serialspublications@vsnl.net
Website : www.seriealspub.com

Contents

Preface ix

About the editors and contributors xi

1. Stagnation, retrogatde change, or positive progress? Vignettes from the journey of the OBC communities in the process of change in India 1
   H.S. Verma & Nadeem Hasnain

PART I: FARMING/SERVICE COMMUNITIES

2. Caste mobility and gilding of rituals: The impact of Gulf migration on Ezhavas of Kerala 21
   Prema Kurien

3. The Kolis of Gujarat: A conspectus 45
   Lancy Lobo

4. Miniscule progress in the midst of mainstream stagnation: The Kurmis of Uttar Pradesh 70
   H. S. Verma & Rakesh Varma

5. Social structure, people's movement and the role of OBCs: A case of Baliapal movement in Orissa 102
   D. R. Sahu

PART II: PASTORAL COMMUNITIES

6. Discarding the composite cultural inheritance and ushering in orthodoxy? Cultural change among the Meos of Mewat 121
   Abha Chauhan

7. Cultural change in a pastoral community: The Gollas of Karnataka 146
   M. Gurulingaiah

8. The Raikas of Rajasthan 170
   Vinay Kumar Srivastava

PART III: FISHING COMMUNITIES

9. The fisherfolk's movement in Goa: A conflict between tradition and modernity — 209
R.B. Patil, Rekha Ramesh Gaonkar & Maria de ceu Rodrigues

10. Elementary structure of desire in South Indian kinship: A case of a fishing caste of coastal Andhra Pradesh — 227
Charles W. Nuckolls

11. Ethnographic profile of Vadabalijas of Andhra Pradesh — 246
S.V. Sudhakar

PART IV: ARTISAN COMMUNITIES

12. Rural artisans in Bhavnagar, Gujarat: A study of their socio-economic conditions — 255
C.N. Ray

13. Urban settlement patterns of artisans in Karnataka: Geographical expression of thought — 279
Jan Brouwer

PART V: OTHER TYPES

14. A rural community in the process of modernization: A study of three Nepalese villages of rural Assam — 293
K.P. Upadhyaya

15. Influence of Gulf migration on the identity assertion patterns: Denominational contestations and the emerging public sphere among the Muslims of Kerala — 307
Shareena Banu C.P.

16. Social isolation and backwardness of an ethnic community — 334
Monirul I. Khan

ANNEXURES: LANDMARK DOCUMENTS ON THE OBC PROBLEMATIC

A. **Findings/recommendations of Commissions/action taken on their reports** — 347

D-1. The First Backward Classes Commission, 1956 and the view of Mandal Commission on the treatment meted out to its report

D-2. The Memorandum of action taken on the recommendations of First Backward Classes Commission report, 1956

D-3. Criteria adopted by the Mandal to identify the SEBCs
D-4. Recommendations of the Mandal Commission
D-5. The adequacy or otherwise of representation of the backward classes in public services of Kerala: Context and important findings of the K.K. Narendran Commission.

B. GOs on reservations for the OBCs 373
D-6. Communal G.Os 1921, 1922, 1928
D-7. G.O. on backward classes by the GoI, dated February 1, 1980
D-8. Statement of the then PM and the OM dated 13 August 1990 (issued by the V.P.Singh Government)
D-9. The OM, dated September 25, 1991 (issued by the P.V. Narsimha Rao Government)

C. Authoritative judicial verdict on reservations 381
D-10. Neeta Verma: Analysis of judgment of the Special Constitution Bench of the Supreme Court on Indra Sawhney case

D. Creamy layer 400
D-11. Report of the Expert Committee for specifying the criteria for identifying of socially advanced persons among the socially and educationally backward classes (Ramnandan Prasad)
D-12. Criteria adopted by the Government of India for the identification of creamy layer among the OBCs
D-13. Comparative analysis of creamy layer criteria recommended by the Uttar Pradesh Expert Committee (Umesh Chandra) and provisions actually made in Schedule-II of the *Uttar Pradesh Lok Sewa Adhiniyam*, 1994

E. Listing of the OBC communities by the Central and state governments 422
D-14. Number of communities listed as the OBCs in the Mandal Commission, States/Union Territories and Central lists

F. Consequential proposals on empowerment of the OBCs in Plan documents 424
D-15. Development and empowerment of the OBCs as viewed by the Working Group on the Empowerment of the OBCs for the Tenth Five Year Plan, 2001

Index 427

Preface

One of the curious but shocking episodes in the realm of social science's investigation and discourse in India especially with reference to sociology/ social anthropology is the utter neglect of what we know and identify today as the OBC communities. This was despite the fact that the OBCs constitute the largest segment of the Indian society. They remain as the single most neglected social-constitutional category even today. The present volume coming in quick succession after H.S.Verma's ***The OBCs and the Ruling Classes in India*** (2005) and ***The OBCs and the Dynamics of Social Exclusion in India*** (2005) will definitely make the social scientists sit up and ponder over their acts of omission.

When one compares the present volume with the two mentioned above one would find that it is in continuity with the themes of the treatment meted out to the OBCs by the ruling classes and the dynamics of social exclusion. The present volume is largely ethnographic in nature, and deals with the 'lived life' of different types of OBC communities – from farming to pastoral and from fishing to service communities. It is not only ethnography in the anthropological tradition but also brings out different facets of social change among the OBC communities of India.

First of all, the editors wish to express their heartfelt thanks to the contributing authors for not only responding to the invitation extended to them but also bearing with them the long delay caused in bringing out this volume. We also thank the Ethnographic and Folk Culture Society for allowing us to reproduce three papers written by Charles W. Nuckolls, Jan Brouwer and Monirul I. Khan that appeared in different issues of their internationally renowned journal, *The Eastern Anthropologist*. We are grateful to Shri Rakesh Varma who helped us in assembling different papers and putting them on the CD in a logical sequence. Last, but not the least, we wish to thank Mr. S.K. Jha and Mr. Vijay Kumar of Serials Publications for producing the volume the way we wished and taking minimal time in producing it.

H.S. Verma
Nadeem Hasnain
Editors

About the Editors and Contributors

Editors

Harnam Singh Verma (b. 1942) is a senior sociologist who has worked in such prestigious institutions as the *NIRD, Hyderabad (1965-1971), CIDCO Ltd, Mumbai (1971-1974), IIM, Ahmedabad (1975-1977), GIDS, Lucknow (1977-1982) and State Plg Com, U.P. (1982-1993).* He has also taught full courses at the TISS, Mumbai *as* a visiting faculty (1971-72,1972-73). He was the Member-Secretary-Coordinator of *the Expert Committee on Creamy Layer* and a Member of the Committee for *Fixation of the Percentage of Reservations for the OBCs*, both appointed by the Government of Uttar Pradesh in 1993.He was a Member, *State Commission for the Backward Classes, Uttar Pradesh and a Member of the Working Group on Empowerment of the OBCs of the Tenth Five Year Plan.* He has authored/co-authored / edited /co-edited nine books, written two dozen monographs, contributed thirty pieces to books edited by others and published 44 research papers in prestigious national and international journals. *Social Change in Rural Areas, Industrial Families in India: An enquiry in to nature of their entrepreneurship, Bombay, New Bombay and Metropolitan Region: Growth process and planning lessons, The OBCs and the ruling classes in India*, and *The OBCs and the dynamics of social exclusion in India* are some of his books that are rated as classics. He has been working on the OBCs for the last 14 years. His email ID is: *harnamverma@rediffmail.com.*

Nadeem Hasnain is a Professor of Social Anthropology, University of Lucknow, Lucknow, India. He is the Honorary Director of *Centre for Social Action and Development*, a multidisciplinary research and advocacy organization for the marginalized sections of Indian society and also the editor of the internationally renowned journal *The Eastern Anthropologist* and the founder editor of *Islam and Muslim Societies: A Social Science Journal*. He has edited and authored several books notably *Bonded For Ever, Tribal India, Indian Anthropology, Shias and Shia Islam in India, Indian Society and Culture: Continuity and Change* and *Islam and Muslim Communities in South Asia*. An academician-social activist, he also regularly contributes to popular English, Hindi and Urdu magazines and newspapers and participates as an expert in panel discussions on the electronic media. His email ID is: csad.lucknow@rediffmail.com.

Contributors

Shareena Banu C.P. is a doctoral student at the Centre for the Study of Social Systems, School of Social Sciences, Jawaharlal Nehru University, New Delhi.

Jan Brouwer is working at the Centre for Advanced Research of Indigenous Knowledge Systems, Mysore, India.

Abha Chauhan has Masters and Ph D degrees in sociology and is presently a Reader in the Department of Sociology, Jammu University, Jammu.Her paper included in this volume is based on her research conducted at the Centre for Women Development Studies, New Delhi. Her areas of interest include social change, family and kinship. Her email ID is: acju@rediffmail.com.

M. Gurulingaiah (b.1967) has been a Senior Lecturer at the Post Graduate Department of Sociology, Mangalore University for the past ten years. He was associated with the Karnataka Urban Development Coastal Environment Project of the KUIDFC and helped in conducting its base line socio-economic infrastructure survey of ten coastal districts. His areas of interest are: stratification and mobility, sociology of the marginalized communities, rural sociology and tribal studies. His email ID is: mgurulingaiah@ rediffmail.com.

Rekha Ramesh Gaonkar has a doctorate in Economics and is presently Reader, and Head, Department of Economics, M.E.S.College of Arts and Commerce, Zuarinagar, Goa. Her research has focused on economic activities of the women, sectoral reforms and changes in different spheres of the Goan economy.

Lancy Lobo is a doctorate from the Department of Sociology, Delhi School of Economics, Delhi University and is presently the Director, Centre for Culture and Development, Vadodara, Earlier, he was the Director, Centre for Social Studies, Surat.He has contributed extensive research on the SCs, STs, and OBCs and minorities in rural and urban Gujarat. He has authored five books and published widely in reputed national and international journals. *The Tahakors of Gujarat* (1995), *Poor in urban India* (jointly with Bishwaroop Das: 2000), *Globalisation, Hindu nationalism and Christians in India* (2002), and *Shoshan ane aatankni aagama adivasio* (in Gujarati with Jayanti Macwan: 2003) are his notable books. He was International Woodstock Fellow in Georgetown University, Washington, D.C. in 2000.His email ID is: drlancylobo@rediffmail.com.

Monirul I.Khan is a Professor, Department of Sociology, University of Dhaka, Bangladesh.

Neeta Verma (b. 1970) has M.A. (Economics) from the University of Lucknow, Lucknow and a Post Graduate Diploma in Human Resource Management from the Barkatulla University, Bhopal. Three of her papers on the OBCs and the Panchayati Raj institutions in Uttar Pradesh, the press and opinion makers in the public discourse on the reservation issue and creamy layer among the OBCs and two monographs on Indra Sawhney judgment and organizational assessment of the Panchayati Raj institutions in Uttar Pradesh have received widespread national and international attention.

Prema Kurien is associate Professor of sociology at the Syracuse University, Syracuse, U.S.A. Her paper included in this volume is based on her dissertation fieldwork and is a much revised version of Chapter six of her book, *"Kaleidoscopic ethnicity, international migration and the reconstruction of community identities in India"* (Rutgers University Press, 2002) which won a book award (2003) from the Asia and Asian American section of the American Sociological Association. Her current research is on religion, ethnicity, and politics among Indian immigrants in the US and she is completing a book,*"Multiculturism and immigrant religion: The development of an American Hinduism" (under contract with Rutgers University Press).* She is also working on a project on Indian Christian Americans, *"Establishing an 'ethnic' Christianity: The challenges facing immigrant Indian churches in the US"*. She has published over fifteen journal articles and chapters in edited books based on empirical material from these three projects. She has also received several major grants and fellowships for her research. Her email ID is: kurienprema@aol.com.

Charles W. Nuckolls is a Professor of Anthropology, University of Albana, Tuscalasa, USA.

Rakesh Varma (b. October 1969) is a member of the Uttar Pradesh Provincial Civil Service (1997 batch) and has M.A. (Anthropology: 1993) and a PGD in HRD (1997). In spite of being a very busy civil servant, he has done pioneering work on project formulation, operationalisation, and computerized monitoring in the areas of urban development, NGOs and self-help groups. *Bhartiya Mahilaon Ke Samvaidhanik Adhikar and Swam Sahayata Samooh Se Swarojgar Tak* are two of his recent books. His email Id is: raakeshebox@yahoo.co.in

R.B.Patil (b July 1960) has a doctorate in Sociology and is presently Professor and Head, Department of Sociology, Shivaji University, Kolhapur.Recently, he has co-edited a book, *Environmental movements in India*. His areas of special interest include social movements, social problems and rural and urban studies.

Chandra Nath Ray has Masters degree in sociology from Kolkata University and Ph D in sociology from Kumaun University, Nainital.He is presently a Professor at the Centre for Environmental Planning and Technology, Ahmedabad. He has collaborated with a number of international agencies in conducting studies dealing with urban and rural poverty. *Liberalisation and urban services: Health and education* and *Politics of rural development: A comparative study of rural development programmes in Gujarat and West Bengal are* two of his recent books. He has organised and also participated in a larger number of seminars and workshops and published over a dozen research papers in reputed journals. His email Id is: cnr96@yahoo.com.

Maria de Ceu Rodrigues has a doctorate in Political Science and is presently Reader, and Head, Department of Political Science, M.E.S. College of Arts and Commerce, Zuarinagar, Goa. She has conducted research studies on electoral reforms, good governance and human rights.

Dipti Ranjan Sahu is a Senior Lecturer at the Department of Sociology, University of Lucknow, Lucknow. He is also Joint Secretary, Ethnographic and Folk Culture Society, Lucknow.

Vinay Kumar Srivastava has a Ph.D degree in Anthropology from the Cambridge University, Cambridge. He is a Professor in the Department of Anthropology, University of Delhi, Delhi. *Religious renunciation of a pastoral people* and *Methodology and fieldwork,* both published by Oxford University Press, are two of his well-known books. He is also one of the three editors of *The Eastern Anthropologist*, published by the Ethnographic and Folk Culture Society, Lucknow.

S.V. Sudhakar is a Professor at the Department of Social Work, Andhra University, Waltair.

K.P. Upadhyaya teaches in the Department of Sociology, Sikkim Government College, Tadong, Gangtok, India.

Stagnation, retrograde change or positive progress? Vignettes from the journey of the OBC communities in the process of change in India

H.S. Verma and Nadeem Hasnain

I

Despite the fact that the OBCs constitute the largest segment of India's population, they are the least studied and most neglected social-constitutional category. For social scientists in India the scheduled castes and scheduled tribes deserved to be studied as underprivileged sections of the Indian society but not the OBCs. They have been, by and large, invisible people.

The moment we talk about the underprivileged sections of the Indian society, the so-called OBC communities come to our mind. But the notion of underprivileged is basically a concept of negation. Logically speaking, unless there is a group or community exclusively having a right, immunity or benefits, for example, a number of privileges there cannot be any community which may be considered as underprivileged. Privilege is a prerogative and privileged communities are those that enjoy this. "Without conceiving a position of privilege (or communities having privileges such as special rights or a number of social-legal exemptions from doing certain obligations or undertaking liabilities), we cannot think of underprivileged communities. A community is underprivileged when it is denied of the enjoyments of normal privileges or rights of a society because of socio-cultural constraints such as low economic position, inferior social status, exploitations, historical antecedents, geo-political location and administrative indifferences"(B.B.Goswami: 1988).

The privileged and underprivileged people and groups can be observed everywhere throughout the world. It has, however, been observed that in the third world traditional societies this distinction is more marked than in the western societies. That is why the concern for the removal of disparities has drawn the attention of social thinkers and political leaders of this part of the world. In India, position and status in *Varnashrama* is an important criterion for an underprivileged social status. All the groups and *Jatis* from the *Shudra Varna* have been socially, economically and politically underprivileged while the *Brahmins* and other 'clean' castes are taken as ritually privileged people. However, religion also sometimes is taken as a criterion for deciding the privileged and underprivileged position.

Before going into the question of identification of the backward classes, it will be necessary to examine the problem of meaning. Also, it will be necessary to appraise oneself about the historical usage of some of the terms. In any discussion on the 'backwardness' of the OBCs, social backwardness is the most important component. The social backwardness of an individual and/or a group is society and time specific. The term 'OBC' was widely used by the British administration, and had come to mean 'other backward castes' by administrative usage. It is used in the Constitution of independent India to designate backward classes other than the scheduled castes and scheduled tribes. Article 15(4) refers to them as "socially and educationally backward classes of citizens", and Article 340 as "socially and educationally backward classes". Article 16(4) mentions "backward class of citizens" while Article 46 refers to "the educational and economic interests of the weaker sections of the people". There has been an increasing judicial concern with the question of the other backward classes (OBCs) ever since special provisions were made for them in the Constitution of independent India. State action for the OBCs has increased and the courts have been called upon increasingly to pronounce judgments on the appropriateness of methodology of this action.

As mentioned earlier in the preceding paragraph social backwardness and its implications have been a matter of academic interest to the sociologists and other social scientists. Social backwardness cannot be understood in isolation. It is an unalienable part of a social structure. The social structure places certain individuals and groups in a particular position of disadvantage. The deprivations accompanying such groups become normative and the value system of the society legitimizes it. The objective economic condition becomes the determinant of social backwardness. The factors responsible for social backwardness may change with changes in the economic structure but its total eradication cannot be achieved automatically. It requires effective institutional intervention in the socio-cultural domain and the politico-economic structure. Through organized efforts the victims of exploitation and deprivation try to break the shackles but the role of the State in such a situation becomes very important. "The state in the interest of overall social development takes actions to change the social structure and create conditions whereby socially backward groups and individuals can overcome their backwardness. The range of actions and ideologies adopted for reducing social backwardness fall in the political arena"(Ghanshyam Shah: 2002).

In the case of the exploitative caste system enjoying legal, religious and cultural sanctions, the role of Indian State becomes paramount. The socio-political exploitative environment of the caste system enabled the ruling classes/castes to continue their dominance and maintain the status quo in their favour. The constitutional framework provided an opportunity to the government to alter the traditional social structure by initiating a number of measures in the social, economic and political domain. But the caste/class character of the Indian state supported by the traditionally privileged castes never confronted the problem head on. Those who controlled the means of production and dominated the society in the past are still in an advantageous position not only to retain their economic hold but also to get more access to new sectors. Though some changes have come about in the agrarian situation in the country vis-à-vis backward castes if not for the *Dalits*/ scheduled castes, industrial entrepreneurship, modern professional occupations and management have a strong western cultural bias impervious to the aspirations of the backward castes and hence the dominance of the upper castes continues.

It is true that all members of the backward castes do not suffer from the same degree of backwardness. Modernization of skills and technology and secularization of institutions help some members in diminishing their backwardness but the crucial question is: can an individual overcome social backwardness without eradicating backwardness of caste as a whole or a large part of the caste? Moreover, many of the scholars look at caste as a determinant of life chances in independent India. The National Sample Survey organization (NSSO) offers the most broad based data sets that provide relatively direct evidence on economic inequality across caste groups. The 55th Round of its survey is of historic importance providing data separately for the OBCs and thus exposing the stark social inequality even after five decades of independence and in the face of loud claims of empowerment of the OBCs. It is true that in the farming sector an affluent, elite class has emerged among the OBCs but what about the large majority of marginal farmers, agricultural labour and the impoverished artisan castes fighting a losing battle in the face of competition from industrialization and lack of institutional support from the governments in power including the so called ruling classes/ parties of OBCs?

The situation becomes extremely contradictory when we find that the so called 'upper *Shudras'*/OBCs have shown reluctance to share power with the lower *Shudras*/SCs. Perhaps, that is why, political scientists such as Kanche Ilaiah describe the OBCs as a 'directionless social force ever ready to be exploited by the ruling higher castes for pursuing their own social-political agenda. Moreover, as Satish Deshpande (2003) rightly comments that "most sociologists (like other academics) were from upper caste backgrounds and they could not call upon the accidental resources of personal experience to overcome the powerful consensual positioning of caste in the past. Thus, Indian sociology was unable to address adequately the forms in which caste was being reinvented as a modern institution, specially its new modes of reproduction and the fresh meanings and functions it was acquiring in urban India".

Thus, the foregoing provides us the background in which we tried to examine various aspects of the process of change the OBC communities are passing through. With the help of 15 papers dealing with peasant/service communities, pastoral communities, fishing communities and artisan communities, we have tried to have some idea of social change among the OBC communities in different states of India.

II

There are four papers in Part-I dealing with the peasant/service communities. Prema Kurien presents the impact of the Gulf migration on the caste mobility and gilding of the rituals of the Ezhava of Kerala. She traces the transformation of the caste system in the past century. From a structure that was so encompassing that it dictated almost every action of an individual, it became a system of stratified, endogamous communities in the post-colonial period. With the movement toward the de-castification of status, it seemed to be moving towards an arrangement that regulated little more than marriage universe of the members. Education, class position and occupational prestige seemed to be replacing ritual purity as indicators of status. The metamorphosis of the caste system went hand in hand with substantial changes in the economic, political and social standing of the main castes in the Cherur region. The Ezhavas, formerly considered non-caste Hindus with few rights and only a little above the slave castes, had become an increasingly affluent section of the society, rapidly becoming educated and politically powerful. With their numerical preponderance, economic, political and social power, they seemed to be taking over as the local dominant caste. This transformation has been concomitant with the changes in the economic, political and social standing of each of the main castes. Kurien argues that this transformation took place due to two principal processes—colonialism and large-scale labour migration. Both processes resulted in the creation of a new structure of economic opportunities in the society at large, one that reversed the pre-existing structure and allowed the lower castes and classes to be the prime beneficiaries. The resultant caste mobility has taken new form based on fundamentally different principles. The empowerment of the Ezhavas seems to have resulted in the emergence of a more open status system.

Organised in five sections, Lancy Lobo offers a conspectus on the Kolis of Gujarat. The Kolis are not a homogenous people. In some parts of Gujarat, they are known only as Kolis without any sub -caste or sub-group name: they are divided in to named sub-castes in some other areas. They are basically rural –oriented. The Kolis have been considered as congeries of aboriginal tribes in the past but now days they are regarded as castes within the Hindu caste system. As an ethnographic category, the Kolis present a very complex history of descent. Many scholars record that they were 'indigenes' and got absorbed in the caste system over a very long period. In the initial stage of this process, they were accorded a low status. The Census operations bear witness to the widespread desire of the Kolis to *Rajputise* themselves. The process of *Rajputisation* among the Kolis has been uneven in different parts of Gujarat: although sizeable in population, the Kolis of south Gujarat are perhaps the least *Rajputised* among the Kolis. From the available evidence, it is possible to isolate two types of Koli settings in Gujarat. In the first, as in north Gujarat, there are immigrants Kolis, called Thakardas or better still Thakors freely arranging marriages among themselves. In the second, indigenous Kolis, called Talapadas, live side -by –side with the immigrant Kolis from an adjoining area, as in Saurashtra, central and south Gujarat. They freely arrange marriages among themselves and are known by several lineage names. Differentiation and stratification has taken place and further groups have crystallized on a regional basis. Without further ethnographic research, intra-Koli rankings at all Gujarat level may be an exercise in futility. There is a Koli –Rajput continuum operational in Gujarat. This has not been of same vintage in different parts and at different points of time. The Koli hierarchy in north Gujarat is simple: at one end are Thakors and at another are the Dabars or chiefly Kolis. In Saurashtra, central and south Gujarat, there are Talpada and Pardeshi divisions. There is an observable hierarchy among the Kolis and the Rajputs. At the lowest level of the pyramid the two-way relationships signify reciprocity among the ordinary Kolis. At the top, however, status groups have crystallized. The *Kshtriya Sabha* structurally began to interact on the political platform by structurally linking neighbouring social units like the Kolis. The Koli –Rajput continuum provided the cultural infrastructure to this political combination. However, the cleavage between the Rajputs and the Kolis remained: the former were identified as upper Kshatriyas and the latter lower ones. After the break up of the *Kshatriya Sabha*, small Koli associations have sprung up all over Gujarat. These express the desire to unite the different status groups among the Kolis so that they can cash on the political platform under the dictum "union is strength". Now a feeling of disenchantment with ritual status enhancement process through Rajput connection has crept among the Kolis. They appear to have discovered the political ground reality that their pooling with the Rajputs largely benefited the Rajputs. Now they are more inclined to secure economic and political benefits even through relegation in the ritual status.

Organized in five sections, the piece by H.S.Verma and Rakesh Varma is an effort at auto-ethnography that focuses on the changes registered in the socio-cultural, educational, economic and political status of the important peasant community of the Kurmis of Uttar Pradesh. After stating the methodology followed in assembling the case study, the first section examines their origins, composition and decomposition in the state including the crucial issue of their relegation from the somewhat ritually respectable comity of the *Vaishyas* to the lowly rated *Shudras*. The second section documents the character of their economic activities, principally how have they have adapted to the changing requirements of the shift from subsistence to commercial agriculture in an unsympathetic environment. The third section sketches their lackadaisical journey in the field of education at a time when the upper castes of the Uttar Pradesh society have moved into the knowledge economy. The fourth section focuses on the political profile of the community probing the possible causes of their less than impressive assertion of community identity despite their larger population size and better resource endowment. The fifth section sums up their socio-cultural status identifying the Kurmi psyche responsible for the progress shown by a very minuscule segment in the midst of stagnation registered by their mainstream.

D.R. Sahu's paper deals with the active participation of the OBCs in the movement against the establishment of National Missile Test Range Center at Baliapal, Balasore in Orissa. This Missile Testing Center project was supposed to displace more than one lakh people spread over 55 villages covering an area of 102 square kilometers. The proposed project could not be implemented due to the people's resistance and their active participation in the movement. Intertwined with the role of different political parties also involved in the movement, it articulates the mobilization of people on the plank of sons of soil.

There are three papers dealing with the pastoral communities in Part-II. Abha Chauhan's case study of the Meos of Mewat, originally Hindus but converted to Islam in stages, examines the relationship of customs, and religion with the nature of change that has been witnessed in the social structure of the Meos. Her analysis first presents life and history and social structure of the Meos: this is followed by an examination of their kinship and marriage rules to show the impact of change, especially of the process of *Islamisation*.Finally, it relates this process with the continuing backwardness of the Meo community in the changing environment of Haryana where other comparable Hindu communities like the Jats, Yadavs, and Rajputs have moved ahead in different fields (i.e.education, farming practices, political participation,etc.).Chauhan argues that the dilemma the Meo society faces today is that it is laying too much emphasis on its un-Islamic customary practices and is trying to undo them. The consequence is that neither the correct and the best Islamic values are being inculcated nor much effort is being made towards the development and empowerment of the Meo community. The Meos have given up some of their customs and practices but rules of kinship and marriage, which are as much due to demands of an agricultural economy and rural society as to their Hindu descent, are foundations of their social structure. These provide them security and stability and, therefore, the Meos are reluctant to change them. Chauhan posits that the Meos themselves need to come out of their secluded life and come closer to other people.

In an elaborate ethnographic account covering the origins, population, stratification, settlement pattern and housing, dressing patterns, names, education, food habits, occupation, marriage, religion, purity and pollution, and social movement, M Gurulingaiah discusses cultural changes registered by the pastoral community of the Gollas in Karnataka. What is the nature of socio-cultural change that has been registered among the Gollas of Karnataka? Without any trace of doubt, the recorded change appears gradual if one takes in to consideration the Gollas as a collective entity. Second, the extent and nature of change has been of different types in different spheres. For instance, far-reaching changes have been recorded in some of the fields whereas not much has changed in certain others. There has been mass spread of education at the lower levels but not much at the higher echelons. In the field of farming, they are in the process of switching over from subsistence to commercial agriculture. Third, segments of the Gollas that have moved to the urban areas and non-traditional occupations have changed their customs and practices and belief systems more appreciably than their counterparts that have remained tethered to the rural areas and their traditional pastoral occupation of cattle rearing. Fourth, compared to their north Indian brethren, the Gollas of Karnataka activated themselves politically very late. However, they have certainly realized the usefulness of political mobilization and mass struggles to obtain what they consider to be their legitimate claims. On the other hand, compared to the dominant communities of Karnataka, the Gollas still remain socially and economically very backward community of the state.

With a change in the socio-economic environment and a specific capitalist-oriented meaning of development, pastoral-nomadic existence in many parts of the world has become extremely precarious. But there has been a conspicuous paucity of studies on nomadic groups. Vinay Kumar Srivastava did a remarkable study of the Raikas of Rajasthan fetching him his Ph.D. degree from Cambridge. Srivastava's present paper is an excellent piece of ethnography of the Raikas mingled with the author's personal experiences of his fieldwork. The paper also contains a number of incisive comments and observations pointing towards trends of social change among this pastoral community.

Three papers deal with the fishing communities in Part-III. Patil,et al analyze the movement of the fisher folk in Goa essentially as a conflict between two diametrically opposed traditions of fishing. Among these, the traditional form of fishing is age-old .It involves deployment of conventional boats, and is community-based. Fish catching is made in the territorial waters through fishing nets. There is abstinence from fishing activity during major part of the monsoon allowing full flow of fish breeding and replenishment of marine resources in the catchment area. It mainly caters to the internal market. On the other hand, mechanized fishing involved huge investment, high technology and complex organization, indiscriminate exploitation of marine resources throughout the year and focusing on the export market. The entry of mechanized fishing and its unregulated pursuit even in the territorial waters has adversely affected the traditional fisher folk communities. This has led to the emergence of the *Goenchea Ramponkarancho Ekvott*(GRE) on the scene and an aggressive fishermen's movement in Goa. Over fishing, low catch, displacement and ecological damage were the main issues on which the GRE carried on the fisher folk movement demanding, among other things, a ban on mechanized fishing within 5 kms from the shore, a ban on night fishing, and a ban on fishing during monsoon season. Patil, et al point out that in spite of repeated pleas of the GRE, the state government did absolutely nothing on these demands until it was forced to enact a fishing regulation act under a directive from a Central Act on the question. Reluctantly, the Goa, Daman and Diu Marine Fishing Regulation Act was passed in 1980 but the state government did not take effective cognizance of violations of its provisions on ban on fishing in shallow waters and fishing during the monsoon. The GRE carried the fight to the higher judiciary from where it obtained favourable orders. It also opposed the Aquaculture Authority Bill 1997 arguing that it was ecologically harmful. Apathy of the government and existence of vested interests are the most significant factors that have made enforcement of the Marine Fishing Regulation Act ineffective and consequently made the fishing issue a perennial source of conflict between the traditional fisher folk and the mechanized fishing industry in Goa.

Charles W. Nuckoll's paper is a highly innovative and deals with a less treaded area of sociology/social anthropology. On the basis of his field work among the Jalari, a fishing community of coastal Andhra Pradesh he has put 'desire' at the center rather than the periphery of kinship which is anthropologically new, and different from other approaches which, these days, tend to emphasize 'power' and define kinship according to the strategies encoded in roles for the acquisition or maintenance of political positions in a field of limited good.The Indians do recognize the individuality as an essential feature of ordinary life, and indeed, display a keen awareness of this unique aspect of personality. The desire for fusion is not unproblematic, since the means available for its fulfillment are contradictory. But that is only part of the problem, since the means for achieving fusion conflict not only internally, but with each other. In Jalari culture, the problem locates itself in sibling relations, in the choices brothers and sisters are forced to make between forms of sibling unity and separation. It is in the domain of sibling relations that work of achieving fusion is supposed to be done, but it cannot be done given the paradoxes embedded in the sibling relationship. The paradox of Jalari kinship is that although brothers must some day separate, the ideology of fraternal solidarity cuts against this, and makes brothers ambivalent about their role in the group and their efforts to divide it. Brothers want to remain together, but cannot, and in fact do every thing they can to bring about dissolution as group. This they then regret. Similarly, brothers and sisters want to remain united, but find this increasingly difficult given their competition among each other and their growing inability to meet each other's needs. Eventually, they go their separate ways, signifying their break in a ritual of chicken sacrifice made at the door of one's sibling. But they always regret it and think that somehow the split might have been prevented. The paper suggests that Jalari kinship is much more than a set of norms and rules. It is a dynamic of unfulfillable desires, and this dynamic is fundamental to the working of the system. The paper suggests a strategy for formulating a theory of paradox in culture.

In the state of Andhra Pradesh two types of fishing communities are in existence. One is a marine fisherman community that lives on the coastal belt of the Bay of Bengal spread over from Srikakulam to Nellore while the other one is inland fishing community. S.V. Sudhakar's paper deals with the Vadabalijas belonging to the first category. The author presents a short and crisp ethnographic account of Vadabalija that also includes some aspects of change in the social organization as well as in the realm of technology.

There are two papers in Part IV on the artisans. Historically, the artisans (i.e. castes providing services and goods for the rural economy) were linked in a hierarchical relationship with the agriculturists who, by virtue of having control over land, were able to keep others dependent on them. While the form of relationships varied significantly over space and time, the exploitative elements were present in most situations. The changes, however, were more significant during the colonial rule, setting the downward trend and the process of de-industrialization. Nevertheless, at the time of Independence, the economy was still vested with a fairly large and widespread segment of rural artisans. The crucial elements characterizing this segment were as follows: (i) Their presence was essential to sustain a self-sufficient rural economy; (ii) Their growth was mainly dependent on the development of agriculture and allied activities; (iii) Frequent drought conditions, therefore, exerted disintegrating influence on the artisan sector; (iv) Servitude and patronage, on the one hand, and a decentralized production system, on the other, constrained mobilization of capital and entrepreneurial skills. Moreover, low social status of some of the artisans further aggravated these constrains;(v) Traditional arrangements of mutual rights and obligations were undergoing constant changes in the light of overall changes taking place in the economy; and (vi) The process of transformation resulted in gradual shift towards urban centres and an advance integration with market economy. Most of the foregoing characteristics have been closely associated with the early phase of capitalist production. As industrialsation proceeds, eventually the artisan based activities especially those scattered over the countryside would disappear. Such transformation also takes place in the less industrialized countries. In their simple form, these changes emerge through transition of artisan industry, replacement of household industry and development of modern small-scale industries along with large-scale production. In the process, the artisan-based production tends to get integrated with the mainstream industrial production by establishing product as well as capital linkages. Thus, a shift from home-based to workshop/factory enterprises and from rural to semi-urban/urban locations is a natural phenomenon and perhaps a desirable goal in the process of capitalist development. Moreover, it can pave the way for an upward mobility as well as social integration among the artisan households. Overall, therefore, the changing pattern of artisan-based production can be positive phenomenon. The crucial question vis-à-vis the foregoing hypothesis is: has this type of transformation been really taking place? If so, has it really proceeded in the same type of sequence as the hypothesis assumes? These questions can be answered only through empirical studies of the artisan groups in different parts of the country.

C.N. Ray carried out his study to develop a socio-economic profile of the artisans engaged in the cottage and village industries in Bhavnagar district of Gujarat to test the foregoing hypothesis.Ray's empirical analysis reveals not only the present poor socio-economic conditions of the Bhavnagar rural artisans but also the crucial reality of their rudderlessness. Traditionally, their growth was dependent on the development of agricultural and allied activities. However, since the character of the Gujarat economy in general and its agriculture and industry in particular have undergone a significant change, the support that the artisans drew from the rural agricultural economy appears to have declined appreciably. The fact that the rural urban differences themselves narrowed down in Gujarat also affected the demand and supply sides of the artisan trade adversely. The expected gradual shifts of the artisans towards the urban centres on the one hand and advance integration with the market economy that was expected to proceed with capitalist development also have not been witnessed. Thus, the artisans find themselves in no man's land: the rural economy is not sustaining them and the urban-industrial conglomeration has not integrated them. As Ray's empirical analysis amply reveals, the artisans know precisely what their problems are but on their own initiative, it appears that the Bhavnagar artisans are hardly in a position to solve them. As some social scientists have rightly argued, does this not call for charting a new set of policy initiatives? There is not much hope from the government side since the mid Nineties both the Central as well as the state governments have continued to neglect both the farm and non-farm rural sectors.

Nomads and artisans of south India especially of the Mysore region have been an important area of study for the sociologists and social anthropologists. Through a case study of settlement patterns of one artisan caste, the Vishwakarmas, Jan Brouwer attempts to gain insight into the settlement dimension of the Indian indigenous knowledge system. He argues that the choice of locale for settlement is neither random nor guided by principles of efficiency, but follows from indigenous conceptualizations that are informed by categories from various domains simultaneously. The data are arranged in three sections referring to the southern, central and northern regions of interior Karnataka respectively. Section two considers the town plan of Mysore city in terms of artisan settlement. Having been the capital of the erstwhile kingdom of Mysore and the later Mysore state, it shows the indigenous model of caste distribution in a more sophisticated form than the other towns of the region. Section three describes the artisans' settlement in towns of central Karnataka and section four considers their settlement in northern Karnataka. Taken together the settlement patterns of the three regions form variations on the same theme guided by the same indigenous categories of segregation and hierarchy. In the concluding section a few aspects of the indigenous settlement plan are contrasted to those found in Europe and on which India's modern state and town planning principles are based. Brouwer finds that the high castes are settled on low terrain; low castes are settled on high terrain; high occupations are settled on low terrain and low occupations are settled on high terrain. Thus, unlike the settlement pattern of rural Karnataka, the elevated areas in the towns are inhabited by the non-Brahmin, non-vegetarian castes while the vegetarian, usually the Brahmin castes, are settled in the low wards. This pattern is just the opposite of the settlement pattern of the Europe. The town planners and resettlement authorities could benefit from the knowledge of these contrasts.

There are three papers in Part IV that deal with assorted OBC communities. One of these covers the Nepalese community; a second deals with the Muslims of Kerala and the third analyses the isolation of the tea plantation workers. The last two belong to very special types of the OBCs. India has got a substantial Nepalese community settled in different parts of the country. K.P. Upadhyaya's paper deals with one such Nepalese speaking community living in Assam for a long period of time and participating actively in the socio-economic and political processes in India and has undergone the process of assimilation with the local Assamese society. Like other segments of the Assamese society, they are also passing through the process of modernization – cultural as well as technological. The author has shown that despite the influence of assimilation, the Nepalese community is still conscious of its cultural and historical roots but this does not come in the way of their socio-cultural and political identification with the local Assamese population.

Shareena Banu's paper looks at the identity assertion patterns of Mopilla and other Muslims of Kerala in the wake of migration to the Gulf countries. She contends that identity should not be seen as a static entity but as a phenomenon that is constantly in the process of construction. For the Muslims in India, religious beliefs and practices are an important part of their ethnicity and these are largely shaped by history and socio-economic events as well as the regional culture. In recent times the Muslims in Kerala are engaged in serious religious polemic and self-introspection in response to various social and cultural challenges. Deciphering this state of interpretive ambivalence is indeed a challenge for scholars and intellectuals.

Although Monirul Khan's paper deals with the tea plantation workers in Bangladesh, it has been included in this volume because of it's conceptual resemblance to similar backward communities of such workers in India on which the editors could not include any paper in the present volume. Moreover, the places of origin of the workers are Orissa, Bihar, West Bengal, Andhra Pradesh and Tamil Nadu. The author is of the view that social isolation of an ethnic community could be outcome its own choice. The interacting relationship between an ethnic community and the mainstream, the former may preserve its cultural purity at the cost of isolation. It means that social isolation is directed to the attainment of a cultural goal of a small community. Although the tribal and ethnic communities may opt for isolation or limited interaction to protect their cultural and economic uniqueness, they may not be benefiting in the long run. On the other hand, social backwardness is a developmental as well as structural issue. Through his case study of the tea plantation workers, Monirul Khan identifies factors that have contributed to the isolation of the tea garden workers. Prominent among these are (i) the inward looking mentality (confining themselves to their own language, religion, and other norms) of the tea workers and the fear of losing their uniqueness, (ii) lack of educational opportunities for a very long period and their consequent lack of outside orientation, (iii) lack of alternate job opportunities intensified their link with the tea gardens, and (iv) lack of any intervention programme from outside world. This prolonged isolation had serious consequences. The tea garden workers not only lost their linkage with their ancestral homes but also have failed to change their living standards and seize the opportunities that could be found outside. Had they been mobile enough, certainly that would have left positive impact on their bargaining capacity. The isolation of the tea garden workers had conferred two distinct benefits to their employers. Greater isolation and lack of mobility has kept the wage rate and the bargaining position of the workers down. Isolation and backwardness should not be perceived as a cultural phenomenon only. It is very much linked to the political economy that operates in the tea plantation's surplus generation process. A few families of the tea garden workers have come out of this general trend. They have rediscovered their ancestral homes, received education and with the help of some NGOs developed skills and switched over to other occupations.

The last part of the collection comprises of Annexures containing what the editors call as the milestone documents on the OBC problematic. These are further categorised in to (a) findings/ recommendations of Commissions enquiring in to conditions of the

OBCs, and action taken on their reports, (b) GOs on reservations for the OBCs, (c) analysis of authoritative judicial verdict on reservations(Indra Sawhney case), (d) creamy layer, (e) listing of the OBC communities by the Central and state governments/Union Territories and (f) consequential proposals for empowerment of the OBCs prepared for the Tenth Five Year Plan.There are five documents included under (a) these deal with the First Backward Classes (Kalelkar) Commission and the view of Mandal Commissin on the treatment meted out to its report,the Memorandum of action taken onthe recommendations of Kalelkar Commission (very clearly showing the diabolical conduct of its Chairman and the Machiavellian logic used by G.B. Pant, then Home Minister); the criteria adopted by the Mandal Commission in identifying the OBCs (first suggested by the cream of mainstream social scientists themselves, adopted by the Mandal Commission in toto and criticised by the same mainstream social science community that suggested such a methodology after V.P.Singh government accepted some of the recommendations ten years later); recommendations of Mandal Commission (apart from 27 per cent reservations,it had suggested quite a few appropriate sets of measures that would have gone a long way in improving th conditions of the OBCs and ones that still remain very much valid even today) and the adequacy or otherwise of representation of the Backward communities in public services of Kerala as reflected in the report of the K.K. Narendran Commission (the only state where this exercise has been undertaken so far and one that proves beyond any trace of doubt that reservations under Article 16(4) have indeed enabled hitherto unrepresented communities to get in services under the state). Four documents are included in (b) These consist of the communal GOs of 1921,1922, and 1928 from the British period and one GO issued by the Government of India in 1980, the OMs issued by the V.P. Singh and P.V. Narsimha Rao governments.Taken as a bunch, they indicate the motives of the governments of their time. Only one paper by Neeta Verma analyzing the historical verdict of the nine judges Special Constitution Bench of the Supreme Court in Indra Sawhney is included in (c). The paper brings out not only the salient points emerging from the historical ruling but,more importantly, also the contradictions contained in the authoritative judgments,some thing that the legal luminaries had avoided to point out. The issue of creamy layer has been a contentious one. This is also one of the areas on which not so glorious role played by the Expert Committee appointed by the Government of India needs a closer scrutiny.That is possible only when one goes through the report of the Expert Committee appointed by the government of Uttar Pradesh in juxtaposition with the Expert Committee of the Government of India. Three documents included in section (d) attempt precisely this exercise. There is no single official list of total number of communities listed as the OBCs by the Government of India and different states and Union Territories: all that they have done is to issue periodically the notifications of newer listings or, in exceptiona cases, deletions from the existing inclusions of the OBCs previously made. A consolidated list has been compiled and included in section (e). The empowerment efforts of the Government of India— or more appropriately lack of them up to Eightth Five Year Plans—is the report of the Working Group on empowerment of the OBCs constituted by the Planning Commission for the Tenth Five Year Plan.A summary of these proposals, most of which did not find approval for inclusion in the finalised vesion of the Tenth Five Year Plan, is included in section (f). This exposes the ulterior designs of the ruling classes. Given the range of their coverage, these documents constitute very significant bunch of historical records on the OBC promlematic,not available in any single collection to date.

This collection contains only 14 pieces and on the basis of such small material, it is clearly hazardous to generalise about the nature, direction and consequences of changes registered by different communities in the country in the post-independence period.This must wait until a more representative number of case studies of the OBC communities are available at some future date.The collectin only provides glimpses of what has happened or, conversely, what has not happened with some of the OBC communities.

References

Deshpande, Satish. 2003. *Contemporay India: A Sociological Pespective*.New Delhi: Penguin Viking.

Goswami, B.B. 1988. 'Towards an understanding of the underprivileged' in S.B. Chakrabarti (ed.). *Social Science and Social Concern*. Delhi: Mittal Publications.

Shah, Ghanshyam. 2002. *Caste and Democratic Politics in India*. New Delhi: Permanent Black.

Part - I
Farming/Service communities

Caste mobility and the gilding of Rituals: The impact of gulf migration on Ezhavas of Kerala

Prema A. Kurien

Introduction

Over the past three decades there has been a large migration from Asian countries to the Middle East, and the available evidence indicates that the migration has resulted in large inflows of money and major changes in the sending communities. Although the economic impacts of the migration have been studied in some detail, much less attention has been paid to the social consequences. Kerala is a good example of a highly stratified society where the traditional stratification system was overturned in a relatively short period of time. This took place as a result of a series of changes that systematically favored the lower castes and worked to the disadvantage of the higher castes. Thus, there was a process of rapid social mobility, both upward (for the lower castes) and downward (for the upper castes) and a fundamental restructuring of society. These economic reversals in turn gradually translated into changes in the status system.

Cherur[2] is a village in south Kerala which had a large out-migration to Singapore from around the 1930's and to the Persian Gulf countries from the early 1970's. The migrants were largely from the lower Ezhava caste. One major consequence was that they had become significantly richer than the higher Nayar caste in the village. The decades of migration brought about major changes in the the caste system of the village and in the inter-caste relationships.

The Indian caste system has generally been viewed as being a rigid and unchanging hierarchy. In practice, however, change and mobility have always been a part of the system. Over the centuries, there have been many castes that have risen or fallen within the caste hierarchy. Conventionally, when a lower caste became affluent or powerful, a process of caste mobility called *Sanskritization* (Srinivas 1968) was initiated whereby the style of life and the customs and rituals of a higher caste were adopted. Typically, the low caste gave up its former low status occupation, adopted vegetarianism and teetotalism, maintained stricter control over the "purity" of its women and took over some of the *Vedic* rites confined to the upper castes, including the wearing of the sacred thread. Generally, these changes were followed by a claim to a higher position in the caste hierarchy than that traditionally conceded to the claimant caste by the local community" (Srinivas: 1968:6). Social mobility took the form of *Sanskritization* or collective mobility since individual or family mobility was traditionally more difficult within the caste system. The achievement of a higher status was usually a slow process, taking several generations and was generally undertaken by castes who were able to advance economically *and* acquire political power. Some of the well known historical cases are the *Kayasthas,* traditionally assigned the status of a *Sudra* caste, who were able to become influential members of the *Mughal* court and who subsequently fought legal battles to have their caste position changed, and the *Noniyas* who were considered almost untouchable but whose economic mobility has since gained them a position among the top few castes of the area (Pandey: 1986:77-78). The *Nadars* of Tamil Nadu are another example. Originally an untouchable caste called *Shanars*, they succeeded in developing a mercantile upper stratum and then claimed *Kshatriya* status and the new caste name in the 1901 census.

In Cherur, the Ezhava migrants had changed their occupation, life style and, as in the case of *Sanskritization*, adopted new rituals and ceremonies. What was different about this case and distinguished it from the conventional processes of *Sanskritization* was that the rituals that the Ezhavas introduced were not those practiced by the higher castes of the area. On the contrary, it was the Nayars and even the Brahmins in the village who were subsequently forced to modify some of their existing practices and to adopt ones more in consonance with those of the Ezhavas.

The new rituals can be studied as a cultural text of a symbolic expression of the emerging social order. My argument is that unlike *Sanskritization* which resulted in *positional* changes of castes within the existing structure, what was taking place in Cherur and the high migrant Hindu areas nearby was a *reformulation of the structure* itself. This was not merely a consequence of the migration but was the end product of a long sequence of changes initiated by colonialism and commercialization. The migration of the past two decades precipitated the transformation of the system by bringing about a reversal of the economic position of the major castes.

In the next section a brief sketch of the traditional caste structure as it existed in the pre-colonial and early colonial period is presented. This is followed by an account of the changes brought about by colonialism and by migration and a description of the new cultural practices. These practices are then analyzed and their social message discussed.

The traditional caste structure (1300 - 1850)[3]

The caste system in Kerala had some distinct features which distinguished it from that prevalent in the rest of the country. Firstly, of the four basic *varnas* in the ideal-typical pan-Indian schema, Brahmans, Kshatriyas, Vaisyas, and Sudras, Kshatriyas were rare and Vaisyas non-existent. The Nayar caste took the place of the Kshatriyas but they were regarded as *Sudras* by the local Brahmins. The Ezhavas came below the Nayars followed by the former slave castes, now called the "scheduled castes". The Christians and the Muslims were the main business and trading communities in Kerala. The Hindu society was traditionally divided into *Savarna* (caste Hindus), *Avarna* (non-caste Hindus) and the slave castes. The Brahmins and Nayars fell into the first category, the Ezhavas into the second and the scheduled castes into the third. Another distinctive feature of the caste system in Kerala in earlier times was that over 50 percent of the population was matrilineal and matrilocal (Kumar: 1989: 517-539).

The caste system in Kerala was also more severe than elsewhere. While untouchability existed in the rest of India, in Kerala, the notion of pollution by contact was taken a step further to include "atmospheric pollution", pollution from a distance and in the case of the lowest castes, even by sight. The specific distances to be maintained between the different castes were stipulated depending on their respective positions in the caste hierarchy. There were other prescriptions and proscriptions imposed on the members of the different castes with the restrictions becoming increasingly severe as one went down the caste hierarchy. Thus, there were restrictions on the access to education, religion, and other institutions, and on the occupations a caste could follow. Each caste also had certain types of hair styles, clothes, jewellery, shoes and houses that they were allowed. Lower castes were obliged to observe specific demeaning forms of address and posture when talking to a higher caste member. There was also a differential justice system for each of the castes.

Brahmins, locally called Nambudiris, were ensconced securely at the apex of the hierarchy and though they constituted less than one per cent of the population, their control over the rest of the society was absolute.[4] Besides being the religious specialists, they were also the largest land owners of the state. They were absentee landlords, the cultivation being supervised by Nayars and performed by the Ezhavas and slaves. The Brahmins had a family structure and life style evolved so as to prevent the fragmentation of their estates and the dissipation of their wealth. It was a patrilineal joint family system in which only the eldest son was allowed to marry. His children were regarded as the legal issues of all the brothers. The rest of the sons contracted liaisons with Nayar women. The Nayar family structure was matrilineal and matrilocal, so the Nambudiris would visit their Nayar wives (polygyny was combined with polyandry, see next page) at night in their own homes. The children born of such unions were Nayars and became the full responsibility of the mother's *taravad* (the Nayar joint family). The Nambudiris led very austere lives, spent mostly in religious learning and observances. Their food and clothing were also very simple.

The Nayars were divided into several sub-castes and occupied a range of positions but those in Cherur were mainly landowners. They owned or leased (from the Nambudiris) most of the wet land in the area. A few were moderately large landowners owning over fifteen acres of land but most had between three to eight acres. As mentioned, they lived in matrilineal and matrilocal joint-families called the *taravad*, headed by the eldest male member. The property and assets of the *taravad* were held in common and could be alienated only with the consent of all its members.

Pre-pubescent Nayar girls underwent an expensive mock marriage ceremony after which they were permitted to contract *sambandham* (agreement) marriages with men of the same or higher status groups. In practice, it is generally only the upper caste Nayar women who married higher caste men. Cross-cousin *sambandham* marriages were generally practiced among the rest of the caste. A woman could have *sambandham* with several men at the same time. Such marriages were loosely structured and could be dissolved at any time by the wishes of either party.[5] The husband had no rights over the woman and her children and little obligation except the provision of small presents.

At least the higher sub-castes of the Nayars performed all the Brahmanical religious observances permitted to them. Pillai (1987) has argued that this process of *Sanskritization* was a means of securing high ritual status which in turn secured them alliances and traditional ritual service relations with highly honored Nambudiri families.

The Ezhava caste formed the largest section of the population in Cherur, and the Hindu population of Kerala as a whole. Their traditional occupation was tending of the coconut palm mainly tapping it for toddy and using its husk to make coir (coconut fibre) products. In Cherur, however, most of the Ezhavas were agriculturists, share-croppers, tenants and the hired workers of the lands held by Nayars. Ezhava women, unlike Nayars, also worked outside the house mainly in the fields in Cherur. Several prohibitions were imposed on this caste since they were considered *Avarnas*. Thus, they could not carry an umbrella or cover their upper bodies (not even the women) and could not wear certain types of jewellery and footwear or use metal vessels and finely woven cloth. They were also not permitted to approach public offices, roads close to temples and houses of high castes. Since they could not approach the regular temples, they had their own temples and priests. Like the Nayars their family structure was matrilocal and matrilineal[6], and they followed most of the ceremonial practices of the latter. Ezhava women married within their caste. Cross-cousin marriages were widespread.

The slave castes were treated like property with no rights over self or family. They carried out the most arduous agricultural tasks in return for a minimum amount of food. They lived on their master's agricultural land and were the caretakers of the property. There were innumerable restrictions on their behavior, the most onerous of which stemmed from the rules which kept them at a great distance from the rest of the society, particularly the Savarna castes. Thus, it was even inauspicious for them to be spotted on the horizon by a high caste member before any important ritual; if that happened, they could be killed on the spot.

Colonialism and the reformation of the caste system (1850-1950)

The process of colonialism has almost invariably resulted in some degree of structural change in the colonized society. Colonialism imposes a new economic system on the society and usually introduces commercialization for the first time. The consequent disruption of the economic structure eventually translates into a change in the social structure. In addition, colonialism gives rise to religious and cultural proselytization. Often there are attempts to forcibly change many of the traditional practices which are perceived to be "barbaric" or "immoral". Both these processes were at work in Kerala during the period of colonialism and resulted in major changes in the caste system.

Most of the changes took place in the latter part of the 19th century and the first few decades of the 20th century. Many of the central features of the caste system in Kerala such as the polgyny of the Nambudiris, the polyandrous and loosely structured *sambandham* marriage system of the Nayars and the institution of slavery were considered immoral by the colonialists and, consequently, abolished over time. Legislation was also passed which permitted the partitioning of joint family land to the individual members. All these laws led to the gradual dismantling of the traditional structure of the caste system. The alienation of land by the Brahmins and Nayars led to a weakening of their economic position. At the same time, the commercialization process introduced by colonialism permitted the participation of the lower castes, particularly the Ezhavas and thus, they were able to improve their situation. With the improvement in their economic position, they sought corresponding improvement in their social position and began to organize and militate against the many disabilities they faced, particularly the restriction against their attending government schools. According to Robin Jeffrey (1976: 146-147), "The growing Irava [Ezhava] aim, unstated but perceptible from the 1880's was to achieve the status of Nairs [Nayars] . . . and they took over several of the customs of the Nairs." At the turn of the century, Sri Narayana Guru emerged as their spiritual leader. He launched a crusade against untouchability and casteism with the slogan "One caste, one religion, one God for mankind". He rebelled against the domination of the Brahmins and the *avarna* status of the Ezhavas by installing *savarna* Gods in the low caste temples, performing the worship rites himself and getting the other Ezhavas to do the same. He tried to *Sanskritize* their religious practices and prohibited the performance of animal sacrifices. He also urged simplicity and the abolition of the traditional expensive ceremonies like the mock marriage, the puberty festival and the festival for the first pregnancy which did not have any religious value. He exhorted the pursuit of education and encouraged the starting of economic enterprises. Thus, his movement gave the Ezhavas a sense of pride in their group and a desire to improve their social and economic position in society. Sri Narayana had a great influence on Cherur and surrounding areas since Sivagiri, where he established his *ashram* was only two or three miles away. The Ezhavas continued to spearhead reform movements and their efforts culminated in the temple entry movement and the 1936 Temple Entry Proclamation which permitted all Hindus, irrespective of caste status, the right to enter temples.

The mobilization of the lower castes provided fertile ground for an incipient Communist movement which gradually gained momentum in the state. The Ezhavas were the largest supporters of the movement and the first general elections of 1957 returned a Communist government to power. The Communists have been an important force in state politics since then, both in and out of elected office. In keeping with their election manifesto, a series of land reforms were initiated. These reforms further impoverished the big landlords in the state, the Brahmins and Nayars. The Communist movement also abolished the last vestiges of the traditional caste system like distance pollution and the differential privileges accorded to castes.

Thus, the caste structure at the end of the colonial period had changed significantly from what it was in the pre-colonial era. The Ezhavas, in particular, experienced a process of social rebirth during the period. They gained access to the institutions and occupations which till then had been reserved for the higher castes and emerged as a significant social and political power in the state. Almost all of the official supports that had propped up the system were whittled away in the course of a century and thus the upper castes no longer had the backing of system to enforce compliance to their dictates. A progressive "unbundling" of the caste structure was set in motion. Though many practices continued relatively unchanged in everyday rural life, especially in areas far away from the major political and social centers, the caste system at the end of the colonial period had become a fundamentally different entity. From an all-encompassing institution which structured every major activity of the life of an individual or group it became little more than a system of hierarchical, endogamous status groups.

Migration and the transformation of the caste system (1950-1990)

The period between 1930 and 1945 during the Depression and the Second World War was one of great hardship in Kerala since the commercialization process had made the state vulnerable to disruptions in the global economy. The first international migration from Cherur started during this period with several villagers setting off for Malaysia and Singapore. Due to a combination of social and economic reasons, the migrants were mainly Ezhavas.

The Brahmins and the Nayars had their land to turn to and their family structure, together with their narrowly defined occupational role and life style did not give them the independence (or the desire) to undertake such a risky venture. At the other extreme, the Harijans were too poor, and too ignorant of such opportunities. The Ezhavas, on the other hand, had only rather tenuous links with the land (since most worked on leased land or as hired labor) a more flexible family structure than the Brahmins and Nayars (they did not have large extended families) and were occupationally more innovative and adventurous since they were used to engaging in a range of occupations (during the colonial period, for instance). Thus, all these factors resulted in the Ezhavas taking the lead in the migration. Some of the Nayars did migrate later (though in far smaller numbers) when they saw the success of the Ezhavas.

The migrants were all male and almost all of them went alone, leaving their families behind. They took up skilled and technical jobs in Singapore and Malaysia. Most of the migrants from Cherur were drivers of heavy vehicles or car mechanics. Because of the time and cost involved in the long journey by ship, the men would come back very infrequently, usually only once in five to six years. But financially, they were able to earn substantially more than they would have at home and this increase in the economic position of many of the Ezhavas initiated some changes in the community.

The Gulf migration from Cherur started in the 1970's, after job opportunities in Singapore and Malaysia had been exhausted. Again, for most of the same reasons as earlier mentioned, together with their prior migratory experience, it was mainly the Ezhavas who migrated, particularly in the beginning. Some Nayars started migrating in the 1980's but by that time better paying jobs were more difficult to get and pay scales were generally lower. As in the case of Singapore, the villagers went mainly for technical jobs. Thus, most of the migrants from Cherur went as mechanics, electricians, plumbers and masons. Gulf migration soon became more widespread than the earlier migration and Gulf jobs also yielded far more than did those in Singapore and between five to ten times the earnings of local jobs. A few of the migrants did take their wives with them at least for a few years but the majority continued to leave their families behind. The 'Gulfites' (as they are locally called) were however able to come home more frequently since the travel was by air and procedures much simpler. Thus, on average, a migrant would come home once in two years. The changes that were slowly beginning to be introduced during the Singapore migration were tremendously accelerated with the second exodus to the Middle East.

The Nayars, as mentioned, had largely continued living off the land during the period of Ezhava migration. But their land holdings grew progressively smaller due to partitioning. The wages of agricultural labor also increased tremendously during the same period for a variety of reasons but primarily due to unionization and the scarcity of labor created by the large scale Gulf migration. Thus, the Nayars gradually became impoverished. Their decrease in economic standing was all the more glaring because of the steady enrichment of the Ezhavas during the same period. At the time of my field-work (over a period of five months in 1990) the differences between the two groups were great and very visible.

The pattern of settlement in Cherur was such that the Ezhavas are clustered together in one area, the Nayars in another and the Harijans in a third. This made the differences between the areas appear even starker. The Ezhavas were on either side of a tarred road and their houses were built on the new 'fashionable' model what was locally referred to as "terraced" houses (houses built completely of concrete and which have a flat concrete roof). Most of them were medium to large in size. Many houses in this area had modern gadgets, electric pumps for running water, gas stoves, fridges, televisions, even an occasional VCR. The people were well dressed, usually in synthetic material from abroad. The young women wore the fashionable "maxis" (nightgowns) when at home. The children were also fashionably dressed. Many of them were sent to the English medium school nearby. Whether or not this was the case, there was a great deal of emphasis on education and almost all the children were sent to tutorial schools for coaching classes after school hours.[7] Expenditure on medical care was another item that has received a big boost after the Gulf migration. Thus the Ezhavas avoided the public, Government run hospitals and went instead to expensive private clinics even for relatively routine matters.

The Nayar houses in contrast were mainly set on the two slopes on either side of a long strip of paddy fields. There were only dirt roads or tracks leading to the houses and the houses themselves were on the older model with thatched or tiled sloping roofs. They were also far smaller than those in the Ezhava area and for most part without the gadgets in the latter. In the matter of clothes too, the two areas presented a sharp contrast, with Nayars dressed in rather drab, old cotton clothes. Almost no Nayar child was sent to the English medium school and few parents could afford to have their children take coaching classes. Many of the Nayars were working for Ezhavas as domestic servants, agricultural workers and launderers.

Migration, like colonialism, introduces a new structure of economic opportunities to the society which in turn eventually affects the social structure. As in the case of colonialism, there is a differential response to the opportunities by the various groups which, depending on the situation, can act to deepen the existing economic inequalities, or, as in the case of the Gulf migration, to undermine and even reverse them. The Ezhavas have been the beneficiaries of the migration opportunities and their economic prosperity has once again given rise to a process of social mobility and consequent structural change in the society at large.

The gilding of rituals

Besides making changes in their life style due to their Gulf affluence, the Ezhavas had also introduced changes in the ceremonial and ritual sphere. In general, rites of gift giving had been inserted in several parts of the older rituals, all ceremonies were conducted on a grander scale, and several new ceremonies had been instituted by Gulf families.

Most of the changes related to the ceremonies connected with marriage. Thus, at the time of my fieldwork, there was often a lavish engagement ceremony at the woman's house, and a tea party on the evening before the wedding. Guests at the wedding eve ceremony (relatives and friends of the bride's family) brought gifts of cash while the bride's family used to defray the expenses of the wedding. This function had been introduced around the late Sixties and from the early Eighties, a similar ceremony was often arranged at the man's house for the relatives and friends of the bride-groom's family, who would also bring gifts of cash.[8] The actual wedding was conducted on a far grander scale than in the past and where it once used to take place in the home of the bride, it was now arranged at the wedding hall in Sivagiri (the Ezhava religious center) with expensive catered meals. Large amounts of gold were given as part of the dowry or the trousseau of the bride[9] (in addition to the bride's property share).

However, the most interesting innovations were the new gold and gift giving rituals interspersed during the course of the marriage and post marriage ceremonies. Some examples of these are given below. The new rituals are in italics:

1. When the groom's sister presented the wedding saree to the bride, *she reciprocated with a gold bangle or a watch* (earlier she would only give a brass vessel).
2. When the groom put on the wedding chain (of gold) on the bride, *she gave him a gold chain in return.*
3. On the bride's crossing the threshold of her new home (the house of her husband's parents), her mother-in-law welcomed her by giving her a lamp. *The bride gave her a gold bangle in return.*
4. When the bride's family went to the groom's house for the first time after the wedding, *her father had to give pocket*

money [English words used] to the bride groom. (Earlier this used to be more of a symbolic gift. At the time of my fieldwork, a fairly large sum of money was given).

5. On that visit or later, when the woman's family came to the man's house to see the kitchen, *they had to take gifts of furniture and kitchen equipment with them* (earlier they only had to give a few cooking pots and some sweets).
6. After staying at the man's house for a few days, the couple went to stay with the woman's family. At this time, *the woman's side was expected to give some gold to the man's sister and had to give an equal amount to the bride.* The man's side would bring clothes for the woman's family *and the woman's side also reciprocated.*

When we examine these new prestations, we see that all of them are from the woman's side to the man's. This pattern of gift giving was introduced by the newly rich families of the bride and the gifts were usually given in reciprocation for ritual services performed by the bridegroom (or someone from his side) during the course of the marriage or post marriage ceremonies.

But wealthy Gulf grooms on their part had started a trend of their own. They generally turned down (as demeaning) the monetary inducements offered by the families of prospective brides and looked instead for such attributes as education and family status. In such marriages, unlike the above cases, the flow of benefits was more equal or the direction was actually reversed. The groom often bore most of the expenses for the marriage (conventionally it was the bride's family which did this); the wedding chain he gave the bride was far more expensive, (in one case that I witnessed, he gave her two chains instead of one) he gifted his in laws expensive consumer items (a color television was common) in the first few years of marriage; he built a luxurious house in a few years time (or sometimes even before getting married) with labor saving gadgets and entirely with his money (here again the conventional pattern was that the woman's dowry went toward part of this expense and her father would have been expected to come forward with more if the couple had financial difficulty).

In one such case, Rajan, a young migrant in Cherur who worked as a mason in the Middle East, had built himself a house even before getting married. Neighbours told me with awe that the house was equipped with everything: television, VCR, mixer, grinder and even a device to lie down and bathe (a bathtub, which until then had not been seen in that region). He subsequently returned from the Gulf during the period that I was doing my fieldwork, married a woman with a Bachelor's degree (he himself had only had five or six years of schooling) at a lavish wedding ceremony that he paid for. After the wedding he took her on a tour of some of the scenic areas in the neighboring states (such honeymoon trips were also a recent introduction in the area).

The social meaning of the new rituals

While the new rituals and prestation patterns had to do with changed wife giver, wife taker relations, they could also be seen as symbolic of the transforming structure of social relations in the area. Marriage was a crucial sphere in which such changes were manifested. Firstly, in India, marriage is the most important and the most public (with the largest number of invitees) life cycle ritual. Thus, it is the best occasion to demonstrate a change in social standing. Perhaps, even more importantly, a marriage in the typical Indian context is arranged by the elders of the two sides and is seen as the formation of an alliance between the two corporate groups. The forging of important and prestigious alliances are fundamental to social and political status and, thus, marriage is socially significant for this reason as well.

The villagers (particularly the non-migrants) felt that the lavishness and all the new gold giving rituals were introduced by the migrants to show off and to assert their position as the new elite. And why did Gulf grooms on the other hand, turn down offers of large dowries? I was told: They have money, what they need now is status, so they try to get girls from good families or who are well educated. It is demeaning for them to be seen to be marrying for money.

In short, the seeming contradiction between these developments in the patterns of marriage exchanges can be explained by the desire of Gulf families (both of the bride and groom) to obtain higher status matches as one of the ways by which they could rise in status themselves (see Osella and Osella: 2000a: 81-116). Thus, Gulf migration had given rise both to hypergamous marriages (where the man's side is of a higher status than the woman's side) and hypogamous marriages (where the reverse is the case). This, however, was a significant change from the earlier pattern where, there was a positive preference for isogamous unions i.e. for unions in which both spouses families are of equal status (Fuller: 1976: 74 75). And hypogamous marriage in particular was anathema in the traditional Indian system (Fuller: 1976: 77). As cross cousin marriages used to be the pattern among the Ezhavas (and Nayars), conventionally the lawful spouse was a relative[10] and there was an overlap between kin and affinal relationships. Cross cousin marriages also meant that wives were *exchanged* between two (or more) intermarrying groups. Both these factors account for the traditional isogamous pattern of marriages and probably accounts for prestation patterns being more or less equal (going by the descriptions given by the respondents).[11] Structurally, there is another major difference between the two types of marriage patterns. Intermarriage between relatives, or 'restricted' exchange, creates smaller, close knit sub groups within the larger community and also serves the function of keeping property holdings within this group. Hypergamy and hypogamy are, however, means of forming alliances with powerful strangers (see Levi Strauss 1969). However, by the late Eighties, cross cousin marriages had fallen out of favor.

Typically, it was the formation of a marriage alliance between two families of unequal status (generally hypergamous marriages) that resulted in the large and continuing flow of prestations from the lower to the higher status family. In such cases, there was no prior kin relationship between the two groups and only a one way affinal relationship, not a reciprocity. In other words, it was clearly the introduction of hypergamous marriages that was responsible for the new gift giving from the bride's side, and vice versa. Hypogamous marriages had brought about the reversal of the prestation patterns in the case of Gulf grooms.

The de-castification of status

The introduction of hypergamy and hypogamy illustrate that the traditional principles underlying marriage patterns were being eroded. What is of even greater significance than the change in the *pattern* of marriage (from equal to unequal status matches) is the change in the *content* of status. Hypergamous marriages in Kerala and elsewhere in India are typically between members of a higher and lower *caste* (or sub caste) or at least of higher and lower family status, or ancestry. However, an examination of the new marriage patterns, and my conversations with the villagers seemed to indicate that it was education (and the income that accrues through having educational qualifications) that was most highly regarded. I was told, if a boy has education, that's what counts nowadays. Then no one looks at family [background] or wealth. (Family status was still quite important but the two criteria were overlapping since increasingly, family status or ancestry referred to the type of jobs that were held by family members in the past or at the present.)

Thus, a good match for a girl was usually considered to be: a doctor, an engineer, a lawyer with a good practice or a holder of a government job (in that order). Many wealthy Gulf families were able to get such grooms for their high school educated daughters. One coir merchant of high standing in the village recounted: My relatives and friends tell me: Look for education, not more wealth [in the bride groom] for your daughter. Education begets education so even your daughter's children will be able to get good positions. Wealth, especially Gulf wealth is ephemeral and can pass away. A woman with a Master's or a Bachelor's degree was considered to be a prize catch for a man and again several migrants with just a few years of education but with well paying jobs in the Middle East were able to marry such women from relatively less affluent families.[12]

The following excerpt from a long conversation I had with women in Muttam regarding marriage practices and ceremonies provides further evidence of the new norms underlying the practice of dowry.

> "Generally, men don't *ask* for a dowry when they contract a marriage. It is considered to be in bad taste and most families will not give daughters in marriage to a man who has any financial demands. But of course, it is impossible to get a girl married without giving anything. The men don't ask because they can generally assess how much gold the family will give the girl and how much her property share is worth. Dowries in the form of cash are generally considered vulgar and are avoided.
>
> Men from the lower classes, however, do make financial demands. Poor people have to give [relatively] large sums of cash in addition to gold and property to get their daughters married since this is what the couple uses to start off in life. A huge dowry [including cash and expensive consumer goods] has also to be given to get a man with a professional or salaried job. One has to give a car to get a doctor or engineer and around

> Rs. 100,000 for a lawyer with a good practice [in addition to a large amount of gold and the promised property share]. *It is only in such cases, where the man is highly educated that the groom's side can make demands and the bride's side has to give what is demanded.*"[13]

In other words, it was shameful for an average middle class person to demand a dowry but poor men did this since they needed the money. Paradoxically, however, it was perfectly justified (even appropriate) for a highly educated person to make extravagant dowry demands! This seeming contradiction makes sense if the cash dowry in the latter case is viewed as a tribute to the high educational and professional status of the groom.[14] Such payments have been described as being groom-price (Osella and Osella: 2000a: 97).

Although it was theoretically possible for a person from a poor family to obtain a professional education and a salaried government job, in general, wealthy families had a distinct advantage. Coaching classes and private schools were expensive and even if the child was successful at that stage, admission into many of the professional and technical courses conducted by private colleges could only be obtained through donations (which ran up to Rs. 300,000 for a seat in a medical college in the late Eighties). Getting a job after earning such a degree was still not easy. Most salaried jobs in Kerala could only be obtained by paying another huge donation (often an amount equal to more than the five year income earned on the job).

Thus, Gulfites could use their money to purchase a comfortable life style and also to buy education as a means of legitimizing and refining their (new) money. In short, over the second half of the Twentieth century, the traditional system had changed to such an extent that not only had the monopoly of the upper castes over the control of income-generating resources been whittled away, but in many ways, status itself had become commoditized.

I have mentioned that it was the Ezhavas who had introduced the pattern of status spending for weddings. The Nayars resisted this pattern at first justifying it by saying: We are careful with money and know better than to throw it around unnecessarily. The Ezhavas are just wasteful spendthrifts. But as their own social position deteriorated and that of the Ezhavas rose, the wealthier Nayar started following the Ezhava model. As a savvy Ezhava woman put it: If an Ezhava gave Rs. 25 as a wedding present, a Nayar would only give Rs.10: if an Ezhava gave a dowry of fifty one pavan, a Nayar would only give thirty one pavan. The Nayars have been trying to catch up only in the last few years. The Nambudiris of the area had fairly simple wedding ceremonies. However, even they admitted to having been forced to modify their practices a little in the recent period, particularly in the case of dowries and wedding gifts. But they still continued to give far less than an Ezhava of equal economic standing.

Interpreting the new patterns

In the previous section, I have described and tried to decode the modifications in the patterns of marriage alliances and in the rituals and ceremonies of marriage introduced by the Ezhavas as a consequence of their newfound affluence. Turning now to the interpretation of these new patterns—I would argue that the modifications symbolized a challenge to the cultural hegemony of the upper castes and are indicative of a fundamental change in the traditional system. If colonialism resulted in a *reformation* of the system, the large scale migration seems to have brought about its *transformation*. I indicated earlier that the caste system at the end of the colonial period had become a structure of hierarchical, endogamous status groups. Although it is still too early to say anything definitive about the long–term implications of the recent changes, my impression was that the caste system, particularly in the migrant areas, was moving toward an arrangement that created and maintained community and that regulated the marriage universe of its members. Thus, my argument is that the new marriage patterns and rituals symbolized a process of the *de castification of status*. This can be seen from the fact that marriages between partners of unequal social status (typically hypergamous marriages) which were earlier based on caste or *ritual purity* were increasingly based on *achieved* qualities such as education, class position and occupational status. Marriages were still arranged within the caste group but the universe of marriage alliances had become larger since sub-caste distinctions had become less relevant. The personal qualifications of the individual and the family generally superseded sub-caste considerations.

The changes were not in the direction of *Sanskritization.* While the new gold giving rituals were structured to fit into the broader Hindu cultural context, they were not in imitation of Nayar (or

Brahmin) practices, particularly of the groups in the area. In fact, it was the Nayars and even the Brahmins who later followed the lead of the Ezhavas. Again, classic *Sanskritization* strategies such as vegetarianism (the Nayars avoided beef and many did not eat lamb either, but Ezhavas ate lamb and many even ate beef) and teetotalism were not introduced and ceremonies such as the puberty festival which many Nayars still continued to perform, were no longer celebrated by the Ezhavas. Furthermore, while the Ezhavas could have had their weddings conducted at the traditionally high caste temple by Brahmins, most preferred to go to Sivagiri and to use Ezhava priests. All the evidence seemed to indicate that the Ezhavas were not aiming to pass as Nayars, to be like them, or even to have Nayar friends. Instead, they were secure and self possessed, with a strong sense of caste identity and pride.

This, of course, was not a change that came about only due to the migration. Other developments in the Twentieth century such as the social reform movements and the Communist movement were also responsible for the rise in the status of the Ezhavas. Furthermore, Ezhava organization and pride were particularly strong in the Cherur region since it was the center of the caste movements initiated by Sri Narayana Guru and had also become a fairly strong Communist base. While many of the traditional features of the caste system existed in other parts of Kerala that I visited or knew about, (even just a hundred or so miles to the north of Cherur) in spirit if not in form, this was not the case in Cherur. In this area, the numerical preponderance of the Ezhavas, their political power and the current economic ascendancy gained by the decades of migration had turned the traditional system on its head and class and education were superseding caste as an indicator of status.

There were other developments that could be taken as indications of this change. For instance, interdining between castes had become fairly common. While there were still some Nayars (mainly older people) who did not dine with Ezhavas, this was not behavior that was condoned even by most Nayars. I was told that most people, particularly those who were educated (considered to be the social elite of the community) would have been ashamed to show that they still held on to such old fashioned rules. Earlier, upper castes invited to an Ezhava wedding would generally only attend the function the day before the wedding when snack items were served (accepting such food from lower castes was permitted even in the traditional caste system). If it was a Nayar wedding, the Ezhavas would be called in to eat after the Nayars had finished and left the hall. The Harijans would be served last and would only be permitted to sit outside the hall. But all those practices had been abandoned and I was told, now, all those who are decently dressed are served food together. I saw this at the wedding I attended.

Again, while the majority of the Harijans lived in separate colonies and were still treated as a low status group, I came to realize that this was as much due to class as caste. A few educated, salaried Harijans lived in the Ezhava area and seemed to be treated as equals. During the initial period of my fieldwork in the area the local pre-school was staffed by two Nayar women: Sarasa and a cook. But by the end of June, the Nayar cook had been fired and a Harijan installed in her place. In November, Sarasa went on leave for a few months and a Harijan teacher was hired for the period. When I asked some of the villagers whether anyone had minded having their child taught and fed by Harijans (something that would have been totally unheard of earlier and would not have been well received in many parts of the state even in the late Eighties) I was told that no one had objected. It is not caste that matters but hygiene.

The existence of hypogamous marriages could also indicate a fundamental change in the traditional role and position of women. Conventionally, through a set of cumulative criteria, all attempts were made to see that the husband has a higher status than the wife. Thus, husbands were older, had more education, a higher paying job (if the woman was also working outside the home) and came from higher status families. The belief was that it was this unequal relationship that made for a harmonious marriage and it was for this reason that hypogamous marriages were forbidden. In a hypogamous marriage the structural inequality between the spouses is disturbed. From my observations, it did seem to me that this worked to the advantage of women since women who married hypogamously were accorded more respect by their husbands and in-laws.

Conclusion

In this paper I have traced the transformation of the caste system in the Cherur area over the past century. From a structure which was so all encompassing that it dictated almost every action of an individual, it became a system of stratified, endogamous communities in the post-colonial period. With the movement toward the de-castification of status, it seemed to be moving towards an arrangement that regulated little more than the marriage universe of its members. Education, class position and occupational prestige seemed to be replacing ritual purity as the indicators of status.

The metamorphosis of the caste system went hand in hand with substantial changes in the economic, political and social standing of the main castes in the Cherur region. The Nambudiris, once considered to be the semi divine local rulers, had become ordinary land lords and salaried workers (though they were still treated with some awe and respect by the villagers). The Nayars had become a largely impoverished group, in psychological and social retreat from the community that they once dominated, and the Ezhavas, formerly considered non caste Hindus with few rights and only a little above the slave castes, had become an increasingly affluent section of society, rapidly becoming educated and politically powerful. With their numerical preponderance, economic, political and social power, they seemed to be taking over as the local dominant caste. This transformation has been concomitant with the changes in the economic, political and social standing of each of the main castes. The Nambudiris who were once almost like semi-divine local rulers had become ordinary land-lords and salaried workers (though they are still treated with some awe and respect by the villagers). The Nayars had become a largely impoverished group, in psychological and social retreat from the community that they once dominated and the Ezhavas, formerly considered non-caste Hindus with few rights and only a little above the slave castes, were an increasingly affluent section of society, rapidly becoming educated and politically powerful.

As a group, the Harijans were still economically and socially marginal in society. Although they no longer faced any legal restrictions, in practice, most of them led their lives in colonies which were separated from the rest of the society. Even in the case of the Harijans, however, those who were able to move out of the colonies and obtain salaried occupations were accorded a far better status.

These changes were effected with amazing rapidity. I have argued that this transformation took place due to two principal processes—

colonialism and large scale labor migration. Both processes resulted in the creation of a new structure of economic opportunities in the society at large, one that reversed the pre existing structure and allowed the lower castes and classes to be the prime beneficiaries.

Until the middle of this century, upward mobility took place through the process of *Sanskritization.* Both the Nayars and Ezhavas had been actively engaged in this process as a means to secure status in the society. But the breakdown of the caste system and the social structure linked with it, together with the large scale Ezhava migration which brought about an economic reversal in the position between the Ezhavas and the Nayars, resulted in caste mobility taking a new form based on fundamentally different principles. *Sanskritization* only resulted in a positional change within the existing structure, but seemed to be taking place as a consequence of the migration was a change in the structure itself, one that has brought about reversals in the caste system and the conceptualization of status.

The transformation of the earlier system was a consequence and a manifestation of a fundamental shift in the power balance between the groups in the society. The caste system had institutionalized the cultural dominance of the economically and politically powerful sections of the society, the upper castes. The system had some room for upward mobility but this was very restricted and only a long-term possibility. The empowerment of the Ezhavas (and to some extent the lower castes in general) through colonialism, marketization, the Communist movement and the Gulf migration, and the concomitant weakening of the position of the upper castes during this period, seems to have resulted in the emergence of a more open status system.

Notes

1. This chapter is based on my dissertation fieldwork and is a modified version of part of chapter 6 in my book, *Kaleidoscopic Ethnicity: International Migration and the Reconstruction of Community Identities in India,* (Rutgers University Press, 2002). The field research was supported by grants from the Center for the Study of Comparative Development at Brown University, Sigma Xi, Taraknath Das Foundation, Indian Council for Social Science Research and the Association for Asian Studies. The subsequent period of writing was partly funded by a Dissertation Fellowship from the Thomas J. Watson Jr. Institute for International Studies, Brown University. I am grateful to all these institutions for their support.

2. The name of the village and its inhabitants have been changed.
3. See for instance, Aiya (1906), Innes 1951 [1903], Logan 1981 [1887], Menon 1967, Jeffrey 1976 for accounts of the early history of Kerala and a description of the caste system.
4. Robin Jeffrey (1976: 11) quotes Nagam Aiya in his 1875 census report as describing the position of the Brahmins in this manner. "His tenants...bow down to him not simply as a landlord but as their royal liege and benefactor...their very God on earth".
5. But in practice both polyandry and divorce were rare, at least after the late 19th century when the scribes of the colonialists studied the issue. See Logan (1981, [1887], 136) and Aiya (1906, 359-360).
6. This was the case for those Ezhavas in the region. The family structure and inheritance pattern of Ezhavas varied across the state.
7. Given the poor quality of the school system in the rural areas, and the fact that the parents did not have much education, it was only with the help of such classes that children could do well in their exams.
8. The earlier pattern when there were no such ceremonies, was that the gifts would be given at the time of the wedding and any money given would go to the boy's family.
9. In practice this was part of the dowry of the girl but in theory, the term 'dowry' in this area referred to cash (and expensive consumer items) given to the bridegroom or his family at the time the marriage was contracted. In addition to the gold (and cash which may or may not be given), the girl got a share of the family property. Here again, in theory the property was to be divided equally between the children but in practice in most poor and middle class homes most of it ended up going to the daughters for their dowries.
10. Cross cousins were however merely the preferred category of spouses. In practice, the choice of the actual spouse depended on the circumstances such as age, availability and inter familial relationships.
11. In fact, it is even hypothesized that one of the reasons for the better position of women in Kerala (and South India in general) is that cross cousin marriages were fairly widely prevalent. (Dyson and Moore 1983).
12. A wealthier family would prefer to obtain a bride-groom who was wealthy and educated. This they were able to do by giving a larger dowry.
13. This is transcribed from a long conversation I had with some Ezhava women in Muttam, Cherur regarding marriage practices and ceremonies.
14. Undeniably it is also partially because of the relatively high salary as well as the permanent (pension benefits) and steady nature of the income that the latter is expected to be able to earn. But income per se is not the

main reason (since Gulfites and businessmen could earn more). What is more important is the fact that income earned through the use of education is seen as "prestigious" or "honorable" income.

References

Aiya, N. 1906. *Travancore State Manuals, Volumes 1, 2 & 3*. Trivandrum: Tranvancore Government Press.

Dyson T., and M. Moore. 1983. On Kinship Structure, Female Autonomy and Demographic Behavior in India. *Population and Development Review*, 9: 35-60.

Fuller, C. J. 1976. *The Nayars Today*. Cambridge, U.K.: Cambridge University Press.

Innes, C. A. 1951 [1903]. *Malabar*. Madras: Superintendent, Government Press.

Jeffrey, R. 1976. *The Decline of Nayar Dominance: Society and Politics in Travancore 1847-1908*. New Delhi: Vikas Publishing House, Inc.

Kumar, G. 1989. Gender, Differential Mortality and Development: The Experience of Kerala. *Cambridge Journal of Economics*. 13: 517-539.

Kurien, P. A. 2002. *Kaleidoscopic Ethnicity: International Migration and the Reconstruction of Community Identities in India*, New Brunswick, NJ: Rutgers University Press.

—— 1994a. Colonialism and Ethnogenesis: A Study of Kerala, India. *Theory and Society*. 23: 385-417.

—— 1994b. The Non-economic Bases of Economic Behavior: Consumption, Investment and Exchange Patterns among Three Emigrant Communities in Kerala, India. *Development and Change* 25: 757-783.

—— 1992. Sojourner Migration and Gender Roles: A Comparison of Two Ethnic Communities in Kerala, India in J.S. Emlen, ed., *Continuity and Change: Women at the Close of the Twentieth Century*, Occasional Paper No. 12. Thomas J. Watson Jr. Institute for International Studies, Providence, R.I.: 43-61.

Levi-Strauss, C. 1969. *The Elementary Structures of Kinship*. Boston: Beacon Press.

Logan, W. M. C. S. 1981 [1887]. *Malabar*. Trivandrum: Charitham Publishers.

Menon, S. 1967. *A Survey of Kerala History*. Kottayam, India: National Book Center.

Osella, F. and C. Osella. 2000a. *Social Mobility in Kerala: Modernity and Identity in Conflict*. London: Pluto Press.

——2000b. Migration, Money and Masculinity in Kerala. *Journal of the Royal Anthropological Institute* 6: 117-133.

Pandey, R. 1986. *The Caste System in India: Myth and Reality*. New Delhi: Criterion Publications.

Pillai, A. K. B. 1987. *The Culture of Social Stratification: The Nayars*. Acton, Mass.:Copley Publishing Group.

Srinivas, M. N. 1968. *Social Change in Modern India*. Berkeley and Los Angeles: University of California Press.

The Kolis of Gujarat: A conspectus

Lancy Lobo

I

Introduction to the Kolis

The Kolis are the single largest caste in Gujarat. According to the 1931 Census, they accounted for nearly 20 per cent of the total population of Gujarat (Lobo: 1986:371). They are spread in almost every village in mainland Gujarat and in most villages in peninsular Gujarat. They also co-exist with the tribal people in some parts of highland Gujarat. Since the Kolis are also found in the adjoining parts of the neighbouring states of Rajasthan and Maharashtra, so the Gujarat tract forms the mid-portion of the *Koli belt* in western India.

The Kolis are not a homogeneous people. In some parts of Gujarat they are known only as Kolis, without any sub-caste or sub-group name: they are divided in to named sub-castes in some other areas. Two main endogamous divisions exist among the Kolis in most parts of Gujarat: *Talpada* (indigenous) and *Pardeshi* (foreign). Some other names like *Idaria Koli, Debaria Koli, and Chumvalia Koli* suggest the places from which they emigrated, though in the place of origin they may not be identified by the same name. There are also groups among the Kolis who are identified by the name of their traditional occupation, as for example, *Pagi* (village watchman). There are some sub-group names that seem to have been honorific patronymics, such as *Khant, Dharala, and Baraiya*. One of the problems in studying Kolis is to find a path in the maze of their group names. In Saurashtra, they are known as *Ghedia, Divechia, Valankiya, Chumvalia, Talpada, Khant and Pagi Koli*. In North Gujarat, they are called as *Thakarda*

(Thakor), Chum valia, Pagi and Indaria Koli. In Central Gujarat, they are named as *Pardeshi, Talpada, Bariya, Bhalia, Khant, Kotwal, Pagi, Patanwadia, Chumvalia, Debaria and Dharala.* In South Gujarat, they are addressed as *Rathwa, Talpada, Matia, Machhi, Kachhia, Mansarovaria and Khedvaya Koli. Vast majorities of north Gujarat's Kolis are known as Thakardas, but of late they prefer to be called Thakors.*

Mention must also be made of another status group of Kolis who have upgraded themselves and are located somewhere at the midpoint of the Koli-Rajput continuum in north Gujarat. These have been called *Palavi Darbars* in social usage and Rajput-Koli Thakardas in official records. The Gazetteer of Bombay Presidency (1901: 238) identifies the following as belonging to this category: *the Solankis of Bankoda, Chaniar, Dekavada and kukvav in Chumval; the Makvanas of Kotosan, Janjuvara and Punar; the Rathods of Ghanti and Vaghpur on the banks of the Sabarmati; the Dabhis of Ghodasar in Charotar; the Chohans of Amliara in Mahikantha, and the Vaghelas of Kankrej.* They were chieftains of one or more villages during the Maratha and British rules. Thus, at one extreme we can find ordinary Kolis, and at another end of the continuum the Koli chieftains who ruled over one or more villages in different parts of Gujarat.

In Gujarat, as elsewhere, some castes are predominantly urban-oriented, many are rural-oriented, and a few are both rural as well as urban-oriented. The Kolis are basically a rural-oriented caste. However, there is regional variation in their occupation. Those who live in the coastal area of peninsular Gujarat generally earn their living by fishing. In mainland Gujarat, however, the bulk of the Kolis are agricultural labourers, tenants and small landholders (Naik: 1981; G. Shah: 1982).

The Kolis have also been considered as congeries of aboriginal tribes in the past, but nowadays they are regarded as castes within the Hindu caste system (Shah: 1955a:109). Traditionally, the Kolis are non-vegetarian in their diet, and their ritual rank is much lower than that of the other meat-eating castes like the Rajputs. In order to grant protective discrimination, the Bakhshi Commission included nearly all the Kolis among the 'socially and educationally backward classes'. The Mandal Commission placed the Kolis under the category of 'Other Backward Classes' (OBC) in 1980.

II

Ethnography of the Kolis

Social science literature on the Kolis, who account for nearly one fourth of the total population of Gujarat, is not at all commensurate with their importance. We shall now attempt a conspectus of the Kolis of Gujarat by examining the available literature on the Kolis from different parts of Gujarat.

There is a prevalent opinion concerning the Kolis of Gujarat that they have tribal origins. For instance, Koppers has cited Bishop Heber, a British religious head and traveler, "*These last (i.e., the Kolis in certain parts of Gujarat) form perhaps two-thirds of the population, and are considered by public men in Guzerat as the original inhabitants of the country, a character which, I know not why, they refuse to the Bheels, who here, as in Malwah, seem to have the best title to it"(Koppers 1943:4) Wilson held that if the Bhils were aboriginals of the hills, the Kolis were the aboriginals of the plains.* Kolis have also been considered as civilised Bhils. *"Bhils and Kolis of eastern Gujarat being almost as hard to distinguish as are the Kolis and Rajputs of western Gujarat and Kathiawad ..." (Koppers: 1943: 8).*

Regarding the Kolis, A. Shah wrote, "Over a 100 years ago, they were-a congeries of aboriginal tribes, but now a days they are regarded as castes within the Hindu caste system" (1955a: 109). To support his opinion, Shah also cites scholars such as Risley, Hutton, and Enthoven (1922). In the Indian context, the word 'tribal' is a disputed one in sociological literature. However, to borrow a term used by Srinivas, what the above- mentioned writers indicate is that Kolis have been 'indigenes' of Gujarat.

The tribals are being absorbed into the caste system through a well-known process called *Sanskritisation,* which has been at work since the earliest times in Indian history. But when the tribals were inducted into the caste system they were assigned low ritual status. The Kolis are less Sanskritised in their life-style, ritual behaviour and practice of the traditional values of Hinduism. For instance, their household and family compositions have revealed that there is greater incidence of nuclear households and relative absence of joint households (Lobo: 1992). Hence, the practice of the Hindu norm of joint living of patrikin and their wives and children is found in a lesser degree among the Thakors of Dhoria. Fraternal joint living is also conspicuously absent, especially after the death of the parents. These norms are present among the upper castes such as the Patels in Dhoria village. Shah (1973) has also reported the same characteristic from the village he studied in central Gujarat. Thakors practice bride price, widow remarriage, leviratic and sororatic marriages, which again indicate their low ritual status in the regional caste. The Thakors of north Gujarat do not have *gotra vyavastha* of the Brahmins, nor the clan system of the Rajputs. They have, what is known as *gamshakha*, which is a collection of agnatic lineages dispersed in a few villages, calling themselves after the name of the village of their common origin. The *gamshakha* is in effect the largest exogamous unit among the Kolis of north Gujarat and also among those that migrated to central Gujarat, such as *Patanwadias and Chumvalias*. The Kolis use the term *gotra* to mean the *Gamshakha.* They also use the term *gol (*marriage circle), to mean the number where they have marital links. The terms *gotra* and *gol* among the Kolis indicate their emulation of the upper castes. Kolis in other parts of Gujarat worship the *mata or Shakti* in her non-Sanskritic manifestations. Commenting on the religious beliefs of Kolis in Kathiawad, Mankad writes that the Kolis are predominantly worshippers. They have one goddess called *Sakat or Shakti.* She would be by their side and would help them in all respects. They choose one of her many manifestations as the family deity and worship her as supreme power in the world. These goddesses play a very great part in settling their everyday troubles The role of the oracle is also extremely important in the religious universe of the Kolis of Kathiawad (1940:245-7).

Silverberg has extensively discribed the lower degree of *Sanskritisation* among Koli Patels of Kasandra village, referred to earlier, in terms of the prevalent traits such as beliefs in phantom spirits, sorcery, magic, 'evil eye' and the spirit medium. He has also mentioned the rising popularity of *bhagat* (a pious man) whose pious devotion to the greater Hindu deities is being accorded high prestige in opposition to the *bhuva* (the spirit medium) (1962:333). Pocock has highlighted the less Sanskritic nature of Baraiya's (Kolis) of Sundarana village in central Gujarat and recorded the Sanskritising tendencies among them.He writes :

"Bhattiji is a god whose services are available to members of all castes, but the Bareia regard him as particularly their own. They themselves claim to be of Rajput origin and in the legend Bareia is Thakurji, respected lord, a title also used to address Rajputs. The Bareia have also surrounded his shrine with a wall with the intention, currently abandoned, of covering it to create a large temple. Without the resources of the wealthy Patidar, they have been unable to decorate it as finely as the shrine of Ashapurimata, but they have persuaded Brahman to officiate and, at least today, there is no hint that blood sacrifice is offered to Bhattiji" (1973:70).

Census operations and status claims

The Census operations bear witness to the widespread desire of the Kolis of Gujarat to *Rajputise* themselves. For instance, G.H. Desai in his comments on Census returns mentions, "some Baria Kolis claimed to be Thakores" (1912:237). He also noted that:

"A section of Kolis left off their traditional occupation of menial labour and took to the making of bricks. They came to be known as Dalwadi or Talvari, that is cutters, because they dug ponds and made bricks. This new and honourable profession gave them a high social status, and in course of time, they came to be known as a new caste of Kolis. They now call themselves Rajputs and have severed all connection with the other Kolis"(1912:244).

Regarding Baria Kolis of Central Gujarat, the Census Says:

"There was a large and genuine movement of central Gujarat Barias to be considered distinct from Kolis, and affiliated to the Rajput. Petitions were received from 32 villages signed by over 1000 persons. Local enquiries confirmed the genuineness of their feeling. Representative Rajput Thakors and other Rajput organisers were asked whether they were prepared to consider Barias as belonging to them. They refused, but admitted having taken girls in marriage from them as from Makwanas and Talbadas. Baria, Khant, Makwana and Talbada are shown separately from the Koli total. Their claim to Rajput status turned down, as the Census was no forum for recording such decisions" (Census Report: 1931:394).

Concerning the Patanwadia Kolis, It is Reported:

"The Barias, themselves an aspiring community, are a caste to which many of the lower caste Kolis (Patanwadia and the like) wish to affiliate themselves as a half way house to the Rajput status. Particularly was this tendency evident in this census, as it was decided that the Barias would

> not be shown under Kolis in the Caste Table. As a result many of these Patanwadias etc., called themselves Baria.It is necessary, therefore, to take the Baria, Khant and Makwana total and add it to that of Koli and allied castes, to find out the true rate of variation..." (Census Report: 1931:60).

The Secretary, Gujarat *Kshatriya Samaj* applied to the local government to issue orders to, "*class the members of the Baria community among Kshatriyas or class them separately as Baria Rajputs... It was ascertained that they are Kolis and not Kshatriyas. Kshatriyas as such have not been separately tabulated" (Census Report: 1931:398).*

The Rajputs were unevenly distributed in different regions of Gujarat. For instance, in south Gujarat they were numerically insignificant. The sizeable Koli population of south Gujarat is perhaps the least Rajputised among the Kolis The dominant castes generally set the model for people in the area and hence one may speculate if the south Gujarat Kolis emulated the Anavils or the Patidars in the relative absence of Rajputs in the area. In south Gujarat a large number of Kolis attach the suffix Patel. Shah (1955a,1955b) and Silverberg(1962) have reported the same phenomenon from eastern and western Gujarat respectively. Apart from the emulation of Patel caste, one may also suggest that in predominantly Koli villages a number of Kolis assumed the position of Revenue and Police Patel of the village, and thus came to be addressed with the appellation of Patel.

Endogamous status groups among the Kolis of Gujarat

There is a broad spread of Koli names in Gujarat. In Saurashtra, these names are Talpada, Chumvalia, Ghedia, Valankia and Khant Kolis whom scholars like Desai (1958), Roy (1983) and Joshi (1984) tend to consider as *jatis,* sub-castes, or endogamous units. Silverberg reports presence of three "endogamous" units of Kolis in Kasandra viz., Koli Patels, Koli Thakardas and Koli Pagis (1962:30). In central Gujarat, the varieties of names that include the Kolis are Baraiya, Dharala, Khant, Pagi, Patelia, Talpada, Thakarda and Thakor (Shah: 1981). In south Gujarat, there are Talpada, Matia and Gulam Kolis (Patel: 1984:3).

Are these names suggestive of endogamous groupings? One may have to wait for further sociological accounts from various regions to give an adequate answer to this question. But from the already existing evidence, one can say that all these names are not indicative of endogamy, the kind of endogamy one finds among Leva Patels, where the endogamous units are very discrete.

We have already seen that the assumption of prestigious names was common among the Kolis.However, assigning prestige to a particular name is a phenomenon that undergoes change with the passage of time. For instance, at one time names like Pagi and Kotwal (watchmen) were prestigious but now have fallen into disrepute. So also names like Baraiya and Dharala were once in fashion but no more.

Shah, who has thrown much light on understanding the caste universe of Gujarat, has this to say, "*The Kolis seem to have had only two divisions in every part of Gujarat: for example, Talpad (indigenous) and Pardeshi (alien) in central Gujarat, Palia and Baria in eastern Gujarat*" (1982:7). The Talpadas are found in the south, central as well as peninsular Gujarat. One hardly comes across the Talpadas in north Gujarat, mainly because there has been no immigration of Kolis from other parts of Gujarat into this region. On the other hand, the reverse is true, as north Gujarat Kolis both from Chumval and Patan have emigrated to Saurashtra as well as to south and are known there as Chumvalia Kolis and Patanwadia Kolis respectively. As opposed to the locals or indigenous, it is this category of Kolis who are considered Pardeshi. The Talpada and Pardeshi do not indulge in marital transactions and have, thus, remained distinct endogamous units.

From the foregoing analysis therefore, *it is possible to isolate two kinds of Koli settings in Gujarat. In the first, as in north Gujarat, there are no immigrant Kolis, and these Kolis are called Thakardas or better still Thakors, freely arranging marriages among themselves*. In the second, *indigenous Kolis live side-by-side with immigrant Kolis from an adjoining area*, as in Saurashtra, central and south Gujarat. Here the *Talpadas, who belong to the same division, freely arrange marriages among themselves and are known by several lineage* names, like Bariya, Dharala, Khant, Kotwal, Pagi, Patelia, Talpada and Thakoro. Shah notes, "I have not yet come across an area where Kolis from three or more different areas live together, excepting in modern, large towns and. cities" (1982:13).

A thought must be given to the maze of names within a division, lest they be mistaken for endogamous groups or sub-castes. In the case of Talpada, in opposition to the Pardeshi division, there is no problem. But how to explain the names among the Talpadas? Some names have occupational connotation, as ,for instance, Pagi and Kotwal (watchmen). In earlier times Pagi or Kotwal carried prestige and eventually they became family patronymics and hereditary. Thus, these patronymics suggest intra-Koli status among the Talpadas, who freely arrange marriages among themselves (Shah: 1977:359). In the same context, Shah points out that these Talpada lineages have now adopted a single name, Solanki, but they do not claim, "to belong to a single exogamous group". Adopting the patronymic Solanki is indicative of upward social mobility after the Rajput model. For the high status Rajputs, Solanki is also a derogatory name. Times have changed and what was once respectable has now become a term of contempt in the case of Pagi. Hence Rajputisation or Kshatriyaisation as a mechanism for status elevation is very much in vogue with the Kolis of Gujarat.

If we consider the Kolis of Gujarat (or even those outside) as a caste, i.e. *jati,* then there are broadly two divisions among them: Talpada and Pardeshi, in most regions of Gujarat. Each division can freely intermarry within itself. But within each division, over a period of time, differentiation and stratification has taken place and further groups have crystallised on a regional basis. Further sociological fieldwork is needed to establish if Talpadas of one region marry with those of another. It is also desirable to investigate if the Chumvalias and Patanwadias, who emigrated from north Gujarat, have maintained 'links with their horizontal group in places of their origin'.

Intra-Koli ranking at an all Gujarat level may be an exercise in futility. Regional intra-Koli ranking of status groups is a possibility in terms of food exchange, purity-pollution concept, Sanskritization, Rajputization, possession of economic and political power, hypergamy and marital exchanges wherever more than two status groups co-exist.

Koli-Rajput continuum

The Rajputs of Gujarat, as shown earlier, are divided into those claiming mythical descent from the Sun (*Suryavarnshis)* and the Moon (*Chandravarnshis)* and a few who claim their descent from the fire-god, *Agni.* Under each of these mythical lines, were patri-clans, like Jadeja, Jhala, Gohel, and Mahida, etc., which were exogamous. Below the clans are sub-clans, sub-sub-clans and lineages. *The Rajputs in general not only practiced clan hierarchy and hypergamy but also regional hypergamy. They also had status groups among them.*

Apart from clan hierarchy, political power and ownership of land gave rise to another kind of Rajput hierarchy that is significant for our discussion on Koli-Rajput continuum. Shah explains this Rajput hierarchy in the descending order (1959:52-58; 1982:10-11):

1. Royal families of large and powerful kingdoms;
2. Ruling lineages of the smaller and less powerful kingdoms;
3. Lineages of owners of large and small fiefs variously called jagir, giras, thakarat, thikhana, taluka and wanta;
4. Lineage of substantial landowners under various land tenures having special rights and privileges; and
5. Lineages of small landowners.

Thus, at the highest status were kings, rulers or *rajavi*, at the second level were Thakor-Sahebs, Thakors or Darbars, at the third were *jagirdars, girasdars(garasiyas), thikhanedars, talukdars and wanta* holders, at the fourth level were substantial landowners and at the fifth level were ordinary low-ranking Rajputs. Shah comments, "*as we go down the hierarchy, we encounter more and more debates regarding the claims of a particular lineage to being Rajput, so much so that we lose sight of any boundary and the Rajput division merges imperceptibly into some other division. In most parts of Gujarat it merged into the various second-order divisions of the Kolis and possibly also into the widespread tribe of Bhils" (1982:11).*

The Koli hierarchy in north Gujarat is simple: at one end are Thakors and at another are Darbars or chiefly Kolis. In Saurashtra, central and south Gujarat there are Talpada and Pardeshi divisions. Similar to the Darbars of north Gujarat, there were chiefly families among Talpada Kolis who married their daughters to low ranking

Rajputs.As we go from the bottom of the continuum to the top, we can observe a hierarchy within Kolis and Rajputs. At the lowest level or base of the pyramid the two-way relationships signify reciprocity among the ordinary Kolis. Here reciprocity means bride giving and bride bringing from nearby villages. At the base of the pyramid there is a general lack of the concept of hierarchy. The concept of hierarchy gets sharpness as one climbs towards the top of the base, where status groups among Kolis have crystallised. From then on hypergamy too follows close on the heels of hierarchy. In the case of Dhoria we observed that while brides are brought in from nearby villages, its daughters are given to far off places. While 36 villages give brides to Dhoria, in turn it gives its daughters to only 12. Both these facts help us to locate Dhoria Thakors somewhere at the middle or upper regions of the base of the pyramid and the continuum helps us to locate the point at which Koli stratum "Darbars" or "Thakors" meet the Rajputs (of low rank) in marital transactions. These Koli chiefs adopted Rajput customs, and traditions, and established hypergamous relations with the low-ranking Rajputs that provided a mechanism for upward mobility to them. The Rajputs, because they practiced internal hypergamy, had the need to recruit women for themselves from below and the families met these demands. It is well established that the incidence of unmarried males earlier among the low-ranking Rajputs and female infanticide among the high ranking Rajputs the incidence of unmarried males were prevalent earlier (Viswa Nath: 1969, 1976). This fits in well with the logic of hypergamy.

There are ethnographic and documentary reports about the Koli-Rajput liaisons, as also Bhil-Rajput marital relations. In central Gujarat, the Rajputs took wives from the Talpada chiefs and their kinsmen" (Shah: 1959:60). Shah also cites references where Bhil-Rajput marriages have taken place (Naik: 1956:18f; Nath: 1960:11-15, 57-75). The highland Bhils have also provided brides to lower Rajputs of Rajasthan and Madhya Pradesh (Arora: 1972:16, 32). Thus, Rajput hypergamy has provided an avenue for the elite sections of Kolis and Bhils to Sanskritise and Rajputise themselves.

The logical end of the inclusion and exclusion process in the Koli-Rajput continuum in central Gujarat comes out strongly in Pocock's writings, "*The leading Baria families in their own way exclude their caste fellows in their attempt to rise in status and these same lower levels include themselves with the higher. Similarly, the Baria as a whole claim Rajput affiliations but their claim is repudiated by the latter who, in their turn, would possibly not be recognised by the Rajputs of Rajputana*" (1957b: 29). Shah has also analysed this phenomenon in his writings (1955b; 1959; 1982).

III

Politicisation of Kolis in Gujarat

The growth of caste associations is relatively a recent phenomenon in India. In the post-Independence period the new opportunities in educational, political and economic spheres were supposed to be caste-free and open to all. But, in fact, they were more accessible to higher castes of learning. This increased their cultural, social and economic distance from the lower castes. As we have seen, the lower castes began to express their desire for upward mobility through *Sanskritisation*, listings in the Census operations and Backward Classes movement. It is in this context that caste *Sabhas* (associations) among the lower castes came into being. These caste associations articulated as well as organised the new urge to mobility. The *Sabhas* also altered the style of life of castes in the direction of *Sanskritisation*. Formation of associations and "heightened caste-awareness" resulted in the increase of "horizontal stretch" of castes (see Srinivas 1972: 98-100).

Shah has pointed out that in Gujarat there were caste associations much before Independence. These were limited to mostly the upper castes, and their main concern was welfare and social reform. The associations among lower and numerically larger castes such as the Kolis are a post-Independence phenomenon. Their express objective was more political than welfare. The elites dominated in these associations while the masses did not participate actively. But in the upper caste associations participation was more or less equal between the caste members (1982).

The involvement of the Koli caste in competitive modern politics could rightly be considered as a process of politicization (Sheth: 1979:178). Rajni Kothari (1965, 1970), Weiner (1967) and Ghanshyam Shah (1975) have studied the phenomenon of political movements of castes, relationship between caste associations and political parties, and the process of interaction between competitive politics and caste with reference to the Kolis of Gujarat.Narendrasinh Mahida, a Rajput, launched *Rajput Bandhu*, (Rajput Brother) in 1946, a publication intended to disseminate liberal-democratic ideas and promote social reform among the Rajputs. Natwarsinh Solanki (not a confirmed Rajput) who was running an association called *Charottar Kshatriya Samaj* became the co-editor of *Rajput Bandhu*. They also started the *Gujarat Rajput Kelavni Mandal* (Gujarat Rajput Education Society) in 1946 for educational activities among the Kshatriyas. Both these key figures broadened the scope of their activities into a movement that not only recruited non-Rajputs like the Kolis into the Sabha, but also brought about a degree of politicization among them.

Economically, the plight of the Kolis in general had deteriorated in many parts of Gujarat. They had also to bear the social ignominy of *haajari* and their educational status was extremely low. But their claim to be called *Kshatriyas* was ever sharpening. 'It was Natwarsinh Solanki who correctly read the situation and saw the signs of the time. He felt it necessary to go beyond the Kheda district and form a Gujarat-wide organisation of not only the Rajputs but also of others like the Kolis, who were claiming Rajput status. Hence in November 1947, Rajput leaders of Kutch, Kathiawar and the rest of Gujarat assembled at Dhrol, and resolved that *Gujarat Rajput Kelavni Mandal* be converted into *Kutch, Kathiawar, Gujarat Kshatriya Sabha*, whereby all the *Kshatriyas* of these areas can become its members and benefit from its activities. The word "Kshatriya" replaced the word "Rajput" in order to facilitate the inclusion of non-Rajput castes like the Kolis (Shah: 1975:43). The *Rajput Bhandhu* was renamed the *Kshatriya Bhandhu*. At its annual convention held on April 13, 1952, the *Kshatriya Sabha* demanded that the government they supported classify the *Kshatriyas* as "Backward Classes"so that they become eligible for the benefits that went with such a classification.

Since the government rejected this demand, the *Sabha* voiced its disillusionment with the Congress. Mahida, a staunch supporter of the Congress, disclosed his frustration in 1956 in these words, "I cannot ask you", he said, "to support the Congress because they have neglected you throughout these years. You are all free to decide according to your own discretions", cites Kothari (1965:41).

For the 1962 general elections, the anti-Congress Patidar Bhailalbhai and his Kshatriya opponent, Solanki, decided on a Patidar-

Kshatriya alliance in forming *the Swatantra Party* to oppose the Congress. The Swatantra Party accepted the *Kshatriya* demands, and *Kshatriyas* came to hold important positions in the *Swatantra* organisation. The *Kshatriyas* of Saurashtra came to realise that the basis of power had shifted from land to organisation of political support, and so worked towards bringing the lower castes like Kolis, Kathis, and Mers into the *"Kshatriya"* fold. Once again the *Kshatriya* movement got a new lease of life. Thus, the political platform brought together a number of castes, which had social and cultural links among them, under the Kshatriya label. Kothari and Maru observe, "*Caste provides not only channels of communication and leadership support for "submerged" sections of society but also important basis for joint and "voluntary" action in the organisation of which the urban-educated take the initiative*" (1965:48). In 1962, the *Swatantra* party emerged as the single largest opposition party in Gujarat and the Congress was routed in many parts of Gujarat. The Congress could not take the *Kshatriyas* for granted from then on. Kothari and Maru conclude their analysis with these words, *"A highly diffuse and plural society is here found to come to terms with the centralising tendencies of a modern polity. By inducing diverse social strata to enter into larger identifications and by providing to political leaders significant communication channels and a relatively stable loyalty structure, such a reorientation of the caste system fills an important place in the emerging infra-structure of modern India" (1965:50).* Before the 1967 general elections the *Kshatriya* caste association was divided between the Congress and *Swatantra.* Mahida went over to the Congress while Solanki remained with the *Swatantra.* A rift also developed between the old guard and younger elements within the *Sabha.* In 1971 on the eve of the fifth general elections, all *Kshatriyas* joined hands together against the Patidars and walked out of the *Swatantra Party*. Different *Kshatriyas* joined different political parties like the Organisation Congress, and the Ruling Congress. Some others contested as independents. The *Kshatriyas* as a group were completely split up in 1972. The Kolis have by and large separated themselves from the *Kshatriya Sabha* and formed independent associations. *Kshatriya Sabha, Kshatriva Bandhu*, and *Gujarat Kshatriya Kelavni Mandal* do continue even today, but their reach, hold, and mass base have been seriously eroded. The greatest impact of the *Kshatriya Sabha* was felt in central Gujarat and its nucleus continues even today. In general, one can say that the *Kshatriya Sabha* structurally began to interact on the political platform by structurally linking neghbouring social units. The Koli-Rajput continuum, discussed earlier, provided a cultural infrastructure to this platform. The Rajput and Koli elites interacted with each other as never before. And yet, the cleavage between the Rajputs and Kolis remained: the former were identified as upper *Kshatriyas* and the latter lower ones. The latter formed their own associations in different regions.

IV

Koli associations in different regions of Gujarat

Not much is known about Koli associations in central Gujarat but it is likely that Societies and Associations of the kind that exist in north Gujarat also exist there. The *Kshatriya Sabha*, with its headquarters at Nadiad of Kheda district, has been the major association in central Gujarat attracting a lot of attention of the Kolis of the region. In the Ahmedabad district, efforts are made to reorganize the Talpada Koli marriage circles for social and educational purposes. For instance, in Dholka taluka 42 village circles have become active in this regard. In Ahmedabad itself, there is one *Uttar Gujarat Thakor Yuvak MandaI* (North Gujarat Thakor Youth Association) at Mitakali. A Sociologist and also an activist, Arjun Patel, a Talpada Koli from south Gujarat, indicated that a number of Kolis had participated in the 1926 non-cooperation movement; in the 1930 *Dandi satyagraha*; and in the Quit-India movement of 1942. From the Olpad and Choryasi talukas alone 91 Kolis became freedom fighters. Koli leaders have been active in social reforms among their folks. A number of caste associations (*Gnati Sangathano*) have come up in south Gujarat: (1) *Dakshin Guiarat Koli Samajsangh, Surat; (2) Shree (Talpada) Koli Samaj (Olpad-Choryasi limited) Talpada Koli Vikas Mandal, Mangrol; (3) Bardoli Taluka Koli Samaj; (4) Shree Saurashtra Talpada Koli Gnati Samaj, Surat,* and so on. The last mentioned association belongs to those Talpada Kolis who have immigrated to Surat from Saurashtra. Patel mentions that the main objectives of these associations are social reform, promoting education, and furthering economic interests of the Kolis. Just as in the case of north Gujarat Koli associations, these too do not avowedly profess any political objective. Kambad, a Talpada

Koli from Bhavnagar, Saurashtra, writes in the book edited by him on behalf of the *Samast Koli Samaj* (All Koli Association), that since 1951 nearly every year meetings were held at different places in Saurashtra, to bring about 'we-feeling' among the Kolis, and to promote all round development among them (1981:453). According to Roy, this association took formal shape on November 20, 1973, under the title, *Shri Samast' Talpada Koli Samai* (The All Talpada Koli Society). Its first convention was held at Chotila (Surendranagar district) where about 7000 Kolis assembled. During this convention the *Bandharan* (constitution) of the association was framed and approved. Briefly, at the village level 5 elected members would compose the "*nath*" or *gramya panch* (village caste council) who have powers to tackle civil and social disputes and offences. The collective representation of a minimum of 5 and a maximum of 12 village "*naths*" or *gramya panches* type can be brought before the "*Hunda*". Roy has traced 13 "*Hundas*" having 106 *grarnya panches*, in what is called, "*Panchal Vistar*", that cuts across portions of Surendranagar, Rajkot, Junagadh and Amreli districts of Saurashtra. These 13 "*Hundas*" constitute the *nath mandal* or the supreme body. It is composed of an elected member from each of the 13 *Hundas*. The *Hunda* is constituted of elected members from each "*nath*" or *gramya panch*. One of the main functions or objectives of the society is "to develop the general standard of the Koli Samaj with respect to economy, culture and education (Roy: 1983:127)". The *Nath Mandal* appears to be purely a programmatic effort and yet, it is significant that Kambad makes no secret about the political intentions of the *Samast Koli Samaj* and their efforts to bring the Talpada associations of south Gujarat and Saurashtra together, perhaps eventually wanting all the Talpadas to unite on a common political platform (1981:465-472). The non-Talpada Kolis, though less organized, are showing signs of stirring up organisationally. Some of the Koli associations in different regions may be only on paper and are really not active, as for instance *Shri Samast Talpada Koli Samaj*. While it may not be active for a number of reasons, what is significant is the aspiration that it embodies for the Kolis. There is an effort at fusion and an orientation to horizontal solidarity. One must also remember the number of Koli associations that may have come into existence to take grants and funds from the government. The *Kshatriya Sabha* was the most ambitious project to unite highly differentiated Kolis and Rajputs. After its break-up, small Koli associations, Societies and Trusts sprung up all over Gujarat under the appellations, "All Gujarat Koli", "All Koli" "All Kshatriya" "All Tal Pada Koli" and so on These express the desire to unite the different status groups among Kolis so that they can cash in on the political platform under the dictum "union is strength". Caste consciousness and "we-feeling" among the Kolis has gained momentum.

As pointed out earlier, one must remember that there is a qualitative difference between Koli associations and upper caste associations. In the latter, participation by members of the caste is extensive as well as intensive. Among the former, participation is by and large restricted to the elite Kolis. They attempt to project their vested interests as those of the entire caste. By welfare activities of Trusts, Societies and associations they build credibility for themselves and build support from caste-fellows in the event of an election.

Kolis as OBCs

Kolis are economically differentiated. They have remained a basically rural-oriented caste. In agricultural skills they are backward as compared to the Patels. In different parts of Gujarat, they are occupationally diverse. For instance, Kolis in coastal Gujarat many earn their living by fishing. Low educational achievements have prevented them from securing good jobs in the job market. Their women are largely illiterate. Most males have hardly gone beyond primary education. Those who have gone beyond the primary have succeeded in securing low category jobs such as policemen, peons, drivers, clerks, and watchmen.

We have already referred to the Bakshi and Mandal Commissions appointed by the governments of Gujarat and India respectively, which included the Kolis of Gujarat among the OBCs. Their inclusion in the list of the OBCs by the Gujarat government met one of their long-standing demands.

Apart from being an instrument for achieving equality, the Backward Classes concept has also served as a device for maintaining balance of power in the political arena in different regions of India. Gujarat has not been the first to indulge in the Backward Classes game. This game was first played in South India in the form of an Anti-Brahmin Movement. In Gujarat the opposition is between the upper castes (Brahmins, Vaniyas and Patels) and the Backward Classes, chiefly the Kolis. The Kolis have sharper political consciousness now than ever before.

In 1975, the Gujarat government reserved 7 per cent of the seats for Scheduled Castes, and 13 per cent for Scheduled Tribes in the Medical Colleges at the suggestion of the Union Ministry of Health. As also mentioned earlier, it reserved additional 5 per cent seats for the 82 listed SEBC communities in 1980. In an unpublished paper Achyut Yagnik (1981) has shown that not more than 5 per cent of the reserved seats were actually filled in by the communities for which they were reserved. In 1981 Gujarat witnessed what has come to be known as the Anti-Reservation Struggle launched by the upper castes. Yagnik comments that the unity consciously achieved on this occasion among all Backward Classes was unparalleled in the social history of Gujarat. Commenting on the 1981 Anti-Reservation Stir, Bose writes "... in India where the role of caste and inherited status have for long influenced the monopolising of the available jobs by the upper castes, the mobility of lower castes is viewed as dangerous by vested interests and hence disruptive of social stability" (1985:138).

The government of Gujarat appointed the Rane Commission that submitted its report in October 1983 and the government decided to accept its recommendation of raising the reservation quota for Backward Classes from 10 to 28 per cent 15 months later. The government set up yet another body headed by a Congress MP, Haroobhai Mehta, to compile a fresh list in which as many as 167 communities were expecting to be included. The Anti-Reservation Stir repeated in 1985 was once again spearheaded by the upper castes. Though the stir was not particularly directed against any caste, at one point it threatened to pose as a confrontation between the Patels and Kolis in some parts of mainland Gujarat. Following Bose's observation, one may say that the upper castes have not taken kindly to the rise of Kolis on the political platform or to their claim in the economic cake.

A trend that has begun to emerge among the Thakors of north Gujarat is that some of the Koli elites are advocating a return to the name Koli. They ask: "What is in a name? What do people gain by calling themselves Thakors?" They add that if Thakors reverted to calling themselves Kolis, they might stand to benefit in terms of positive discrimination. In fact, the MLA of Kadi constituency held a meeting at Detroj prior to the Lok Sabha elections in, December 1984, where he advocated the idea of reverting to being called Kolis. At the moment, ordinary Thakors of north Gujarat certainly welcome positive discrimination but do not like to do away with the appellation "Thakors". The elite Thakors do not bother with appellations when it comes to securing economic benefits.

In contrast, many of the Darbars of north Gujarat welcome compensatory discrimination, even if it means taking on the Koli appellation. They are in a fix because they had declared themselves as Rajputs in the earlier Census and so are not eligible for 'reservations'. Thus, the Kolis see no contradiction or double-facedness in calling themselves *Kshatriyas* and wanting to be included among the OBCs. At the same time, they have even come to develop a vested interest in backwardness. The Kolis, who actively Sanskritised themselves after the Rajput model and claimed the *Kshatriya varna*, and succeeded to a great extent, have been seeking inclusion among the OBCs for securing economic benefits. The Kolis sought upgradation of social status earlier but their inclusion among the Other Backward Classes although giving some economic benefits involves status degradation. While there is a contradiction in this behaviour in the eyes of an "outsider", the Koli himself refuses to acknowledge or does not want to recognise the contradiction. Srinivas has explained this contradiction as follows:

> "In traditional India Sanskritisation" was not only of great importance for the ambitious caste but was difficult of achievement, as there were both religious and legal sanctions against taking over the ritual and style of life of the twice-born castes... But with the increase in spatial mobility and urbanisation, and with more and more castes participating in the new educational and employment opportunities, fear of boycott and physical violence by the dominant castes diminished if it did not disappear. Sanskritisation came to be seen by the lower castes as an adjunct to other and more important things, such as education, prestigious employment, and political power. They also saw that by itself it was of extremely limited value in raising the position of a caste" (1972:94).

One cannot draw a firm conclusion from this contradiction and say that ritual status has lost its relevance and secular status has gained prominence. Both ritual as well as secular statuses assert themselves according to the context of a situation. For instance, common or shared ritual status i.e.Kshatriya is emphasized by Koli leaders when they want to unite a highly differentiated Koli caste for political ends. If the context were securing economic and political benefits, the Kolis would relegate their ritual status and highlight their economic status.

V

Koli power in Gujarat

Forbes made the following observation in Rasmala more than a 100 years ago:

> "The numbers of the Koolees would have rendered them formidable had they been capable of union, but though they had a strong fellow-feeling for each other, they never regarded themselves as a nation, nor ever made common cause against an external enemy" (1856:442).

Forbes was largely correct except in claiming strong fellow feeling among them. This fellow feeling is not the type of feeling for horizontal solidarity and unity that we are going to talk about, which is a post-Independence phenomenon.

The picture of the Kolis around Independence was one of a dormant majority in Gujarat. Though their political ambitions manifested themselves in history, they were sporadic, occasional and unsystematic. But since Independence they have been on the road to modern politicisation. We have earlier mentioned the actors responsible for it: 'one man, one vote' principle, the growing consciousness of numerical strength, increasing attempts to form caste associations, sustained efforts at *Kshatriyaisation,* and the Backward Classes movement. If in 1952 there were only 4 elected Koli members then in the 1980 general elections there were no less than 40.

A couple of decades ago it was unthinkable that a Koli in north Gujarat could have fellow feeling towards another Koli living 10 miles away unless he was related to him through kinship. Today it is no exaggeration to state that not only does a Koli feel solidarity with another from the same region but also with those of other regions. How could this caste consciousness or horizontal solidarity come about in a caste so spread out and so diverse? This solidarity was possible because Kolis shared some similarity as a community. From this similarity was born identity. Not that there was no caste-identity in earlier times. It was there but fuzzy, diffuse and limited to some areas. Agents who kept up this identity were the cultural specialists such as

Barots and Targalas. The former fostered caste identity in a limited way with their mythography and genealogical devices and the latter with folk stories.

The persons primarily responsible for bringing about horizontal caste-identity in modern times were the Koli political leaders, through caste associations, Backward Classes movement and competitive politics. Caste associations and caste-specific 'societies' are as much instruments of projecting the economic interests of the dominant group as those of the entire caste. In order to elicit the support of the ordinary members of the caste, the Koli elites foster a sense of "we-feeling" through a variety of ways. Welfare programmes of caste associations such as loans, scholarships, hostels, schools, books, doles to widows and orphans convince the poorer members that it is for their welfare. Terms such as "*All Koli Samaj*", "*All Gujarat Thakor Samaj*" and "*All Talpada Koli Samaj*" indicate the serious attempts to bring the Kolis together.

The ordinary Kolis of one region may not have occasions to interact with those of another. But elected representatives of the Kolis at taluka, district and State levels have many opportunities to meet each other. Fellow feeling and caste-solidarity is generated first by these Koli leaders and then disseminated in their respective regions. Common political strategies are hammered out at these meetings. Prior to Independence, a meeting of the Koli leaders of all the regions was a remote possibility, but now it is an empirical reality. These leaders motivate caste consciousness and caste loyalty among the ordinary Kolis. Quite often, it is held that equality paves the way for identity. But different groups can share one common identity.

One must understand the community aspect of caste in order to what is happening to the Kolis of Gujarat. Common ritual status of the *Kshtriya* is highly desired by the Kolis despite existence of economic and political inequalities among them.

Koli political unity has cultural implications. One must recall the Koli-Rajput continuum referred to earlier. Kolis of all regions at the lower level of Koli hierarchy have more diversities than those at its top layer. The Koli leaders usually come from this top crust. Irrespective of their regional background, these leaders share a common culture in a great measure than those who are at the base. The Kolis of the top crust meet each other quite often and interact frequently and chart out political strategies. These top crusts Kolis also have a common source of influence, viz., the Rajputs. They give daughters in marriage to low-ranking Rajputs as pointed out earlier. Rajputisation has been greatest among these Kolis. These Kolis act as a link between the Rajput and Koli cultures.

Because of the inclusion and exclusion processes operative among them, the relationship between the Koli elites and the Rajputs has been a dialectical one. The Rajputs are constrained to accept Koli women in marriage because they practice internal hypergamy. Having accepted Koli women, the Rajputs are in danger of loosing Rajput status. By giving their daughters to the Kolis can claim the Rajput status. Yet,the situation is very fluid and rests on claims and counter-claims. The relationship between the Rajputs and Kolis has always been an uneasy one. When it is convenient to include the Kolis among the Rajputs, the latter have not hesitated to do so. For instance, the story of the *Kshatriya Sabha* bears testimony. Being just 5 per cent of the total population of Gujarat, the Rajputs realised that in 'one man, one vote' culture it is highly desirable to include Kolis in the *Kshatriya Sabha*. Having included them, the Rajput elites were niether ready to count them as equals nor share the spoils of power in its heyday. The Rajputs were called upper *Kshatriyas* and the Kolis the lower ones. The *Kshatriya Sabha* fell apart mainly because of the dialectical nature of relations between the Kolis and Rajputs.

Even today, the royal Rajputs will not accept the Koli elites who have secured high secular status such as professionals, bureaucrats and politicians. They will not have connubial relationship with the Koli elites. But the Koli elites will keep trying to upgrade their social status. It is said that they are trying to capture symbols of status such as participating in fine arts, attending cultural shows or presiding over such displays. These were the monopoly of the upper castes wherein elite Kolis are trying to seek entry.

Prior to Independence, most of the Koli chiefs composed the Koli elite. Since Independence many ordinary Kolis have attempted to become elites themselves. As mentioned earlier, Kolis had participated in some of the movements led by M. Gandhi. Gandhi was successful in bringing a certain degree of political awakening among the Kolis all over Gujarat. A number of Brahmins and Vanias inspired by Gandhi set up *ashrams* in many rural and remote areas in all parts of Gujarat.

These *ashrams* acted as nuclei for furthering the process of Koli awakening and a small number of them got educated. Many of those who benefited from such institutions were drawn to urban centres and secured lower level jobs such as drivers, peons, clerks, teachers, police and so on. Their children pursued further education than their parents. There was a snowballing effect in terms of education and availing newer job opportunities. Hence, the Kolis today have an increasing number of professionals like lawyers, schoolteachers, middle level government officials, etc. These could be rightly called the modern Koli elite. Though the number of elite Kolis is small, the role they play for the Koli masses is significant. They give the Koli masses a new confidence and self-esteem as a caste. With Kolis in the bureaucracy, the masses feel that they have some one in the centres of power who can get things done for them. So also the presence of a Koli school principal is a powerful factor in a locality. Irrespective of regions, the Koli elites meet each other oftener. Their presence in the urban centres is on the rise. Hence, traditionally rural-oriented Kolis are making inroads into towns and cities in Gujarat.

The Koli unity and political power reached its peak in the 1980s when Madhav Singh Solanki, a lower *Kshatriya*, became the Chief Minister of Gujarat. The ruling Congress party in Gujarat has its core supporters drawn from the KHAM (Kshatriya, Harijan, Adivasi and Muslim) groups.The Kolis are the single largest caste represented at different political levels in the KHAM alliance. The KHAM combine is basically lower strata combine, and the line of battle is drawn between the lower strata and the upper strata in Gujarat politics. The upper strata composed of the Brahmin, Vania and Patel, who have been elites in every aspect, have been seriously threatened by the KHAM on the political platform. The lower strata want a share in the new opportunities in the educational, economic and political spheres. The Backward Classes game can only be understood against this background. It is the KHAM combine under Solanki that increased the reservation quota of the Backward Classes and also made many other caste groups eligible for such benefits. The anti-reservation stir all over Gujarat has been a result of reaction of the upper castes to the increasing dominance of the lower strata in the political sphere.

It is obvious that the Kolis, who in the past were either in the militia or indulged in looting and dacoity, have now changed their fields of action and arenas. The increasing antagonism and hostility between Patels and Thakors is but a symptom of changing power structures. The same phenomena have been recorded for other levels such as taluka, district (Lobo: 1986). Loss of vertical unity in a region is an inevitable consequence of increased horizontal solidarity. In Gujarat, the rise of the Kolis in politics has intensified tension between them and the traditionally power-wielding upper castes such as the Patels, Brahmins and Vanias. Hence, one can observe structural changes afoot in the society in Gujarat as well as in Indian society. Thus, numerically preponderant but lower castes in many states of India like the Kolis are staking claims for political power in their respective states.

The Patels in Gujarat derived their power initially from landownership and then attempted to secure power on other axes, such as electoral politics, business, industry, commerce, and bureaucracy. The Kolis in the post-Independence era have realized that their axis of power lies in their numerical strength. It is through their numerical strength that the Kolis are attempting to capture other axes of power. But can they possibly wrest power from the bureaucratic, industrial, business and commercial elite, who are generally from the upper castes? True, the Kolis have increasingly threatened the upper castes in their political position. But numerical strength alone is not sufficient to gain strategic foothold in other arenas.

In fact, the ex-Chief Minister, Madhav Singh Solanki, on taking office, admitted that he was unable to fulfill his electoral promises made to his caste fellows. Electoral power alone is insufficient to bend the upper caste elites, or to make them share their power and privileges with others. Until there is sufficient representation of the Kolis in the bureaucracy, which will not come till the Kolis take to education in good measure, power gained through electoral politics may remain largely inconsequential and the upper castes can play with their fragile unity secured with great effort. Every dominant group elicits electoral support from its poorer members, but the former may not share the spoils of power with them. The case of the *Kshatriya Sabha* well illustrates how the Rajput elites played games with the Kolis. Needless to say, the Koli elite may play the same game with ordinary Kolis, which may give rise to new internal cleavages or sharpen the old and existing cleavages.

References

Arora, G.S. 1972. *Tribal-class encounters: Some aspects of folk urban relations in Alirajpur Tehsil,* Hyderabad, Administrative Staff College of India.

Bose, P.K. 1985. "Social mobility and caste violence: A study of the Gujarat Riots" pp. 137-147 in Centre for Social Studies, *Caste, caste- conflict and reservation, Delhi, Ajanta.*

Desai, G.H. 1912. *A glossary of castes, tribals and races in Baroda state*, Baroda, State Press.

Desai, I.P. 1973. *Water facilities for untouchables in Gujarat*, Bombay, Popular Prakashan.

Desai, I.P. 1973. *Untouchability in Rural Gujarat*, Bombay, Popular Prakashan.

Enthoven, W. 1922. *Tribes and castes of Bombay,* 3 Vols., Bombay,Government Press.

Forbes, A.K.1856. *Ras-Mala: Hindu annals of western India with particular reference to Gujarat,* London, Richardson and Co. Reprint used: Delhi, Heritage Publishers, 1973.

Gazetteer. 1923. *Gazetteer of the Baroda state,* Vol. II, Bombay, Times Press.

Koppers, W. 1943. "The Kolis in northwest central India". *Ethnos: 1-2:* 1-18.

Kothari, R. 1970. " Federation for political interests: The Kshatriyas of Gujarat" in Rajni Kothari (ed.), *Caste in Indian Politics*, New Delhi, Orient Longman.

Kothari, R. and Maru, R. 1965. "Caste and secularism in India: Case study of a caste federation, *Journal of Asian Studies*, 25: 33-50.

Lobo, Lancy. 1992. "Household and family among Thakors in a north Gujarat village, *Sociological Bulletin:* 41 (1&2): 49-66.

Lobo, Lancy. 1995. *The Thakors of north Gujarat, A caste in the village and the region*, Delhi, Hindustan Publishing Corporation.

Mankad, B.L. 1940. "A sociological study of the Kolis in Kathiawad", *Journal of the University of Bombay*, 9(I): 224-269.

Naik, T. B. 1956. *The Bhils*, Delhi, Bharatiya Adimjati Sevak Sangh.

Nath, Y.V.S. 1960. *Bhils of Ratanmal: An analysis of the social structure of a western Indian community*, Baroda, The M.S.University of Baroda.

Roy, S. 1983. *Koli culture: A profile of the culture of Talpad Vistar*, New Delhi, Cosmo Publications.

Shah A.M. and Shroff, R. G. 1959. "The Vahivancha Barots of Gujarat: A caste of genealogists and mythographers", pp. 40-70, in Milton Singer (ed.), *Traditional India: Structure and Change,* Philadelphia: American Folklore Society.

Shah, A. M. 1955a. "A Dispersed hamlet in the Panchmahals", *The Economic Weekly:* 7: 109-16.

Shah, A.M. 1955b. "Caste, economy and territory in central Panchmahals", *Journal of the M.S. University of Baroda:* 4(1): 65-91.

Shah, A.M. 1973. *The household dimension of the family in India: A field study in a Gujarat village and a review of other studies,* Delhi, Orient Longman.

Shah, A.M.1977. "Lineage structure and change in a Gujarat village" pp. 339-367, in M.N. Srinivas, et al (eds.), *Dimensions of Social Change in India*, Delhi, Allied Publishers.

Shah, A.M. 1982. "Division and hierarchy: An overview of caste in Gujarat", *Contributions to Indian Sociology*: 1(1): 1-33.

Shah, Ghanshyam. 1975. *Caste associations and political process in Gujarat*, Bombay, Popular.

Silverberg, J.M. 1962. *Peasant behaviour and its caste-relevancy: The Kolis of Kasandra,* Unpublished Doctoral Dissertation. Michigan, Microfilms International.

Srinivas, M.N. 1972. *Social Change in Modern India*,(Indian edition) Delhi, Orient Longman.

Viswa Nath, L.S. 1973. "Female infanticide and the Lewa Kanbis of Gujarat in the Nineteenth century", *Indian Economic and Social History Review*: 10: 386-404.

Yagnik, A. 1981. "Caste war in Gujarat", *Lokayan Exchange*, Unpublished Typescript.

Miniscule progress in the midst of mainstream stagnation: The Kurmis of Uttar Pradesh

H.S. Verma and Rakesh Varma

The ethnographic accounts of Kurmis, a pan Indian OBC community and one of the important peasant communities of Uttar Pradesh, provided by the colonial ethnographers, notably William Crooks and Russell and Hira Lal, are useful in a very limited sense but far from complete [2] While one may discover traces of bias and gaping holes in the narratives in what they do discuss, what is even more significant is what they conveniently leave out from their exercise i.e., dimensions such as participation in political activities, leadership, relationship with other communities, material culture, nobility, education, relegation from *Vaishyas* to the *Shudras,* treatment by different set of rulers during the *Moghul* and British periods, and differentiation among the Kurmis of different cultural areas,etc.[3] Organized in five sections, this effort at auto-ethnography focuses mainly on the changes registered in the socio-cultural,educational,econmic and political status of the Kurmis. After stating the methodology followed in assembling this case study, the first section examines their origins, composition and decomposition in the state including the crucial issue of their relegation from the somewhat ritually respectable comity of the *Vaishyas* to the lowly rated *Shudras*. The second section documents the character of their economic activities, principally how have they have adapted to the changing requirements of the shift from subsistence to commercial agriculture in an unsympathetic environment. The third section sketches their lackadaisical journey in the field of education at a time when the upper castes of the Uttar Pradesh society have moved into the knowledge economy. The fourth section focuses on the political profile of the community probing the possible causes of their less than impressive assertion of community identity despite their larger population size and better resource endowment. The fifth section sums up their socio-cultural status identifying the Kurmi psyche responsible for progress shown by a very minuscule segment in the midst of stagnation registered by their mainstream.

I

Methodology deployed

This case study has been assembled using inputs from a large variety of sources. The most important set of informants among these are the personal detailed discussions of the authors with six categories of Kurmis (i) the Kurmi common man who is poorest of the poor, (ii) the Kurmi well to do farmer residing only in the interior and largely inaccessible areas, (iii) the well to do Kurmi who continues to be a farmer but has also a foothold in the small towns and in non-farm occupations especially small trade and having close contact with the larger cities, (iv) the Kurmis who have largely settled down in the urban centres and are in non-farm occupations, especially in teaching,law,medical practice, engineering, and government employment at higher levels, (v) the Kurmis occupying political positions at different levels in the Panchayati Raj institutions, and urban local bodies, the State Legislature, and the Parliament and in voluntary organisations,and (vi) the Kurmi government officers serving in far flung areas of the state and responsible for law and order and implementation of development programmes and ,to that extent in live touch with the latest ground level empirical realities. These inputs have been obtained from different geographical terrains in which the Kurmis are concentrated in Central and Eastern Uttar Pradesh.The personal background of the authors vis -a-vis OBC problematic also helped a great deal.[4] Second important set of sources was the adversarial counterparts of the six categories of Kurmi informants listed above. These were drawn from the so-called upper castes to provide the counterpoints and act as checks on the information offered by the first set. As is evident from the foregoing, the material for this case study was not collected in one time sequence but spread over a period of roughly thirty years and has constantly been updated. The third set of information has been culled from colonial and the oral and written ethnographic accounts of the Kurmis by the Kurmis themselves. Its veracity has been verified using different techniques.

Origin, composition and decomposition:The Kurmi view

Most reputed historians of Indian culture and race trace its roots in the Aryans who had two streams i.e. *Surya Vansh and Chandra Vansh.* It is posited that the Indian social organisation was rooted in the basic *Kshatra Dharma* which took upon itself not only the responsibility of protecting the society, but also carrying out the farming operations that developed the important institution of joint family and decided the preeminence of the peasantry in the country. The Kurmis were among the first set of *Vaishyas* removed to the status of *Shudra* communities to set up their caste association known as *Akhil Bhartiya Kurmi Khastriya Mahasabha* and articulate their own perception of their origins and ancestry (J.P.Verma: 1988). J.P.Verma's account of the Kurmi heritage is pieced together from the oral tradition of history and sketched from the authentic information gathered from the people drawn from different parts of the country. Collaterally, it is corroborated by other verifiable but irrefutable facts. From his account, it emerges that the early Indian society had two major streams: one group consisted of peasant *Kutumbi Kashatriyas* and the second one comprised of those who had the responsibility of protecting the life and property of the population from the enemies and frequent invaders. In the later period, the second stream assumed the status of rulers and came to be called as the *Kashatriya* rulers although some of the leading lights of the second category *Kutumbi Kashatriyas* who were mainly engaged in farming operations also became rulers—albeit of lesser proportions—from time to time. The reverse flows of not so well to do among the *Kashatriyas* to the *Kutumbi Kashatriyas* and to the profession of farming also continued. However, eventually the cultural practices of the two assumed orthodox forms and the two groups became separate communities.

The term Kurmi is derived from *Kutumbi,* and *Kunbi* that in turn were derived from *Kutumbi* and *Kutumbini*.The *Vyas Smriti*, considered to have been written in the 13th Century, calls them *Kutumbin*.Since the *Kutumbin* were supposedly beef-eaters, it treated them very low and indicated that even seeing them was sinful. Any one who talks to them must take a bath to purify himself. Thus, it is believed that farming fraction of the *Kutumbi Khastriyas* was known as *Kutumbis*. As the community migrated to different parts of the country and settled down at different places, in course of time, its name acquired variants such as *Kunbi*, *Kunabi*, and *Kurmi*. Consequently, the community formed different lineages and clans that eventually became sub-castes/communities. The 1891 Census enumerated 1488 sub-castes of the Kurmis. It is quite difficult to authoritatively determine the original and the extended roots and stems of this family of the sub-castes of the Kurmi communities. Although the Katiyars, Gangwars, and Sachans among the Kurmi sub-castes are the ones that have gained some presence in the urban centres, notably in and around Kanpur, and the Malls (both Sainthwars and Patanwars) in some of the eastern Uttar Pradesh districts, in reality 11 major endogamous Kurmi communities are prominent in terms of importance, population size and social –economic significance in the state of Uttar Pradesh.These are: 1. Baiswar, 2. Gangwar/Gangapari, 3. Gujarati, 4. Jaiswar, 5. Katiyar, 6. Kharbind, 7. Mall (Sainthwar and Patanwar), 8.Radh, 9.Singraur, 10.Shakya/Maurya, and 11.Umardaha.

1. Baiswar: This sub-caste is named so because they were initially called *Bais* Kurmis.This branch was originally living in and around Kannauj.About a thousand years ago, they were attacked by their enemies and left that area and, after clearing jungles in Lucknow, Kanpur, Hardoi, Barabanki, Sitapur and Lakhimpur Khiri districts, settled down there. Because the Bais community lived in this area for a very long time undisturbed, the area became known as *Baiswara* and its residents came to be called as *Baiswars*. In 1193 when the Delh's king Prithviraj Chauhan was defeated by Gori, groups of defeated Kashtriyas, in retreat and roaming as small armed brigands, started attacking and annexing fertile tracts in the hands of the Baiswars.As several Gazetteers of the *Baiswara* area record, the *Baiswars* suffered several and repeated evictions and kept on shifting northwards. Quite a few of the *Baiswar* families were *Zamindars* holding as many as 12 villages as their estates.

2. Gangwar, Gangaparis: Originally, the Gangwars/Gangaparis lived in the Gangwadi area of the former Mysore state. They had even established their own estate which had its headquarters in a city called Talkund.This state was under the tutelage of Chalukyas but later became independent. Several rulers tried to annex their foothold but failed to do so. Eventually, Rajendra Chol First succeeded in defeating Gang king Rakshamall in 1004.The Gang state still survived as a small principality. Between 1076 and 1147,Chood Gang established a very powerful state and was also responsible for starting construction of the Jagannath temple that was completed by later Gang kings. The Gang state was finally annexed by Akbar.Several members of the ruling Gang family, their officials and general category of Gangs left Mysore and settled down in the riverside area of the Ganges. Even in Farrukhabad there were several Gangwar Zamindars in the Kayamganj and Shamshabad areas of the district that were later taken over by the Muslims. The Gangwars occupy a special position among the Kurmis. Quite a large number of the Gangwars are found in Bareilly, and Pilibhit districts although a smaller number is also scattered in Shahjahanpur, terrai area of Farrukhabad and Etawah. Physically, they are well built, and quite tall. Being very cordial in their behaviour, they have been in the forefront of linking different branches of the Kurmis.From amongst the numerous Kurmi branches, the Gangwars have given the largest number of Kurmi members to the Uttar Pradesh Assembly as well as the Lok Sabha.They are also better represented in the civil services than any other Kurmi branch.

3.Gujarati: Originally, this branch came from Gujarat. Presently, they are found in Raebareli, Basti, Bahraich, and Faizabad districts. Compared to the other branches of the Kurmis, they are well to do. They belong to several lineages that are known by their village names. Presently, Bahraich district has their largest number. The Gujaratis call themselves Chaudhary and deem themselves superior to other branches of Kurmis.

4. Jaiswar: Unlike most branches of Kurmis that settled down at one particular place and consequently came to be named as such, although more in numbers compared to the other sub-castes, the Jaiswars are widely scattered. The Avadh Gazetteer records their origin to Kannauj.The Jaiswars claim that Yashodharman belonged to their community. Given the established prowess of outstanding warriors of the rulers of this descent, they came to be called as 'Yashovars'. In the latter period, this word got converted into Jasover and still later

Jaiswar.On the other hand, Herbert Risley records that the Jaiswars who were very expert riders of horses, went out from the Jais area of Raebareli district and are consequently called Jaiswars. Shivram Singh's *Kurmi Kashatrya Itihas* attributes the Jaiswars to be descendents of the ruler Yashdhawal.However, he does not provide any details of the time, place of this rulership and, therefore, his claim lacks supporting evidence.

5. Katiyar: The Katiyars are found in the Katiyari area of Farrukhabad district. They were originally living in Maharashtra and migrated to their present place of residence some five to six hundred years back due to constant harassment by the Muslim rulers. Unlike many other branches of Kurmis, the Katiyars are very self respecting, assertive, progressive and free from narrow- mindedness. They are better educated and are outgoing type, have ventured out in non-farm occupations including white-collar jobs and in trade and commerce.

6. Kharbind: This branch of the Kurmis is found in Raebareli and was known for its valour and fighting qualities. It had withstood several Kashatriya onslaughts and used to always carry swords. They were called *Khadagbandhs* (those carrying swords), which in course of time came to be called *Kharbind.*

7. Mall (Sainthwar and Patanwar): There were three such original branches of the Malls. The first was based at Kuskawati, now known as Kasya (Kushinara); the second was in Kashi and the third in Pawa.Historians trace the present day Padrauna as Pawa.This link is established with the legend that Gautam Buddha was in Pawa just before his death. Thus, Kushinagar should be in the vicinity of Pawa, the area now known as Kushinagar.Two other branches of Malls came into existence later on and these are called Sainthwar and Patanwar,so named due to their origins to places named Sainth and Patan. The ancestors of the erstwhile 'rulers' of Padrauna are stated to be Malls.

8. Raadh: This branch is found in Bahraich.They were known to be great warriors and had successfully repelled the attacks of legendry Alha-Udal on their *Gaanjar* area.

9. Shakya, Shakiya, Maurya: The *terrai* area of the northern track of Bihar had republics of the 'Moriya' Kutumbis.The Moriya were a branch of the Sakiya lineage who had settled down in the Himalayan *terrai* due to mutual acrimony. The powerful Magadh rulers, who were later called the Mauryas, later captured their settlements. Despite poisonous written Brahmin propaganda terming the Mauryas as the *Shudras,* most responsible historical accounts treat these republics including that of Chandragupta Maurya as 'Moriya Kashtriyas'. In the latter period, these Moriya Kutumbi Kashatriyas came to be called as Morao or Murai.Although eventually they emerged as a separate caste altogether, William Crookes treats Mauryas as branch of the Kurmis, not as a separate caste.

10. Singraur: The Singraur relate themselves with the sage Shringi.William Crooks feels that they were originally from Singrauli.They are found in Allahabad, Banda, Fatehpur and Mirzapur districts. The local society treats the Singraurs with respect and in Allahabad and Banda, they are even called Thakur Saheb.

11. Umarhada: This branch resides in 150 villages of Ghatampur Tehsil of Kanpur Dehat and Bindaki Tehsil of Fatehpur districts. It is believed that their ancestors came from Hadauti area of Rajasthan where they were constantly engaged in unending fights with either the Kashatriyas or, the Moghuls .So much so that their females too were participating in the wars. As a result, their bangles in their right hands used to get smashed. Eventually, they decided to discard glass bangles and began wearing silver *Mastika* (Mathi) in their right hands that soon became a cultural symbol of the community. This practice continued until 1930s when an internal reform movement against it began and continued for the next 14 years. The practice has waned but has not disappeared totally. The Umarhada are now a fairly progressive sub-group among the Kurmis.

Relegation from the ranks of the Vaishyas to the Shudras

The earliest *Varna* categorization listed those in trade and commerce and farming as the *Vaishyas*.The word '*Vish*', from which *Vaishya* has originated, means land. Consequently, *Vaishya* meant some one who was owner of the land. William Crooks also lends his support to this view by calling *Vaishya as* one who occupies soil. Thus, since the Kurmis were owners of land and were engaged in farming, they were such *Vaishyas* who were carrying on the trade of farming but were not conducting trade and commerce. Only those that were warriors and rulers were called the *Kashatriyas*.

The Kurmis were not called *Kashatriya* since most of their branches were not warriors and rulers. The Kurmis were known more as *Kutumbis* and the adage of either the *Kashatriya* or the *Vaishya* was not very prevalent in their case. Eventually, the use of term *Kashatriya* for the warriors and rulers and *Vaishya* for those engaged *only in trade and commerce* gained more popularity and wider acceptance. That the Kurmis were indeed *Vaishyas* is also confirmed by the treatment of the community as the *Vaishyas* in the neigbouring Nepal. When the Kurmis go to Nepal on pilgrimage to the temple of Lord Pashupatinath in Kathmandu, they are addressed as *Vaishya* by the *Purohits* of the temple. What, however, contributed to their eventual relegation to the ranks of the *Shudras* was their tendency to overthrow the corrupt and amorous kings and replacing them with the '*Ganrajyas*' (republics) at many places. India possessed many such republics before the rise of the famous Magadh Empire. As is well known, these were people friendly and participative governing systems. Several authoritative historical treatises confirm that these republics were controlled by communities, and not by single rulers. Jain and Buddhist literature give a listing of the names of such *Ganrajyas.* These listings refer not to the place or region but different communities that established them first and later controlled them. When the invaders annexed these *Ganrajyas*, the winners handed the controlling communities some of the worst penalties and indignities. Oral history accounts collected from different parts of Uttar Pradesh indicate that different branches of the ruling Kurmis not only lost their assets of land and other properties in these periodic campaigns, but were also repeatedly evicted from their successive new settlements after they had cleared the jungles, developed the fields and began settled agriculture. This broke their back, literally weeded out their warrior tendencies and they were more or less forced to accept their fate of being only staple hard working farmers. While other loser communities were not as fortunate and were assigned to perform degraded tasks, and consequently became untouchables, the Kurmis escaped this fate. However, even the Kurmis were relegated to the *Shudra Varna* and were no longer considered part of the *Vaishya Varna*.

The reality of Kurmi origin

The fact that emerges very clearly from the dispassionate analysis of the entire foregoing ethnographic narrative is that the Kurmis were indigenous original inhabitants of the Indo -Gangetic valleys and were, apart from good farmers, also not too timid as warriors. However, since their lanlord, small time chieftain elements were eliminated successively by the invaders, dispossessed by the Moghuls and the British and finally dispossessed of their large tracts of lands under the Zamidari Abolition Act, their mainstream, that was more or less forced to accept the status of the ritually low *Shudras* as docile, submissive, yet hardworking and largely inward looking but still self-respecting farmers. It is notable that a thinker, social-political reformer of the stature of Ram Swaroop Verma came from the ranks of the Kurmis and one who, when compared to such illustrious thinkers and social reformers as Narayan Guru, E.V.Ramaswamy Naicker, Jotirao Phule and Babasaheb Bhimrao Ambedkar, provided as good an ideology of *Arjak and Arjakisation*, the Kurmis did not show much enthusiasm either towards his ideology or that of these great men and kept themselves tuned to the *sanskritisation* route. They have not rediscovered their roots of being the indigenous original inhabitants of the country.

II

Economic status

It is significant to note that in spite of repeated evictions, the Kurmis remained confined to the fertile tracts of river valleys of central Uttar Pradesh. Their hard working nature enabled them to carry on settled agricultural operations. However, the Moghuls first and the British later carried a land tenurial system that did not confer them freehold rights of ownership of the lands that they were cultivating. The methodology of collecting rents through a system of Zamindars, and the deployment of intermediaries by the latter kept them at the receiving end of a lot of exploitative mechanisms. Their earlier loss to the invaders and the latter subjugation to the rulers and their intermediaries led to development of a submissive and docile mentality among the Kurmis.Farming was rain fed and totally at the mercy of the nature; there was no protection from floods and famines; repeated epidemics of cholera, Kalazar, malaria, and plague took their heavy tolls. The British did initiate cultivation of opium, and sugar cane in the terrain inhabited by the Kurmis but the promotion regimes of both these commercial crops were such that were heavily loaded against the cultivators. The sugar factories were, for instance, not bound to purchase the entire crop of sugar cane that the farmer was contract bound to sell them. In fact, the opium cultivators continued to receive their payments of opium yield from the concerned government Department in their open begging bowls at the opium collection offices in places like Barabanki right up to the middle Seventies. During the Second World War, there was acute shortage of such items of common use as cloth, kerosene, sugar, cement and the farmers were required to supply their quotas of grains to the government and used to receive supplies of these essential items from the ration shops in return.

The British constructed the Ganga canal irrigation system in western Uttar Pradesh first and the Jats and the Gujjars benefited from it much earlier than the Kurmis because the Sharada canal system bringing in assured irrigation to the tracts where Kurmis lived was constructed much later. Consequently, the Kurmis were late in their switchover first to intensive agriculture and still later to commercial farming. Compared to communities such as the Jats, and Gujjars of western Uttar Pradesh, these historical events were responsible for the relatively late prosperity of the Kurmis.Another contributory factor of the Kurmi backwardness was absence of educational facilities in the Oudh part of the then United Provinces of Agra and Oudh which kept the Kurmi worldview closed and narrow.

In what follows, we would describe the changing nature of the practice of farming by the Kurmis in Uttar Pradesh.Broadly, this analysis could be arranged in to four distinct phases: pre-1947, post - independence of intensification up to the 1980, post -1981 switchover to commercial farming up to 1990, and post-1990 suction of local farming economy in the globalised world.

Pre-1947 phase

Farming for the Kurmis in this phase was a working equilibrium of human skills with the ecological system. The seeds were locally produced and remained available with every Kurmi farmer. The seeds were not susceptible to diseases and there was no need to replace them with newer ones every three-four years. The output from the farms was absorbed on the farm, or, in domestic uses for the human beings and animals. The instruments needed for agricultural operations were locally made and were also serviced locally by different artisan communities under the prevalent *Jajmani* system. Animal and human energy was used in maximum number of farming operations. The Kurmis had a vast repertoire of indigenous knowledge and skills in carrying out farming. This enabled the Kurmis to respond to the needs of three sub-systems: (a) their families, (b) their farms, and (c) their larger village communities and the outside world. The success of the Kurmis depended very much on their ability to harness the resources of their families and their strategies of managing their farm and their relationships with the others. The Kurmis had very few innovators, even early and late adopters of innovations: their bulk comprised of what Everett Rogers (1960) terms as "the laggards", the category that adopts new innovations after its superiority had been demonstrated beyond any doubt and was writ large in the actual behaviour of other peers. This label of 'laggards' was more or less apt for the entire herd of Kurmis living in various locales of the big state of Uttar Pradesh.

1947-1980 phase

This phase saw the operation of programmes such as the Grow More Food, Community Development, and new farming technology (i.e., high yielding varieties, chemical fertilizers and pesticides, etc). This resulted in slow change of the nature of farming being carried out by the Kurmis in various locales. It was never simple acceptance or, rejection of an advocated or demonstrated option: rather it involved complex process of adaptation, homogenisation with the traditional methods for quite a while before making or, not making a total switchover. Equally important was differential response of the Kurmi community to the introduced changes in different areas. The acceptance of the older and newer varieties of seeds of the principal crops of wheat and paddy, for instance, varied from an initial 40:60 to 20:80 in the last part of this phase. The output of the newer varieties was generally sold in the market and the one from the traditional varieties was generally retained for own consumption. The usage of agricultural implements, especially the tractor, the diesel pump set and the thresher picked up as the intensity of cropping increased and demand of local agricultural labour increased. The non-owners promptly used quite a bit of this newly acquired machinery on hire. This was the phase when the Kurmis, helped by the grant of freehold rights to the leased lands that they were cultivating for a very long time, invested on their farms, used the new technology and prospered.

This also led to their forays in non-farm ventures such as trading by some of them in the nearby towns in some areas of the Kurmi belt.

The 1980-1990 phase: The switchover to commercial farming

During this phase, even the late adopters and laggards among the Kurmis switched over to commercial cropping involving three crop combinations. The Murao community had been present among them all along and although possessing very small holdings were carrying on exceedingly well with the help of multiple crops, notably vegetables. It was difficult for the mass of Kurmis to emulate the multiple cropping patterns adopted by the Muraos instantly. However, good returns from the main commercial of sugar cane crop became uncertain due to closer of several sugar mills in the Kurmi belt and a lot of malpractices prevalent in the Cooperative Cane Development Unions and the Cane Development and Sugar Industry Department of the state. Kurmis had to begin experimentation of multiple cropping through trial and error. The first crop that caught the imagination of the Kurmis was potato. Sometime in the early Eighties, this adoption of potato as an alternate commercial crop to sugar cane began and the area under potato shot up. Potao requires adequate storage facilities that did not exist in their area. This crucial deficiency meant that the potato growers had to take their crop output to distantly located cold storages for storage. Quite often this created overcrowding and law and order problems requiring intervention of the police. Cold storage owners also charged exorbitant rates and in league with the bureaucracy indulged in so many exploitative practices. Not familiar with the peculiarities of marketing the stored potato produce, quite a few of the new Kurmi entrants ended up in paying higher storage costs and getting lower prices for their stored produce. Compared to other crops, potato also required considerably higher labour costs both at the time of planting as well as at the time of maturity. The prices of potato also followed a cyclical pattern giving good returns to the producers only once in three-four years. The Kurmi converts to potato crop soon found out that with higher cost of cultivation and uncertain returns in three out of four years generally, it was not a very attractive proposition to cultivate potato. They had yet to learn the finer steps of marketing potato produce in lean and glut seasons. Another disadvantage was the loss of the wheat crop since the farmer could either cultivate wheat or potato. Potato cultivation had to be cushioned with a crop that was less costly input cost wise and less cumbersome output disposalwise. Mentha provided this finer balancing edge.

Beginning in the late Eighties, cultivation of mentha began in the Kurmi belt. It so happened that in a single year in early Nineties, the prices of mentha oil per litre shot up to as high as Rs. 1800.Although subsequently its price has generally hovered around only at Rs. 300 per litre, it became a popular crop that almost cent per cent Kurmi farmers began planting it. It is a short duration crop and the farmer can plant paddy after he has cut the mentha .Its cost of cultivation is not as high as for instance that of potao. The only additional equipment that the farmer has to purchase, install and operate is the distilling tank that has long life and is locally manufactured. Its cultivation does not require many skills either. The produced mentha can be preserved for quite some time. It is literally cash since one can sell it in smaller or large quantities as the situation requires and receive down payment instantly. On the negative side, distilling oil from the mentha plants causes environmental pollution in the villages and soil fertility erodes very quickly. However, given the tangible gains that it offers the Kurmi farmers are not unduly worried about these disadvantages. Cultivation of mentha has made triple cropping almost a universal practice in the Kurmi belt.

Cultivation of green chillies started in the early Nineties in some small pockets of the Kurmi belt. However, given its requirements of sandy soil, deft and repetitive sequencing of plucking, spraying of the nutrients and pesticides thereafter, higher costs of cultivation including hired hands, necessity of carrying it for marketing on each plucking day, and very volatile prices— depending upon the arrival of agents from the local and export markets—, it is not every one's cup of tea. Consequently, it has remained confined to small number of Kurmi farmers and geographically to a tiny patch that meets its requirements. The switchover in the crop combinations that are now in vogue among the Kurmi farmers are: A-1=Wheat+ paddy+ sugar cane; A-2=sugar cane + potato; A-3=sugar cane +wheat; B-1=wheat +mentha + paddy; B-2= wheat + green chillies + paddy; B-3=potato + mentha +paddy. It is important to note that among these the first three are not replacement crop combinations: all that they amount to are planting of a crop on additional plots that was not being done earlier on.

Conversion to triple cropping meant that the Kurmi farmers are having no lean periods in their farming calender. The number of farming operations and their complexity has also increased. In turn, this has necessitated putting in larger number of own and hired man hours into farming activities. Since farming is carried out in harmony with the weather and follows a set sequence of activities peculiar to chosen crops, the needed steps have to be taken by all farmers at the same point of time. A natural consequence of this convergence of demand on human labour has seen skyrocketing of the agricultural wages. New labour cost saving equipments such as the potato seed planter have been getting growing acceptance among the Kurmis. Those not in a position to purchase them use them through on hire system. A second cost escalating phenomenon is irregular supply of power. This has forced the farmers to go in for bored tube wells to ensure regular supply of water to their crops. A third cost escalating factor is declining fertility of the soil and growing incidence of attacks of pesticides, fungus, and other crop debilitating diseases requiring extensive use of pesticides and chemicals. Fourth, multiple cropping reduces fertility of the soil and constantly requires use of heavy doses of chemical fertilizers. In aftermath of the withdrawal of subsidies on them since the early Nineties, these are very expensive but have to be used to ensure good harvest. Thus, triple cropping might have increased gross incomes of the Kurmis but net returns on them have not been as substantial as commonly perceived. Whereas sugarcane cultivation yielded only one set of the incomes, non-sugar cane cropping patterns have given at least two of these thereby increasing the incomes of the farmers substantially. In addition, the latter also provide wheat from the third crop for domestic consumption. This development had a very salutary effect even on the big farmers who began reducing the area under sugar cane and alternately adding acreage to multiple cropping mechanisms. Cumulative effect of this development was reduction of area under sugar cane in the intensive sugar cane belt in which the Kurmis dominate. Economically, the multiple cropping has certainly enabled the Kurmis to come out of the logjam they had landed themselves in earlier on. However, it does not mean that they have insulated themselves from the losses routinely inflicted by the natural calamities. They retain those vulnerabilities and crop insurance remains a pipe dream for them even in 2005.Nevertheless, since the majority of Kurmi branches live in the areas that have facilities of assured irrigation, multiple cropping provieds some balancing cushion of recouping the losses of one crop— at least partially— with moderate returns from the remaining ones. The Kurmis are consequently some what better off now than they were before when they were cultivating the single long duration crop of sugar cane. Although the amount varies in case of different categories of Kurmi farmers, all of them owe debts to the banks, cooperatives, relatives and businessmen. Thus, it is clear that the indebtedness of the Kurmis persists in spite of current larger incomes. However, this indebtedness is not as crippling as it was before their switchover to multiple cropping. Certainly, this has prevented recurrence of acute distress syndrome of suicides, seen in large numbers in Andhra Pradesh, Karnataka, Maharashtra and elsewhere.

The post - 1990 phase

The introduction of the Diversified Agricultural Project with the financial assistance of the World Bank and a clutch of income generation activities in the rural areas in the Nineties set the stage for a paradigm shift in the fortunes of the farmers. However, although a lot of borrowed money from the World Bank has been sunk in these projects, the paradigm shift either in the Uttar Pradesh agriculture or in the income generating activities in rural areas in the non-farm sector has really not materialized. Several initiatives focusing on sugar cane, potato, vegetables, fruits and floriculture were required to guarantee a fair return to the farmers. Santosh Kumar Gangwar did try his level best to kick start ethanol from sugar cane as the Minister for Petroleum but his more assertive Cabinet Minster Ram Naik thwarted his moves under the overawing influence of the oil companies especially from the private sector. The upper OBC communities like the Kurmis, Jats, Gujjars, and Lodhs stood to gain the most from production of ethanol through molasses. However, ethanol should be produced straight from sugar cane and not as a bye -product through the molasses.[5]

It has been demonstrated that excellent vodka can be produced from potato crop. Uttar Pradesh produces large quantities of potato. The Kurmis as the prominent farming community suffer losses from its cultivation in two-three out of every four continuous years.

However, while continued import of vodka continues to satiate its demand, no initiative has been taken to begin production of vodka indigenously to guarantee good returns to the farmers.

The Directorate of Horticulture, Uttar Pradesh undertook a project to organise marketing of the famous Lucknow mangoes in the foreign market in an effort to give the mango producers a decent return and save them from the clutches of unscrupulous exporters. The project required establishment of a export processing, storage, standardization, branding and transportation and marketing network for this purpose. The resultant Nawab brand has gained a foothold in the foreign markets and its producers are beginning to receive good returns. While this is welcome, similar facilities for the integrated marketing of other fruits and vegetables remains unaccomplished.[6] Consequently, exotic qualities of vegetables produced in Uttar Pradesh are getting marketed by private exporters but exploiting the primary producers from Kurmi and other communities.

Floriculture is yet another line of farming that has immense possibilities but it can yield good returns only if there is excellent marketing network, both inland as well as export, in place. While a very small number of innovative and imaginative farmers have begun this line near the metropolitan cities of Pune, New Delhi, and Kolkata which have a guaranteed market for such produce, there are obvious limits on such farming for simpletons like the Kurmis who are not as educated as these lines of farming require.

From the foregoing discussion, it would appear as though the Kurmis as masters of traditional farming are not quickly seizing the newer opportunities in the advance and exotic farming. Other communities that have demonstrated acumen in opretionalising new ideas before the others think about them have generally picked up these opportunities. Second, the shift of the Kurmis into trade and commerce is confined to only a very small number of small towns in some of the districts where they are concentrated (see H.S.Verma: 2005): they are yet to make their visible presence in the larger urban centres as well as the KAVAL towns of the state. Third, very few Kurmis have entered into the servicing sector, an opportunity structure area developing very fast in the rural areas and waiting to be tapped to its vast potential. Economically, the Kurmis do not appear to be showing the crucial entrepreneurial streak that is seen among the leading segments of the Marathas of Maharashtra and the Patels and Pattidars of Gujarat.

III

Educational status

Education is a mobility multiplier using which the *Kayasthas* migrated from the ranks of the *Shudras* and are now treated as parts of the ruling class if not of the upper castes even by the so called upper castes. However, as demonstrated very vividly by Karen Leonard (1994), this cultural shift has been accomplished over a very long period spanning centuries, not decades. Educationally, the Kurmis belong to a deprived environment. They lack skills, and attitudes appropriate to negotiate complex environment of education requiring cognitive and adaptive strategies for meaningful learning. Level of aspiration is a critical aspect of an individual's motivation since it determines his effort towards attaining goal as well the degree of his adjustment. It has been observed that well-adjusted persons tend to have a critical estimate of themselves in relation to demands of the environment and, hence, have a fairly relativistic level of aspiration. While trying to receive education, the Kurmis find themselves in a complex environment and perceive themselves as a "self-imposed failure"in this enterprise. Therefore, they are extremely cautious and do not want to take risks. The Kurmi children grow up in home environment that does not afford them the kind of early childhood experience that enhances the development of appropriate cognitive, linguistic, motivational and social-emotional skills or, competences for success in the school. A sense of inferiority prevails among them. The mainstream of the Kurmis does not appear to have even seriously launched itself on the grueling task of educational empowerment of the community. The drawback that the Kurmis have in this sector is the absence of social capital. A very tiny section among them did well educationally in the early Fifties and entered the educational sector either as teachers in the Primary or Secondary schools. Children of only this tiny fraction have had the benefit of an educational environment conducive to educational excellence at the family levels. The better ones among these children have gone in to professions such as medical and engineering: those not so bright but with some 'connectivity' in corridors of power gained entry into lower levels of bureaucracy as clerks and assistants. Thus, the numerical strength of the Kurmis coming to these sub-streams of white-collar positions was insignificant. Yet, it was beneficial to the following generations in as much as it facilitated a change of scene and provided an opportunity to live in urban areas and interact with those that were in the middle class. They were not in a position to enroll themselves in the convent schools but the educational institutions to which they went for their education were decidedly superior to the vernacular ones not even properly staffed in the rural areas. In the meanwhile, the Kurmi concentrated areas, undeveloped educationally, were producing sub-standard pupils who were faring not too satisfactorily in the institutions of higher learning. The present structure of educational institutions in the state of Uttar Pradesh is such that does not foster excellence, except for the privilengtsia (H.S.Verma and Neelima Verma: 1986).

The educational structure itself is discriminatory. There has been enormous expansion of the government run educational system so much so that now the government does not have enough funds to provide needed number of teachers in all of its schools. Consequently, more frequently one teacher 'teaches' a flock of 200-300 students in a Primary School in rural areas of Uttar Pradesh. Primary School teachers used to teach until middle Seventies: now, a large number of 'non-teaching' tasks (i.e., distribution of food grains /conducting Census enumerations, carrying surveys for various state government agencies including the State Election Commission, etc.) have been lobbed into their laps consuming their time. Given his extended workload, the single available teacher is no longer available to teach his flock full time. The World Bank funded *Sarva Siksha Abhiyan* has brought in the scheme of deployment of *"Siksha Mitra"*, a hastily trained 'teacher' at the princely honorarium of Rupees two thousand per month on a contractual basis. In effect, the Primary School teacher has now graduated to the status of the 'boss' who attends to the 'non-teaching' tasks and teaching in the Primary Schools is generally in the hands of the *Siksha Mitra*.There are several other drawbacks in the government Primary School system. However, the scheme of distribution of food grains to the enrolled students has certainly enabled the enrolment to rise to dizzy heights but the foundation of education edifice has become totally woblly. The majority of the Kurmi students begin their educational careers from this less than reliable launching pad: only a limited few are lucky to have the benefit of a privately managed English medium schools located in a nearby town.

The *Madhyamik Shiksha Adhiniyam, 1921*, as amended up to date, governs the Secondary education in Uttar Pradesh. There are four categories of educational institutions under the system in vogue: (i) government, (ii) recognized and aided, (iii) recognised but unaided and (iv) unrecognized and unaided schools. The fourth category has grown by leaps and bounds in recent years. While some of these, especially those established by sound professionals and employing good teachers and located in the larger urban centres, are good offering some what tolerable quality of secondary education and imparting other personality development skills, the great majority belongs to the unscrupulous educational mafia hands. In the latter cases, what these institutions offer is a very wide range of paid for facilities (i.e., facilitating copying, promotion in junior classes of six to nine and eleven, substitution of actually written official answer books with written answer books containing solved answers, proxy candidates, leakage of papers, audio dictations using mobile phones/other devices, etc) of passing High School and Intermediate examinations without possessing the necessary educational knowledge. This comes at a price and it has more or less pulverised the clean education institutions from the other three streams. The mainstream of the Kurmi students cannot afford the third variety and only a limited few gain entry into the first one: resultantly, they have no choice but to mainly enroll themselves in the second and fourth. Therefore, it comes as no surprise that the general levels of knowledge and ability of the vast majority of the Kurmi students at these levels are of a very low standard, one that does not prepare him/her adequately to join the university system where teaching makes an abrupt switchover to selective, perfunctory coverage of the opted subjects and unaccompanied by guidance from the teachers. If one adds absence of any guidance from the family in their educational journey and lack of social capital in the community as a collectivity to the foregoing handicaps, it becomes possible to correctly gauge the grim empirical ground reality in which the Kurmi students pursue their education. Nine tenths of the Kurmi students drop out either at the High School stage or, Intermediate. They are mortally afraid of English, mathematics and science, subjects that are essential for their journey in to the knowledge society that is emerging in the country.

University education in Uttar Pradesh is a curious mix of the useful, the sub-standard and the totally useless. The state has three Central Universities in Aligarh, Benaras and Allahabad.There is an IIT at Kanpur and an Indian Institute of Management at Lucknow.Among the state universities, Lucknow, and Gorakhpur are general type of residential universities with affiliation of degree colleges in these very cities and there are three agricultural universities at Kanpur, Meerut and Faizabad and a medical university each for medical and dental education is located at Lucknow: rest of the universities and deemed universities—their number is quite large—are of affiliating type, ones that have an administrative campus in the places they are headquartered and offering affiliation to all the degree colleges located in the districts that are covered under their geographical jurisdiction.Theseare the universities that get only minimal government funds and largely sustain themselves through the 'self financed courses' route. A comparison of the existing faculty positions for the UGC segment of courses with those for the 'self-financed' ones makes it clear that the latter possess very meagre number of full time faculty positions. The residential universities have also dived full stream into this mechanism. One very serious consequence of this development has been the shift of emphasis of attention of the university teachers to the teaching of the UGC stream of courses for which they are in regular employment. They draw salary from the UGC stream but teach more in the 'self financed ' ones since the latter involves cash payment for each lecture. Consequently, they tend to neglect the UGC stream pedagogy. These developments have tremendous implications for the Kurmi students. First, almost ninety per cent among them join an affiliated Degree College in a small / medium town where each subject has most probably only one teacher. The choice of subjects is also very limited. This teaching is in the Hindi medium and the teacher does not prepare his lectures. Most often, his teaching material has not been updated for decades. The Kurmi graduate/post graduate emerging from the portals of such institutions can hardly compete satisfactorily with those coming out from the residential universities. Previously, the Kurmi students were not successful in securing PG admissions in the residential universities but the 27 per cent reservation, in place since 1994, has given them (as well as members from the other OBC communities) an entry option.

However, the manufacture of merit in the Uttar Pradesh universities is in the hands of the so called upper castes and it is almost impossible for the meritorious among the Kurmis, who had shown their prowess at the High School and Intermediate levels, to get good marks at this level: these are generally earmarked for the wards of upper caste teachers who constitute as much as 98 per cent in some of the faculties/ subjects (H.S.Verma, Ram Abhilas Verma and Jay Singh: 2005). Students from Kurmi—and all OBC, SC, ST and minority communities—face discriminatory treatment and counseling even in the coaching institutes, established and run by the upper caste Degree college and University teachers in almost all the important large towns in Uttar Pradesh, both in the class rooms as well as outside class even though they pay as much as the others. The cumulative impact of the foregoing conditions in the education sector, from the Primary to the university level, is seen in the dismal performance of the Kurmi candidates in the civil services examinations, in the results of entry examinations of the IITs, IIMs, CPMT, and other professional courses of prestigious institutions in the country. The frequently cited examples of odd selections to these courses from the Kurmi and other OBCs, SCs and minorities are more examples of exceptions rather than a rule.

To sum up, the Kurmi tryst with education in Uttar Pradesh, it would be more accurate to state that their journey in this field has more of a notional significance: there are more literates among them now than there were six /seven decades earlier. However, the journey thereafter appears to get choked after High School. Among those who go beyond High School, close to 98 per cent go to the Arts stream. Among those who join a PG degree, over 80 per cent do not secure a First Class. Among those who complete a PG end up without getting any job. Consequently, education as a mobility multiplier does not operate in their case. How does a community like Kurmi secure a foothold in the emergent knowledge economy?

IV

Political status

Politically, the Kurmis have been far more active in various phases of modern Indian history than what the colonial and post-Independence historiography basing itself primarily on the records of the administrations has tended to depict. Our collation of the material from the direct descendents of the actual Kurmi participants in the historical political events at various points of time and their collateral verification from others indicates the prominent role played by the Kurmis in each phase. This analysis may be periodised for the sake of clarity: (i) Kisan struggles against the Zamindar-British combination, (ii) suction/incorporation in to the freedom struggle, (iii) post-Independence vacillation and splintered chronological entry and participation in to Lohia's Socialist Party, Congress, BJP, SP, BSP, and Apna Dal.

The Kurmis like Gudar Ram and Jai Ram Verma (from Tanda in Faizabad now in Ambedkarnagar district), Awadh Sharan Verma Lallaji,and Jang Bahadur Verma (from Fatehpur and Nawabganj areas of Barabanki),Hargovind Verma (from Laharpur in Sitapur), and Baba Ram Chandra Das (Raebareli-Pratapgarh) started and carried on their stout shoulders the Kisan struggles of the Twenties , Thirties and Forties in these and some adjoining central Uttar Pradesh districts. These struggles were directed both against the then *Zamindars* as well as the British for whom the former acted as the intermediaries. These struggles were so fierce and bold that the entire country took note of them. The British suppressed them with great deal of ruthlessness including massacres, imprisonment and other barbaric methods of torture. However, their periodic eruption and fierceness forced the British to change some of the atrocious exploitative tenurial practices of the *Zamindars*. In their eagerness to appropriate the leadership of these struggles both Gandhi and Nehru appeared on the scene but instead of getting the grievances of the peasants redressed they ended up in sidelining the peasant issues. Masses in these areas never forgave these two stalwarts of Indian freedom struggle for what they did to these Kurmi leaders.

While leaders like Gudar Ram passed away, and Ram Chandra Das remained imprisoned for quite some time, others were co-opted in to Congress and carried quite aggressive freedom movement in these districts upto the middle Forties. However, Lohia (1960) records that as it became clear that independence was going to be granted to the country, marginalisation of Congress cadres of subaltern background and socialist/communist ideology was set in motion. Resultantly, important Kurmi freedom fighters from central Uttar

Pradesh excepting a few like Jai Ram Verma, found themselves outside the Congress. Kurmi ruling families like that of CPN Singh of Padrauna, which had gala time during the British rule, came over to the Congress.[7] A large number of them made their entry in the first general elections as MLAs of the Socialist Party. Some others like Ram Swaroop Verma, an ideologue of great significance, tried to reform the entire backward class of communities by activating the *Arjak Sangh;* Udal and Ram Chandra Bakhsh Singh continued in the Communist Party of India and Ram Asrey Verma remained an independent MLA for long durations. However, excepting Ram Swaroop Verma, these were political actors of only local significance: they could not play any significant role in the political emancipation of the Kurmis in the Uttar Pradesh polity. The Congress willfully neglected development of such constituencies that repeatedly returned Kurmi MLAs in central Uttar Pradesh.It transferred them in to reserved category in some cases. This intolerance of the Congress was responsible for roasting alive of Awadh Sharan Verma Lallji at a meeting in Baddupur in full day light in the early Fifties and murder of Hargovind Verma much later in the Eighties in Laharpur, Sitapur.Among those Kurmi leaders that still remained in the Congress, Bal Govind Verma from Lakhimpur Khiri got a Deputy Ministership at the Centre and Ram Pujan Patel (Phoolpur, Allahabad) remained only an ordinary MP. However, a potential Chief Ministerial candidate, Jai Ram Verma's inappropriate decisions to switch sides from and to Congress not only jeopardized his chances but also ended in considerable humiliation of a promised Ministership by Rajiv Gandhi but denied the same for a while by sugarcoated Brahmin Narayan Datt Tewari.Not getting their due in the Congress, most newly emerging Kurmi leaders were joining the Socialist Party. Some of these leaders like Beni Prasad Verma from Barabanki also became Ministers in the state during the short tenure of Janata Party in 1977-79. Beni Prasad Verma was in fact performing the tasks of a party manager for Mulayam Singh Yadav and had gained considerable prominence. He later became a cabinet Minister in the Devegouwda government at the Centre and was mainly responsible for development of the telecommunication infrastructure that ushered in the communication revolution in the country in such a short duration. There was a large-scale shift of the Kurmis to the BJP some time later. This saw emergence of some Kurmi political actors having limited local influence that the BJP encashed in its march towards capture of power in Uttar Pradesh first and then New Delhi. These included men like Ugrasen Chaudhary (Bahraich), GL Gangwar (Pilibhit), and Santosh Kumar Gangwar (Bareilly), and Vinay Katiyar (Farrukhabad). Other Kurmi leaders had also emerged on the scene. Chaudhary Narendra Singh, a protégé of Chaudhary Charan Singh, had been lured away from the *Bhartiya Lok Dal* and *Kisan Trust* and rewarded with a Ministership by the Congress but quite a few of the others had gone over to the BJP. In the midst of all these new comers, men like Ram Prasad Chaudhry (Kaptanganj:Basti) and Yadunath Singh (Chunar:Mirzapur) kept on winning their seats purely on the basis of their guts and grass root grip of local support. The BJP, in fact, provided the largest number of berths to the Kurmi candidates in the Assembly elections in the Eighties and Nineties Indeed, it would not be far fetched to state that the Kurmis were very cleverly kept in the forefront of the Ayodhya campaigns both before and after the demolition of Babri Masjid by the RSS and the BJP. Quite naturally, when the BJP shared power in Uttar Pradesh, quite unusually for this state, under the 'social engineering' route devised by the then General Secretary of the BJP,K.N.Govindacharya,the number of Kurmi Ministers was also relatively generous by the mere token standards of the Congress. Among these, Om Praksh Singh,Vinay Katiyar,and Ram Kumar Verma were prominent. The BSP when it 'arrived' in Uttar Pradesh used Kurmis as a focal community in its initial period of ascendancy with Barkhu Ram Verma,Jang Bahadur Patel,Ram Lakhan Verma and Sone Lal Patel as its torchbearers. But as Kanshi Ram and Mayawati are nothing but merchants of vote banks and indulge in the business of milking levers of political power, each of the Kurmi leaders was used and discarded as and when they considered it necessary. Sone Lal Patel, humiliated at a public gathering of the BSP in Kanpur decided to form his Apna Dal, supposedly a Kurmi but a 'lose-lose' Party, to wean away Kurmi votes from the BSP/other parties, in effect ended up in causing maximum political damage to the corporate interests of the Kurmis in Uttar Pradesh.There was an opportunity in the Eighties when Chaudhary Ajit Singh of Bhartiya Lok Dal had offered Chief Ministership to Beni Prasad Verma if he left SP and joined him. Beni Prasad Verma spurned this offer. With the emergence of Amar Singh in the SP, the Kurmis like Beni Prasad Verma were marginalized. Consigning Beni Prasad Verma and Kurmis to obscurity, Mulayam Singh decided to realign the caste arithmetic of his party and cultivate the Kshatriyas.At this point of time, with Kalyan Singh out of the BJP, there was a live chance for another senior Kurmi politician, Om Prakash Singh, who had been a Minister every single time BJP came to power singly or in coalition and had also been General Secretary as well as the chief of the state BJP on earlier occasions, to grab his chance of Chief Ministership from amongst the BJP stalwarts when Rajnath Singh got bumped off. However, he could not utilize this opportunity. The use of political power at the Central and state government levels by the Kurmi men while in power has been at most token. No '*Asar*' (influence), no power, no say even if made Party Presidents,as is the case with most political parties at this moment, makes the Kurmi leaders useless to their constituencies and they lose respect among their own community.Only men like Chaudhary Narendra Singh and Beni Prasad Verma knew how to put upper caste bureaucrats in their proper places and take work: others could not even fix appointments with the Chief Minister for their supporters,not to say getting their orders executed even from their own Departmental Secretaries. Politics is the art of 'getting things done'. The Kurmi leaders, almost in every political party, lack the attitude and *Asar* to get things done. In most cases, their *Asar* is less than even that of the Corporators of other castes. As discussed elsewehere, this is a larger malaise afflicting the OBC politicians which is equally caused due to the deployment of 'caging strategies' both by all the mainstream political parties in India but more so by the Congress, BJP, and BSP. Politically, the Kurmis have excelled only when used very cleverly in oppositional modes as puppets on a chain remotely controlled (H.S.Verma: 2005 B).

Contrastingly, the Kurmis have come up in large enough numbers now in the Panchayati Raj institutions but not in the urban local bodies. These include not only the reserved seats but also quite a few unreserved ones. This emergent Kurmi leadership can be analytically categorised into three sub-types. The first variety is one where power is exercised only as a surrogate in the shadow of the dominant upper caste tyrant of his area. This is a 'command performance' where the Kurmi office holder is not free to do what his own personal interest demands: rather he is serving the interests of others as a dummy. The second variety is just the opposite. He is occupying the seat of power on his own and uses it for his own good. The third variety is a mixture of the first and the second: this type has certainly achieved some foothold and to that extent some of his decisions are 'autonomous' while overall he functions as a part of larger chain of coalition partners sharing the fruits of power. Numerically, the largest numbers of Kurmi incumbents of PRI positions in Uttar Pradesh belong to the second category. This is a positive development on the political front for the Kurmis.

Overall, at the moment politically the Kurmis find themselves lost in the political whirlpool of Uttar Pradesh. When different political parties want to extract maximum mileage out of the Kurmis, they promise them moon. Once they achieve their goal, the Kurmis are dumped and promises given to them are quietly overlooked. The latest example of such a technique is the one used by the SP with Dadua.In return for total support to the SP candidates in Dadua land, the Robinhood type dacoit was promised a ticket for his brother, Bal Kumar from the Karchhana Assembly constituency of Allahabad. However, once the Parliamentary elections were over and the SP had reaped a rich harvest of Parliamentary seats from the Banda region, Bal Kumar was left in the lurch. Even smaller communities are politically far more assertive than the Kurmis.It turns out that they are good enough to be fully used by the Congress, BJP, BSP, and SP: they have not learnt to extract their pound of political flesh. It is indeed true that all the upper castes and even the SCs have treated the Kurmis only as means of achieving their political goals/objectives. However, politics is the game of the possible and the Kurmis have to learn the tricks of the political trade. If they look inwards, they would discover that it is their corporate psyche that is responsible for their miserable political fate.

V

Present social-cultural status

The Kurmis have attained a much better socio-economic-political status in parts of Bihar and Nitish Kumar symbolizes that pivotal position. Characteristically, this type of Kurmi does not suffer from the 'follower by birth' syndrome. He is his own man and no Brahmin,

Bhumihar, Kashtriya or Kayastha can get away denying him his well earned due. He is reasonably educated; he has outside orientation and knows his strengths and weaknesses. He has done reasonably well in all walks of life. Better still, he has learnt to negotiate the rough and tumble of the troublesome and anarchic Bihari society. In that part of Bihar, therefore, he would take his part of the cake.

This is not so in Uttar Pradesh. As the preceding analysis pertaining to economic, educational and political status of the Kurmis indicates, the Kurmi mainstream has remained stagnant. *Why has the Kurmi mainstream stagnated in Uttar Pradesh?* There are several reasons why the Kurmis find themselves sidelined in the society, economy and polity. But, the *principal set* among these causatory factors is *their own psyche*. The Kurmis are known to be a simple, god fearing, hard working peasant community, one that earns its bread with a great deal of sweat, lives a very frugal life and is not known for any coping skills, particularly managing their dealings with the outside world. Due to this handicap, quite often they end up easily squandering their hard earned earnings to the guiles of the traders, lawyers ,policemen and others. Second, with some exceptions, the leading branches of the Kurmis possess a *closed mind set*, lack outside orientation, and continue to be more or less *tethered only to their farm, home and hearth, things local* and aloof to what ever is happening in the outside world. They continue to be a people who *rarely act proactively* and as a corporate entity *react only when they could not help avoiding* the catastrophe facing them. This *cocoon tendency* limits their day-to-day behaviour with things non-farm, non-local and shows almost total lack of entrepreneurial streak in comparison to the other farming/peasant communities. Quite often they wait for some others to take the lead in any thing new and for the results to show. Once it is clearly demonstrated that the idea in question is feasible and profitable, reflecting a *sheep mentality* the entire horde of the Kurmis would plunge for it. The third attribute of the corporate identity is *not easily venturing out for any common cause* that does not have immediate and direct individual benefit to them. In their worldview, this is supposed to be an enterprise best left to others. Fourth, once asked to amplify why he was not giving as much importance to the Kurmis in his party, Mulayam Singh Yadav remarked in one of his very apt and matter of fact closed door meetings that the

Kurmis would seldom come to the aid of some one from their own flock if the latter is in 'trouble'. In fact, they would privately enjoy his discomfiture. On the other hand, the Yadavs, he stated, would come to help a Yadav in trouble without even being asked to do so. The Kurmis have also displayed the habit of more often fighting each other more than jointly taking on a common adversary. At the corporate level the consequence of this fratricide has been disastrous for the Kurmis in social, economic and political arenas. It is not without significance that while the Jats, and Lodhs, population wise all one per cent or even less strength communities in the state of Uttar Pradesh, had succeeded in getting the position of Chief Ministership, despite being close to five per cent population strength community the Kurmis have failed to do so despite the presence of a galaxy of capable Kurmi political leaders in almost all leading political parties of the state. Fifth, the Kurmis have immense pride in their profession of farming and continue to treat it as the 'best' occupation and consequently have been *very complacent in trying out trade and commerce, civil services, and other activities such as the widely expanding services sector in the rural areas.* The logic of this peculiar behaviour is beyond comprehension. Their population has been increasing steadily but their landed assets remain stationery. Consequently, if they expect to prevent their growing pauperisation, they have hardly any choice but to look for pastures new. Sixth, the position of the person in today's society is judged on the basis of multi-utility vehicles, sophisticated fire arms, a convoy of henchmen surrounding you and a lifestyle that flaunts money and power. Most Kurmis, even if they can afford all these, are so miser that they would go nowhere near these materialistic posseessions. Seventh, the Kurmi mainstream would go to any one when needing any favour: after the accomplishment of the requested deed, an overwhelming majority would not even show the courtesy of offering a 'thank you'. This typical trait of not showing *required courtesy and gratefulness* has caused unlimited damage to the image and prestige of the community. Eightth, an average Kurmi looks down upon all those of his community members who have achieved the distinction of becoming doctors, engineers, architects, high civil servants and in general reached a very high level of academic eminence while he has remained where he was. He just cannot digest their progress.

Notes

1. This depends largely upon the researcher's ideological location and commitment to the cause of the empowerment of the OBCs.
2. The dimensions covered are very impressive. These include: 1. Numbers and derivation of name; 2. Functional character of caste; 3. Sub-castes; 4. Exogamous groups; 5. Marriage rules, betrothal, the marriage-shed or pavilion, marriage cakes, customs at the weddings, walking around the sacred post, other ceremonies; 6. Polygamy, widow marriage and divorce; 7. Impurity of women; 8.Pregnancy rites, earth eating; 9. Customs at birth; 10. Treatment of mother and child; 11. Ceremonies after birth; 12. Suckling children; 13. Beliefs about twins; 14. Disposal of the dead; 15. Funeral rites; 16. Burning the dead,burial; 17. Return of the soul; 18. Mourning,shaving and presents to Brahmans; 19. End of mourning; 20. Anniversary of the dead; 21. Beliefs in hereafter; 22. Religion, village gods; 23. Sowing the Jawars or garden of Adonis; 24. Rites connected with the crops, customs of cultivation; 25. Agricultural superstitions; 26. Houses; 27. Superstitions about houses; 28. Furniture; 29. Clothes; 30. Women's clothes; 31. Bathing; 32. Food; 33. Caste feasts; 34. Hospitality; 35. Social customs, tattooing; 36. Caste penalties; 37. The cultivating status; 38. Occupation. The accounts were assembled as parts of Census operations carried out with the help and assistance of the Revenue staff consisting of Tehsildars, Kanoongos and Patwaris.The division of labour was such that the presiding officer, who was by definition British, wrote the 'analysis' on the basis of 'information' and figures collected by the Indian menials.
3. Actually, these precisely are the most crucial items in correctly appraising the socio-political status of a community in a society.
4. The fact that the first author was associated as a Social Planner in the State Planning Commission between 1982 and 1993 and toured the state extensively in that capacity, assisted the state government in Indra Sawhney versus Union of India in the Supreme Court (1990-1992) and thereafter was a Member of the Creamy Layer and Percentage Fixation Committees of the state of Uttar Pradesh (1993) and State Commission for Backward Classes, Uttar Pradesh (1993-1996) and the Working Group of the Central Planning Commission on the Empowerment of the OBCs for the Tenth Five Year Plan (2000-2001)facilitated receipt of privileged information and in exchange of sensitive details, normally not available to a purely academic researcher. Later his association with the Uttar Pradesh Rural Water Supply and Environmental Sanitation Sectoral Reform Project as a Consultant in 2000-2001 required him to carry out a research study in 40 villages from 18 districts of Uttar Pradesh and

Uttranchal enabled a focused discussion with the grass root realities of this community at the lowest level.

Similarly, the second author had grappled with the grass root realities of the Kurmi issues in some finer details during his postings in Hardoi and Raebareli districts as a PCS officer.

5. Even G.S. Bhatt (2002), a scholar known for his Brahminical views, concedes this point that in Uttar Pradesh a few of Kurmis had small estates; quite a few of them were *Zamindars* and were deprived off their *Zamindari* first by the Moghuls and later by the British; that in spite of these periodical dispossessions (*Bedakhali)* by the ruling class reducing their number drastically some among them still survived as *Zamindars* until the enactment of *The Uttar Pradesh Zamindari Abolition Act* passed in the early Fifties. It is also recorded part of history that some of these Kurmi nobles were forming part of the inner circle of the Lucknow Nawabs, sided with them and played notable part in the freedom struggle whereas most other fair weather friends from the Muslim, Khastriya and Brahmin nobility, quickly abandoned them and went along with the British.
6. This switchover should not be mixed with sugar policy but treated as part of energy policy and energy industry. Oil companies should enter into long-term supply contracts with ethanol factories and work out a suitable price band. Brazil has successfully carried out such a strategy of using ethanol and petrol-ethanol mix as fuel for its transport needs.
7. Steps such as the opening up of the Flower Auction Centre and Fruit and Vegetable Mart by the *Rajkiya Krishi Mandi Utapadan Parishad* at NOIDA, announced on June 5,2005 by the Government of Uttar Pradesh would empower the innovative farmers in general and the Kurmis in particular. However, benefits from such experimental, non-traditional farming shall remain confined to a very small segment of innovators, not the ordinary farmers. Therefore, the kind of "farmers smiling all the way to the bank" stories for instance filed by *The Times of India* on June 6,2005(see box below) would be mind blowing exaggerations and totally misleading about the improvement in the economic status of farmers in Uttar Pradesh.

The Times of India Report, Dated 6th, June 2005
Farmers Smiling All the Way to the Bank

Lucknow: Farming of medicinal and aromatic plants has turned into big business now, Gone are the days when farmers barely had enough to cover themselves with a loincloth. One square meal of wheat-bran *chapatis* and onion was a luxury. Now, we have farmers like Raj

Bahadur of Hamirpur, Barabanki. He doubles up as a general merchant along with looking after his ten large farms, where he cultivates medicinal and aromatic plants like germaniium, peppermint, artimicia, menthol, primrose, lemon grass, citronella and khas. The Central Institute for Medicinal and Aromatic Plants (CIMAP) provides knowledge of these plants to farmers. 'I earn around RS 50,000 per month by cultivating plants like limon grass, citronella and sugandha. Huge farms are not required for such farming. About 10 kilograms of germanium can be cultivated in as little as one acre of land and it can be sold for RS. 4000 per Kg" said Raj Bahadur.The added advantage is insects and pests keep away from such plants. Moreover, these plants are not affected by weather artrocities. In fact, there is no harm if these plants are not harvested once ripe, which means no hassles of regular labourers.

"It is profitable farming, which gives us a recurring income. Once lemon grass is planted, it can be harvested after every three months for four years and low maintenance is a big advantage", said Raghvendra,a farmer from Sitapur. He further added that dry leaves of plants like artimicia are sold for Rs. 20 per Kg. and around 25 quintals of output is generated per acre".

8. Married into the Nepalese royal family, CPN Singh truly believed that he was indeed a Kshatriya.However, as the judgment of the State Commission for Backward Classes, Uttar Pradesh argued so clearly, the irrefutable evidence was that they were a Kurmi sub-caste and had been 'admitted' in to the comity of the Kshatriyas only as tactical measure to gain social-political advantages: the exchange of brides from the Kshatriyas to the Santhwars and other social intercourse that is the normal practice of one single community was not taking place. Once the Sainthwars themselves realized the folly of this unequal 'union' they disassociated themselves from the Kshatriyas. CPN Singh was instrumental in getting the inclusion of Sainthwars as a sub caste of the Kurmis into the list of the OBCs in Uttar Pradesh reversed when Narayan Datt Tewari was the Chief Minister in 1989. He killed himself in a family fratricide some time in the Eighties and his family could not stop the inclusion of the Sainthwars in the OBC list as a sub-caste of the Kurmis a second time.

References

Bhatt, G.S. 2002. *Themes of Indian social Thought*. New Delhi: Jawahar Publishers and Distributors.

Crooks, William. 1974. (Reprint). *Tribes and Castes of northwest provinces and Oudh.*Delhi: Cosmo.

Leonard, Karen. 1994. *Social history of a caste: The Kayastha of Hyderabad.* Hyderabad:Orient Longman.

Lohia, Ram Manohar. 1960. *Marx, Gandhi and Socialism.*Hyderabad: Navyug.

Risley, R.H. 1981 (Reprint). *The tribes and castes of West Bengal.* Vol. I. Calcutta: Firma K.L. Mukhopadhyaya.

Rogers, Everett M. 1960. *The diffusion of innovations.* Glencoe: The Free Press.

Russell, R.V. and Hira Lal. 1916 (Reprint 1993). *The tribes and castes of central India.* New Delhi: Asian Education Service.

Verma, H.S. 2005 A. 'Dilution of the exclusivity of the *Vaishya Varna*: Changing composition and character of the business community in a small town' in H.S.Verma (ed.), *The OBCs and the dynamics of social exclusion in India.* New Delhi: Serials Publications.

Verma, H.S. 2005 B. ' The OBC identity and treatment of the OBCs by mainstream political parties in India' in H.S.Verma (ed.), *The OBCs and the dynamics of social exclusion in India.* New Delhi: Serials Publications.

Verma, H.S. 2005 C. 'From sugar cane to potato, mentha and green chillies: The impact of shift on the socio-cultural lives of the OBCs' in H.S.Verma (ed.), *The OBCs and the dynamics of social exclusion in India.* New Delhi: Serials Publications.

Verma, H.S. and Neelima Verma.1986. Educational transformation in Uttar Pradesh: A pattern analysis' in R.T.Tewari and Ashutosh Joshi (eds). *Development and change in India.*New Delhi"ashish Publishing Company.

Verma. H.S, Ram Abhilash Verma and Jay Singh. 2005. 'Power sharing by different social categories: Exclusivity and exclusion in Uttar Pradesh prior to the introduction of 27 per cent reservation for the OBCs' in H.S.Verma (ed.), *The OBCs and the dynamics of social exclusion in India.* New Delhi: Serials Publications.

Verma, J.P. 1988. *Bhartiya Kurmi Krashak Ka Itihas.* Vols II. Lucknow and I: Akhil Bhartiya Kurmi Kashtriya Mahasabha.

Social structure, people's movement and the role of OBCs: A case study of Baliapal movement in Orissa

D.R. Sahu

The present paper tries to articulate the active participation of OBCs in the successful people's movement against the National Missile Test Range Centre that emerged in Baliapal, Balasore district of Orissa. This project was likely to displace more than 1,00,000 people spread over 55 villages covering an area of 102 square kilometers. Due to the people's resistance, the project could not be implemented.

After independence, India began its tryst with destiny by subscribing to the path of rapid industrialization and modernization and pursued the growth-oriented development. Social scientists often critically termed this development paradigm as post-colonial ambitions of the new Indian elite. However, these state sponsored development programmes sometimes forcibly acquired huge land areas covering many villages. Consequently, these did not enthuse the local people since their survival and identities were threatened by such projects. These projects invited stiff resistance and protests from the affected communities, and resulted in a confrontation between the people and the state. Further, these protests and confrontations also attracted response from social activists, intellectuals, voluntary organizations and political parties. The intensity and fierceness of these protests has been of such a nature that in some cases it has successfully prevented the state from proceeding with the implementation of the project.

Our society has been witnessing many such protest movements and resistance concerned with the issues of environment, women's rights, consumerism, land rights and many others. The affected groups are not only challenging the state and its policy decisions but also the legitimacy of bureaucratic and political institutions. Chipko movement, Appiko movement, Narmada Bachao Andolan, BALCO movement, environment in Chilika, and people's movement in Baliapal, Orissa and many similar protest movements are the examples from recent times.

Movements in Orissa

Sociologically, Orissa can be divided into two parts on the basis of its history and socio-economic conditions – the coastal districts and inland districts. The former are fertile, agriculturally rich and have high proportions of the upper caste population of Brahmins, Karanas and the peasant castes. These caste groups have produced most of Orissa's leading politicians and prominent citizens. The inland districts are hilly and covered with forest. These are inhabited by various tribal groups and are materially very poor. This area contains one of the highest proportions (more than 42 per cent)of scheduled tribes and scheduled castes. During the colonial rule, the coastal districts were under the permanent and various kinds of semi-permanent settlements. These *Zamindari* settlements only encouraged pauperization of the peasantry and agricultural labourers and consolidation of upper caste landlords (PUDR: 1988). Further, in the tribal areas, the colonial state gave rights to the kings to collect revenue through intermediaries known as '*Gauntia*'. However, after independence, all these *Zamindari* systems were abolished by the Abolition of Estates Act, 1951 that gave rights over land to permanent and some type of occupancy tenants. Subsequently, land ceiling was introduced in 1973 through an amendment.

Orissa could not make much progress even 58 years after independence, and continues to be termed as a backward state. The state is characterized by low productivity, very few industries, prevailing mass poverty, natural calamities including super cyclone of 1999 and frequent floods. However, some development in Orissa can be seen after the installation of large development projects of mineral based industries (Rourkella steel plant, NALCO and BALCO), big irrigation dams (Hirakund, Rengali and many others), defence projects (HAL in Koraput, Saintala, Air Force base, Charbatia, Naval Training Academy, Chilika, Intermediate Test Range (ITR), Chandipur), power projects

(NTPC Talchel, Gopalpur) and many other projects. Except Baliapal, all these projects have led to massive displacements uprooting people from their native habitat, disrupting their life pattern, taking their only sources of livelihoods and, of course, their lands.

Political economy

The Balsore district is situated in the northeastern part of Orissa bordering Midnapore district of West Bengal on the north, Mayurbhanj and Keonjhar districts on the west and Bay of Bengal in the south. It is also the smallest district with a geographical area of 3634 square kilometers and its population is 1,696,583. This district has an impressive literacy rate of 57.64 per cent that is quite high in comparison to some other districts of Orissa. Density of population is also quite high i.e. 458 per sq. km. in comparison to the 203 sq.km. of the state. Historically, the district was known as one of *Mughalbandi* areas of coastal Orissa during Maratha rule. Earlier to this, during Mughal rule, this area flourished due to overseas trade and commerce through seaports like Balasore and Pipili. European traders, particularly Portuguese, Dutch and English initially came for trading and subsequently they settled down in the area. East India Company acquired the area in 1903 and formed a part of Cuttack district. Finally, Balasore became an independent coastal district only in 1836 along with Cuttack, Puri and Ganjam (Biswal: 1987). However, the district is relatively prosperous than the other parts of the state (Patel: 1988). Rice is the staple crop of the district. Other major crops grown are oilseeds and pulses. Besides, coastal areas grow a variety of cash crops mainly groundnut, cashew nut, coconut, betel nut, betel leaf (*Paan*) and all types of seasonal vegetables.

Though inadequate for rabi crops, three rivers including Subarnarekha, Budbhabalanga and Baitarni and their tributaries provide rudimentary facilities of irrigation. People mainly depend on ground water, drawn through very expensive diesel pumps. The coast canal, built by the British in 1885, provides irrigation support only from October to March: rest of the time it carries saline water. However, recent introduction of high yielding varieties of seeds (HYV seeds) and credit facilities from the block through Gram Panchayat under Panchayati Raj programme have had some impact. The district also produces large quantities of sea fish and fresh water fish from the rivers and ponds. Industrially, Balasore has started making its presence felt largely because of many small-scale industrial units. Birla Tyres and Orissa Plastics are some of the bigger industrial units along with aqua based and ceramic industries. In 1995,the district reported 116 industries that employed 7563 employees (District Statistical Handbook: 1995).

Baliapal formed part of the *Mughalbandi* areas during Afghan period. Earlier to this, during Aurangzeb's rule, *Murshid Qulikhan-I* governed as *Subedhar*, a bigger portion of Midnapore of West Bengal (adjacent to study area) was taken away from Jaleswar Sarkar of Orissa and in subsequent years, the river Subarnrekha was made the southern boundary of Bengal. During the *Mughal* period, this area was used as a military base because of its sea routes and port facilities. As they had to sacrifice their agricultural land, the local people vehemently opposed the construction of coast canal by the British in 1855. The coast canal divides the Baliapal block and Subarnarekha river divides Baliapal and Bhograi blocks. People of Baliapal normally go to the adjacent district of West Bengal for shopping purposes by simply crossing the river through boat. Similarly, people from West Bengal, particularly from Contai, Midnapore and Dantan come to weekly markets located in the villages of Baliapal for trading purposes through this short cut canal root. Baliapal is a thickly populated block and has an area of 233.65 square kilometers with 240 villages that have 24,716 households in 22,454 residential houses. The scheduled castes and the scheduled tribes constitute about twenty and five per cent of its population respectively.

Paddy is the staple crop in this region. Productivity levels are high due to the use of HYV seeds. The area is very vulnerable to natural calamities like land erosions caused by frequent changes of direction of flow of its stream by the river Subarnarekha on its way to the sea and, cyclonic floods and entry of saline water. Along with cultivation of paddy and the agricultural labour, many people of Baliapal, especially those living in the coastal villages, depend on fishing. Cultivation of the cash crops-vegetables, groundnut, betelnut, cashewnut, coconut and most importantly betel leaf has significantly improved the economic status of the people of Baliapal. The land in two geographically distinct parts of Baliapal is used for different purposes. Whereas the area nearer to the sea produces all cash crops i.e., the betel, coconut, groundnut and cashew nut, the other side is used for non-commercial crops.

Caste–class dynamics

The villages in Baliapal area have more than twenty-three Hindu caste groups, a few Santhals and a Muslim population. Ritually, the Brahmins are placed at the top of the hierarchy. Numerically, politically and economically the Raju, Khandayat, Barajia and Mahesh or Gola, all peasant castes (OBCs), are powerful and command more prestige than other caste groups in the area. They constitute the dominant castes. Other than these caste groups, there are *Vaishnavites* influenced by Sri Chattanya's *Bhakti* movement particularly in the eastern part of Baliapal. These people belong to this sect, locally known as Vaishnav. Although they are not part of the local caste hierarchy but over the years people of this sect have been identifying themselves as one of the Hindu caste category. The *Vaishnavaties* are strictly vegetarians, do not cultivate and do not even plough like Brahmins, propagate Sri Chaitanya's philosophy through '*satsangs*' and *bhajans*, lead a simple life and distinctly present themselves by making an anchor mark with the sandal wood paste *tilak* on their nose and three lines on their forehead and both the arms and silently chant *Bishnu sahasra nama*. However, in course of time, they have taken to agriculture and cultivation of cash crops but so far they have restricted themselves to vegetarian food and they do not plough. Jena (1991) has presented a ritual ranking of such caste groups i.e. Brahmin, Vaishnav, peasant castes – Khandayat, Mahesh Raju, Gauda, Sundhi, Teli, Tanti, Dhoba, Ketua, Barika, Radhi, Kumbhara and Kamara (OBCs) all service caste groups and Kandara, Kodma, Mahuria, Kuranga and Domo – all scheduled castes. However, there is no unanimity among scholars on the caste hierarchy indicated by Jena. Hadi, Kandara, Kodoma, Mahuria, Kuranga and Doma are considered as untouchables for their menial jobs. The above caste groups are not considered under socially permitted caste group *Chala Jati*. There is a distinct social distance from the higher caste groups.

Nineteenth century records indicate that the Khandayat and Raju were traditionally peasant castes. Over the years, the migrants from Contai, Midnapore and Belda areas of West Bengal, particularly Barajia and Mahesh or Gola caste groups, joined these caste groups.

Further, they had harvesting land rights called '*Amal nama Patta*' declared by the then *Zamindars.* Currently, these lands are cultivated particularly for cash crops (Patel: 1989). For a long time, these dominant caste groups remained as peasant castes. However, cultivation has no more been the monopoly of the dominant castes as non-cultivating castes particularly Brahmins, fishing communities, *Vaishnavaites* and even tribal people have entered into the cultivation of cash crops because of its low investments and high returns. There are four castes from fishing communities such as Keutas, Ujiyas, Jhalis and Khejalis. During the fieldwork, it was observed that some of them have changed their old caste names i.e., Keutas as Kaivartas and Ujias as Bhumijas and Sunaris as Kamilas (Goldsmith).

Teli (oilpressers), Gudia (sweet maker), Tanti (weavers), Kumbhara (potters), Barika (barber), Dhoba (washerman), Gauda (milkman), Sundhi (liquor maker), Domo or Pana (bamboo makers), Hadi (scavengers and drumbeaters) and Mahuria (flute players) have also started cultivating paddy and all kinds of cash crops. As compared to people from the other parts of Orissa,the life style choices of the inhabitants of Baliapal villages including their food habits, housing pattern, family rituals are quite distinct. Except for the Domas, Panas Keutas and Santhals, the housing patterns are strictly not on the basis of caste groups. However, a clear-cut distinction exists between socially permitted caste groups (*Chala Jati*) and socially prohibitive caste groups (*Achala Jati*) and the tribals (*Adivasi*). Though they do interact with these A*chala Jatis* by maintaining a proper distance, however, all *Achala Jatis* live in a cluster preferably on the outskirts of the village or periphery or roadside of the village. The cluster of the houses of these caste groups and tribals are known as *Sahi*(Hamlet) bearing the name of each caste such as Hadi Sahi, Kandara Sahi, Santhal Sahi.

All middle and upper middle class families maintain two houses, one each in the paddy fields and the other near cash crop fields nearer to sea. These are locally known as *Pahighar* (second home) or *Bali Ghara* (a thatched house in the cash crop area). Households engaged in betel vine cultivation, cashew nut, coconut, groundnut, mango and betal nut, nearer to the coastal sea areas, have small open and thatched houses. Men, including their children and women, go early in the morning to their respective cash crop areas along with mats and food materials. Throughout the day, they engage themselves in the dressing of the *pana* leaves in the *Pana baraja*, collecting cashew with cashew fruits during the harvesting period. Women prepare lunch by cooking the food and look after the garden (*Baadi).* They even carry their cows and cattle along with to their respective *baadi*. Except the tough work like watering the betel leaves, which is normally done twice or thrice a week by the hired labour, most of the cultivators prefer to do this personally since *Pana* requires skilled and intensive nurturing.

Almost all the affluent households from the upper and the middle caste groups have typical house structure locally known as *pheraghara.* Besides, there are number of *pucca* houses and brick houses thatched with tiles (cement or clay). It was observed that most of the houses are clay structures thatched with paddy straw, locally known as '*kuta Chapara*'. As observed in the villages under study, houses are located in the middle of the homestead land. All the households have open ground plastered with clay and cow dung known as *Khala badi* in front of the house with a boundary *(Bedha)* made of branch of bamboo trees and other locally available plants. The coconut trees barricade every house, which gives them a green look. Whenever any guests arrive, they are served green coconut (*daba*) water either in '*kansa*' or steel glass.

The front portion of the house i.e. *Khalabadi* is used for thrashing of grains and keeping the mound of the straw (*kuta gadi*). The cattle shed is normally found near the entrance or one side of the house. All the traditional houses, particularly houses of upper middle and rich class families, are found with grain storage facility known as '*Amara Ghara'* typically prepared with the bamboo and plastered with clay and cow dung. Near the cattle shed, every house has a storage facility for cow dung, which is used as manure for the cultivation purposes and other household uses. In some of the traditional houses, an indigenous technology for processing the grains, locally known as *Khinki* are also found. Normally, women do grain processing through this *Dhinki.* It is installed with the help of a heavy log and it is placed in the front verandah. In the backyard, most of the households have small ponds for multiple uses. Generally, womenfolk of the house take bath and having a pond in the house determines the status of the household and provides privacy to women folk along with cleaning of utensils and washing clothes. Variety of fish is also nurtured in the pond. Fish is a staple diet for all families except the *Vaishnavas*. Due to easy availability of all kinds of fish including sea fish, lobsters, prawns and crabs, most of the people are non-vegetarian. Similarly, due to the large-scale cultivation of betel, and betel nut people of this area have the habit of chewing *paan*. Even the children are found to be *paan* chewers. More or less, *paan* is considered to be the part of the culture of Orissa. Older women of every family keep themselves busy with the preparation of *paan* with some home made *paan masala*. It is also considered to be the part of delicacies of family. Moreover, the structure of the family is found to be 'joint' but in recent times, nuclear set up is preferred by the younger generation.

Different castes groups in villages

Upper Castes:	Brahmin, Karana (Kayasth), Khandayat, Raju, Teli
OBCs:	Gudia, Teli, Gauda, Barika, Radhi, Sundhi Mahesh, Gola, Gudia
Scheduled castes:	Ketua, Dhoba, Tanti, Hadi, Kumbhara, Kamara, Kandara, Pana, Kuranga, Madhuria, Bhurnija.
Scheduled Tribe:	Santhal

Dynamics of the movement

The movement has a mass character and support from all political parties due to the ideology of home, hearth and common identity i.e. "*Bheeta Maati*', (home and hearth) which was found to be the basis of this struggle. All the interest constellations centered on the production process and as perceived by the local people,the land is the nature's gift which have crystallized in the form of an ideology of *Bheetaa Maati* (Patel: 1990). This ideology is restricted to Baliapal block where 45 villages were to be acquired in the revised scheme against the 13 villages acquired in Bhograi block. As already discussed, the area has excellent natural resources and the cash crop economy and it is known for its dominance of the market for the locally grown products (cashew nut, coconut, and especially betel vine). The specific nature of *paan* cultivation attracted the lower and non-cultivating castes and they strengthened the ideology of *Bheeta Maati*. The increased demand of *paan* led to the growth of market and trade. Consequently, the market forces facilitated caste-class dynamics and ideology of *Bheetaa Maati* and the crystallization of the protest.

The government, on the other hand, claimed that the project would trigger development in the region by initiating the process of much desired industrialization and modernization. Industries would be set up along with an Industrial Training Institute (ITI) to train the local youth. It would enable them to find skilled jobs in those industries. Further, the government promised to provide jobs to at least one person from each project-affected family. Besides, the government promised to implement a comprehensive rehabilitation programme, which would provide a modern and developed context of living to the people of Baliapal (Department of Public Relations: Orissa).

Rejecting this government view, the leaders of the movement expressed the view that the area is already a developed one. The development experienced by the people has been initiated by people themselves and is suitable to the local socio-cultural matrix. Unemployment and starvation are unknown to the people in this area. Every one in the family, from children to the aged, is gainfully engaged. The leaders claim that a child who peels off ground earns around Rs. 15 a day and an adult or old person, who either plucks betel leaves or arranges them in the basket, earns around Rs. 20 to 25 a day. So the older and the dependent too are not a liability either on the family or the community. Scarcity of the labour rather than the wage rate is an issue in the area. The extinction of *paan* economy would destabilize the cross section of the community. Various groups engaged in the *Paan* cultivation and trade would be out of job. The labourers who specialize in setting up structure for the betel vine yard, those engaged in plucking and arranging the betel leaves, the artisans who make bamboo baskets for the export of betel leaves would all be left without any viable means of livelihood. Even if they are provided with jobs in any of the proposed industries, they would find it difficult to adapt to the unfamiliar requirements of the new occupation. The peasants who survive on the cultivation of *Paan* will become paupers.

The leaders further stress that whatever may be the amount of compensation, there is no avenue and opportunity of investment where the people will get the same kind of returns as they are getting now. This is true even for those cultivators and fisherman who are not linked with *paan* economy. For them, the natural resources of the region give enough of livelihood so that they prefer staying here rather than working as contract labour as many of their brothers have migrated to various parts of the country in search of job.

The Gola and Raju caste groups (OBCs) of the area initiated the cash crop production by encroaching the common property land and the seacoast land. The outsiders, particularly the Bengali traders, initiated the *paan* cultivation but subsequently they were eliminated and replaced by the local traders. The local peasant castes found this cultivation in a small patch of sandy land more profitable. Since this cultivation requires intensive care and low investment, upper caste peasants were attracted to this production as a result of which the land consolidation process of local people was put on the backburner. Consequently, production process increased the demand for the agricultural labourers in the region and small cultivators and landless labourers met this demand. Gradually, they used the knowledge and started producing *paan.* Small cultivators produced *paan* in their homestead land and landless labourers produced it by encroaching the seacoast land. Similarly, migrant Santhal tribals also became *paan* cultivators. The increase in the demand of such production resulted in the increased rates of wages. This production process also attracted the outside traders, particularly from Jaleswar and the neighbouring areas. The spread of the market has led to peasantisation process. In a way, the market forces brought many changes in the region particularly the quality of life and life style choices of the people irrespective of their caste and class status. The sustenance of cash crop i.e. *paan* economy gained momentum due to the demand of this product in northern and western parts of India. This production process empowered the local people economically and politically and their involvement in the protest became obvious. Further, these groups provided resources to the mobilization process.

When leading Oriya newspapers announced the government's intention to acquire land for the establishment of National Missile Test Range, it was the influential local OBC *paan* traders who initiated the protest and resistance to this move. Earlier to this, the then Chief Minister of Orissa announced this project as a development package to the people of Baliapal and Bhograi blocks of Balasore district, However, official announcement by the Chief Minister in July 1980 did raise the eyebrows of local people especially the educated youth. They informally started mobilizing the local people to oppose the move of the government. After the announcement of the government decision to acquire land of the villagers in the month of October, with the support of local traders local Congress (I) supporters attempted to form a committee known as *Kshepanastra Ghati Paratirodh Samiti* (KGPS) in December 1984. It is worth mentioning here that the Jaleswar Assembly constituency was with the then Janata party leader, Gadadhar Giri and the state was under Congress (I) rule. Local Congress (I) supporters mainly *paan* traders were from the OBC groups, who raised their voice against setting up of the National Test Range in the region. Due to assassination of Indira Gandhi, and resultant wave of sympathy, the Congress (I) could win it by putting a new candidate, a young lecturer in Government College, Judhisthir Jena but only with a very thin margin. Another reason why the people of Baliapal voted in favour of Congress was the hope that the ruling party would help in shifting the test range from Baliapal. But post-election stance of the Congress (I) in the state as a ruling party was different as a result of which, Congress (I) lost its influence and leadership in the *Kshepanstra Ghati Pratirodh Samiti* and the leadership went to Gadadhar Giri, a socialist member of Janata Party and Assembly representative from the constituency for more than two terms. The *paan* traders dominated the reconstituted KGPS. The emergence of a formal organizational structure (KGPS) under Giri's leadership increased the resistance. Jena in his study revealed that earlier to KGPS, there was a *Dakshin Kshepanastra Ghat birodh Samiti* (DBKGBS) run by the local youth of south Baliapal. However, their mobilization process could not muster much support from the people of Baliapal. The leaders of DBKGBS soon realized their limitations and merged their organisation with the KGPS. Giri initially led this organization along with the *paan* traders. In the mean time, *Gannanath Patra*, a local youth, former socialist, a liberal, associated with the centrist Janata party, who had a grass root political base as a member of Naxalite group and a member of the united Center of Communist Revolutionaries of India – Marxist Leninist (UCCRI-ML), joined the KGPS. The KGPS committee created various fronts to mobilize the people of Baliapal namely, student front, youth front, women front and fishermen front. Two prominent individuals (Gadadhar Giri and Gananath Patra) along with the support of the local people created an assertive political entity. Giri's mass appeal and long standing political commitment mobilized all sections of people and Patra's strategy of organizing various fronts greatly strengthened the protest. Irrespective of caste, class, gender and political affiliations, people of Baliapal joined hands together to protest against the government's decision under the strong leadership of these two strong and charismatic personalities of the area.

The economic structure and political entity facilitated the ideology of *Bheeta Maati* – home, hearth and belongingness -- and such ideology articulated an ethnic expression with an emotional and cultural attachment for the land, which is the nature's gift to the people of Baliapal. However, activists with the help religious and mythological stories legitimized this ideology of *bheeta maati* and mobilization process became more effective through such stories. The struggle for the land, the symbol of nature, and the productive land of the people of Baliapal fought against the state agency.

The fishing community, one of the major OBC communities, also articulated the ideology of *Bheeta Maati* by creating a fishermen's front known as *Matsya Jibi Gana Samukhya*. More than thirty thousand fishermen and women are engaged in fishing in the confluences of Subernrekha and Budhabalanga rivers with the sea. More than 10,000 traditional boats are engaged in fishing. It is the fishermen, engaged in fishing, and fish trading along with the female counterparts who cater to local weekly and nearby markets. More than one thousand people from Baliapal go to different markets daily for transporting fish. Though government had a plan to rehabilitate fishing community in another fishing zone i.e. *Kasaphala* but it could not practically accommodate such a large number of fishermen. The front was of the opinion that over generations the skills have been acquired through sheer experience. The long acquaintance with the sea of this region have made them more comfortable with definite knowledge with regard to the movement of different fishes in different seasons and even the movement of air.

There is a unique system for the fishermen prevailing in this area, known as camping '*pala*'. It means a small straw and bamboo-thatched cottage in the seacoast. Generally, *pala* is owned by the owner (*malik*) who invests the money in boats and nets and take care of the marketing of the fish. Interestingly, owners of the *pala* are the upper caste people from Baliapal i.e. *Khandayat*, *Raju* and *Gola*. The fishermen are from *kaivarta* caste locally known as *Ketua*. These caste groups join the owner as fishermen or some of them become the partners in the fishing business. Each *pala* has a membership of twenty to thirty people. Over a period of time, this *pala* system has improved the quality of life of the fishing community. However, this fishing community has also subscribed to the ideology of *bheeta maati*. For them sea is their mother (*maa*) which protects and fulfills their basic needs. These foregoing 'fronts' strengthened the protest by showing their solidarity with *Kshepanstra Ghati Pratirodh Samiti* (KGPS). The grass root leaders, Gannanath Patra, and Gadadhar Giri of the KGPS, managed these fronts.

Conclusion

The articulation of this ideology of *Bheeta Maati* brought out the economic, political, social, cultural and environmental dimensions of this protest movement. However, the ideology articulated by the KGPS and various fronts during the process of collective action focused more on economic issues than cultural and environmental issues. Patel (1989), in her analysis, rightly described that the mere use of land for peaceful purposes remains a weak impulse in the agitation. If we look at the ideology of both the groups i.e. KGPS and UCCRI-ML, we find commonality in terms of goal set i.e. to oppose the government decision for setting up a missile centre at Baliapal, but they differ in their orientations, approaches and perspective. The KGPS under the leadership of Giri criticized the logic and rationale of project in a thickly populated area and demanded its shifting to a no man's land. The KGPS was apparently concerned about their own area, people and the fertile land. On the contrary, UCCRI (M-L) under the leadership of Patra, questioned the very logic and basis of conceiving such a project for facilitating nuclear war in the world and make India a pawn in the 'super power' war politics. For them, it is a protest that is not confined simply to the local issue of Baliapal; rather it is treated as a movement opposing nuclear armament. Patra in his statement in a leaflet revealed "although the people of Baliapal have started the struggle to protect their homes and hearths, their struggle is also a struggle in defense of world peace and opposed to war of Indian ruling class and their treaty bound master Soviet Union. Today, the Baliapal people are in a just struggle, which is not only in their own interest, but also in the interest of all peace loving people throughout Orissa and the country as a whole". Further, they are of view that in the present day world, Soviet Union and United States have been projected as the two 'super powers' contending national test range as apart of the Soviet strategy in collaboration with the Indians to establish its hegemony over the South East Asia (Patra: 1986). He argues that Orissa has been turned as the biggest armoury in India. Besides the proposed NTR in Baliapal – Bhograi area, already ten vast areas, mostly along the east coast, are under the control and use of the Ministry of Defence.The extent of the land these unproductive projects have captured, the amount of natural and people's wealth they have destroyed, the total number of people they have displaced and the magnitude of the burden they have brought for a backward, drought-stricken and cyclone prone state like Orissa are beyond assessment. However, the very project is a contradiction between the non-alignment policy and nuclear policy that India advocated and practiced in the past. The project does not serve either the national or the people's interest; rather it is designed to serve the interest of the imperialistic powers and the ruling class of the country. The consequences of such projects are borne by the poor people in the name of altruistic value. The movement by the local people is a struggle for the macro cause of peace, anti-imperialism and anti-nuclearization as asserted by the UCCRI (M-L) leader. According to UCCRI (M-L), the characterization of the movement, "the struggle being waged by the people of Baliapal-Bhograi area is of immense political significance. They are raising voice against evictions, which in essence, is a struggle to defend their right to live. They are raising voice against the danger of the nuclear holocaust which, in essence, is a struggle against production and use of most destructive weapons in the modern world which destroy natural as well as human wealth on a massive scale. They are struggling against the attempts of 'Super Powers' to drag India into their war preparations, which in essence, is a struggle against war and for world peace. Thus, the struggle for life and the struggle for world peace are closely and inseparably linked and merged into one here" (Call of Baliapal 1986).

Glossary of Oriya words

Andolan : Movement

Achala Jati : Socially prohibited caste groups

Adivasi : Tribal people

Amara : Separate space used for the storage of grain in the house

Anabadi	: Barren land
Badi	: Cash crop areas
Baithaki	: Meeting
Bedha	: Boundary
Bhajana	: Devotional song
Bheeta maati	: Ancestral place
Chada	: Sandy cover on the agricultural and homestead land
Chala Jati	: Socially permitted caste groups
Chapara	: Thatched house
Chua	: Small pond near betel vine yard
Daba	: Green coconut
Dhinki	: Manual grain processing
Gachha	: Tree
Ghara	: House
Ghati	: Defence base
Hata	: Market
Jaanla	: Small shrimp collected from sea
Jati	: Caste
Jatra	: Celebration of festival
Khala Badi	: Front open space of house used for multipurpose use
Kuta	: Straw
Pahi Ghara	: Make shift home in the cash crop area
Pana	: Betel
Pana Baraja	: Betel vine yard
Sahi	: Cluster of house on the basis of caste group
Samudra	: Sea
Sankha	: Conch shell
Sarakar	: Government
Satsang	: Religions meeting
Thali	: Plate
Tilaka	: Sandal paste put on the forehead
Utkala Divasa	: Orissa Day

References

Biswal, B.B. 1987. "*Baleshwar ra iteebruttee*'. Jaleswar: Biswabrahma Publishers.

Call of Baliapal. 1986. Red Flag Publications No. 1

Census of India. 1991. General Economic Tables, Series 16, Orissa, Part III. A and B.

——1991. *Social and Cultural* Tables. Series 16, Orissa, Part IV, A

——1991. *District Census Handbook:* Baleshwar District. Series 16, Orissa, part XIII, B.

Jena, N.R. 1991. "Discontent, Conflict & Resistance in Baliapal". Unpublished Ph.D. Thesis, Chandigarh University.

Mittal, A.C. 1962. *An Early history of Orissa*, Benaras: Jain Culture research Society

Patra, Gannath. 1986. *Support the Just Struggle of Baliapal People Against Proposed Missile Base.* April 14 (Leaflet).

——*1986. Oppose Setting up of the Missile Base in Baliapal area*. May 26 (Leaflet)

Patel, Sujata. 1989. "Baliapal Agitation–Socio-Economic Background". *Economic and Political Weekly* 26(12): March 25

——1989. "Agni, Cyclone and Baliapal Agitation". *Economic and Political Weekly* 25(25): June 24.

——1989. "The Baliapal Struggle and Displaced Communities". *The Times of India*, December 13.

——1990. "Bliapal Agitation: Leaderhsip Crises". *Economic and Political Weekly* 26 (23): June 9.

People's Union for Democratic Rights. 1988. *Bheeta Maati: A report on Baliapal missile base and people's struggle*. August, Delhi.

Sahu, D.R. 2004. 'Caste, Tribe and Peasantry in the emergence of a People's Movement', *The Eastern Anthropologists*: 57(1).

Part - II

Pastoral communities

Discarding composite cultural inheritance and ushering in orthodoxy? Cultural change among the Meos of Mewat

Abha Chauhan

Introduction

The processes of social change tend to open-up closed and rigid groups and re-align them into new forms. Unlike earlier times when the identities of many of these groups and communities were (and in some cases are still) based on local social structures and customary practices irrespective of caste, religion and ethnic ties, today one finds greater assertion of one's identity on caste and religious basis irrespective of the culture and custom they shared once.

For the Meo community of Mewat region in Haryana, 'religion', which is Islam in their case, has become an important aspect of new identity which is constructed, contested and reproduced in the emerging scenario of cultural and identity politics. The flow of goods, capital, people, information, ideas and images across national boundaries and the emergence of new social networks and institutions has facilitated this process. With the improvement of communication and other developments, the Meo began to feel that they could no longer remain isolated from the outside world. A step in this direction would be to forge links with the Muslim community outside Mewat (Weekes: 1984: 520). Besides this, with the weakening of the caste ties and the decline of *jajmani* system in which the Meo occupied dominant position, their privileges have been severely curtailed. For instance, the members of the Scheduled Castes, who were once their clients, but have themselves taken the advantage of reservation policy and improved their status, are no longer willing to give the Meos the same respect and privilege.

The internal tensions within the Meo society due to customary practices on the one hand and the Muslim personal law on the other and external threat to their identity as Muslims as a result of growing animosity between the two religious communities - the Hindus and the Muslims - have placed the Meos at the cross-roads. To move away from the customary practices akin to Hindu castes and come closer to the Islamic way of life seems to be the best option. But much less emphasis is being given to the development of the Meos and on their educational and health status, especially of women and children. Though large number of *Madarsas* have come up all over Mewat and much larger number of girls than before attend them religiously, their general apathy towards education, of girl children in particular, is widely evident and alarming. Slowly and steadily the people of this heroic, brave and self-respecting community are falling behind the neighbouring communities of Rajputs, Jats and Yadavs to whom they resembled very closely in most of the socio-economic matters earlier on.

This paper argues that the process of Islamization will place the Meo community in a vulnerable position, and then it would be far more difficult to wave-off the tag of 'backwardness' that has come to be associated with it, unless factors facilitating change and development are widely accepted and implemented. The Meo is now identified under the category of Other Backward Classes (OBCs) in Haryana which stood at 74 till 2001 (Sharma: 2002: 36 - 63) and unless a special care is taken, the Meo would be left behind and the advantages including those that come with reservation will be taken by the other OBCs. Though the Meos are included in the OBC list both in Haryana and Rajasthan , a study of the Meo community in its totality requires data from both states. The analysis in this paper is based only on a study of Meos of Gurgaon district in Haryana and, to that extent, it cannot be deemed to be representative of the empirical reality of the Meos of the entire Mewat cultural region.

The analysis presented will begin by focusing on the life and history of the Meos and their social structure followed by an examination of their kinship and marriage rules to show the impact of change, especially of the process of Islamization. It will relate this process with the backwardness of the Meo community. Although it does offer some suggestions for the amelioration and empowerment of the Meos but adds the caveat that one should be careful in providing solutions to the problems of such communities that are placed in fuzzy situations and fighting on several fronts.

The Meos of Mewat: Life and history

The Meo is an agricultural community, with ninety two per cent of its total population of nearly 20 lakh living in some 1200 villages of Mewat region. Mewat is not an administrative but a cultural region, 70 kms. southwest of Delhi and comprising of districts of Haryana, Rajasthan and Uttar Pradesh. The major portion of the Meo population lives in the States of Haryana (Nuh, Taoru, Nagina, Firozepur Jhirka and Punhana blocks of Gurgaon district, Hathin block of Faridabad district) and Rajasthan (Tijara, Kishangarh , Alwar and Lachhmangarh blocks in Alwar district and Deeg, Kaman and Nagar in Bharatpur district). Mewat is known as the land of the Meos though a considerable number of them reside outside Mewat also and many other caste groups stay in Mewat region.

Agriculture is the main occupation of the Meos with animal husbandry being another source of livelihood for the people. Sixty per cent of the families own land, most of them belonging to the category of 'small and middle peasants' (5-10 bigha). Nearly 80 per cent of the total land is cultivated and the agricultural and irrigation facilities as well as agricultural technology have improved considerably over the years (Vohra, et.al: 2001). In one of the earlier studies it was noted that about 85 per cent of them have not taken to any of the improved agricultural practices. (Ali: 1970:114). It was also noticed that the area available to the average household was too meagre to raise agriculture above the subsistence level. With the result a large number of people lived at the subsistence level and had to borrow each year and repay at higher rates of interest at the next harvest. They remained at the mercy of the local *Sahukars* and their condition worsened with a single draught (Rathee: 1971: 42-43).

Many previous British writers like Risley (1901) and Crooke (1975 [1907]) claim that the Meos are a tribal group. The decennial Censuses of the British period listed them under the category of 'tribe'. It was only in 1901 Census that the Meos were listed separately from the

Minas (Risley and Gail: 1901: 560-566). Even today one finds prevalence among them of those practices like bride price (money paid to the bride's father by the bridegroom's side at the time of marriage),'levirate ' (marriage of widow with brother of deceased husband) or '*jhagra'*(compensation paid by the second husband to the first at the time of divorce),albeit declining, which are associated more with the tribal *or* peasant communities, classified as the 'backwards' than those of the higher castes. In fact, the customs of widow remarriage and divorce make the Meo different from higher castes. It must, however, be mentioned that these were common practices in the erstwhile Punjab (present Haryana and its Mewat region included in that) followed by dominant Hindu communities like the Jats and Yadavs. It is reported that the Meos followed all the major customs of the Hindu Jats of the region, like the *Karewa* (levirate), as well as the same avoidance pattern of *got* (patrilineal clan) and village observed for marriage alliance as the Hindu Jats (Chowdhry: 1994: 38).

The Meos enjoyed high social prestige as well as economic and political power in the past owing to their Rajput origin. They were placed higher in the regional social hierarchy and were, therefore, the *jajmans* to the various Hindu and Muslim servicing castes (Jamous: 1996: 182-183). They were referred to as the *zamindars* since they were the owners of land. Besides this, they were also the *Chaudharis* of their territorial clans and lineages and *Lambardars* of their villages or the section of the village and assisted the government in revenue collection. Though the importance of these positions has declined, they are still significant in various ways. Like the *Chaudhari of a Pal is* important not only in the meetings of that particular *Pal* but also in Meo *Panchayat* which still holds importance in settling disputes of Meo society.

The history of the region suggests constant struggle and battle of the Meos with the Mughals, the British or other princely rulers. Shail Mayaram is of the view that 'the Meo past is the history of their marginalization' where this 'erstwhile ruling group was reduced to the status of landlords in the 13th Century' and 'by the 18th Century the dual pressure of the *Mughal* empire and the powerful regional kingdom of Jaipur had reduced them to much small peasants' (1997: 27). They suffered the trauma of partition and the successive governments in India after Independence could not attend to the problems of the Meos and the community could not throw up the right type of leadership from among its own ranks. This resulted in their neglect and backwardness (Rathee: 1971: 42). These factors continue to exist and take on new forms wherein different groups appropriate their needs and interests at the cost of the Meos.

The Meos were originally Hindus; when and how they were converted is still unclear. Opinions vary with regard to the time of their conversion. It seems probable on the basis of popular belief that they were converted in stages; first by Salar Masud, son of Mahmud Gazni's sister in the 11th Century, by Balban in the 13th Century followed by Firozeshah Tuglaq in the 14th Century, and again during Aurangzeb's reign in the 17th Century. At times, conversion to Islam was part of the settlement after the defeat. Bahadur Nahar, a Hindu Rajput ruler of Mewat, embraced Islam in the 15th Century. Other Rajput families followed the lead, and the clan of the *Khanzadas* was established (Weekes: 1984: 519).

This shows that the Meos originated from various Rajput clans at different points of time. For instance, Salar Masud who reached Mewat in 1002 AD converted many Meos to Islam who were of Tunwar clan divided into *5 Pals*, viz. Kalesa, Derwal, Landawat, Ratawal and Balut. Hemraj, who invaded Mewat was defeated and slain by his army that subdued the Meos, agreed to pay *Jazia* and some of them accepted Islam. These Meos were divided into other 7 *Pals*- Dahngal, Saingal, Demrot , Panglot ,Dhulot and Nai (the last 5 being of Jadun Rajput clan by origin) (Rose: 1980 (1919) : 82). The presence of Meo *Pal and gotra* by these names and their adherence to the kinship rules reflect their Rajput origin.However, the prevalence of other *gotras* among the Meos suggests that they originated from various other castes as well, like the Brahmin, Bania, Gujar, Jat and some other lower groups. There are grounds for believing that many of them sprung from the same stock as Mina, a tribal group as several of the respective clans are identical in name, like Singal , Dulot, Pundlot. Dehngal and Nai. A story told of one Darya Khan (a Meo) and his ladylove Sisbadani (a Mina) seems to show that formerly they intermarried (Gazetteer of Ulwar: 1878). Thus, the view that the Meos were converted to Islam over a long period of time and they originated from several Hindu castes seems to be the most plausible one (Aggarwal: 1971: 37-38).

In earlier times, Mewat was part of an extensive kingdom ruled over by the Jadun clan. Muhammad Ghori broke their power in 1196, and under Firoz Shah III they were converted to Islam. Babar annexed Mewat and during the decay of the *Mughal* empire Gurgaon district (including Mewat area) was torn between contending powers of Nawab, Ahir and Jat rulers in different principalities. The district passed to the British with the rest of the country ceded by Sindhia in 1803 but left in the hands of native assignees. In 1857, they rose in revolt and the Meos fought bravely against the British. However, with the fall of Delhi, the different principalities also fell and were annexed. Gurgaon (including Faridabad then) remained the part of Punjab at the time of Independence. This was till 1966, when the State was divided into Punjab, Haryana and Himachal Pradesh. Mewat region is a part of Haryana now comprising of five blocks of Gurgaon and one block of Faridabad (blocks mentioned earlier).

The Meo identity was constructed differently during various regimes. During the *Mughal* empire they were described as *'mufsid'* (rebel) and as 'criminals' during the British rule. To the Hinduising princely State of Alwar and Jaipur, the Meos became 'Muslims', a construction readily embraced by the pan Islamic leadership. The process of Islamization, thus, gained momentum and started having wider circles of influences as discussed later in the paper.

Meo social structure

The Meo is a patrilineal and patrilocal community where name, descent, succession, and inheritance pass in the line of males. A person is a member of his descent group; succession to office and inheritance of property follow the same rule, and residence is patrilocal.

As the Meo is an agricultural community, the joint family is the ideal type among them. Most of these are lineal in structure, i.e. a man and his wife living with their sons and their families. Collateral joint families (several brothers and their families living together) also occur to a considerable extent. At a given point of time, the family is at a particular stage of 'development cycle'. It is sometimes nuclear, say with the demise of the eldest patriarch; at other times it becomes joint, as with the birth of the child of a third generation. In Mewat, land remains undivided as long as the father is alive. When grown-up, the daughters are married off in different villages and occasionally visit their natal homes. Marrying one after the other, the sons stay together till the family becomes too large. After some years of marriage of the second or the third son, usually the first son shifts his dwelling and hearth with his wife and grown-up children. But the land still remains undivided on which all women and men of the family put in joint labour. It is also seen at times that even with the death of the father, the sons continue to share the agricultural land or live separately. Sometimes when the father is alive, the sons or one of the sons live, and cook separately, but work jointly on agricultural land.

Marriage among the Meos follows the rule of caste endogamy, clan and village exogamy. The bride's father or brother usually takes the initiative. The principal elements of marriage include the engagement or *sagai* accompanied by gift giving from the bride's side to the groom's side, the marriage proper which includes the ritual preparation of the bridal couple, the ritual service by the paternal aunt, the gift of the ceremonial presentation or *bhat* by the maternal uncle and other ceremonies in which the groom comes forward to take on *dan*, his future wife and the dowry. *Mehr* (amount given or promised to be given by the bridegroom to his bride) is given at the time of *nikah* (marriage), which takes place at the mosque in bride's village after the *barat* (marriage party) reaches bride's house. The *milni* (meeting of relatives from both the sides) ceremony, the *salam* (official seeing and blessing of the bridegroom by the bride's female relatives), the *bidai* (send off of the bride to her husband's house after marriage) are the other ceremonies that take place at bride's house. Some ceremonies take place at the groom's home once the *barat* reaches there like *muh dikhai* (seeing of bride's face by female relatives at the bridegroom's house) and *valema* (a feast once the marriage is understood to have been consummated). *Gauna* (final departure of bride) is subsequently performed.

As can be seen, ceremonies like *salam and valema* are Islamic while others are customary. The latter is the more recent inclusion, i.e. feast after marriage by the bridegroom's family. As prevalent among the rural people of north India, the Meos like their neighbouring Hindus used to feast the entire village before the departure of *barat*. Many still do, or try to combine the two, but the trend definitely is towards change.

Since the Meos follow customary law in matters of descent and succession as well as in other matters like residence, maintenance and adoption, women do not own moveable property or have any ownership rights on them, though they have right of maintenance in their families, both natal and marital. Being a dominant agricultural community where possession of land has been an essential asset, its ownership has been restricted to the male line. This was facilitated by the feature of Meo social structure of village exogamy, which made it necessary for the daughters of the village to move out. Having a son or sons, therefore, so that the property could be passed to the next generation in a male line was considered to be almost essential. In case of an absence of a son, the most preferred step was to adopt one and usually the adoption was made from the patrilineal joint family or the same clan. However, usufruct rights have existed for women who play a very important role in Meo economy and maintenance rights are granted to women, which become more important in case they become widow (Shamsh: 1983: 152-156). Therefore, even though women do not have similar rights to property that are granted to them under the Muslim law they have right to maintenance even after divorce. The Meos also have right of adoption unlike the Islamic law and like it also the provision of divorce, polygyny and remarriage. In this sense, the features like, name and inheritance rights, maintenance and adoption constitute structural elements of Meo society and so far little attempt is made by the people themselves or outsiders to touch upon these aspects. Similarly, joint family or nuclear extended family, clan and lineage systems and kinship and marriage rules based on them are the important structural components of the Meo social fabric. These rules also make them closer to their Hindu high caste origin, especially those related to lineage and clan exogamy maintaining substantial distance in arranging marriages of which they have been quite proud. The details regarding the ancestors are kept updated by a Brahman genealogist or the *Jagga* while the *Mirasi* performers sing in *jas* (praise) of the clan ancestor during marriage and other ceremonies. Shail Mayaram has given an account of Meo myth and ritual to show that the theme of the descent of the Meo clans from Hindu Gods or heroes appear again and again in their oral tradition (Mayaram: 1997: 255).

It is for this reason that despite the many changes that have come about in the Meo society, the people have always opposed —and very staunchly—any attempt to change these structural elements. For instance, the move by certain Muslim organizations like the Tablighi Jama'at (T.J.) and influential individuals to start parallel-cousin marriage (between children of two brothers) among the Meos completely failed. But they 'have not given their campaign for reform of these aspects of Meo culture' (Jamous: 1996: 194).

Not only do these aspects structure the Meo society, but various other institutions and practices, which are related to them, also provide organizational base to the whole social fabric. Some of these are secular in character;some others are religious and still others which can be placed in between the two. Those that are religious, like the ritual of *kuan pujan* (worshiping of well) have been given up, while the more secular ones like the *bhat ceremony* (gift given by maternal uncle to his niece or nephew) are still continuing. Those in between have either been adopted partially or not at all. For instance, *burqa* signifies Islamic element, but Meo women do not observe it (though they maintain *purdah* in their patrilineal homes) as they have always learnt to treat the men in their families, clans and villages as their consanguine relations with whom they should not marry. Here we see that structural principles of clan and village exogamy (explained ahead) not only define the relationships and interactions among people, but also determine various cultural aspects as well.Therefore, any change in these cultural elements which is not detrimental to their social structure is tolerated and accepted, but which goes against it or which attempts at hitting at the very base is opposed ,at times vehemently. The fact that many of these structural principles are not in contradiction to the Islamic injunctions, the Meos find no justification, not even the religious ones to change them. On the contrary, they have reasons to stick to their customary rules, which have been followed by their ancestors since generations. For instance, Islam has very few marriage prescriptions and allows marriage between wider circle of blood and kin relations, but it does not say that one should not marry outside one's clan or village.

It is also important to keep in mind that though several of the customary practices of the Meos were closer to neighbouring Hindus castes, many of them were not identical to the high castes, or more particularly to the Brahmanical ideology. Consequently, as the economic conditions of the Meos improved with better irrigation facilities in the region, Meos started leaving many of the features, which were identified with the lower groups and started adopting those of the higher ones. For instance, giving up of bride price or *ther* marriage and taking on the dowry as well as levirate form of marriage.

However, besides the importance of Brahmanical values, modern forces of change in the form of education and employment are also playing an important role, which are vital in determining the change in the structural aspects. Such changes are, however, slow as only a dent is made and if allowed to occur in a gradual manner with induction of some positive (like spread of secular education, increase in awareness about the quality of life, importance of health, hygiene and nutrition and women's empowerment), more desired changes would follow. Similarly the role of religion could strengthen in doing away with some of the ills like spread of dowry and exorbitant expenses (as is being done at certain levels) and at the same time not allowing the misuse of the tenets of Islam by its very followers. However, not much attention is paid to the latter. This has come to light in the cases of divorce occurring more frequently among the Meos than ever before and their opposition to the new changes justified mainly on the basis of religion. This point is discussed in greater detail later.

To understand the structural changes in the context of Meo kinship and marriage rules, it is important first to understand how they have been operating in the Meo society. This will inform us that why despite more than thousand years of Meos conversion to Islam these could not be changed.

Kinship and marriage rules

Caste endogamy

By and large, the Meos marry within their own caste. Though remarriage is allowed both for women and men, the first marriage between the unmarried couple is the most preferred one. In case of second marriage, late marriage or in a situation of poverty, men marry non-Meo Muslim women from outside Mewat. Second marriage or marriage with the non-Meos are not held in high esteem or follow the same rituals. Due to socio-economic and demographic factors, the number of women in Mewat has always been lower than that of men. Because of this and the industrious participation of women in rural economy, they were always sought for. This could have led to the institution of bride price, which came to be associated with a negative connotation of selling the daughters. As it was difficult to find girls for marriage, the early marriage norm became established. There were many cases of bridegrooms being older than their wives. Many widowers remained unmarried until they began seeking girls from outside Mewat. The cases of polygyny and divorce, especially on the part of males, were indeed few. It must be stated that though marriage with non-Meo women may not have the same status, it is regarded as a perfectly legal alliance and the children born to such a couple have a similar legal status.

There is some change in the rule of caste endogamy where educated male Meos have started marrying non-Meo educated Muslim women from outside Mewat. Such marriages are given status and women receive respect. So it is education of the people that has made a difference but the fact that Islam does not oppose such marriages has provided an incentive. For Meo women it will take a much longer time to initiate such steps due to higher rate of illiteracy and low level of awareness.

Clan exogamy

The Meo is divided into a number of patrilineal clans and the mythical founding ancestor of each is considered to be the descendent of a Hindu divinity. This is evident from their oral tradition, which becomes visible during occasions like marriage. There are 13 main clans called *Pals* which are also territorial units believed to have descended from the Rajput clans. There are also 52 or more clans called *Nepaliya*, i.e. without *Pal* territory. Each *Pal* is divided into a number of villages as each clan or *gotra* is divided into lineages. The marriages between the *Pal* and *Nepaliya gotra* occur frequently and there is no status difference between the two categories. The heads of these *Pals* are no longer important as they used to be, though their voice is still heard and considered in the formation of marriage alliances and settling disputes regarding them.

Earlier the Meos followed four-*gotra* rule, like the neighbouring Jats, but now they have restricted it to only one. Similarly, many other rules of *gotra* exogamy regarding other relations have been given up in the course of time. Today no one remembers if such rules ever existed. However, the people are very particular about the one-*gotra* rule that they follow and any attempt to change this has met with little success. In the 1960s, the *Maulvis* of three villages tried to arrange marriage between children of two brothers. The Meos not only boycotted the marriage but also butchered one of the *Maulvis*. Today, it can safely be said that in the villages of Mewat there are not even one per cent cases where the rule of *gotra* exogamy is broken or not followed. There are, however, some people who have taken initiative in this direction, but so far little success has been achieved regarding this rule.

Prohibition of marriage between cousins

It is not enough to say that *gotra* exogamy is the rule as marriage prohibitions extend beyond one's *gotra*. Besides marriage of a man with the daughter of his father's brother, he is not allowed to marry the daughter of his father's sister', daughter of his mother's brother and daughter of his mother's sister'. The latter three forms of cousin marriages are outside the man's *gotra*, but are nevertheless prohibited. It can, therefore, be said that the rule among the Meos in forming marriage alliance is - no marriage between cousins- cross of parallels, even if they belong to different *gotras*.

According to *Riwaz-i-am,* a Meo man cannot marry any woman where relationship with him is close enough to be traceable, and also a woman whose relation is traced through consanguine kin (Wilson: 1882). It was noticed in the mid 1970s that the Meos avoided both cross cousin and parallel-cousin marriages. Though no definite rule has been there, any person with whom a cousin relationship can be traced cannot be married (Aggarwal: 1976:278). As late as in the 1980, Jamous noticed that no one could marry any parallel or cross cousin (1996:189). A niece following her paternal aunt was considered to be a preferential marriage.

It is only in the late Eighties and early Nineties that a change has come about in this structural rule of the Meos, which is extremely significant. *The change is that the Meos have accepted and started practicing what in anthropological parlance is referred to as matrilateral cross-cousin marriage, i.e. the marriage between a man and daughter of his mother's brother.* In Mewat today, no one will oppose this kind of marriage and though still rare one can hear of instances where a woman is the sister of bride's father as well as her mother- in-law. Islam, which does not object to such marriages, the increasing demand of dowry on a plea that the *Shariat* does not allow dowry and extravagance and ill treatment by the mother-in-law are considered to be the important reasons for giving dowry. Some people also felt that the ties between the families of brother and sister are strengthened, though recent conversations with the Meo women reveal that, with such marriages, animosity between the mother and her daughter-in-law (her brother's daughter) is growing.

Religion, thus, is an important source of change here, though that of customary rule circumscribes its impact as only one form of cross-cousin marriage is allowed and the others opposed, the reason for which lies in the other kinship rule, that of a wife-giver and a wife-taker one (discussed ahead).

Village exogamy

Earlier it was the practice for the Meo not to marry a woman of the village of his mother, but this rule is changed now and there is no problem in arranging marriage alliance in the mother's village. In fact, this is possible in the same family now. With the change in the demographic structure of Mewat and shifting of population, it is difficult for people to avoid territorial unit of *Pal and Thamba* but as social units the rule is adhered to. Though one village is usually a one-*gotra* village, it is possible when for example, a son-in-law comes to his wife's village and settles there and the number of his family members grows in a few years time. If he has to seek a groom for his daughter then he must move to some other village.

In every village of Mewat, fictitious kinship relations among inhabitants occur and a woman will either be a daughter or a daughter-in-law of the village. All relations irrespective of caste and communities would be accordingly maintained and gifts exchanged even when people make visits to other villages. The Meos do not take girls from the villages to which they give their own. Though this rule could be synonymous with the *gotra* rule of wife-givers and wife-takers (explained ahead), it is followed even if this synonymy does not occur. For example, if *gotra* A from village I gives girls in marriage to *gotra* B from village II, it cannot take girls of *gotra* B from anywhere (this is a gotra rule). But if there are girls of other *gotra,* for example, C or D in village II from whom as a rule, *gotra* A can take girls, it will not do in this case (rule of village exogamy). The entire village II acquires a status of wife-givers (Sharma: 1969:183).

Till as late as in the 1960s it was noticed that the father and the son do not marry in the same village (Aggarwal: 1971:118). According to S.L. Sharma 'permitted to marry in his mother's natal clan, the boy must not look for a mate from his mother's village' (1969: 183). In a later study by Jamous, it was noticed that no man could repeat the father's marriage, but it was possible to repeat the paternal grandfather's marriage (1996:189). Over the years, there has been a distinct and clear-cut change in this rule. The first change was, when the restriction of father and son marrying in the village was lifted. Very few people remember that such a rule existed though it is mentioned in the *Riwaz-i-am*. A consistent trend is observed where brides are taken from the same *gotras* over generations. This shows that despite these changes, the concept of village as a unit of consanguine relations has not declined at all. The village is an extremely important place for the people in Mewat irrespective of their castes and communities. For women, the natal village remains as important as their affinal village throughout their lives and various occasions are utilized to maintain this link. The above description also shows that some types of changes in the structural elements of Meo society were always occurring and some of the rules, not found relevant, were given up.

Wife-givers as different from wife-takers

Though gotra and sub-clan or lineage based one, this principle corresponds largely, but not always to the territorial divisions. Therefore, women on marriage not only move from some particular villages to some other particular ones, but also from some specified gotras to some other equal ones. In this sense, the marital relationship amongst the Meos follows a pattern of marriage alliance and to use Dumont's terminology, has a *diachronic dimension* as marriage ties are repeated and transmitted from one generation to another, even if they do not follow positive marriage rules.

Thus, though the rule of *gotra* exogamy prevails where a Meo can find his/her marriage partner in any other *gotra* than his/her, the choice is quite restricted. The rise of these inter-*Pal* clusters is explicable with reference to the demographic fact of the distribution of *Pals* and the social fact of contacts with the affines of one's local friends and fellows. All the *Pals and gotras* have their respective concentration areas and it is the consideration of adjacency that plays a vital role in effecting these inter-*Pal* linkages. One's contacts with the affines of neighbours and friends further facilitate the development of this pattern of marriage links (Sharma: 1969:183)

Every clan or *Pal gotra* is subdivided into a number of groups called *Thamba.*The exogamy and this rule actually operates at the village level. The exchange of girls will never take place between two *Thambas, i.*e. if a *Thamba* A takes girls from another *Thamba* B, no girls will be taken from B *Thamba.* But from the other *Thambas* of the same *gotra* A can take girls if the rule allows this. There are several such configurations occurring among Meos and in this sense, it can be said that similar to the 'inter-*Pal* alliances' are formed 'inter-*Thamba* alliances'.

The change in this rule that wife-givers cannot be wife-takers can be seen in Mewat to day where approximately 4-5 percent of all marriages do not observe this rule. The change has particularly come in the urban areas where such aspects as education, employment and better economic status are playing more important role. Since new choices in selection of mate have been added, the choices have become restricted especially with few educated and well-employed people. With increase in them, more changes are expected to come about.

As the choices are becoming limited, it is just a matter of time when more space would be required and this would be given by crossing the barrier of customary practices and opening alliances with Muslims at a wider level. The Islamization process, with lesser restrictions would only facilitate this move as is more evident in the urban areas of Mewat.

The Islamization process

The Meos were rather known for their ignorance about Islam in the days gone by as their adoption of it was at best nominal (Powlett:1878). They practiced only a few customs of the Muslim tradition, notably male circumcision, *nikah* (marriage) and the burial of the dead (Aggarwal: 1971: 42). There are certain matters, however, in which the Meos follow Islamic rules quite strictly besides circumcision and the burial rituals. *Nikah* is the Islamic element necessary for every Meo marriage, which is essentially accompanied by *mehr*. Apart from these features, during occasions like birth of a child, marriage festival or any other ceremony, the Meos have started following Islamic customs like *aqiqa* (after the birth of a male child), or *salam or valema* ceremony as mentioned earlier. Their participation in the Hindu festivals and the visits to the *mela*, the mausoleums or *dargah*, or even of their own saints have been reduced considerably. The Meo women often talk about worshipping of the village well and local deity after marriage or the birth of the child, which they no longer follow.

As seen earlier, besides the changes in the cultural aspect, i.e. in the form of rituals and ceremonies, changes have also come about in the social structure of the Meos. Hence, some alterations in the kinship rules have been witnessed. This is mainly due to the Islamic injunctions, which do not attain a good fit with these rules. The role of religious organizations, the rising number of mosques, large number of *Madarsas* and rising number of students in them also show a clear shift. The people have become more religious in offering *namaz*, in keeping *roza* and going for *haj*. These are the things most emphasized by the Meos and most of them follow these religiously. A person returned from *haj* is highly respected and called *haji*. A large number of people participate in Jama'at and other Muslim congregations. Many of the students who go for higher education opt for either Aligarh Muslim University or Jamia Millia Islamia and there they realize and at times feel ashamed of their customary practices which have many un-Islamic elements. A Meo teacher at the Jamia Millia Islamia did not appreciate our effort to study the customs of the Meos and said that he is not different from other Muslims and does not follow the customary rules of the Meos.

The origin of these changes can be traced since the pre-partition and partition days when the Meos began to be closely identified as 'Muslims'. The role of the Alwar State in dealing with the Meos, of some members of organizations like the Arya Samaj trying to forcibly re-convert them, and the discrimination by the local Hindus of the Meos when they returned to their villages from Pakistan were some of the important reasons that forced the Meos to have a closer alliance with the Muslims at large. Some scholars have given a vivid account of the experience of the Meos at the time of partition as narrated by themselves (Mayaram: 1997). Opening of the office of Muslim League and campaigning for Pakistan and talking of Muslim state in Mewat by some Meos educated at Aligarh Muslim University further sharpened the differences (Maheshwari: 2003: 84). About 25 per cent of the Meos left for Pakistan, abandoning their land and houses and forfeiting their claims to land and property. Though quite a number of them came back, they could not regain the same monopoly of ownership of land and prestige that they enjoyed once.

From the mid 1930s, the Meo began to come under the influence of Tablighi Jama'at (T.J.), a Muslim religious revival movement started by Maulana Muhammad Ilyas of Nizamuddin, Delhi. The movement became active after 1947 and the Meos were urged to abandon their Hindu customs and adopt Muslim practices. Under its influence the Meos gave up many of the Hindu rituals, ceremonies and festivals. The activities of Tabligh are increasing day by day as large numbers of people go for Jama'at. Besides the distant travels undertaken by males, the neighbourhood meetings for women are also held that are occasions for the committed to assemble and for others to be drawn in. These meetings are held frequently in some places; in others, they are less frequent. In this way Tabligh offers opportunity for women to congregate (Metcalf: 1998: 112).

The changes are most visible in the recent years with the increase in the number of *Madarsas* and the number of children, particularly girls attending them. A large number of mosques have come up in the area as well. The people have become more religious in offering *namaz,* keeping *roza* and going for *haj*. A large number of people now participate in Jama'at after going through some training. The T.J. adopt peaceful methods and preach people the tenets of Islam and not to follow those that are un-Islamic. As Meos are rural and rustic people following several customary practices, the educated and more refined Meos ask them to leave the present social life of *jehalat* (backwardness) and become more religious.

Besides the efforts made by the T.J., some educated Meos have come together and they organize regular *Panchayat* meetings. Meo *Panchayats* are huge congregations in which lectures and discussions are made on how Meos should come closer to Muslims at large and abandon the un-Islamic features in their culture. The Meo *Panchayat* held in May 1999 at Firozepur Jhirka took up matters pertaining to dowry problem and excessive expenditure incurred during marriage and other occasions, besides other issues. As a result of these efforts, some of the Meos have stopped the practice of dowry and started performing marriage without taking *barat* and leaving the girl at the bridegroom's house after simple *nikah* ceremony. Locally, they call this *ladki ko ghar kar ke aana* (leaving the daughter at her residence).

There are, however, few such cases and poorer people usually undertake these. The Meos still prefer to give (and take dowry) as it constitutes a mark of prestige, status and wealth and taking of *barat* during marriage, which involves many customary rituals and ceremonies. The reason for this lies somewhere in their associating dowry with higher castes as much as they relate bride-price with the lower groups. The practice of bride-price common among the Meos earlier has been promptly given-up by the Meos as their economic condition improved. Only poor people, or those who have many daughters or who marry from outside Mewat or for whom it is a second marriage might go for such marriages. The Meos do not look at this phenomenon with respect and call it as *ladki par paise lena*. The educated Meos do not approve of either of these practices and try to convince the others not to follow them. The number of Meos who listen to them is increasing.

Thus, one can discern certain reasons for Islamic revival in Mewat. First reason can be traced to the time when India was partitioned in 1947 to give the Muslims a separate State. At that time, *the antipathy between the Hindus and the Muslims was heightened* and there was a large-scale violence. For the Meos, this produced an urgent need to have an identity of their own to cope up with the crises producing threat to their existence. When the normal situation returned, the Meos began to reassert their identity as Muslims.

The second reason has to do with the *decline in the dominant caste status and the high social prestige* of the Meos as well as economic and political power associated with it. Some recent sociological studies (Aggarwal: 1971; Jamous, 1996) have shown that the Meo is a caste category characterized by endogamy, hereditary membership and hierarchical position in relation to other castes. This dominant position of the Meos in the social hierarchy makes them reluctant to give up their caste status. But now with the weakening of the caste system, decline of *Jajmani* practice, changes in the occupational structure of the Meos and other castes, and commercialization of agriculture, the privileges of the Meos have been severely curtailed.

The third reason for the Islamic acceptance is that with *the improvement of communication and other developments*, the Meos began to feel that they could no longer remain isolated from the outside world. A step in this direction would be to forge links with the Muslim community outside Mewat (Weekes: 1984: 520). Jamous notes that the Meos still want to keep their local identity and local relationships though they are experiencing an increasing sense of solidarity with other Indian Muslims. They try to react to the new changes by mobilizing both the forms of their identity - as a Rajput caste and a Muslim community - even if these imply conflicting values (1996: 199). How long they will be able to sustain this conflict is to be seen as the drift between the two communities has widened. The situation 'changed even more since the mid 1980s, and after the Ayodhya incident in 1992, the animosity between the Muslim community and some of the Hindu groups has grown dangerously' (Jamous: 1996: 194-195).

The end of 1992 and the beginning of 1993 saw many incidents of arson and looting, demolishing of religious places and burning of houses and shops from both the sides. This led to divergence and divide between the Hindus and the Muslims and destroyed centuries old amity between them. These differences between the two communities have made the Meos insecure and vulnerable and more conscious of their identity. Families are mortgaging land at a low price to send their sons to Gulf countries for employment. The best building in any village is the mosque for which money is coming from outside sources (Maheshwari: 2003: 87-90).

Backwardness among the Meos

Independence made very little difference to the condition of the Meos. Mewat remained a backward region, despite efforts made by various government and non-government organizations like the Mewat Development Agency (MDA), which initiated many programmes for the development of the people of Mewat. This can be seen in comparison to the rest of Haryana (Imtiaz Ahmed, quoted in Maheshwari :2003).

About 40 per cent people are below the poverty line in Mewat, while the figure for Haryana as a whole is 10-15 per cent. Percentage of workers in industry in Mewat is 2.70 whereas for Haryana it is 11.53 and for Gurgaon it is 35.23. Net area irrigated to net sown area is only 19.7 per cent in comparison to that of Haryana which is 53.3 per cent. Similarly, the literacy rate of Haryana is 36.14 per cent and it is 21.77 per cent in Mewat.Gurgaon has 35.23 per cent literates. Again the female literacy rate of Haryana is 22.30 per cent, whereas that of Mewat is only 6.84 per cent .For Gurgaon, the figure stands at 20.09 per cent (Ibid: 2003: 55-56). The literacy percentage of Meo women stands anywhere between 1.76 and 2.13.

In a recent research study of three villages in Mewat, it was seen that the literacy rate for the whole Meo population was 39.5 per cent and for Meo women it was only 2.7 per cent. This shows that there is a huge gap between Meo male and female literacy rates. In many villages of Mewat one finds not a single woman literate. Village Ghata in tehsil Firozepur Jhirka, one of the villages of this study, for instance, had zero per cent literacy as far as Meo women were concerned. (Abha Chauhan: 2001).

It is seen that there has been a general increase in the level of education and general awareness regarding the importance of education of the girls in Mewat during the last decade, but this change is miniscule and very slow one. The male preference for sons is still prevalent and the stereotype perceptions (like education will not help the work that they do; that the girls do not have to earn and finally they have to get married and leave the home) are very much evident. It is seen that the Meos do not mind spending money on education of their sons but they hesitate in sending their daughters to school even where the education is given free of cost.

On the other hand, small girls attend *Madarsa* very regularly. Though more than half of their mothers never went to these religious institutions, today one finds hardly any Meo girl who does not go to a *Madarsa. What* is significant is that many of them do not attend any school. Again there are misconceptions regarding education of the girls among the Muslims.These are not only due to general illiteracy among the Meos but also on what Islam has to say about education of the women. A deeply religious Muslim youth in village Karheri of Nagina block stopped sending his sister to the Educational Center run by an NGO, Adi Gram Samiti exclusively for girls as he considers it wrong for Muslims to learn what he called 'Hindi'. On the other hand, a Meo government employee tried to explain to them the relevance of *talim* for women in Islam (personal communication). Unfortunately, such voices in Mewat are far and few. For a community which is yet trying to establish its credentials as true Muslims and which is still criticized quite often for its un-Islamic practices, it is easy to succumb to the pressure of those who propagate backwardness among them in the name of religion instead of concentrating on their socio-economic development and growth. Those who wish to bring them under Islamic fold often call the customary practices of the Meos as un-Islamic and castigate those Meos, who stick to them, rather ostensibly as *jahil.*

Similar is the case regarding the health status of the Meos, especially of the women who suffer due to large number of pregnancies, child birth and low nutritious food and poor hygienic conditions. The sex ratio in Mewat though slightly better than that of Haryana (867) is nevertheless appalling at 883.5 (1991 Census). The maternal mortality rate of 470 per lakh live births, infant mortality rate of 80/1000 and high incidence of TB and anemia speak of low health status of women and children. The average family size in rural Mewat is 9.5;women have their first child before 20 and by the time they are 30 they start looking old with 5 children on an average. It is not uncommon in Mewat to find a woman of 20 and her mother of 42 giving birth to children almost at the same point of time. Therefore, the reproductive years for women in Mewat have a long span and as their work in the agrarian economy is nearly indispensable, they quickly start their work again after delivery. This creates health problems in later stages and sometimes immediately.

The people in general are very suspicious of the outsiders, especially those who ask them questions related to their family size and number of children. The women in general subscribe to the view that the children are gifts of God and they cannot interfere in his decisions. However, on deeper probe and informal conversations with the women it became clear that many of the Meo women want small family, they do not wish to have more children if they have, say 3-4 or even 2 in some cases. Some of them will not even mind abortion or any other form of contraceptive, though tablets are most preferred methods. Lack of information and awareness, deficient infra-structural facilities, attitude of the officials and general apathy and callousness of the people regarding women's health status which stem from the patriarchal structure of the Meo society are some of the reasons for this state of affairs. But it was also noticed that the women are quite wary of the husbands and other male members of their society who are in-turn fed by the religious leaders. Many women stated that they do not tell their husbands about their wishes as well as their decisions who they know will always oppose them. But it is they who as women have to suffer the most, not only in carrying and giving birth to children, but also in bringing them up and perform scores of other related chores.

Conclusion

This is the dilemma of Meo society today in which more emphasis is laid on their un-Islamic practices and on undoing them. The consequence is that neither the correct and best Islamic values are inculcated, nor much effort is made towards their development and empowerment. For instance, no one talks of women's inheritance rights or right to property according to *Shariat*, or on the other hand, a few want them to take advantages of modern education and development programmes and use religion to defend their actions. In fact, some freedom to women granted in the customary law is being taken away like divorce at women's initiation. Since Meo is an agrarian community women do not wear *burqa*, and observe *purdah* only in their husband's house and village (village exogamy and also *gotra exogamy* make this possible), people go for adoption and settlement of various problems through community or village *Panchayat.*

On the other hand, a few customs like *levirate* and bride price are loosing importance with time and the Meos do not feel reluctant in giving up these. But the rules of kinship and marriage are foundation of their social structure, which provide safety and stability to them, and therefore changes in them are vehemently opposed. *Many outside Muslims who often criticize Meos for following Hindu practices do not understand this aspect. These rules are not religious in nature and require no rituals as such but are customary (as many practices followed by the Hindu castes in Mewat region are very different from those in Mitakshara law) and demand of an agricultural economy and rural society.* With the modern pressures, perhaps they will go away as has been seen in the cases of some changes in the kinship rules. But opposition of those on the basis of religion without alternative mechanism would relegate the Meos and station them as 'backwards' as the trend also suggests.

The development efforts for the Meos need to be accelerated without always bringing in religion which has more constructive role to play as far as the Meo social life is concerned, but again by not always opposing their customary ways. For instance, it is noticed that in Mewat region of Haryana, during *nikah* the consent of the girl is not taken directly but through her father in the village mosque, the marriages are not registered and, therefore, divorce becomes easy, sometimes the boy refuses that he was ever married to avoid paying maintenance, or refuses to give divorce to the girl who desperately seeks it. There are many such areas of concern in the sphere of civil laws or more accurately personal laws of the Muslims where efforts are required to be made and can be taken up by the intelligentsia and well-known religious and legal advisers.

The general attitude of neglect and antipathy by the government is not different in this area; it is more as this area is not politically of much relevance. The people of Mewat comprise a mere 3 per cent of the population of Haryana and do not count much in terms of votes. Only sixty per cent of posts are normally manned. Absenteeism among employees is endemic and most of the employees think of Mewat as punishment posting *(kalapani)* and their residences are outside the area (Maheshwari: 2003: 86). Some people come to Mewat to make money, while some others start social work to earn money through development funds that flow to Mewat in huge amounts. Unless the image of Mewat as 'backward area' and of the Meos as *jahils or* 'backwards' do not change, there is very little that one can do.

And to change this, besides the efforts on the part of the government and non-government organizations, *the Meos themselves need to come out of their secluded and devoid life through such means as education and employment, development initiatives and decision making processes and not be circumscribed and relegated by the narrow confines of religion.* The provisions granted to them by virtue of being placed in the category of 'OBC' must become advantages for them. Others also need to bring the Meos closer to the people in general and build trust in each other so that the animosity between the two religious communities does not force them to retreat. A situation of one step forward and two steps backward must be avoided at any cost.

References

Aggarwal, P.C. 1971. *Caste, religion and power*, New Delhi, Shri Ram Center for Industrial Relations.

Ali, Hashim Amir. 1970. *The Meos of Mewat: Old neighbours of New Delhi*, New Delhi, Oxford.

Chauhan, Abha. 2001. *Gender, kinship and marriage alliance: The Meos of Mewat* (unpublished report), New Delhi, CWDS.

Chowdhry, Prem. 1994. *The veiled women: Shifting gender equations in rural Haryana 1880-1999*, Delhi, Oxford University Press.

Crooke, William. 1975 (1907). *The native races of India*, Vol. III, Delhi, Cosmo Publications.

Jamous, Raymond. 1996. "The Meo as a Rajput caste and a Muslim community" in C.J. Fuller (ed.), *Caste today*, New Delhi, Oxford University Press.

Maheshwari, Belu. 2003. "The Meos of Mewat : Perspective on ethnicity and nation building", *Social Change*: 33(1).

Mayaram, Shail. 1997. *Resisting regimes: Myth, memory and shaping of a Muslim identity*, Delhi, Oxford University Press.

Metcalf, B.D. 1998. "Women and men in a contemporary Pietist movement: The case of the Tabliqhi Jama'at", in Patricia Jaffery and Amrita Basu (eds.), *Appropriating gender*, New York, Rutledge.

Powlett, P.W. 1878. *Gazetteer of Ulwar*, London.

Rathee, C.R. 1971. "Meos of Mewat : An economic analysis", *Mainstream: Annual Number.*

Risley, H.H. and Gail, E.A. 1901. Census *of India*, Vol. I, Part I, Delhi, Superintendent of Government Press.

Rose, M.A. 1980 (1919). *Glossary of the tribes and castes of the Punjab and N.W.F. Province*, Vol. III (L-Z), Delhi, Amar Prakashan.

Shams, Shamsuddin. 1983. *Meos of Mewat: Their customs and laws*, New Delhi, Deep and Deep Publications.

Sharma, S.L. 1969. "Structural continuity in the face of cultural change", *Eastern Anthropologist*: 24(2): May-August.

Sharma, S.R. 2002. *Protective discrimination: Other Backward Classes in India*, New Delhi, Raj Publications.

Vohra, M.B.L., M. Kaur and R. Gulati. 2001. *A report of a baseline survey to examine the socio-economic status of people of Mewat,* HIPA, Gurgaon.

Weekes, Richard V. (ed.). *1984. Muslim peoples: A world ethnographic survey*, London, Aidwych Press.

Wilson, J., 1882. *Codes of tribal customs of twenty-one tribes*, Lahore.

Cultural change in a pastoral community: The Gollas of Karnataka

M. Gurulingaiah

Karnataka occupies the centre tableland of the Deccan plateau. Since it comprises of various racial elements including the indigenous, the various religious movements and regional customs, the Karnataka culture has been described as an anthropological museum. According to the 1991 Census, with an area of 1,91,791 sq.kms, Karnataka had a population of 44.977,201 with 22,951,917 males and 22,025,284 females. The sex ratio of population was 961 females per 1000 males. It had a literacy rate of 47.05 per cent. It ranked eighth among the 25 states and seven Union Territories in the Indian Union both in respect of the geographical area as well as population. Karnataka contributed about 5.8 per cent of India's population (Karnataka Gazetteer 1996:55).

Maharastra and Tamil Nadu states in the north and south and the state of Andhra Pradesh in the east bound the state. Geographically, the territorial length and breadth of the state extends to about 750 kms from north to south and about 400 kms from east to west. The state is divided into three important geographical regions: the coastal region, the *Malnad* and the *Maidan* (plains). The coastal region is about 200 miles long and 8 to 20 miles broad in the north and 30-40 miles wide in the south. Several ridges and spurs of the Western Ghats, some of which run into the western sea, traverse this low-lying coastal region. The *Malnad* area runs across the state from the north to the south and ranges in elevation from 1,000 feet in the middle to 8,000 feet in the south. The *Malnad*, literally meaning hilly region, is confined to the tracts bordering on the *Western Ghats*. It is a land of splendid hills and forests presenting the most diversified and charming natural scenery. The fertile soil and perennial streams clothe the valley with lush greenary. The *Maidan* (plains) region is a rolling plateau. The northern part is about 1,000 feet to 2,000 feet above sea level, while the eastern part rises to as much as 3,000 feet.

Who are the Gollas?

The Gollas are one of the most backward communities of Karnataka. The Golla is a traditionally pastoral community whose occupation is tending cows and selling milk and milk products. They occupy a low position in the Karnataka society and are considered to be very simple minded to the extent that they are some times described as '*Erry Golla*' meaning dullard Golla. Taken together with several allied castes, it is estimated that the Gollas constitute about two-tenth of the total population of India. The castes coming under this category are to be found in different parts of India and are known as the *Ahir* in the Punjab, Haryana, Himachal Pradesh, Delhi, Uttar Pradesh, Madhya Pradesh, Bihar, Gujarat and Rajasthan, the *Gopalas and Sadagopa* in Bengal and Orissa, *Govali and Gopala* in Maharastra, *Golla* in Andhra Pradesh and Karnataka and *Idayan and Konar* in Tamil Nadu. Two things are common to these cognate castes. First, they claim to be the descendants of *Yadu* dynasty (Yadava) to which Lord Krishna belonged. Further more, many castes in this category have a set of occupations around the cattle (Rao: 1987:124).

Population

The Census reports do not give the population figures of the Gollas and the places where they are distributed across the state. However, we do know the fact that the Gollas are dispersed throughout the state of Karnataka but relatively large concentrations of them are found in the *Maidan* districts (plains) like Chitradurga, Tumkur, Bangalore, Kolar, Bellary and Raichur. According to the Third Karnataka Backward Classes Commission Report (1988), the total population of the Gollas in Karnataka was 5,85,314. They constitute about 2 per cent of the total population of the state. The state caste association of the Gollas, however, claims that their population is about 35 lakhs.

Origin of the Gollas

Golla means cowherd. Golla is a contracted form of 'Govala' that is derived from Sanskrit 'Gopala' or cowherd. Govli or Gouliga is another form of the same word. Gopala means some one who is a keeper of cows ('Go' means cow, 'Pal' means keeper). The names that they themselves use are 'Yadava Kuladavaru' (Yadava dynasty) or Krishnana Kuladavaru (Krishna dynasty), as they believe that Krishna who was of the Yadava race was brought up among the women of their caste known as *Gopis.* They also style themselves as people of *Gokula* (cow-tribe), either because they trace their origin to a cow or because they are professional cowherds. The caste titles they affix to their names are *Golla, Golla Gowda* (Iyer:1988:219).

The Gollas, an offshoot of Yadavas, have migrated from northern India and settled down in Karnataka, and are having their own colonies called *Gollara Hatties*. These *Gollara Hatties* are not shown in the revenue records. The ancients believe that the Gollas originally came from the forests located near the present day city of Delhi. Another legend states that their original place was the neighbourhood of Delhi. Unable to bear the intolerable persecution of the Muslim rulers, the Golla chieftains decided to migrate to the south. Weary from the wanderings they had to undergo in deeper south, they finally settled down in Bangalore, Chitradurga, Tumkur and Bellary districts of Karnataka. There are some ethnographic studies conducted on the Gollas (Shearing: 1974; Thurston: 1909 and Iyer: 1931) that have revealed that they have typical social structure and political organizations. According to them, the original place where they settled down was Uttaragatti and its neighborhood near the bank of river *Yamuna.* To avoid persecution by the Muslim rulers in Delhi, their chieftains migrated to the south during 16th century A.D.Two brothers, Uru Gollas and Kadu Gollas or Hatti Gollas, are stated to be among them. During the course of their wanderings, they mingled with various castes and gave birth to many sub- divisions among them.

Stratification

There are more than 28 divisions (sub-sects) among the Gollas and they are called Kadu Golla, Hava Golla, Dasa Golla, Vidya Golla, Bajanthri Golla, Helava Golla, Peddathi Golla, Kuri Golla, Gangh Golla, Karma Golla, Kanchi Golla, Gowda Golla, Puja Golla, Hanuma Golla, Hasu Golla, and Kettahatti Golla, etc. Among these divisions of the Gollas, the Kadu Golla is one of the dominant divisions and they differ from the other divisions in the practice of their customs, rituals and pollutions. They do not mingle with other divisions especially with Uru Gollas. Neither do they intermarry nor mix together. But now days, even the Kadu Gollas and Uru Gollas are gradually forgetting their differences and organizing themselves for the upliftment of Gollas in the state.

Settlement pattern and housing

According to Hoebel, the spatial arrangement of the subgroups of a society in relation to each other, to their environmental resources, and to the pattern of other societies can easily enable an observer to discern their relationship with the life of a community. Observing the settlement pattern of the Gollas, one can discern the impact of socio-economic-cultural and geographical environment on their lives. Hoebel also notes that the house types are variable in structure, depending upon the nature of the local climate and materials, the kind of subsistence economy indulged in, and the nature of the social organization of the society and the kind of aggressive threats it must face from the enemies. Thus, the settlement pattern and housing powerfully represent the past and present life. The Gollas live in the middle region of Karnataka state (particularly in districts of Chitradurga and Tumkur) which is famous for tending the cattle and sheep and rich '*Gomalas*' and plain land (1976:126).

Generally, the Gollas live in a small village consisting of some 30-40 households. There is a headman for each such village that often consists of families belonging to a single exogamous division. Most of the Gollas in Karnataka live in thatched hut houses. These are built with mud walls plastered with clay. The flooring is done with mud and doubled with cow-dung and the roofs are constructed with coconut leaves and bamboo. Pillars support their huts. Mud walls are some times employed to support the thatch but the uses of pillars ensure longevity. Earlier on, the Gollas did not possess the habit of using the door for their houses but now they do so. The shape of the roof may be gabled or rounded, but that of the temple house is always of the latter type. The roof may consist of clay, leaves and bamboo. Structurally, the houses are of two types: circular and rectangular. The houses are either one or two roomed and consequently provide very small covered space. There is no separate allocation of rooms for cooking, dining, and storing necessities.

Everything is accommodated inside the limited space of the houses itself.

The Gollas who have migrated to the cities and towns have started imitating neighbouring castes in their house designs there. Now they decorate their houses with the use of modern paint. Recently, the Gollas have started constructing tiled and RCC houses. These indicate the status of the inmates.

Dressing patterns

Elderly men among the Gollas wear a piece of cloth around the waist and cover themselves with a blanket. Some of them also wear trousers. Traditional women don't have the habit of wearing a blouse. But they like coloured saris. They wear bangles of bronze. They do not comb their hair but just tie them together. The women don't use *kumkuma*. The widows apply some ashes on the forehead, and wear glass bangles. In this regard, Thurston indicated that their females don't wear the bodice (*ravike*) usually put on by the women of the country. Nor do they remove or break the glass bangles worn at the wrists in their widowhood, as is done in other castes. But widows are not allowed to remarry (1909:287). Among other communities as soon as a woman becomes a widow she has to break her glass bangles. But that is not the custom among the Gollas. They don't shave off their heads either. They say that their husband is Krishna. "According to the advice given by Krishna we are not going to wear blouse". In this regard, Iyer indicates that the Gollas are of dark brown colour and are average heights. The dress of males consists of a waistcloth, turban and an upper cloth, which may be either a blanket or of thick cotton stuff. Their women generally wear a white cloth, bordered with red fringe either of lines or flowers or a coloured sari. They don't use *ravike*, and ascribe the omission to Krishna's act of tearing off this part of their dress in his *Raas* with the *Gopi* maidens. The cloths used in marriage by the bride and bridegroom must be made by the weavers, but they have no such *Swadesi* scruples with respect to articles of ordinary wear. The male members wear gold earrings, shaped as cobra and use silver wristbands. Before the marriage women wear silver wristlets, but after they are married they substitute a '*Gollakadaga*' on the left wrist. They don't wear *kumkuma*, but widows sometimes put on *vibhuti (1988:240-241)*. Now there is a significant departure in the dressing practice among both the males and the females of the Gollas.The young females wear *kumkuma.* They continue doing so even after the death of their husbands. These days the married women wear various types of dresses and ornaments. Today men and women of the Golla community wear modern dress without hesitation. This is a new trend among them.

Names

Names of the Gollas are quite amusing. Karadi, Kariya, Huliya, Jadiya, Giriya, Chitta, Junjappa, and Kendaiah, etc.are frequently used male names. The women have names such as Rangamma, Chittamma, Kariyamma, Chinnamma, Maramma, Sannamma, Thimmakka, and Jadiyamma, etc. The practice of giving one name for day-to-day purposes and another for purpose of ceremonies does not exist among them. But today like many other castes, they consult an astrologer and *panchanga* (calendar) and choose the day and time of celebration of naming the child. Now, due to the interaction with other castes and influence of north Indian Yadavas, the typology of names in use has also changed considerably. They use the names like Siddalingaiah, Prakash, Nataraj, Krishnappa, Manjunatha, Shankara, Basavaraj, and Deevith Yadava, etc. for males and Lakshmi, Parvathi, Sharada, Gawri, and Akshtha Yadavas, etc for the females.

Education

Until very recently, the Gollas least preferred education. For learning the traditional chores of the Gollas, the child was not required to sit for hours together in the school. It was enough for the child to be in and around the village where the fundamental activities of an adult life take place. The child could learn by playing with the playmates or by using certain instruments of the adults, by helping the adults in various activities or listening to legends and stories. The child used to acquire the knowledge of life as a by-product of living with one or the other members of the community who could be the agents for development of skills and learning their roles. Mainly the family, kin groups and community members imparted this kind of traditional education to the child. The knowledge of cultivation, sheep rearing, cattle tending, construction of house, internalization of customs, traditions and practices etc., were imparted to the child by the elder members. The child learnt at an early age the methods of cultivation, sheep rearing and cattle tending. The child accompanied the adult members of the community when they went for cultivation and sheep rearing. So the company of the adults enabled the child to acquire the skills early. The child also learnt the method of cultivation at an early age by helping his/her parents. Besides this, the female children get training regarding cooking and housekeeping by their active involvement in this work with the elder female members of the family. Children of both sexes acquire knowledge about their customs, traditions and various other aspects of their life by constant observation and participation. The elder members also take the younger members of the household along with them when they go to the nearby market to sell their products or to buy consumer goods. *It is found that 90 per cent of the Gollas are illiterates and in most of the cases the maximum limit of their educational attainments is Primary or High School. Only a limited few among them have succeeded to acquire higher education. This indicates their continuing educational backwardness in the state.*

Since many of the customs, traditions, occupations, beliefs, practices, and attitudes, etc. have been disappearing gradually, the process of child socialization has also changed. Now, most of the younger members don't know the traditional cultivation, sheep rearing and cattle tending. The parents evince keen interest on pre-school training. Now they have started enrolling their children in the *Anganavadi* (non-formal pre-primary facility) class and later they send them to *Ashram School* (residential school of the Government). So the children spend quite significant part of their child lives at school and learn various non-Golla community skills, beliefs, and practices and carry them to their village.

The accessibility to schools in a nearby place is one important reason why the Gollas send their children to the school. Most of the *Gollara Hatties* in Karnataka are situated away from the city, even from the town, where the transport and communication system is hardly adequate. But now due to the efforts of the Government, primary schools have been established in each *Gollara Hatti* or in a nearby village and most of the Golla children have availed off this benefit. For example, one *Ashram School* has been established in Honnagondanahally near Sira. Most of the Golla children around that place have got enrolled in this school. About ten-years ago, the Golla children had to walk more than 15 kms to reach a school. The situation has changed appreciably now. *Considering the historical backwardness of the Gollas in the field of education it is natural to find only a gradual improvement in their educational accomplishments. Now not only their literacy rate has registered an improvement but, more importantly, their level of education has also increased. However, educational mobility is found to be relatively poor and slow.*

Food habits

The Gollas take both vegetarian and non-vegetarian food. They eat *ragi*. In fact, it was staple food for them. On the food habits of the Gollas, Iyer records that their staple food is *ragi*, and they are allowed to eat flesh, fish, fowl, hares, sheep and rabbits. It is, however, considered pious to avoid all animal food, and when they partake of it, they never cook it in their houses, but resort to a tank, or watercourse, out side and carefully cleanse and purify all the utensils used in the process (1988:240). They like grams very much. They eat mutton, chicken and even bandy coots. Since they have their cows, they also consume milk, curd, butter and ghee. However, the Gollas do not eat beef since they offer *puja* to the cows. Today most of the Gollas eat rice and it is becoming their staple food.

Occupation

The hereditary occupation of the Gollas is tending cattle and sheep. On this issue, Iyer indicates that *the original occupation of the Gollas seems to have been confined to sheep and cattle breeding and it continues to be their occupation even now.* They are backward in agriculture and cultivate only such crops as are needed for their own use and can be easily raised. A Golla without cattle would be misnomer and this association is so well recognized that all the Okkaligas choose him by preference to officiate as the *pujari* of the cattle goddess, Katamma, at the Sankaranthi festival (1988:235-236). But they have not remained untouched by the waves of occupational change in the wider society due to the educational progress and influence of other neighbouring castes. *Today most of the Gollas have started practicing cultivation on their own land. Some of them do possess irrigated land.* Compared to the earlier intensive use of manual and animal power in their farming operations, now they have adopted more complex techniques. They are employing more efficient techniques to conserve and rejuvenate soil fertility. They used animals to plough their fields earlier on: now they are deploying the tractors. They have also started using iron plough, hoe, harrow, sickle and a few farmers also use machines to lift water, apply fertilizers, sow hybrid seeds and spraying weedicides/pesticides. To replenish the fertility of the soil, green manure and chemical fertilizers are being used. On the recommendation of Horticultural Department, they use hybrid seeds frequently. A few Gollas have begun use of drip-irrigation for their coconut and areca nut plantations. The Gollas of Tumkur and Chitradurg districts are, however, still rooted in their traditional occupation of sheep rearing and cattle tending.

The Gollas feel that their traditional occupation, especially sheep rearing, gives them more income. It has been observed that those who are continuing sheep rearing are satisfied with their occupation. Most of the Gollas who are living in rural areas, at least each family possesses one or two cattle or sheep. Gollas farmers grow food crops like *ragi*, paddy, *jowar* and commercial crops like ground nut, areca nut, mango and cotton. Due to lack of irrigation facility, most of them depend on the rain for agriculture. *Thus, slowly occupational mobility is taking place among the Gollas in the state.*

Marriage

Marriage among the Gollas is a religions duty, and it takes place only after puberty. According to Iyer, marriage among them is generally adult, but infant marriage also may take place (1988:224). Marriages of the girls immediately after attainment of puberty are common among Gollas, particularly those who combine sheep rearing and cultivation. Further, Iyer records that a woman should not die unmarried. It is not imperative that the husband should be older than the wife. If an unmarried woman becomes pregnant by a man within the caste, she will be given to him in marriage. Both the woman's father and man have to pay a fine, which is utilized for feeding the caste men (1988:224). Now they have no traces of practice of capturing wives from other castes. But in past days, the Gollas had the habit of stealing the bride forcibly. They used to catch hold of a girl found alone and make her a wife. But this custom is not in existence now. *Today, the marriages are traditionally ceremonised.*

Polygamy is recognized, but polyandry is unknown. It is said that a woman may be married to one younger in years. A man may marry daughter of his maternal uncle, or daughter of his elder sister, but may not marry either his mother's sister, or her daughters. Thus, relatives such as the mother, sister or daughter are avoided in marriage. Exchange of daughter is permitted, but not encouraged. From a similar belief, marriage of two sisters is also avoided. All are not prohibited from inter marriage based on differences in local position, occupation, or religious belief. Men are generally married when they are twenty-two years of age. Parents or elders arrange marriages.

Thurston stated that the marriages among them are performed in a temporary shed erected outside the village, and the attendant festivities continue for five days, when the marrying couples are brought into the village (1909:287). However, now most of the marriages among the Gollas take place in the house of the bridegroom and continue for five days. In some places, the marriage booths are erected with twelve posts, and '*Ariveni*'. The ceremony of marriage is very simple, and it can take place on any convenient day. A *Puja* known as '*Kalasa Puja*' has to be performed in the houses of the boy and the girl. They make an offering of milk to the deity. Then grains of rice are used to farm designs on the ground known as *rangoli*. Once the day for the marriage is fixed, they have to wear *Kankana*. This ceremony is held outside the house. During this time areca nut is put in pots and it is covered with cow dung and the *Hatti Gowda* (village headman and *Yajamana*) seals it with their rings. After fixing the day for the marriage, they break open the seal, and then the areca nut is given to all together with beetle leaves. The bride and the bridegroom are seated on a plank in front of the village temple, and the *pujari* sprinkles the milk of the sacred sheep (*Jennige Kuri*) on them, and ties a string of block beads, known as '*mangalya*' (*Tali*), round the bride's neck, and puts a chaplet of flowers on the bridegroom's head. The father of the bridegroom pays the balance of the *tera*. The bride then puts a brass and silver bangle on her arms and two rings (*Kalungura*) on her feet.

They never invite a Brahman during the marriage, and the reason given is that on one occasion the Brahman invited pronounced the hour fixed for the marriage to be inauspicious, and put them to the inconvenience of delaying the ceremony. Interestingly, they seem to attach more importance to the actual ceremony. For the latter, any day may be chosen, while for entering into the contract, they are scrupulous in selecting on auspicious time. The married couple has to bathe and put on newly washed clothes supplied by a washer man and indeed a marriage has to be put off if no washer man is available to supply washed clothes. The amount paid as *tera* is Rs. 14 for the first marriage. A man who marries for the second time has to pay Rs. 20, and to give the bride one of the jewels that had been worn by his previous wife (Iyer 1988:226). During the marriage, there is another custom known as "*mudde* t*heerisuvadu*". The Gollas prepare six nice balls with rice, grapes, sugar, cow dung, milk and honey and mix with jaggery. Among these, two are called '*Gowda Muddhe'*, and '*Boovda Muddhe'*. After the nuptials, three delegates are requested to come forward to consume the *boovada muddhe*. At first, people from both sides eat *muddhe*, jokingly inquiring who will eat more. Then they discuss how strong the bride is, how strong is the groom? No one comes forward to eat the *muddhe.* And then the *muddhe* are given to the Gowda and to the delegates of the village.

There is another special feature about their marriage. This is known as "*Aruni"*. They cover pots with lime and red mud. Then they fill them with rice and jaggery. They keep four or five such pots ready. These are called *Aruni* pots. Considered as holy vessels, these are kept in one corner of the marriage *pandal* and are worshipped. The place where these *Aruni* pots are kept is called '*Aruni Gudlu'* (pot hut). The *poojari* and the Gowda are the important people during the marriage ceremony.

Rules of marriage

Marriage among the Gollas is subjected to a number of rules, and regulations. These deal with the issues such as who should or should not marry, residence of spouse after marriage, how marriage should take place, and where it should take place, etc. These rules and regulations guide the individuals and make it easier to acquire a life partner.

The Golla marriage is, by and large, monogamous. There are definite marriage rules, with regional variations, relating to prohibited degrees of marital relationships, endogamous prescriptions and exogamous restrictions, preferential unions and the like. The Gollas prefer to marry within their kin. Ideally, there is vast field to select their life partner. But for practical purposes, they have some preferences and proscriptions. Marriage between the children of siblings of opposite sex (cross-cousin marriage) is commonly practiced. It means that a young man can marry either his mother's brother's daughter or his father's sister's daughter. The obvious reason for this practice is to have personal security, affinity and maintenance of relationship. Moreover, in order to perpetuate their community, their group, most of the Gollas go for preferential marriages within their own kin.

Endogamy is a rule that insists that the Gollas marry within certain social groups with which an individual recognizes himself as a member. Exogamy is another rule, which insists that they marry outside a certain social group. An individual or group who violate these rules is punished. If they perceive that the violation is serious threat to their social life, they may punish by keeping away such violators from social gatherings. By tradition the Uru Gollas and Kadu Gollas are separate endogamous group and intermarrying among them was a taboo. Now days in spite of this barrier, a few inter-group marriages are also taking place.

Lineage, and clan are strictly exogamous units, where one should not select his partner from his own lineages. The Gotra among the Golla is characterized by the principle of exogamy for marital unions. As each clan or Gotra is considered within the same Gotra, a marriage within the same Gotra is considered incestuous. Although in principle, the Gotra is exogamous, but in practice, deviation is not certainly ruled out. There has been frequent insistence on the strict observance of such rules in meetings of the caste councils. But there are exceptions to the rule of the universality of clan exogamy. Due to consent by parents and no choice in their own clan, clan exogamy is relaxed in some places especially in the cities; change of clan for a particular marriage purpose is possible. As they follow the patrilocal rule of residence, after the establishment of the marital relationship, the bride resides in her husband's place and associates with latter's kin group. This not only entitles her to the status of a housewife but also permits her to participate actively in all rituals in the household of her husband. Her incorporation into the husband's *Gotra* and the leasing of social recognition connecting her to her natal family results from the transformation consequent to marriage. Generally, the Gollas select their partners from their own village or near by villages. But today, the process of selection has changed. Usually, the Gollas celebrate marriages at the groom's residence. But now days due to the influence of other neighbouring dominant castes, few people opt for bride's home and marriage hall in the cities.

Martial payment (*Tera*)

Martial payment among the Gollas is basically in the form of price that is locally known as *Terina Hana*. The dowry system and bride price are two entirely different and in fact contrasting practices. The parents of the bridegroom pay the bride price to the parents of the bride. This practice is usually popular among some of the socially backward communities in India. The amount of bride price among the Gollas is nominal and fixed at Rs.12. This amount has to be paid to the parents of the bride by the parents of the bridegroom in the name of *Tera.* The traditional Golla society had no dowry system and if some one took it, he had to face stiff criticism of the community. But now due to urbanization, the practice of dowry is slowly creeping into their community although not to any significant extent. This payment is usually made in the form of gold and silver ornaments, clothes, and utensils, etc. Some times it is also in cash. Thus, although taken in a token form, the Gollas have not shed their ancient customs i.e. bride price.

Inter-caste and inter-religious marriages are not socially recognized and approved among the Gollas. If any one marries a girl or a boy from any other caste (high/low), such a party would be excommunicated from the community and the village. The parents of the offending party have to pay a fine (*Danda*) and also offer a feast to all members of the village. Such couples are not encouraged to participate in any social/ritual activities of the community. However, now the situation is slowly changing on this issue. Some of the educated youths have shown their interest in inter-caste marriages. There are some instances of such inter-caste marriages. The widow remarriage is not socially recognized and approved. On this issue, Iyer (1988) stated that the widows are not permitted to remarry. Indeed, it is believed that on loosing her husband, a woman becomes the bride of the tutelary deity. Consequently, she keeps on her bangles and *tali* just like other married women. In the past, the Gollas had numerous customs associated with the performance of marriage ceremonies, but the presence of Brahmin priests and the elaborate rituals conducted by them were not present among them. But *now some changes have taken place in marriage ceremonies among the Gollas living in the towns and cities. Changes have also occurred in the associated rituals and in the food pattern.* In earlier times during the marriage ceremonies, the traditional food that was exclusively prepared for the occasion was served with rituals that were called *'Kulada-Uta'* (community feast). The items in this feast included meat of the goat offered sacramentally and cooked *Ragi*-balls. Sweets were not served. But recently, this has been replaced by common food that is offered in the marriages of other communities without a tinge of ritualistic flavour. This food includes items like boiled rice, sweets and other items. Now the Gollas have also started inviting guests from the other communities through invitation cards: the practice was totally absent in the past. There are also changes in the dress worn at the time of marriage rituals of a few families that are settled in the towns and big villages: they are not wearing traditional community dresses. They wear pants and shirts and in some cases coats and shoes. Unlike the past, *the Gollas living in the cities are now using the services of Brahmin priests to conduct their marriage ceremonies. Another change in the marriage ceremony is that the marriage is now celebrated for only two days instead of five days or one week earlier on. However, the Golla marriage rituals are intact in the remote and secluded areas.* But as they interact with the people from the other communities and have to invite outsiders in case of the big towns and the cities, the inevitable change has taken place. This proximity with the newer people and their practices has resulted in the introduction of some new practices and modifications of traditional marriage rituals of the Gollas.

Religion

Religion may very well be said to constitute the whole life of the Gollas and they have a strong belief in the existence of deities and spirits. They are entombed in the wombs of superstition. They believe in various deities, ghosts and spirits guiding every walk of their life. Religious beliefs of the Gollas are characterized by the practice of ancestral worship, and practice of ritual deity worship during the festivals. They worship many gods and goddesses, and they consider themselves belonging to Sri Krishna's clan. The Gollas worship Krishna under the names of Venkataramana, Rama, Ranga and Vishnu. Their deities include Junjappa, who is much respected, and Chikkannaswami, Kyatedevaru, Chitradevaru and Butappa. Junjappa, their prime deity, is a glorified cowherd and is regarded by them as a later incarnation of Sri Krishna.

There are main and common gods for the Gollas. When they worship the main gods and goddesses, it will be a grand celebration. During such celebrations, the whole village gives a fine appearance. Gollas have many male gods but the Chitradevaru, Junjappa, Yettappadevaru, Kyatedevaru, Butappa, Thimmappa, Halappa, Eramuddappa, Puralahali Butha etc., are the important gods. Gowrasandrada Marakka, Kareobenahalliyamma are the goddesses worshipped by them. Among the male gods, Junjappaswami Devaru, is seen in Hagalavadi once annually. On this occasion, all their caste men, including some of the upper castes, gather.Next to Junjappa Swamy, the Gollas have great devotion to Chikkannaswamy. There is a temple in Hebburu- between Bangalore and Tumkur— at which Junjappa is worshipped under the name of Chikkannaswamy. A temple of leaves or straw is constructed. A scared bull, known as Pattada Basava, is dedicated to the temple, and is privileged to graze in a field, undisturbed by any of the Gollas and also other castes. It is believed that having been cured of the possession of evil spirits, even some members of other castes (including the Brahmins) have become devotees of this deity. Such families do not allow women during their menstrual period to enter their house, and if accidentally they do so, a penalty is paid to this shrine. Unless they do so, they believe that they will be afflicted with boils, or be bitten by snakes, or stung by scorpions. In some parts of the Chitradurga district, Kyatedevaru is worshipped, and an annual *jatra* on a small scale is held in its honour. In the month of Chaitra (April-May), a *jatra* in honour of Butappa is held, at which only the members of the Golla caste attend to show their reverence. This deity has no special temple, and his figure engraved on a stone is set up underneath a shady tree. The worship is conducted by a *pujari* (priest) of their caste (Iyer: 1988:234).

The Gollas also worship their ancestors. They believe that soul of their relatives come close to their houses during the time of the festival when they beat the drums. In fact, no function or festival is held without drums. They also worship '*Alagu*'. *Alagu* is the *puja* of the sickle. If any important person dies, a special *puja* is performed in the name of the person. This is known as '*Alagu Puja*'. They recall their ancestors and other relatives, who had died long back, and offer golden cobra and scorpion ornaments to them and perform *Puja* to them.

On the whole the Gollas are prime devotees of their ancestors and cultural heroes of their community. They have temples for different gods. They decorate their deities with various ornaments. They light 101 lamps during *Deepavali* festival. They worship cows during Basava Jayanthi. The cows are given a good bath on that day, decorated with colour and colour paper on the body and taken in a procession in the evening.

The Gollas worship many local deities (non-vegetation gods and goddesses) like Butapa, Yattappa (cultural heroes), Polegdamma, and Maramma, etc. But today some continuities and changes can be found in the realm of religion among them. The old deities, viz., Junjappa, Chikkannaswamy, Buttappa, continue to be the supreme deities and they also continue to celebrate some other festivals adopted from the neighbouring castes especially the Lingayats.

Besides worshipping their cultural heroes (deities), today the Gollas have also adopted the worship of several Hindu mythological gods like Manjunath, Mallikarjuna, Shiva, Lakshmi, Ganapathi and many other gods and goddesses. Earlier, the Gollas constructed temple with leaves. Today due to the influence of other castes, they have begun constructing temples with stone and cement. Nevertheless, most of the Gollas continue participating in the community festivals very actively. In addition to these, they celebrate some *Jatra* in honour of the deities like Bevinahalliyamma, Maramma, Halappa, and Chikkannaswamy. It is a fact that even though they are economically backward and face financial difficulties, this hardly affects their enthusiasm in celebrating their festivals in the *Gollara Hatties*.

Purity and pollution

Puberity is a sign of basic alteration of the biological state of a girl. It is the time of the final attainment of the functional sex organs and the development of secondary sexual characteristic. Certain ceremonies are practiced when a girl experiences her first menstruation among the Golla community. The first menstruation of the girl is called as '*maineredavalu' or Doddavaladavalu or Ruthuvadalu* by Gollas. That means that the girl has attained puberty. On their first menstruation, the girls live outside the limits of their village for 21 days in a hut of green leaves erected exclusively for this purpose. She is prevented from looking at any man or the sun during the period of menstruation. Staying at a little distance from the hut, some female relatives give her company in the night. Her bed consists of *margosa* leaves and dried grass thinly spread over them. At the end of the period, except clothes and vessels, all the materials used by her are burnt. The clothes and vessels are washed before being taken back into the house. While returning home after bath, she carries water in small pots with which she washes the feet of their *pujari* (priest) and elderly male members including her father. This is done as a gesture of respect to the elders and also as an indication that she is no longer under pollution. Then the pujari (priest) gives her spoonful of five products of the cow known as '*Panchagavya'* (cow-dung, urine, butter, curds and milk) and makes her to chew some *margosa* leaves. Afterwards, the *pujari* declares that she has got rid of pollution. During subsequent menstruation periods, she remains outside the village only for three days. It is believed that a man becomes impure if the shadow of such a woman falls on him.

During this period, the physical contact of this hut or the concerned girl by others at any time is deemed to lead to ritual impurity. The person who touched her has to take bath, purify him\herself. The girls are given a separate plate and a tumbler that are to be cleaned by her. She should not enter into house, village, temple and other ritual places before completing 21 days and the performance of the purification ceremony. During this period, any member of the household sends special food for her. She is also given nourished food like soaked, bangle gram, copra, coconut, and jaggery to eat. In some places, especially the towns and cities, the Golla females under menstruation do not maintain physical segregation. This practice of segregating a menstruating female has been gradually disappearing.

On the last day of seclusion, they invite washer man to terminate the pollution. He/she supplies washed clothes to the girl. After her bath, the girl puts on the clothes provided by washer man. After purification is over, in the evening they perform puberty ceremony.

The Gollas call this ceremony as '*Vasage Hakuvadu*', which means that a girl who has attained puberty enters into the house. All the relatives and the caste members are invited to attend the function on that evening. The concerned girl takes the bath and wears a new sari and blouse presented by her maternal uncle. The father of the girl has to give a feast to the relatives and caste members on that day. Then '*Muttaideyaru*'sing some folk songs appropriate for the occasion. At the end of the ceremony, the *Muttaideyaru* (married women but not widows) are offered turmeric powder, *Kumkuma*, betel leaves and nuts. From this day onwards, she is regarded as grown up women and she wears saris.

During her subsequent monthly periods, she will be in the state of 'uncleanliness' for three days. During this period she will be kept outside the village and should not enter into the village, home and temple. On the third day she takes bath and purifies herself. During this period, the woman has to observe certain taboos (i.e., not touching others, not letting her shadow fall on the others, not comb her hair, not apply *Kumkuma* on her forehead, not participate in sacred activities, and not talking to any one, etc).

Today, due to spread of modern education, efforts of the community leaders and interaction with people of other castes, most of the Gollas consider the menstruation as a biological process and do not feel that it pollutes. They no longer feel that there is need of keeping the concerned female out of the village. Therefore, most of the practices associated with puberty and menstruation have disappeared. Now they believe that celebrating this kind of ceremony is very expensive. Excepting some parts of the Tumkur and Chitradurga district, in all parts of the state the Golla girls attaining puberty do not inform caste members, and their relatives. The concerned girl just takes bath and remains engaged in her routine activities. No purifying or any other kind of ceremony is conducted. Previously, after puberty the Gollas immediately used to stop the concerned girl attending her school or colleges. But today, if girl attains puberty they do not stop sending her to the school /college and she can continue her education.

Birth pollution

The life of an individual starts with his birth. The Gollas have got peculiar tribal customs pertaining to childbirth. When a women delivers a baby, both the woman and the baby will be kept out of the village for a period of three months in a specially erected thatched hut (*Banathi Gubba*) and no one will be allowed to touch either the mother or the child even when they suffer from any illness or disease. They consider that the woman becomes impure after childbirth. That is why, when a woman feels the first pain of labour, she is sent out of the village into a little leaf or mat hut about half a kilometer away from the village. On this issue, Iyer states that childbirth is looked upon by the Gollas with great fear, as if some impending evil, and is extremely detested, owing to the anxious days, which the woman in childbed has to spend. When labour pain comes on, the woman goes out furlongs off the hamlet, to a part of the jungle where a shed of leaves and grass has been newly erected for the purpose. A woman of the Bedar caste attends upon her as a midwife. The mother is considered impure for three months after accouchements, the impurity diminishing in degree day by day. If any person touches her during these intervals, he will catch the contagion, and will have to remain outside for a similar period, and on the occurrence of such a contingency, the mother and her child are not allowed to enter the house until they obtain the permission of their deity. The *Yajman* of the caste, being supposed to be the trusted servant of the deity, announces its decrees, learning them in his dreams, or interpreting them by signs observed during worship (1988:228-229). The woman's husband generally makes a little hut about fifty yards from her, and watches over her; but he may not go near her on pain because of the fear of being outcasted for three months. Food is placed on the ground near the hut and she takes it. On the fourth day of the childbirth, the mother of the woman goes to her, pours water and cow urine on her and shifts her to a new hut near the village. On the ninth, fifteenth and thirtieth days, she similarly moves to another new hut and again once in each of the two following months. On the ninetieth day, the headman of the village calls the woman to come out of the hut. Then the mother and child take bath and dress up in new washed clothes, go to the village temple where the *pujari* (priest) touches their mouth with drops of milk of the sacred sheep (*jennige kuri*) and then accompanies her to her house, where a purifying ceremony is performed. The villagers do not allow even people of the Health Department to look after the mother and child during delivery time. Due to this reason, the death rate during childbirth is very high. If any individual goes to her help, he is ostracized. The mother and child are not allowed to enter the house, village and temple unless they have completed three months outside the village in a small hut. After the purification ceremony of mother and child, the materials that have been used to construct the hut are thrown way.

Earlier during the pollution period, except mid wife none was allowed to enter or even touch that hut since it was believed that physical contact of any person might cause ritual pollution of that person. But now, the situation has changed due to educational progress, occupational change, influence of other castes and efforts of the community leaders. Educated couples oppose these taboos at the time of childbirth. The delivery takes place at home, inside the village or in the hospitals. The touching of the child and/or the mother by any person is no longer considered as polluting. However, some of the orthodox community leaders are still following this custom. Today if there is any difficulty in the normal delivery, pregnant woman is taken to the hospital and take the assistance of the doctors. Soon after childbirth the umbilical chord is cut by using knife or freshly cut piece of a large jungle *reed.* The placenta is buried under a milk-oozing tree or under palm tree. Previously, there was a taboo on taking assistance at the time of delivery but today mother or old women of the community or other relatives or *Soolagitti* or doctors can assist in the delivery of a child. Now the ritual impurity (*sutaka)* after the childbirth has been reduced from three months to nine days. However, in Sira, Pavagada and Madhugiri taluks and some other parts of the state the belief of ritual impurity at the time of childbirth still persists. But the Gollas, living in the cities completely ignore this traditional belief.

After stipulated time of ritual pollution, the ritual purification used to take place. They invited a Brahmin or a Lingayat to the house to perform purifying rituals. Today in most of the cases the washer man does not act as an agent of purification. Traditionally, the priest (*Pujari*) suggests the name for the child of their own deities. But today like many other castes, they consult an astrologer and *panchanga* (calendar) and choose the day and time of celebration and naming the child. Thus, today most of the educated youths even in the villages are not interested in maintaining pollution (*sutaka*) at the time of delivery. Community leaders, organizers and officials today are persuading the Gollas to get rid of this evil. The majority of the younger generation is responding favourably to this plea. Some of the youths meeting me during my fieldwork in the village stated that in order to overcome such superstitions, we should kill our *pujari* and *patelas* (village head man) because they are mainly responsible for the persistence of this evil tradition. Recently, the Government of Karnataka has started constructing small single room houses (*prasoothi gruha*) outside the village for delivery, puberty and menstruation purposes. But this programme of the Government helps to foster/ maintain this unscientific custom. To overcome this problem completely, it requires creation of scientific awareness among the Gollas.

Social movement

The Gollas in Karnataka suffered from economic, political, ritual, educational and civic disabilities. The former Chief Minister of Karnataka late Devaraja Urs stated that the economic and social conditions of the Gollas were as bad as those of the scheduled castes and scheduled tribes. The Gollas in Karnataka started organizing themselves by forming caste associations in order to overcome their ritual, economic and political disabilities and also agitated against inequalities, discrimination and deprivation. This process led to their widespread and collective mobilization and, in turn ,these assumed the shape of a social movement. The emergence of awareness among the Gollas materialized through a gradual process with different degree of intensities at its different stages. The Yadava consciousness among the Gollas of Karnataka existed even before independence. However, systematic organization, collective mobilization and launching of agitations took place long after independence especially after 1990s. The strongest movement of the Gollas in Karnataka started in the 1994. The Government of Karnataka appointed the Third Karnataka Backward Classes Commissions on 9th March 1988 under the Chairmanship of O.Chinnappa Reddy (one man Commission) and the Commission submitted its report to the Government. The Government headed by M. Veerappa Moily implemented the Chinnappa Reddy Commission report on 20th April 1994. After the implementation of the report various communities belonging to non-dominant and some dominant backward castes such as the Vokkaligas (dominant caste) strongly opposed and agitated against the report. The Gollas also launched a strong movement against the recommendations of Chinappa Reddy Commission, because the First Karnataka Backward Classes Commission (known as Havanur Commission) had treated the Gollas as backward tribe and they were enjoying the benefits that were provided to the nomadic and semi-nomadic castes without any income restrictions under the regime of Devaraj Urs. But, the Chinnappa Reddy Commission (Third Karnataka Backward Classes Commission) placed the Gollas in the category II (Backward caste) instead of placing in the category I (Most Backward Caste). Consequently, the Gollas were denied all facilities such as reservation in the admission to technical schools and collages and other educational facilities like free scholarship, economic benefits like subsidy to purchase bullocks, and cattle that they enjoyed until then. Then the Gollas from different parts of the state collectively mobilized and organized under the leadership of notable community leaders S. Siddppa and Dr. Dwarkanath and others protesting against the recommendation of the report and demanding restoration of their listing in to the category I.

For the first time in the history of movement of the Gollas, they collectively mobilized and strongly protested against Chinnppa Reddy Commission report and Veerappa Moily Government on 18th July 1994 at Bangalore. The Gollas alleged that by placing them in the category II the Government had deprived them of all the benefits due to them in various fields. In addition, the Gollas alleged that the category II comprised of many communities that were economically and socially stronger than the Gollas. In their view, placing the Gollas in that category was unscientific and unfair. The agitation and its agenda received wide coverage in the newspapers and other mass media and helped the Gollas to put their case of being victimized very effectively. As a result of the movement of the Gollas, the Government of Karnataka issued an order No. 150 BCA 94, dated 17th September 1994, placing Gollas in the Category-I of most backward caste as was the case in the previous Government orders giving them all the attendant benefits. According to the said order, the percentage of reservation for the other backward castes (OBCs) of Karnataka under Article 15(4) and Article 16(4) of the constitution for education and government jobs is fixed out at 32 per cent as follows:

Backward Castes	Education	Jobs
Category I	4 percent	4 percent
Category I A	15 percent	15 percent
Category II B	4 percent	4 percent
Category III B	4 percent	4 percent
Category III B	5 percent	5 percent
Total	32 percent	32 percent

Now the Gollas are being treated as the most Backward Caste and are placed in category I. Today they are claiming reservation in educational institutions especially medical and technical institutions and in appointments in various departments without income restriction.

Conclusion

What is the nature of socio-cultural change that has been registered among the Gollas of Karnataka? Without any trace of doubt, the recorded change appears gradual if one takes in to consideration the Gollas as a collective entity. Second, the extent and nature of change has been of different types in different spheres. For instance, far-reaching changes have been recorded in some of the fields whereas not much has changed in certain others. There has been mass spread of education at the lower levels but not much at the higher echelons. In the field of farming, they are in the process of switching over from subsistence to commercial agriculture. Third, segments of the Gollas that have moved to the urban areas and non-traditional occupations have changed their customs and practices and belief systems more appreciably than their counterparts that have remained tethered to the rural areas and their traditional pastoral occupations of cattle rearing. Fourth, compared to their north Indian brethren, the Gollas of Karnataka activated themselves politically very late. However, they have certainly realized the usefulness of political mobilization and mass struggles to obtain what they consider to be their legitimate claims. On the other hand, compared to the dominant communities of Karnataka, the Gollas still remain socially and economically very backward community of the state.

**The author is grateful to Prof. Jogan Shankar for his invaluable guidance in this study.*

References

Gurulingaiah, M. 2000. 'Yadava movement in Karnataka', *Samaja Shodhana*: 9 (2).

Gurulingaiah, M.2002 'Educational structure and mobility among Kadu Gollas of Tumkur District', *Samaja Shodhana*: 11(1-2).

Hoebel, Adamson, 1976. *Cultural and social Anthropology*. New Delhi: McGraw Hill Book Co.

Iyer, L.K.A. 1988. *The Mysore tribes and castes* (5 Volumes). Delhi: Mittal Publication. Vol. 3.

Karnataka,Government of. 1996. *A handbook of Karnataka*. Bangalore: Government of Karnataka.

Karnataka,Government of. 1986. Second Backward Classes Commission (O Chinnappa Reddy: Chairperson). *Report*. Bangalore: Government of Karnataka.

Lakshminarayana, H.D. 1976. *India's villages at cross roads*. New Delhi, National Publishing House.

Rao. M.S.A. 1988, *Social movements and social transformantion*. New Delhi: Manohar.

Sheering, M.A. 1974. *Hindu tribes and castes*. New Delhi: Cosmo Publishing.

Thurston, Edgar. 1909. *Castes and tribes of south India*. Madras: Government Press. Vol. 3.

The Raika of Rajasthan

Vinay Kumar Srivastava

Enumerating certain areas that require urgent research, Shah (1969: 156-7) notes the 'conspicuous absence of studies of nomadic groups such as Banzaras in several parts of India and the Bharavads and Rabaris in Gujarat.' Although Shah does not include the Raika of Rajasthan (also known as the Rabari) in his list of the communities that require study on a priority basis, we agree with him that on the whole, social anthropologists and sociologists have paid little attention to the study of pastoral-nomadic and semi-nomadic groups by comparison to agricultural communities. Also, pastoral groups have received marginal attention in our planning and development programmes where emphasis has largely been laid on the issues of agriculture and industrialization (Salzman, 1985: 1-8). Guided by the policy of 'grow more food', the tracts of land that hitherto had been pastures were colonized for agricultural purposes (see Jodha, 1988). Between 1956 and 1987, common property resources, for example, decreased by 32 per cent while the net cultivated area increased from 28.6 per cent in 1951 to 47 per cent in 1981 (Köhler-Rollefson, 1995: 116). The expansion of agriculture was interpreted as a yardstick of development, but that was not the case with an increase of animal herds.

With a change in the socio-economic environment and a specific capitalist-oriented meaning of development, pastoral-nomadic existence in many parts of the world has become extremely precarious (Srivastava, V.K., 1987: 317-8; Dyer and Choksi, 1997: 218). The synergism that once obtained between agriculturalists and pastoralists – with the animals (the 'vacuum cleaners' as they are called since they eat up almost every vegetation available in the field after it has been harvested) providing the ready-made manure to agricultural fields – is gradually breaking down (Agarwal, 1985). Köhler-Rollefson (1995: 115) writes in the context of Rajasthan: 'Peaceful co-existence is replaced by an increasingly belligerent struggle for land, or access to it, between agriculturalists and pastoralists and among animal herders belonging to different castes.' Realizing the difficulties of keeping cattle wealth in ecologically altered situations, certain pastoralists are contemplating giving up their traditional occupation (Srivastava, V.K., 1999). At this juncture, it is urgently required that ecologically sound programmes are devised for them. This would be possible if there are available intensive sociological studies of animal husbandry, and the ways in which they manage their environment and extract resources for survival (Srivastava, V.K., 2005).

Pastoralism is a way of life that results from the dependence of a community upon its livestock (Salzman, 2004). The members of a pastoral community survive on animal products – they subsist on milk (and its products) and may eat the meat of their domesticated animals. If pastoralists are in touch with markets, they may sell milk and animals to their buyers, but they retain with them a few pints of milk for domestic consumption.

Similarly, the entire herd of animals is never disposed of except in cases of distress sale. An optimum number of animals essential for further growth of the herd is always retained. This explains the prohibition in many pastoral societies against the sale of female animals. This taboo is magico-religiously protected in certain grazier communities, while in others, the local councils, concerned with the issues of social control, impose strong sanctions against those violating it.

Pastoral people may refrain from eating the meat of their domesticated animals, but they may occasionally eat those animals (and birds) that they themselves do not tend, or they may only consume the transvalued (or 'blessed') food of meat. Some may claim to be strictly vegetarian. However, both these groups of pastoralists may continue to sell their domesticated animals to those who buy them mainly for slaughterhouses, for meat. Thus, although they themselves do not kill their animals for food, they sell it to those who kill them and sell their meat. It may be said that their living depends upon the 'consumption' of their domestic animals' meat, blood, and hides.

Besides milking female animals, consuming meat, blood and hides, and converting of milk into dairy products, the pastoralists also use animal hair and wool. Animals are used for carrying or pulling loads and riding; they are the source of mechanical energy. An important traditional fuel is cake cut out of animal excreta or droppings. Many settled pastoral people sell animal manure to neighbouring peasants (see Fratkin, 1997).

Agricultural communities also domesticate animals, and many pastoralists have land holdings on which they may cultivate monsoon crops. As men attend to grazing duties that cannot be suspended (or relaxed) even for a day, the pastoralists face the acute problem of organizing labour for agricultural work. Either a few males of the herders' kin group are relieved for cultivation; if it is not possible then the land is leased out to peasants on a soft economic bargain; or, women of the pastoralists organize agricultural work, engage male labour and get the chores done, and also look after the market operations; and if nothing works out, the land is left fallow.

Thus, whether a society is to be termed pastoral or not depends upon how central are animals to its existence. For instance, the maximum number of camels is found in the district of Sri Ganganagar (Rajasthan) and their owners are rich peasants, but neither this district nor the camel owners can be called pastoralists because agriculture is central to their economy and not animal herding. Camels, used for pulling carts and sometimes used as traction animals, support agricultural economy. Köhler-Rollefson and Rathore (1996: 34) note that because in India camel utilization is almost exclusively transport-oriented, there is a distinct separation between camel producers and camel users. The former are pastoralists, the latter are not; they may be agriculturalists, merchants, or transporters of goods.

Pastoral nomadism and semi-nomadism is an ecologically appropriate technique in arid and semi-arid parts of western India, forest and hilly regions in central India, and sub-mountainous regions in north India (Rao and Casimir 2003). Pastoral nomadic and semi-nomadic groups have evolved their own suitable methods for upbringing the locally available genetic stocks. For this, they have not been dependent upon foreign assistance and imported technology. But maintenance of the livestock at one place for a long period of time is difficult as the carrying capacity of the local eco-system is limited. It may not sustain the pastoral pattern of land use for a long time; hence migration in search of grazing lands and water becomes imperative for the existence of a herd.

According to the estimation of the *Statistical Abstracts of India* (1980, new series, no. 25), there were 50 million livestock and 34 million people managing it. In 1992, Rajasthan had 11.6 million cattle, 12.2 million sheep, 15.1 million goats, 7.7 million buffaloes, 73 thousand camels, and 19 thousand donkeys. The district of Kutch (Gujarat) in 1989 had an animal population of 1.72 million by comparison to a human population of 1.05 million (*Report of the Government of Gujarat,* 1989). However, the exact number of nomadic and semi-nomadic families is not available in India. The census officials do collect data on occupational categories but not on their nomadic or settled state (Bose, 1975: 1), but some classifications of breeding tracts of animals in India have been advanced (Makhijani, 1957), and based on the census data, some have attempted the distribution of Indian pastoral castes (e.g., Sopher, 1975: 198-200).

Pastoralism is differentially associated with nomadic existence. But pastoral groups in India have their 'permanent villages' to which they return after completing their grazing expeditions. Some of them combine pastoralism with agriculture. In Kutch, it is estimated that on average five thousand Rabari families migrate each year in search of grazing lands for their animals, taking with them about 40 thousand cows and oxen, 700 thousand goats and sheep, and camels and donkeys; and they start returning to their villages just before the onset of rain. In Rajasthan, there are several non-pastoral nomads also – such as trading nomads (Banjara, Ghattiwala Jogi, and Gowaria), artisan nomads (Gaduliya Lohar, Sansi, and Sattia), and other types of nomads who live by providing entertainment to other communities or offer certain 'supernatural services' (such as Nat, Kalbelia, Jogi) – who are now in different stages of sedentarization.

Mainly spreading from western Rajasthan to the Kutch region of Gujarat, the Raika-Rabari hamlets survive in a harsh climatic zone. The rainfall, for example, in Kutch is a measly 350 mm, and during 1984-87 it was less than 200 mm. In Rajasthan, the mean annual rainfall varies from 100 mm on the Indo-Pakistan border and 210 mm at Jaisalmer to about 350 mm to 400 mm in parts situated more towards the eastern region. The Rajasthan Canal Project has affected the irrigation potentiality of some areas in Bikaner, but on the whole the villages yield a single crop and its success depends upon the rain. The District Gazetteer of Jaisalmer (p. 4) notes:

> The entire area is barren and dreary, the only variations on the landscape being a few hills and many sand dunes...No other part of Rajasthan is as life-less and forbidding in appearance...There is hardly any variation owing to lack of water. There are no permanent water sources and the inhabitants consequently lead a nomadic life, grazing sheep and cattle, shifting from one green patch to another. There is an endless struggle for survival which is reflected in all aspects of life of the inhabitants.

By comparison to the rest of India, Rajasthan is thinly populated; however, the *Resource Atlas of Rajasthan* (1994) records that the population of this state has increased from 16 million in 1951 to 44 million in 1991. In its western part, the population growth has been significantly high; in fact, Thar is the most densely populated desert in the world.

But the thorny vegetation of the entire area has supported a significant population of both sheep and camel. Salzman (1986: 50) writes that less than 5 per cent of the village population in Rajasthan owns about 50 per cent of livestock. With regard to the camel population, Rajasthan has 72 per cent of the 1.10 million camels in India (*Annual Report of the National Research Centre on Camel*, 1987: 3). The sheep can subsist, and often flourish, on coarse feed not relished by other domestic animals. A similar ecological adaptation applies to the camel. What is admired by camel-tenders (and also by people in general) is the 'camel's fortitude under conditions of extreme heat and its ability to cross vast expanses of desert without drinking' (Köhler-Rollefson 1993: 180).

The Raika combine camel and sheep in their herds in varying proportions. But in Bikaner, Jodhpur, Pali, and Kota, we have come across Raika hamlets having several large camel herds. Flocks of sheep also exist in these hamlets. As we move towards Bikaner, camel herds are larger whereas sheep herds are smaller; in Pali, camel herds are smaller but sheep are tended in large numbers. In Marwar, although the herds – especially the migrating ones – do have a couple of camels, which are the beasts of burden, the Raika mainly specialize in sheep breeding and tending. Similarly, the Raika of Jalore and Sirohi are predominantly sheep-breeding communities. The exceptions are certain Raika hamlets (such are Jojawar in Pali, Ghum-ki-dhani in Kota) famous in Rajasthan for collective ownership of large camel herds numbering two to three thousand animals. Köhler-Rollefson, in one of her papers (1995: 118), mentions an exclusively camel-oriented Raika community in Pali which not only had a 'collection of memorial stelae depicting camel-mounted ancestors' but also self-made clay camels with which the local children played. The Rabari of the district of Mandsaur (Madhya Pradesh) breed camels; they do not keep sheep but buffaloes and engage in crop cultivation (Köhler-Rollefson and Rathore, 1996: 34). Although the traditional image of Rabaris as camel-breeders still holds in Gujarat, their economy has diversified. They breed the world's best tropical cattle (Westphal-Hellbusch, 1975; George, 1985; Choksi and Dyer, 1996).

As human beings impose a hierarchy on themselves, so do they on their animals. The kind of animal a caste domesticates has a bearing on its social status. A common observation in north India is that pigs are domesticated by castes below the line of purity. Further, the hierarchy of animals is not reducible to notions of economic advantage. Had it been so, perhaps the buffalo (which yields a large quantity of milk of richer quality) would have been more sacred than the cow. We need to know the cultural patterns of a society for understanding the way in which it arranges its animals in an order of rank.

In Rajasthan, in addition to the pan-Hindu concept of sacred cow, the camel is placed very high in animal hierarchy. But it does not mean that it is an object of veneration in the same way as the cow is; for instance, there is no concept of the 'unreturnable gift (*dan*) of the camel' as it is of the cow (what is called *gaudan*). To be specific, the camel is kept high in the secular hierarchy of animals. In times when modern transport facilities did not exist, the camel was the mode of conveyance in the desert (and even today is), because of which it has aptly earned the reputation of being the 'ship of the desert'. Köhler-Rollefson (1993: 185) states that the 'greatest impact of the camel was its role in opening up vast expanses of desert to human exploitation.' The princely lineages kept camel armies. The dromedary warriors won many wars. Bulliet (1975) writes that the system prevalent amongst the Assyrians was to put two riders back to back on a camel. One of them guided the camel, the second darted arrows at adversaries. In Rajasthan, the Maharaja of Bikaner, Ganga Singh, had his own camel corps named after him. It served in Somaliland, Egypt, and other countries and was complemented by the colonial administrators (Singh, Karni, 1974). The *Administrative Reports of Bikaner* (19134) noted that in 1914, the camel-breeding establishment of the Maharaja comprised 1,636 she-camels and offspring. There were 49 stallions also. It was disbanded in 1929 and the 'imperial camels' were auctioned.

Although Marwari language does not have as many names of the camel as it is in Arabic (where there are six hundred words meaning the camel), its importance in social life is well known and researched. The love lyrics of Rajasthan (such as in the stories of Dhola Maru, Mahendra Mumal, Nihalde Sultan, Amala Khimvaji) eulogize the camel's role. About the camel which every evening drove Mahendra from Amarkot to Mumal's palace in Lodhra, and brought him back, it was said:

> (The camel) With small ears, a dense growth of hair on its tail, having long legs;
> (by the time you say 'no') it reaches Nagore, (while you 'glance') it drops (you) at Jaisalmer.
> And, if its bridle is loosened, (within a split second) it brings news from Delhi.

The camel which took Dhola to Pugal was 'as fast as the wind,' ate not the 'thorny grass' but a particular vegetation called *nagarbel*, and drank the 'holy water of the Ganges' (Singh, Ram et al., 1997: 132).

Although not revered, the camel is indirectly attributed with sacredness. Goraksha Samhita records that Kalakarni, a female deity, has the camel as her mount. Some sort of debate exists with respect to the name of this deity; some prefer to call her simply Ustravahini Devi ('the goddess that rides the camel'). Icons depicting her have been found from Orissa and Bengal in the east to Rajasthan and Gujarat in the west (Srivastava, V.S., 1981: 182). One of her temples is in the town of Bikaner.

The camels were owned in the past by royal lineages and rich castes. A peasant family aspired to own a camel. Besides serving as a traction animal and for ploughing sandy soils, its ownership also raised the status of a family. Even today, rich peasants (and transporters) own camels, for it costs on average not less than seven to eight thousand rupees. Although peasants own camels, the Raika carry out the tasks of camel tending and breeding, and looking after their health care system. There may be individual camel specialists from other castes (and I have heard of a Rajput in Bikaner, who holds the expertise of tracing the lost camels through their pug marks), but no community, except the Raika and Sindhi Muslim, has occupational specialization regarding everything pertaining to the camel. In social contexts (like in Marwar, Jalore, Sirohi) where the herds are predominantly of sheep, the knowledge of the Raika about the camel is not less. As said previously, the migrating herds invariably have camels. A Raika family, whether in Bikaner or Pali-Marwar, aspires to own a couple of camels. Besides the utilitarian aspects to which the camel may be put, its ownership, as is the case with peasants, raises the prestige of the family. Many Raika say that tending camels is their moral duty. Against all odds and meager economic benefits, the Raika think they must domesticate camels rather than letting other castes take over their traditional occupation.

Besides being concentrated in the states of Rajasthan and Gujarat, the Raika inhabit certain villages in Haryana, Punjab, Uttar Pradesh, and Madhya Pradesh. According to a Raika leader of Haryana, there are at least 32 villages in Haryana that have a sizable Raika population; Kaithal village of Kurukshetra and Bhirdana of Hisar have around 150 houses each. However, these Raika are not like their counterparts in western Rajasthan and Gujarat. They do not live at the outskirts of the main village. A common saying about the Raika of Rajasthan is that their hamlet (*dhani*) is always 'outside' the village and they have little to do with the other settled and non-pastoral castes. The Raika of Haryana, by comparison, are an integral part of the village. They constitute one of the occupational castes specializing in agriculture. Animal tending in their case is not remarkably different from what is found in other agricultural castes. In the district of Bikaner, our estimate is that there are thirty-six villages with Raika hamlets; the largest of them like Gadhwala and Amarpura in Bikaner tehsil, Udasar Raikan in Nokha, Bajju and Charanwala in Kolayat, and Jaitpura in Lunkaransar, have forty to fifty houses each. In Jodhpur and Pali-Marwar, there are big hamlets having more than one hundred houses each. In Jalore and Sirohi, the number of Raika households in a hamlet is quite large. A report released in 1989 (during the time of the general elections) noted that a majority of voters in Jalore consisted of the Raika, Meghwal, and the Kumhar. Some big hamlets of Jodhpur and Pali (like Bagri in Sojat Road) have Raika of different sub-castes, although in so far as we know no competition exists amongst them.

So far no authentic information exists about the total Raika population in Rajasthan, or in India, as a whole. The earliest census report on the castes of Marwar dates back to 1891. According to this report titled *Report: Mardumshumari Raj Marwar,* there were 98, 406 Raika (52,808 men and 45,598 women) in Marwar. The second document, *Report on the Census of Marwar and Mallani,* taken on 26 February 1891, recorded 122,668 Raika/Rabari (60,756 men and 61,912 women), and they were included in the Group (classified as XXVI) of Shepherds and Wool Weavers of the Class D of Artisans. The figure of 122,668 people is of the Rabari in both Marwar (Jodhpur) and Mallani (Barmer) regions. Marwar had 112,096 Rabari (55,261 men and 56,835 women), while in Mallani there were 10,572 Rabari (5,495 men and 5,077 women). As compared to the Raj Marwar Census, the second report included 13,690 more Rabari (2,453 men and 11,237 women) in Marwar. Discrepancy between these two figures is difficult to explain. An intriguing fact is that in the second Report there were more women than men.

The Gazetteer of the Bombay Presidency (vol. 5, 1888: 80) reported 13,371 Rabari in Kutch. Census 1891 listed 898 Rabari in the United Province. Ibbetson (1914) recorded 3,881 Rabari in Punjab (2,825 in British Territory and 1,056 in Native States). In Census 1931, 135,820 Rabari/Raika were recorded in Rajasthan. This gives an indication that perhaps the figure given in Marwar-Mallani census could be more accurate than the one given in the Raj Marwar Census; however all census material is fraught with the problem of reliability.

The contemporary situation is that no department (governmental or otherwise) in Rajasthan has an exact knowledge of the total population of the Raika. An official of the Social Welfare Department, Bikaner, told me in 1989 that the Rabari were not less than three hundred thousand in Rajasthan and Gujarat. Westphal-Hellbusch (1975: 124) estimated their number to be between 350 and 440 thousand people. In the district of Kutch, they are estimated to be around 90 thousand (Dyer and Choksi 1997: 217). According to a Raika leader of Jodhpur, Rajasthan had in 1991 around 2 lakh Raika families (c.f. *League for Pastoral Peoples,* n.d.). Assuming the average

Raika household/family to be four, it would mean that Rajasthan had eight lakh Raika in 1991 which seems to us an inflated figure. A moderate estimate is that both Rajasthan and Gujarat have around five to six lakh Raika/Rabari.

The Raika trace their origin from the Sanskritic Hindu deity, Lord Shiva. A detailed version of this myth has been recorded in the Raj Marwar Census. I present below the myth as the Raika and their genealogists (called Rav-ji) narrated it to me. Notwithstanding the regional variations, in structural terms, the myth as recorded in 1891 and as detailed out to me in 1989 remains the same, although differences do exist in its finer aspects. The Raika recalled having learnt it from their ancestors as well as their genealogists.

Lord Shiva was in deep meditation for twelve years in a place called Chikal Nadi in the Himalayas. His consort, Parvati, engaged herself in various playful activities. From the clay of Nadi, she made a few objects having legs, the torso, eyes and face. After Shiva emerged from meditation, his eyes fell on the clay model and he smiled on Parvati' s skill.

Parvati, then, wanted Shiva to infuse life (*sajiv*) in all clay objects she had made. Shiva readily agreed, and one by one, the 'clay toys' awakened to life. (In these terms, the myth says, the faunal world came into existence.) Finally came the turn of a Parvati's strange creation, the object with five legs, the fifth one stuck to its belly. Shiva was reluctant to grant 'life' to it. He told Parvati that the five-legged animal would face grave difficulties in its movements once it came to life. But Parvati – exemplifying the quality of female stubbornness (*triyahata*) – refused to listen to her husband, insisting that the 'toy made from clay' should be granted the benefit of 'flesh and blood'. Shiva yielded to Parvati's insistence, endowed life to the five-legged object, and uttered, 'Utha', meaning 'get up'. From that time, the animal was named 'Unth', the camel.

But the animal could not move as the fifth leg hindered its movement. Touched by the animal's suffering (*kasth*), Parvati requested Shiva to make the fifth leg disappear (*amit*). Shiva said that once the camel had four legs, it would create problems for the divine couple, but Parvati's insistence was relentless, emphasizing once again the characteristics of *triyahata*. Once again succumbing to his consort's request, Shiva pushed the fifth leg upwards – it emerged as a hump (*thumbi*) on the back and its base formed the boss (*aidar*). At this point in the story, the Raika and their genealogists point to the morphology of the camel. The hump and the boss are considered as the marks (*chinha*) that Lord Shiva left on the camel's body.

Once the camel had four legs, it started running swiftly, often disappearing in forests and wilderness. Parvati found it difficult to control the animal's movements. She once again beseeched Shiva for creating a man who would look after the camel, take it out for grazing. For his 'vehicle' (*vahana*), the bull (*nadiya*), Shiva had already created a man called Charan, whose descendants came to constitute the caste of Charan. For looking after the camel, Shiva created a man from his locks. Ibbetson (1914: 269) writes that the first camel-man was made out of Shiva' s sweat. The Raj Marwar Census records that he was created from the 'dirt' of Shiva's skin, hence he was named Chamar (meaning 'leather'), and the clan (*got*) assigned to him was Samar. Since the man was created from Shiva's body (hair, skin, or sweat), he also came to be known as Dewasi, in whom 'dwells the god', 'one who has been created by the almighty'.

Although the Dewasi had a divine creation, that is to say, he was created asexually, he was still a human body, an ensemble of drives and passions, and desires, emotions and sentiments. Soon, he started 'urging for a woman'; the myth says, he desired to be 'coupled' (*jorey ban-na*). He approached Shiva with this request – 'to be coupled' in the same manner as Shiva and Parvati were. Shiva advised him to go to the river and 'touch' any of the celestial nymphs (*pariyan,* singular *pari*, from Indra's kingdom) who descended to the earth for bathing. The myth further says that once human beings touch these fairies, they are rendered 'useless' for the heavenly kingdom and will not be permitted entry.

As advised by Shiva, the Dewasi reached the river and waited for the arrival of the fairies. The nymphs descended, took off their clothes, and when they were about to enter the river, the Dewasi came from behind and took away the clothes of one of them. Running away with the clothes of a celestial being amounted to 'touching' her. Seeing the man escaping with her clothes, the fairy chased him exasperatedly, yelling out: 'Oh Mortal! Oh, Man of the World (*mrtu lok*)! You have rendered me ineligible for the World of Gods (*devalok*). Now you marry me.' In the meantime, the Dewasi had reached the place where

Shiva meditated. The fairy that was named Gavri also followed him. Shiva advised Dewasi to marry Gavri. Ibbetson (1914: 269) records that the camel-man had picked up the clothes of two fairies and was chased by them. Both these women reached Shiva who advised one of them to marry the camel-man and the other was bestowed on the Charan. Blessing the first Raika couple, Shiva charted out ten principles (*dharma*) for them to be followed religiously (see Srivastava, V.K., 2000).

The first Dewasi couple gave birth to seven daughters and a son (Ibbetson, 1914: 269); but according to the Raj Marwar Census, Gavri had one son and twelve daughters. The son retained the clan name, Samar, of his father. When the Raika's daughters (seven or twelve) grew up, the problem concerned their marriage. From which groups should the spouses of these girls be sought? As there was no other Raika family, endogamous unions were ruled out. The Raika approached Shiva for help in this matter who asked him to place his request for prospective bridegrooms before the Bhatti Rajput king, Lakhoji Phulaji. Through the divine technique, the king had already been informed what he was expected to do when the Dewasi reached him for help. The king asked the Dewasi to select bridegrooms for his daughters from his army. The bridegrooms were from different Rajput subcastes; thus, although the daughters' children were Raika, they belonged to the subcastes of their respective fathers. The Raj Marwar Census says that since all these marriages were against the principle of caste endogamy, the progeny thus produced bore the name 'Rabari' – meaning 'outside the established way'. Following this myth, if we ask, 'who are the Raika/ Rabari', the answer is: they are the descendants of the daughters and the son of the first Dewasi couple. The myth is silent about the group from which the spouse of the Dewasi son was sought, however there is no doubt that his descendants belonged to the Samar clan regarded as the highest amongst the Raika. A schoolteacher in Bikaner told me: 'The Samar are the original people; we bow before them.' The myth of the Raika origin explains the affinity between them and the Rajput, the evidence of which is available in political alliances, economic exchanges and in general social life.

It is clear from above that the Raika are also known as Rabari (however, its spellings may vary: Rebari, Raewari, Rahwari, Riwari, Rabarri; John Smith in 1993 had suggested to me that the word 'Raika' should be written as 'Rayaka') and Dewasi. The term principally used in Gujarat is Rabari; they are mainly sheep breeders and are included in the list of the Scheduled Tribes of Gujarat. They are also known as Mogha (meaning 'mute') in Gujarat because the first Raika was forbidden to speak to his wife, so says the myth (c.f. Tambs-Lyche, 1997: 155). In Rajasthan, they are largely called Raika, but when we move southwardly, the terms Rabari and Dewasi appear frequently. Combining both the terms – Raika and Rabari – one of the caste associations of these people was called All-India Raika-Rabari Association and had its head office at Sonepat in Haryana. In Rajasthan, the Raika are included in the list of the Other Backward Classes and Semi-nomadic Tribes, and the name by which they are identified in the list of the Semi-nomadic Tribes is not Raika, but Rabari.

Why are these people called Rabari? The Raj Marwar Census offers two reasons. The first is (we had stated it earlier) that the daughters of the first Raika were married to Rajput men and such marriages defied the norm of caste endogamy – 'outside the established rules' – and thus these people came to be called Rabari. Westphal-Hellbusch (1975: 125) has translated *raha* as 'outside' and *bari* as 'way' – 'outside the way'. The Rabari of Gujarat also believe that as the marriage of their common ancestor – Shamar or Shambal – was with the celestial damsel, the *devaputri*, they came to be known as Rah-bari, 'outside the usual path' (Enthoven, 1922: 253).

The other reason is in terms of another myth. The Dewasi's work was to look after the camel and take it out for grazing. One day when he was returning from the forest after having grazed the camel, it became dark; he was hungry as well as feeling cold. He saw a flicker of light from some distance. Reaching there, he found a corpse burning. An earthen pot (used for carrying water to the cremation ground) was also lying there. The Dewasi collected the camel's milk in that pot, drank it, and as he was feeling cold and tired, he slept close to the burning corpse.

When the Dewasi did not return home till late night, Parvati became very anxious. She requested Shiva to search for him in the forest. Shiva meditated for a while and took Parvati to the funeral ground where the camel herdsman lay fast asleep. He woke him up saying the following words: 'Utha, Bhoot, Rabari' ('Get up, [you]

Ghost, Rabari'). In this myth, the meaning of the term *raha* is 'custom' (or *reet)* and *bari* means 'outside'. The Dewasi was called Rabari because what he did (by sleeping in the cremation ground, near the burning pyre and drinking milk from the pot associated with death impurity) was 'outside' the customary practices. He was also called Bhut because the place where he slept was usually the abode of ghosts. The common point in both reasons given by the Raj Marwar Census is that these camel herders came to be known as Rabari because they did not abide by the existing conventions. Moreover, as we said earlier, the hamlets of Raika/Rabari are generally outside the main village, because of which they have acquired the reputation of being the 'people of outside' (*baharle log*). Enthoven (1922: 253) writes that once the first camelman had a large family, Shiva asked him to shift from the heaven and 'live outside', thus he acquired the name of 'Rabari'.

But, it may be noted that some sources give a different meaning to the term Rabari. Crooke (1896 orig., 1975: 201) and Ibbetson (1914: 269) say that this word is probably derived from *rahwar* meaning 'quickpaced, active'. A pharmacist in Sojat Road (Pali) conjectured that it could be a corrupt form of the word *darbari*, the courtier. He supported his conjecture with a commonly known fact about the Raika that they – being the 'imperial graziers' – were close to royal lineages; hence they were a 'type of courtiers'. During my field work I was also told that the term Rabari consists of two Persian words, *rah* and *bar*, respectively meaning 'way' and 'burden'; combining these two, it would mean, 'one who carries the burden of the way,' or 'one who leads a burdensome existence.' It also means a 'guide', 'friend on the way', being derived from the Persian word, *rahbar*.

The term Raika, we noted previously, is mainly used in Rajasthan. The Raika had special occupational relations with princely lineages of Bikaner, Jodhpur, and for some time, Jaisalmer. According to Westphal-Hellbusch (1975: 126), the Rabari in western Rajasthan acquired the special duty of a 'camel-riding messenger' because of their association with the princely kingdoms, and thus added a special name Raika to their Rabari caste. Raika is a prestigious name. We may accept the suggestion that the term denotes an 'occupational meaning' – the Raika represent a 'professional name' (Westphal-Hellbusch, 1975: 126). It is also believed that the term Raika is derived from the name of a fairy that married the first Dewasi. She was named

Raie or Raika – that is why, her children came to be called Raika. Please remember here that her name is Gavri in the Raj Marwar Census. Such confusions are bound to exist in mythical and oral literature. The anthropological task is to juxtapose these varied and deviant details rather than endeavouring to reconcile them.

Let us have a look at the surnames used by the Raika. The uneducated (and those in traditional occupations) do not use any surnames. In a face-to-face village community, every one knows the caste of the other. A caste (especially in Rajasthan) can easily be identified by its dress patterns, jewelry and ornaments, shape of houses, furniture and other material cultural things, the style of living, etc, or, in other words, what Galanter (1984:8) called the 'common round of life'. For instance, a Raika male can be identified by his style of tying the turban, the long plait (*choti*) he keeps (the Raika of Godwar region keep the tonsure with long hair on the occiput), the stick (*lathi*) and a small pitcher (*handia*) for carrying water, the bag for keeping tobacco, a metal bracelet in right hand and also an anklet in left leg, etc. A Raika woman is identified by the type of skirt she wears – it generally has eighty pleats (*assi kali ka ghagra*)—the armlets (*chura*) adorning both lower and upper arms, and the head-dress (*ati*). The regional variations are however found in all these diacritical signs of the Raika caste.

In multi-caste villages, the Raika males are addressed with a lot of respect – the honorific suffix 'ji' is added after each name, including those of younger people (like Harji, Devji, Sugnaji, Kishnoji, Mulji), to the extent that 'ji' becomes a part of the person's name. The second name generally used by Raika men is Ram; in recent years, the younger generation has started using the term Singh, which is mainly used by the Rajputs (on this see, Srivastava, V.K., 1999).

The educated Raika and those in urban-based occupations (such as school teachers, policemen, white-collar workers) are not only conscious of their caste and community, but also more regularly use surnames. Dewasi and Raika are frequent choices. In Bikaner, the preference is for the term Raika; in Jodhpur and Pali, the term Dewasi is preferred. Rarely do the educated ones in Rajasthan use the term Rabari. Some use the name of their clan (*got*) as surname, like Bhim, Bar, Aal, etc. Although their affnity with the Rajput is not questioned, rarely do the Raika use Rajput surnames. However, I know a Raika originally from Uttar Pradesh (Mathura district) who uses 'Rajput' as his surname. Some Raika from Uttar Pradesh also use the title 'Chaudhury', which the Jat generally use. In Gujarat, many educated Rabari choose to use Desai as their surname. I know some Raika families settled in Mount Abu (but originally from different areas of Rajasthan) who also call themselves Desai and have established their matrimonial relations with Rabari of equal standing in Gujarat. A cursory glance at the pages of the Rabari caste magazine published regularly from Mehsana (Gujarat) may familiarize one with diverse surnames that the educated Rabari and Raika use.

Proud of their glorious historical links with princely lineages, the Raika (both educated and illiterate) maintain that their caste has its own identity and the attempts to merge it with any other group are erroneous. They concede the generally held beliefs (such as, the Raika emerged from one of the Rajput groups, or some Rajput groups were amalgamated into the Raika, or Raika and Rajputs go together, assisting each other) but assert that they are different from other castes. Such a commitment has an important bearing upon their caste association.

A difficult area in sociological research pertains to the social history of a caste. Historiography, it is well known, has paid more attention to the governing classes. Now with the rise of subaltern history, the focus in many studies has shifted to the governed people and small communities. For constructing the social history of the Raika, I perused quite a few Sanat Parwana Bahi, Haqiqat Bahi, Dastoor Quamvar, and other archival materials. At every step of this endeavour I received guidance from the staff of the state archives at Bikaner. But whatever information I gathered dealt with the relations of Raika with the centres of power. Observations on their style of life were dispersed and not of much use and virtually nothing concrete existed about their migratory history in the archival papers, however I was able to collect some articles that illuminated certain aspects of the Raika history.

Archaeological evidence points out that camel breeding was essential for small kings. Since Iran was not suitable for camel breeding, the camel herders must have always been in search of appropriate landscapes. Northwestern province is believed to be the area from where the Raika are supposed to have entered India. Sherring (1879 orig., 1974: 246) writes: '...most of them (Raika) have the peculiar Persian physiognomy. One of their family names is Aga, which seems to support their Persian descent.'

In one of the earliest studies of the Rabari of Gujarat, Mankad (1939: 31-2) said that these people were first the inhabitants of Baluchistan. As that country was rocky, mountainous, sandy and barren, the Rabari began domesticating dromedaries. They trained the camels for long journeys, milked them, and prepared clarified butter for domestic consumption as well as sale. From the camel's hair, they also made coarse cloth. In course of time, the Rabari population increased and they started moving to other areas. Through the northwest, they entered Marwar. The climatic condition was agreeable to camel tending and breeding. But like Baluchistan, Marwar proved a 'very limited field or a small country' for them. Therefore, they migrated to Kutch and from there to Kathiawad. The Rabari did not change their occupation in Baluchistan, Marwar and Kutch, but when they came to Kathiawad, great changes started surfacing among them mainly because of the impact of the local occupational groups and the environment.

There are other sources that believe that the Raika are not the autochthones of Rajasthan. Both mythical and historical sources point to their exterior origin. One of the myths of Rabari origin I heard was that they originated in Kailash, the sacred mountain where live Shiva and Parvati, and their work was to tend camels. Once, the Raika couple annoyed Shiva, as a consequence of which they were sent to the earth. From Kailash, they traveled southwards and finally settled down in Kutch. Their descendants then dispersed westwardly towards Marwar. Some of them went to Mewar also. Another common theme in Raika migratory history is that they moved southwardly a thousand years or so in order to escape the tyrannous Muslim rulers of Sindh (Westphal-Hellbusch, 1974). Further, Westphal-Hellbusch (1975: 125) writes that the Raika claim to have given 'shelter to many Rajput clans who had been put to flight by Islamic conquerors.' Although such 'historical tales' cannot be taken as authentic, there is 'little doubt that the Rabari traveled far and were separated into several groups. Each of them had to adapt it to local surroundings and neighbours, thus affecting this way-of-life, customs, and status' (ibid.: 125). Elson (1979: 23) writes that the descendants of the first Rabari 'are said to have lived in Haryana until about a thousand years ago. Need for additional grazing land forced (them) to leave their original home, and they wandered through Rajasthan, Sind, and Gujarat before arriving in Kutch.' About the Rabari of Punjab, Ibbetson (1987 reprint: 258) writes that their home appeared to be Bikaner and the Rajputana desert.

The affinity between the Raika and the Rajput is supported by Tod's study of the Annals of Jaisalmer (1832: 169-231). According to these Annals, the Rabari are the descendants of the Bhatti tribe who later came to be known as the Rajput. The Bhatti were a branch of the Yadu (or Jadoo) race believed to have ruled from Yamuna to Dwarka (Tod, 1832: 169). According to Tod's information, Tunno – the ancestor of Rao Jesal after whom the kingdom was called Jaisalmer – had five sons, Beeji Rao, Makur, Jeytung, Allun, and Rakecho. Allun, the fourth son of Tunno, had four sons and the descendants of his eldest son, Deosi, 'became Rahbarris (who rear camels)'. The genealogy in Jaisalmer is traced from Lord Krishna, the incarnation of Vishnu, and the Rabari are believed to have originated in the nineteenth generation (Tod, 1832: 185-6). It is further said that the descendants of Makur became carpenters (Suthar) while those of Rakecho were the merchants (Bania). At no place does Tod explain why the descendants of Deosi became Rabari?

The Raika submit that the most appropriate name of their caste is Dewasi because they are the 'progeny' of Lord Shiva. As they generally live outside the main multi-caste village, they acquired the name Rabari (*abadi se bahar*, 'outside the population'). They preferred to dwell away from the villages, in their own hamlets (*dhani*) because of their occupation of animal breeding rather than being the abettors of 'permanent impurity'. The Raika say that they are well versed with the routes and paths that are not known to the others; I often heard the people from other castes calling Raika the 'knower of routes' (*rastey ke jankar*). In addition, the Raika are popular for 'searching the things'. For this quality, they are often called *khoji* ('one who searches [the lost objects]'). They can trace the lost animals by examining their pugmarks on the sandy soil (for this ability, they bear the name of *pagi*, 'one who reads the foot marks'). Traveling with herds through wilderness, barren tracts of land and dense forests, they possess a rich knowledge of routes, the grazing lands, and know the villages *en route* and their people.

For all this knowledge, along with their traditional occupation of camel tending, they were employed by the princely lineages. I came across many entries in the court records of the tasks the Raika carried out for the royalty and the payment, grant, and reward they received for that. The task to look after the 'imperial herd' (*rajsi tola*) was always entrusted to the Raika: the camel herd of the state of Bikaner was under the supervision of the Raika of village Gadhwala, and the Raika of Nokh supervised that of the state of Jaisalmer. The Raika were also the confidants of the kings and other members of the royal family. The Gadhwala Raika remember that Maharaja Dungar Singh desired to see either of the following two in the morning: a white cow or Chaina Raika; both were equally auspicious to him. The Raj Marwar Census summed up the position of the Raika in the following words: 'They (Raika/Rabari) have a great power to search the things. They are the good riders of the camel. Employed by the states of Jodhpur, Bikaner, and Jaisalmer, they look after camels. They work as messengers and it is through them that important papers and documents are sent.' Writing on the postal system, Sharma (1970: 166) observed that the 'Raika and Mirdhas were employed to convey confidential letters and they were handsomely rewarded after they had delivered letters.'

Against the background of the contribution the Raika made to the royal houses, they were attributed with a set of characteristics that continue even today in their descriptions of their caste. The Raika are trustworthy and loyal, capable of undertaking any task howsoever difficult. One of the best-known cases is of Maharaja Jaswant Singh of Jodhpur who died while fighting on the Kabul border. Ramdas, a Raika, brought the news of his sad demise to Jodhpur. Carrying the Maharaja's turban (*pagri*), he reached Jodhpur from Kabul in thirteen days. He was rewarded for this service. Another example can be taken from the royal lineage of Jaisalmer (Chand, 1891). Vijaya Rao became the Maharaja of Jaisalmer in 820 AD. In 836 AD, he was blessed with a son, Devraj. The king of Bhatinda sent the marriage proposal of his daughter with Devraj, and the Jaisalmer king readily accepted it. In 841 AD, the marriage procession left for Bhatinda, but the enemy's army attacked it en route. The guests from Jaisalmer suffered heavy casualty. A Raika named Neg came to Devraj's rescue. He escaped with that five-year old royal heir, and left him to the safe custody of a Purohit called Devayut. Then, the Raika reached Jaisalmer and informed Devraj's mother about the attack, and the whereabouts of her son. Neg Raika's valorous act is still remembered and commemorated.

For the Rabari of Porbundar, Sherring (1879 [1974]: 233) wrote that they, together with the Mahars, constituted the 'national militia and were a body of soldiers, called the Sword of the State.' In Rajasthan, there are individual Raika cases of valour, but organization of the whole community on the lines of a 'national militia' did not take place.

The image of a trustworthy Raika can be gathered from the folklore of Rajasthan. Some stories in Vijay Dandetha's famous *Batan Ri Phulwari* have a confident and brave Raika character, Ratna Raika, who sacrifices his interests for the sake of others, executing each task given to him with skill and speed. Almost every Rajput hero, now venerated, had a Raika confidant. Pabu-ji, Goga Chauhan, Ramdeo Baba, could accomplish difficult (and almost impossible) tasks because a Raika was always with each one of them.

For example, take the story of Pabu-ji Rathore. He is believed to have brought the camel to Marwar from Lanka. When Pabu-ji's elder brother's (Bura-ji's) daughter was getting married, his mother asked him about the gift he had thought of giving to his niece. Pabu-ji said: 'I shall give her an animal found in Lanka called *rati bhuri sande* ('red-grey camel'). No one knew about this animal. Although he had promised, he had no clue where this type of animal lived in Lanka. He asked his officers, ministers, and other brave people to volunteer for the task of tracing it. None came forward. Finally, Harmal Raika volunteered and succeeded in bringing home the whereabouts of the camel. On Harmal's advice, Pabu-ji went to Lanka to bring the animal to Rajasthan.

Because of their association with the royal houses, the Raika (in Bikaner and Jodhpur) occupied a position next to the Rajput in the village hierarchy. Such a status of these people is accepted even today. With the decline of royal states, the economic position of the Raika was also severely affected. They are aware of this fact and regret for not acquiring cultivable land, and become peasants, during Maharaja Ganga Singh's (1887-1943) reign. Other migrant groups to their area, especially the Jat, gradually came to acquire land and shifted to cultivation. A Raika woman from Bikaner told me: 'The Raika remained a simpleton. He ran into a great loss. He never acquired the land. He confined his work to domesticating the camel. We thought that those glorious days would always remain.'

In Haryana and Punjab, the Raika, like the other dominant castes of village India, have adopted agriculture as the mainstay of their existence. The educated people have taken up new occupations. The Raika *jati* periodicals – Gopalbandhu (published from Mehsana, Gujarat) and Raika Jagriti (from Sonepat, Haryana)—often publish lists of the Raika/Rabari in various white-collar professions; an analysis of these lists shows that a majority of them are from Haryana, Punjab, and Gujarat. In village Bhirdana (of district Hissar), for four times the Sarpanch (Headman) of the Village Council (*panchayat*) was a Raika. From Kaithal (district Kurukshetra, Haryana), a Raika family has immigrated to England. And, one who looks after the All-India Raika-Rabari Association as its Mahamantri (General Secretary) is from Sonepat.

Similarly, in Gujarat, the Raika have made good progress on all fronts. A Member of the Parliament, as mentioned earlier, was from this community. Important differences exist between them and those from Rajasthan. In Gujarat, the Rabari are broadly included in the category of the Bharwad. Sherring (1879 [1974]: 277) has used the term Rabari as equivalent to Bharwad. The latter in Eastern Gujarat are divided into three groups: Motabhai ('big brother'), Nanabhai ('younger brother'), and Rabari. Their inclusion with the Bharwad has been accepted by the Rabari, although the latter do not have marital relations with any of the Bharwad groups: it is because of this inclusion that Westphal-Hellbusch (1975: 127) concluded that in Eastern Gujarat, the Rabari were 'dissolving as a recognizable ethnic unit.'

In Rajasthan, some Raika have taken up new professions, but their number is not large. A former Raika teacher is now in the State's account service. The first Raika to have become a veterinary doctor is from Pali district. Recently, a Raika man finished his graduation in engineering, and is now preparing for the Civil Services Examination. After obtaining a degree in medicine, a Raika man from Pali had sought employment in a Delhi hospital, and has now gone abroad to pursue a degree in psychiatry. There are many well-known Raika teachers, and those active in State politics, but the community, on the whole, has remained pastoral, variously combining agriculture with it, and having a negligible representation in the State's decision making institutions. The recent announcement of reservation for the socially and educationally backward classes (Other Backward Classes), it is hoped, might bring about certain changes in their life.

Here, one may notice two levels of differences: firstly, the kind of animals the Raika/Rabari domesticate varies with the geographical area they have come to inhabit. In Bikaner and a part of Marwar, the camel herds predominate, although they may also keep sheep and goats. In Pali, Jalore and Sirohi, sheep and goats are mainly raised; a migratory herd (*dang*) may have a couple of camels. Camels and donkeys accompany a *dang* as 'beasts of burden'. Similarly, the Rabari in eastern Kutch and northwestern Saurastra have switched to sheep and goat breeding. In northern Gujarat, they have resorted to agriculture, selling of animal products, or work for wages. In Barda Hills and Gir Forest (Junagarh), the Rabari are buffalo-breeders.

Secondly, in accordance with the geographical areas the Raika/ Rabari historically occupied, they have developed some kind of affinity with the local groups that have a higher ritual status. The Rabari of Bikaner, Jaisalmer and Marwar were employed by the Rajput kings – they were the latter's 'camel-riding messengers,' 'imperial graziers,' 'royal camel tenders' – and as a result, their occupational association with the Rajput inspired them to consider themselves as 'having emerged from the Rajput caste.' Their attempt certainly was not to claim the Rajput status (as was the case with the Grasia of Udaipur) – there is no evidence of Rajputanization among them, but the Raika assert that 'Raika-Rajput have always been together.' Such a claim comes mainly from the camel-tending Raika.

Those who predominantly had sheep have remained deprived of the imperial patronage. Their association with the Rajput was not of the same kind as was of their brethren working for the imperial lineages. The sheepherders maintained their identity of the Rabari, however they have often switched over to the term Dewasi. In Gujarat, as we saw, they were linked with the Bharwad and other occupational and pastoral castes. Because of living in Rajput dominated areas, the Raika of Uttar Pradesh have started using Singh as their second name and Rajput as their surname. Landedness has also inspired them to take up the title Chaudhury that is generally associated with the Jat.

In Haryana, Punjab, and Uttar Pradesh, the Raika do not live outside the main village, although the Raika houses may be clustered together as is the practice with the other castes. In Rajasthan, the Raika invariably live outside the main village in their own hamlets locally known as *dhani.* (It is also called *Raika bas* – the 'place where the Raika live.') Sometimes, these *dhani*s are a few kilometers away from the main village (or, even a small town) – and if it is big enough, it almost resembles a village. Now, because of expansion of the main village, the space that separated the village (*gaon*) from *dhani* has significantly reduced in Gadhwala; the *dhani* is just across the road that leads to Kilchu. (Gadhwala, Kilchu and Kotari had common Village Council some years ago, but now, Kilchu has its own body.) Bagri *dhani* or the one close to Sojat Road, both in Pali-Marwar, almost resemble a village. As noticed previously, the reason for such an aloof existence is not the defiling status of the caste as is the case with the ex-untouchable (Harijan) castes. Traditionally being associated with raising the livestock, they required habitational sites close to grazing lands. Keeping large herds of animals within the village was not possible, therefore to avert any nuisance that their animals might cause, the Raika preferred to establish their hamlets outside the compact village.

A *dhani* is usually a kin-based group comprising all those who claim a common descent. In a big *dhani* a couple or more of such descent lines may be present. Sometimes one may come across the households of recent Raika arrivals in a village. Although marital relations may not be established between them, the ties of *bhaichara* (brotherhood) are always extended. The Raika say they can seek abode in any Raika *dhani* in any village, anywhere in Rajasthan, by simply pronouncing their identity, and anyone denying them this privilege is liable to be fined or even excommunicated by their caste council.

The Raika live in multi-caste villages. Though a *dhani* is a closed group in spatial terms, it is not self-sufficient. For various services, the Raika depend upon other castes with which they have patron-client relations, the payment being made after harvesting or shearing of sheep. For a wide variety of goods and commodities, they depend upon the local markets. On occasions of marriage and death, the inter-caste relations manifest in full form and exchange of gifts takes place. Fictive kinship relations are extended to castes of higher and equal rank in a village. An incoming bride has a 'fictive father' and 'fictive brother' in her 'village of procreation' – the term *dharmela* is used to encompass all these fictive kinship relations. The services of the Brahmin are sought on ritual occasions and with Rajput, Jat, Khati (Carpenters) and Mali (Gardener), the Raika share smoke-pipe (chillum), food and water.

According to the Raj Marwar Census, the Raika are divided into two groups: Maru and Chalakya. The Maru think that they should only use the title Dewasi because of their claim of superiority over the Chalakya. A crucial difference between the two according to the Census is: the Maru do not domesticate sheep or goats – they restrict their specialization to camel tending and breeding. A Chalakya herd predominantly has sheep, followed by goats, and sometimes cows and buffaloes. They keep camels for carrying the load.

Further, Maru Raika were patronized by Rajput princes, and perhaps, because of this, they refrain from using the term Rabari for themselves, which connotes an inferior status. According to the Maru, the Chalakya are ritually polluted, and are indifferent to the rules of purity and pollution. Hypergamy is practiced between the two groups: the Maru may marry Chalakya daughters but they do not give their own to the inferior group. As the Chalakya women wear brass (*pital*) ornaments, the group is also called Pitalya. The Raj Marwar Census also noted the diacritical differences between the two. The head-dress (*ati*) is worn by married Maru women only. The Maru men wear a long loin cloth (*dhoti*) stretching up to the toe while Chalakya have a shorter one.

The term Chalakya has been used in the description of Raika by Westphal-Hellbusch (1975), and a couple of other general accounts by people influenced by the Census reports. But the Raika of Pali-Marwar and Bikaner do not use this term to refer to the other group. Neither is the term Pitalya used, however, I did come across the phrase *pital pehannewale log* ('those who wear brass') often used for these people.

The distinction is made according to the area — the Raika of Godwar are called Godwara and are regarded as inferior to the Maru. Thus, there are Maru, Godwara and Kutchi (or Kasiya) Raika – the Maru inhabit Bikaner, Jaisalmer and Marwar regions. The Godwara are mainly concentrated in Godwar, though their hamlets are also found in Marwar. Those from Kutch are called Kutchi and are distinct from the others in their dress and hairstyles. Keeping tonsure and a long bunch of hair on the occiput is one of their characteristics. Since the Rajasthani Raika do not have marital or other relations with those of Gujarat, they are less informed about them.

Presently, the animals they domesticate do not distinguish Maru and Godwara. The Maru keep both camel herds and sheep flocks; and today, as keeping sheep is much more economically viable than camels, even the traditional camel herders have started rearing sheep. Those who keep big flocks of sheep are constantly on move; the camel-graziers generally live in permanent villages. But in case of large camel herds, they also follow a migratory way of life. Take the case of the Raika *dhani* of Jojawar, having a collective ownership of thousands of camels, where camel herds return to the *dhani* only for shearing. The Maru Raika in Marwar tend flocks of sheep more than those in Bikaner. Marital relations between the Maru and the Godwara are almost absent – so far I have not come across a case of hypergamy. Diacritical distinctions are pronounced – the married Chalakya women do not wear the head-dress. There is neither commensality nor marital relations between the Maru and the Chalakya. Some Maru also say that the Chalakya did not originate from Lord Shiva.

Indian anthropologists have observed that the term *jati* is used by people for various levels of segmentation of their group – what the sociologists call caste or subcaste is referred to as *jati* by the people. Different identities precipitate in different situations. When a Raika interacts with a Jat, he is a Raika, but when he is related to a Godwara, he is Maru. Each of these groups (Maru, Godwara and Kutchi) is further divided into units which people call *jati* or *khanpa;* the latter are also used as surnames. In turn, each of these *jati*s (or *khanpa)* is divided into exogamous groups, locally called *got* (which is a corrupt form of *gotra,* some believe it to be equivalent to 'clan'). The Raika are an endogamous group, and so are Maru and Godwara. The Raika avoid the father's *jati* or *khanpa* and those of the mother's brother (mother's *khanpa* before marriage) and father's mother's brother (paternal grandmother's maiden *khanpa)* for marriage. So, to reiterate, the Raika are divided into Maru, Godwara and Kutchi. Each one of them is further divided into *jati*s or *khanpa,* such as Aal, Bar, Bhim, etc. Then, each *jati* (or *khanpa)* is divided into *got* – exogamous patriclan. The entire system looks like a pyramid; like a segmentary lineage system. As one moves down the pyramidal structure of the Raika caste, the number of the units increase and their ethno-history becomes blurred.

The Raj Marwar Census collected the information on the Raika from the genealogists of Godwara Raikas who lived in Bijapur in Pali. It listed 103 *khanpa* names of the Raika – quite a few of which are compound names having Rajput or Brahmin caste names as suffixes, like Bar Chauhan, Bhakra Chauhan, Khatana Solankhi, Kalatara Brahmin, Aal Bhati, etc. These compound caste names emerged because of the marriages of the first Dewasi's eleven daughters with the Rajputs and of the twelfth with a Brahmin.

The Raika are Hindu. The Raj Marwar Census records that those 'who sing their paeans' – the group called Dadhi – were earlier Raika and Hindu, but on one occasion, they dined with the Muslim, and so, were excommunicated. These outcast Raika came to constitute a separate caste category called the Dadhi. Today, this myth of some Raika's conversion to Islam is not remembered. The Dadhi are the Raika's minstrels, singing their praises and commemorating their heroes on the occasion of marriage. They have a caste-wise specialization – there are separate Dadhi of the Bar, or the Aal, or the Bhim, etc. The Dadhi are not the genealogists of the Raika as was noted by the Raj Marwar Census. The genealogists of the Raika constitute a caste called the Rav, who are honorifically called Bhai Bhat-ji or Rav-ji; they are Hindus and keep on traveling to different Raika villages. Their records are lugged on camels and in this process they up-to-date the genealogies of their clients. Most of the Dadhi have moved out of their traditional villages, working as labourers at construction sites and other developmental projects. But at the time of marriage, they return to the villages of their patrons and sing their praises when the marriage procession (*barat*) arrives and when guests (*barati*) go to the dining space (*pandal*) to eat.

Lord Shiva is the Raika's chief deity. The places of penances of various renouncers, called *dhuni*s they visit, invariably have Shiva temples. On Mondays, the Raika observe fast and visit Shiva temples. On ritual occasions, when opium water is prepared for collective consumption, Lord Shiva is invoked. The Raika of Rajasthan worship both Shiva and Parvati, but in Gujarat, the worship of the goddess has primacy over that of the god. Mankad (1939: 54) writes:

> Rabari are goddess worshippers. The Goddess they worship is called Mammai. It is believed that she is mute... (She) is the Goddess Parvati in her angry mood towards God Shiva. It is said that when God Shiva went away to practice penance, Parvati did not approve of his going away to take *samadhi* and determined to remain mute... Her priests are expected not to speak. They are called Moghas or the mutes.

The Census of India, 1961, monograph on Village Pachhatardi in Gujarat (p. 8) adds:

> The goddess which the Rabari worship is known both as Jog Maya and Mungai, *i.e.* the dumb goddess... Each Rabari village (*nes*) has a sanctified place or a temple for the worship of the goddess... in all the religious ceremonies, only the males of the tribe participate... The tribe has almost an implicit faith in the powers of the goddess and in certain contingency, emergency or illness, seek protection and help from this source.

Mummai Mata has her mediums on which she descends and predicts amongst many things the time of rains, which the peasants are always eager to know. The dominant caste of Porbundar, Mer, considers Mummai Mata as the patron-goddess of their saints (Trivedi, 1961, quoted in Tambs-Lyche, 1997: 160). Mummai Mata's temple may not be accessible to outsiders. To cite here Tambs-Lyche's (1997: 160) experience in a Rabari village:

> I once tried for hours to impress the Rabari of Loj - a coastal village near Mangrol - to let me see the 'dumb' goddess. At length they allowed me a glimpse of her, but against the dark background, I could see very little.

This also supports the observation that the Rabari not only wish to lead an 'aloof' existence, but are also skeptical of the outsiders.

An important deity of the Raika of Rajasthan is Pabu-ji, the Rathore Rajput hero who brought the camel in Marwar from Lanka. Every Raika hamlet has a temple or a platform (*sthan* or *than*) dedicated to Pabu-ji, which is looked after by a local elder. On every ritual in the house, an offering of sweets and coconut is made to him. A Pabu-ji temple has the idols of Roop Nath-ji and Dema-ji, both of whom are related to him. Especially during the life cycle of a camel, its illnesses and other contingencies, the people make offerings to Pabu-ji for its safety and fast recovery.

The local deities – such as Bhairon-ji, Mama-ji, various mother goddesses, and the ancestral spirits – also descend on their prime worshippers, who are called *bhopa.* The Raika say that Pabu-ji does not descend on his 'servitor' (*sevak*) or *bhopa,* however Roop Nath-ji and Dema-ji do. Besides being diviners, the *bhopa* specialize in local medical practices.

An important observation about the Raika concerns the concept of renunciation. It is quite common to come across in the villages of Rajasthan the Raika renouncers who are presently looking after some shrines, or have been elevated to occupy the seat (*gaddi*) of their teacher. Once they are initiated in a system of renunciation, they give up their original name and acquire a new name, with the title of their order suffixed to it. Having local popularity, they provide supernatural help to people of all castes.

For looking after the caste affairs and maintaining its internal unity, the Raika have a caste council, locally called *thikana* or *panchayat.* The literal meaning of the word *thikana* is 'place', but for the Raika, it means 'the place where they assemble to sort out their differences and plan for some sort of a community-oriented action.' Earlier, the *thikana* was only for arbitrating conflicts, but now with a gradual crystallization of their caste consciousness, it takes up collective action for the benefit of the entire caste. If a rest house (*dharmashala*) or a school is to be built, the *thikana* will play an important role in raising funds, and may even entrust some of its members to supervise the task of construction.

On average about fifteen villages constitute a *thikana,* of which the bigger one (having a sizable population of the Raika) is generally chosen for holding council meetings. Although the term *panchayat* may give the impression of a body of 'five' men that plays a decisive role, it is not true. It may consist of a large number of councilors (*panch*) (Srivastava 2004). Among the Raika, no formal election takes place for the position of a *panch.* Whosoever attends the council meeting is a *panch.* These meetings continue for a lengthy period of time, sometimes for days, and not everyone can possibly attend them. Those who have to take animals out for grazing, or those who are employed, have no time to attend council meetings. Of all the members who attend the meetings, some may be more vocal, persuasive, or active; thus every member of a *thikana* is a *panch,* but not everyone is equally influential, charismatic, and endowed with political resources (oratory, farsightedness, organizing skills). Each *thikana* has the office of a treasurer, who is one of the active, literate members. He maintains accounts and keeps a record of the meetings. In case the minutes of a meeting are to be circulated in the form of a pamphlet, a practice that has become common in recent years, he takes the charge of getting them printed and circulated. The treasurer is appointed by the members of the council, and is paid a token sum for his work.

Many conflicts are taken up by the *thikanas*. Cases of elopement, adultery, betrayal of a marital commitment, or defiance of caste rules and principles, are arbitrated by the council. The guilty are fined; in the past they were punished corporally, and if the offence is serious, they may be excommunicated. Anyone keeping any relations with them is also liable to be dealt accordingly. For the guilt of a person, his whole family and the kin group are ostracized. With great difficulty, a person is assimilated to the caste fold – he has to pay a heavy fine; he has to organize a communal feast for all in which clarified butter is lavishly served. Money collected through the recovery of fine is spent on acquiring objects, like cooking utensils, for the entire community; some money is also donated to the poor people for the marriage of their daughters. Recently when a Raika was contesting an election for the Rajasthan legislative council, financial help was also provided to him by the *thikanas*.

Today, the traditional council has come under criticisms. The Raika youth say that *panchayati* (active participation in council meetings) is a full time engagement of those Raika men who have nothing else to do. Their male descendants and their wives have taken up all economic and domestic works. The result is that these men have plenty of time at hand to devote themselves to other tasks; and one of them is to 'do *panchayati*'. The educated and employed men are extremely critical of those who are active in caste councils. The word *panchayati* is not spoken with respect. The critics feel that conservatism in their caste and the sustenance of oppressive institutions in their society is because of their caste councils. For them, *panchayati* is a strategy of punishing the individuals who are forward looking and want to bring about change in their society.

Traditionally the Raika knew only one breed of the camel – the Bikaneri, also called Jheenpa – but now because of their association with the National Research Centre on Camel (NRCC), they have come to know the characteristics of other camel breeds. The Raika of Gadhwala are advantageously placed – about a dozen of its males work in the NRCC, and have gradually acquired an elemental idea of the sort of researches that are going on there. Certain aspects of the scientific knowledge are integrated with their traditional practices of camel management. As a result, they know the distinction between the Jaisalmeri, Kutchi, Mewari, and Arbi breeds of the camel and know that through eugenics, the local breeds can be improved upon. However, in practice, they prefer an intra-breeding between the Jheenpas. At one time, the Gadhwala Raika were proud of their herds and asserted that the best camels in Bikaner were bred and tended by their hamlet, and they fetched a handsome price. As more and more Raika have taken up jobs offered by the encroaching educational and urban frontiers, there has been a decline in the number of camel herds, nevertheless, as said earlier, each household dreams to keep a couple of camels.

In 1991, when fieldwork was carried out in Gadhwala, it had four camel herds (*tola;* plural *toley*); the biggest of which had around two hundred camels. But, it did not mean that the Raika owned all of them; in the above-mentioned *tola*, the grazier owned only forty animals. The rest were of the other castes. Here, the Raika make a distinction between the *dhani* (the owner) and the *charwaha* (the grazier): the former owns the camels but has no time or skill to take the animals out for grazing. The grazier is a specialist – he knows where the kind of grass the animal eats is available; he knows the sources of water in forests and the wilderness; he has a thorough knowledge of the animals' problems and illnesses and administers traditional medicines. The owner needs the animals at the time of ploughing, or to pull the cart. Thus, during the months of *chaumasa* (the agricultural season), the animals go back to the owner, who uses them for ploughing his agricultural fields, or loans them to others for various tasks. In case the owner has a regular occupation of cart pulling, he keeps the animals with him; and stall-feeding is arranged for them. The graziers have complete right over the camel's hair and milk. None of the products is for the markets as the Raika are religiously prohibited from either selling the wool or milk. They are also prohibited from processing the camel milk into curd. The Raika believe that they can keep themselves away from many illnesses by consuming camel milk. Incidentally, in one of the recent studies that the Indian Council of Medical Research (ICMR) carried out, it was found that the Raika have not reported even a single case of diabetes and have an amazing tolerance to glucose. One of the hypotheses that the ICMR has advanced is that it could be because they drink camel milk, and in terms of this practice, they are different from other communities in their neighbourhood (*The Indian Express*, 13 March 2005).

For grazing a camel, the grazier charges Rs. 40 for one year. A sum of Rs. 20 is charged for the forest department on whose land the animals graze. And, in case the animal destroys the crops of a peasant, the fine levied on it is also to be paid by its owner. The relations between the owner and the grazier are hereditary; they break down in the most adverse situations. Thus, every camel bears the marks (*khenga*) of the owner as well as the grazier. Although the demographic composition of a *tola* is in favour of females, the male calves are equally valued because they are more efficient for riding, pulling the cart and the plough. Maintaining the camel population for generations, the Raika have constructed a whole system of practices concerned with the camel. In fact, pastoralism requires more of skills than objectively transmitted techniques.

I remember one of my stints of fieldwork of early 1990 with the Raika of Pali-Marwar. At that time, I was living with a Raika family in the hamlet of the village of Pachunda Kalan (of Sojat Road, Pali-Marwar). My host from this hamlet, who was also one of my key respondents, was a veterinary doctor. On holidays and the days he was on leave from work, he often took me to meet his relatives and affines in other nearby villages. He mostly preferred to be in the company of the other educated people of his community, who in any case could be counted on fingertips, maybe because he thought he could communicate with educated people far more easily than with herdspersons.

In one such visit to the village of Rajadand, I came in contact with a schoolteacher, who was the younger brother of my key respondent's son's prospective father-in-law. After the usual, pleasant conversations, he vexed me with a question (that in fact many anthropologists have reported of having been asked in the field) as to how my work was going to be of any help to them in the issues of the uplift of their community. A conversation pivoting on my role and the expectations from fieldworkers who throng their areas took an interesting turn when the school teacher said that the government had been unkind to the Raika of Rajasthan, for they have not been included in the list of the Scheduled Tribes while their brethren in Gujarat had been enjoying this status for a long time. When someone intervened with a comment that the camel-breeders of Gujarat, those who are Scheduled Tribes, call themselves Rabari, and not Raika, the schoolteacher said that there was no difference between the Raika and Rabari, and moreover, he observed, a Member of Parliament from Gujarat from this community chose 'Raika' as his surname. In Rajasthan, at that time, the Raika were included in the list of the semi-nomadic tribes.

The schoolteacher then defined my role – it should be to prepare a petition on behalf of the Raika of Rajasthan urging the government to consider them for granting the status of Scheduled Tribe. I was also advised to fix up as soon as possible a meeting of the Raika notables with the concerned politicians and government officials in Delhi. The schoolteacher wanted me to spearhead this movement on behalf of his people, because having worked with them, I was closely acquainted with the 'harsh reality' of their existence. Although ideally no anthropologist would like to involve himself in such issues – or become a 'spokesperson' of the community–such situations are unavoidable. Notwithstanding the premises of a dispassionate understanding, value-neutrality, and objectivity, the fieldworkers get entangled in all matters of 'working with the community'. I also drafted a petition, arguing why Raika are a 'tribe' and belong to the same stock as the Rabari of Gujarat, and therefore, they should be accorded the status of a Scheduled Tribe in Rajasthan, along with the other tribes, such as the Mina, Girasia, Bhil, Saharia, etc. However, before the petition could be moved, the Raika came to be included in the list of the Other Backward Classes (OBCs) of Rajasthan when the V.P. Singh government accepted the recommendations of the Mandal Commission Report on the OBCs in 1990. A semi-nomadic community became an OBC, as a consequence of which the demand for a Scheduled Tribe status came to be shelved. However, it is far from being dead, and as I have learnt from my periodic visits to the field areas, many educated Raika feel that their status as an OBC has not really helped them in any concrete ways as it was expected, and perhaps, their designation as a Scheduled Tribes would have had far-reaching consequences. For the herdsmen, these administrative designations do not have any implication for their occupation and problems. They are more concerned with the availability of grazing grounds for their animals and better economic deal for the pastoral products (milk, animal hair, live animals, etc) that they contribute to the market.

References

Agarwal, Anil. 1985. Beyond pretty trees and tigers. *South Asian Anthropologist*, 6 (1): pp. 25-40.

Bose, A.B. 1975. Pastoral nomadism in India. In: Leshnik and Sontheimer (Eds).

Bulliet, R. 1975. *The Camel and the Wheel.* Harvard University Press, Cambridge.

Chand, Lakhmi. 1891. *Tawarikh Jaisalmer.* (In Marwari.) Chirag Rajasthan Evam Rajputana Gazat Yantralaya, Ajmer.

Choksi, Archana and Dyer, Caroline. 1996. *Pastoralism in a Changing World: Patterns of Adaptation Among the Rabari of Kutch Gujarat.* Issues paper no. 69. International Institute for Environment and Development, London.

Crooke, W. 1896. *The Tribes and Castes of the North-Western India.* Cosmo, Delhi (Reprint) (1975).

Dandetha, Vijay. 1987. *Batan Ri Phulwari.* (In Marwari.) Rupayan Sansthan, Borunda.

Dyer, Caroline and Choksi, Archana. 1997. Research report: literacy for migrants, an ethnography of literacy acquisition among nomads of Kutch. *Compare.* 27(2): pp. 217-29.

Elson, V.C. 1979. *Dowries from Kutch: A Women's Folk Art Tradition in India.* Museum of Cultural History, California.

Enthoven, R.E. 1920, 1921, 1922. *Tribes and Castes of Bombay* (Vols. 1-3) Cosmo, Delhi (Reprint).

Fratkin, Elliot. 1997. Pastoralism: governance and development issues. *Annual Review of Anthropology*, 26: pp. 235-61.

Galanter, Marc. 1984. *Competing Equalities, Law and Backward Class in India.* Oxford University Press, Delhi.

George, Shanti. 1985. *Operation Flood. An Appraisal of Current Indian Dairy Policy.* Oxford University Press, Delhi.

Ibbetson, Denzil. 1914. *A Glossary of the Tribes and Castes of the Punjab and North-west Frontier Province* (Vol. 3). Civil and Military Gazette Press. Lahore.

Ibbetson, Denzil. 1987. *Punjab Castes: Races, Castes and Tribes of the People of Punjab.* Cosmo, Delhi (Reprint).

Jodha, N.S. 1988. *The Decline of Common Property Resources in Rajasthan, India.* Pastoral Development Network Paper, 22c. Overseas Development Institute, London.

Köhler-Rollefson, Ilse. 1993. Camels and camel pastoralism in Arabia. *Biblical Archaeologist,* 56(4): pp. 180-8.

Köhler-Rollefson, Ilse. 1995. Rajasthan's camel pastoralists and NGOs: the views from the bottom. In: *Social Aspects of Sustainable Dryland Management.* Daniel Stiles (Ed.). John Wiley & Sons Ltd., England.

Köhler-Rollefson, Ilse and Rathore, H.S. 1996. The Malvi camel: A newly discovered breed from India. *Animal Genetic Resources Information,* 18: pp. 31-42.

Leshnik, L.S. and Sontheimer, G-D. (Eds). 1975. *Pastoralists and Nomads in South Asia.* Otto Harrassowitz, Wiesbaden.

Makhijani, H.J. 1957. *Nomadic Cattle Breeders in India.* New Delhi.

Mankad, B.L. 1939. Rabaris of Kathiawad - a social study. *Journal of the University of Bombay,* 7: pp. 31-79.

Rao, Aparna and Michael J. Casimir. 2003. Nomadism in South Asia, An Introduction. In: *Nomadism in South Asia.* Aparna Rao and Michael J. Casimir (Eds). Oxford University Press, Delhi, pp. 1-38.

Salzman, P.C. 1985. Cooperation in herding castes. Paper presented in *Workshop on Cooperative Enterprises and Rural Development in India.* Department of Sociology, University of Delhi.

Salzman, P.C. 1986. Shrinking pasture for Rajasthani pastoralists. *Nomadic Peoples,* 2: pp. 49-61.

Salzman, P.C. 2004. *Pastoralism.* Colorado: Westview Press.

Shah, A.M. 1969. Urgent research in social anthropology: Some points for discussion. In: *Urgent Research in Social Anthropology.* B.L. Abbi and S. Saberwal (Eds.). Indian Institute of Advanced Study, Simla.

Sharma, G.N. 1970. *Rajasthan Studies.* Lakshmi Narayan Agrawal Educational Publishers, Agra.

Sherring, M.A.: 1879. *Hindu Tribes and Castes.* Cosmo, Delhi (1974).

Singh, Karni. 1974. *The Relation of the House of Bikaner with the Central Powers,* 1465- 1949. Munshiram Manoharlal, New Delhi.

Singh, Ram, Pareek, Suryakaran and Swami, Narottamdas. 1997. *Dhola Maru Ra Duha.* (In Hindi and Marwari). Rajasthani Granthagar, Jodhpur.

Sopher, David, E. 1975. Indian pastoral castes and livestock ecologies: A geographical analysis. In: Leshnik and Sontheimer (Eds).

Srivastava, V. K. 1987. Some issues in the anthropology of development. *Man in India,* 67(4): pp. 317-34.

Srivastava, V.K. 1999. Renunciation from Below. In: *Institutions and Inequalities, Essays in Honour of André Béteille*. Ramachandra Guha and Jonathan Parry (Eds). Oxford University Press, Delhi, pp. 171-208.

Srivastava, V.K. 2000. Social anthropology of pastoral nomads, the Raika *jati* and its dharmic order. *Journal of Human Ecology,* 11 (4): 281-98.

Srivastava, V.K. 2004. The Indian village. In: *Issues and Themes in Anthropology*. Vinay Kumar Srivastava and Manoj Kumar Singh (Eds). Delhi: Palaka Prakashan.

Srivastava, V.K. 2005. Review of Aparna Rao and Michael Casimir (eds), *Nomadism in South Asia*. *Anthropos,* 100 (1): pp. 290-2.

Srivastava, V.S. 1981. The iconography of the Ustravahini Devi. In: *Cultural Contours of India.* V.S. Srivastava (Ed.). Abhinav Publishers, New Delhi.

Tambs-Lyche, H. 1997. *Power, Profit and Poetry, Traditional Society in Kathiawar, Western India.* Manohar, Delhi.

Tod, James. 1829, 1832. *Annals and Antiquities of Rajasthan, or the Central and Western Rajpoot States of India* (Vols. 1 & 2). Routledge and Kegan Paul Ltd., London.

Westphal-Hellbusch, S. 1974. *Hillduistische viehzuchter im Nordwestlichen Indien. I: Die Rabari.* Duncker und Humboldt, Berlin.

Westphal-Hellbusch, S. 1975. Changes in meaning of ethnic names as exemplified by the Jat, Rabari, Bharvad, and Charan in northwestern India. In: Leshnik and Sontheimer (Eds.).

Official Publications

1888. *Gazetteer of the Bombay Presidency.* Bombay: Government Press.

n.d. *What is the future for the pastoralists of Rajasthan? A Proposal and Action Plan.* League for Pastoral Peoples (with Lokhit Pashu Palak Sansthan).

1891. *Report of the Census of Marwar and Mallani.* Jodhpur Government Press.

1891. *Report Mardumshumari Raj Marwar (Raj Marwar Census).* Jodhpur: Census Press.

1913-4. *Administrative Reports of Bikaner.* Bikaner: Government Press.

1987. *Annual Report.* Bikaner: National Research Centre on Camel.

1980 *Statistical Abstracts of India.* Government of India Publication.

n.d. *Village Survey Monographs, Village Pachhatardi.* Census of India, 1961. Gujarat: Superintendent of Census Operations.

1966. *District Gazetteer of Jaisalmer.* Government of India Publications.

1989. *Report of the Sub-committee for Studying the Problems and Suggesting the Remedial Measures for the Salinity Ingress in the Banni Area of Kutch District.* Gandhinagar: Government of Gujarat Water Resource Department, Central Design Organization.

1994. *Resource Atlas of Rajasthan.* Department of Science and Technology, Jaipur.

Part - III

Fishing communities

The fisher folk movement in Goa: A conflict between tradition and modernity

R.B. Patil, Rekha Gaonkar and Maria Rodrigues

Introduction

In recent years, fishing activity all over the world has experienced a dramatic transformation in terms of mechanisation, motorisation, commercialisation and so on. In India too, fishing sector has been affected by this global pattern of modernisation. In an effort to provide cheap source of protein to improve the health of the people, the government put considerable emphasis on expanding the fishing sector during the Fifties. From 1960 onwards, however, this focus shifted largely to increasing the fish production for boosting the exports. To achieve this objective, it adopted the policy of providing subsidies for trawlers and improving the port facilities (Johnson: 2001:1096). Thus, today's fishing activity is characterised by indiscriminate exploitation of marine resources through huge investment, high technology and complex organisation to meet the needs of national and international markets.

This modernisation process of fisheries in India has affected the traditional fisher folk in several ways. The community-based fish catching occupation of these fisher folk has come under severe pressures of mechanization and commercialization. The traditional fisher folk community normally belonging to low economic and caste groups are marginalised since skills and resource-wise they are ill-equipped to carry out mechenised fishing. The problem of displacement, depletion of marine resources and ecological disturbance are the direct outcome of the deliberate modernisation process initiated by the government.

The policy of subsidies, concessions and special facilities pursued by the government to promote and encourage export oriented mechanized fishing has led to the dualistic kind of development of the fisheries sector. This can be largely attributed to the development of mechanized fishing at the cost of the traditional fishing. The deep-sea fishing and aquaculture have increased the woes of the traditional fisher folk. This phenomenon has created simmering discontentment and unrest among the traditional fisher folk communities. Consequently, many well-organized traditional fisher folk organisations have emerged in the coastal states of India to protect the interests of the artisan fisher folk (Johnson: 2001:1096)

In this paper, an attempt has been made to understand the genesis of the traditional fisher folk movement in Goa. In doing so, it throws light on the ideology, leadership, mobilisation and other aspects of the movement. It also deals with the study of modernization of fishing activity in Goa and its impact on traditional fishing community. It is largely based on the information derived from the secondary sources like books, articles, newspapers and also booklets, souvenir, pamphlets etc published by the Goenchea Rampankarancho Ekvott (GRE)[1] and some personal informal discussions with the leaders of the GRE.

Fishing in Goa: Some facts and figures

Goa has a coastline of 104 kms. and about 250 kms. inland waterways and 4000 hectares of marshy lands along the banks of its numerous estuaries (Government of Goa: 2000:1). This has provided a vast potential for fishing activity in Goa. There are 8 talukas and 42 villages (marine) involved in fishing (Directorate of Fisheries, Government of Goa: 2000). There are about 8000 fishermen households with a population of about 48,000. The average size of the fishermen family is 6 (Sehara, et al: 1992:242). The table below gives information about fish production and mechanised and country crafts in Goa.

A short description of fisher folk community would be useful for a fair understanding of fishing activities in Goa. The fisher folk in Goa belong to both Hindu and Catholic religious communities. Among the Hindus, the *Kharvis* and *Gabits* are the prominent fishing communities. The Hindu fishing community is largely found in the northern part of Goa.

Fishing vessels and fish catch

Year	Fish Production (in Tonnes)	Estimated Value (Rs.in lakhs)	Mechanised Crafts	Country Crafts
1961-62	17,000	78	4	4125
1970-71	36,616	900	110	3600
1980-81	25,715	985	186	2887
1985-86	27,711	1250	600	2450
1990-91	56,225	2850	707	2000
1992-93	97,014	4750	764	2000
1995-96	85,418	5400	880	1980
1997-98	94,547	6608	1056	1840
1998-99	70,710	10061	1092	1890
1999-00	63,440	9068	1092	2194
2000-01	68,133	15793	1128	1963
2001-02	73,135	16544	1128	1963

Source : D'Souza, Joe. 2002. "Fishing woes to the fore", *Goa Today*, 37(4): 17.

The *Gabit* fisher folk communities live in the Konkan region of Karnataka, Goa and Maharashtra. They consider themselves the original inhabitants of Goa (Mandal : 1993 : 112). The *Gabit* community is mainly located in the coastal areas of Canacona, Salcete and Pernem talukas of Goa (Ibid). As most of them are landless, they are the tenants of their landlords. The elders teach the art of fishing to the younger generation. After reaching the age of ten, the boys are taken to the sea to assist in the catch. The community is not educationally advanced. The *Gabits* are non-vegetarian. Though, their staple food is fish curry and rice, they occasionally eat meat of goat, sheep, hare, deer and fowl. There is a clear division of labour among the *Gabits* based on sex. Men are involved in fishing and women are generally engaged in selling the fish caught by the male members. They are also engaged in collecting the shellfish. The *Gabits* mostly live in the joint families. However, in recent times there are signs of their disintegration leading to the emergence of nuclear families. The *Gabits* follow the Hindu law of inheritance. Marriages within the *'kul'* are prohibited and the monogamous forms of marriages prevail in the community.

The Catholic fisher folk, locally called Kharvis, are mostly settled along the coastal belts of Salcete, Mormugao and Tiswadi Talukas.

Their mother tongue is *Konkani* written in the Roman script. A few persons of the older generation have some knowledge of Portuguese language too (Rao: 1993). The *Kharvis* mostly belong to the Catholic *Shudra* caste. Like their fellow fisher folk communities, the staple food of the Catholic Kharvis is rice and fish curry. Meat, vegetables and milk also constitute an important part of their diet. The *Kharvis* practice monogamous system of marriage. The parallel-cousin marriages are normally not permitted. Though arranged marriages are a common practice, marriages by consent are also prevalent. Legal divorces are allowed and both widow and widower re-marriages are permitted (Rao: 1993). The joint family is a common form among them but in line with the recent trends, the joint families are disintegrating giving way to the emergence of nuclear families. The influence of modernisation and westernisation is largely responsible for this social change. Many of the young and moderately educated *Catholic Kharvi* boys are migrating to the Gulf countries to earn fast money. This money is normally used to construct their own R.C.C. bungalows and to establish their own business, which ultimately ends up in the break up of the original families.

Fishing is a traditional and primary occupation of the *Kharvis* that is usually carried out by a group of about 25 fishermen. Each group has a nickname like *Chayabe, Dumgale, Pequeno, Baro, Chadenkar, Marale, and Kodibiyale,* etc. Each group owns a fishing boat, net and big shed on the seashore. The license for fishing is issued in the name of the group. All members of the group share the day's catch equally (Rao: 1993). The *Catholic Kharvi* woman plays multiple roles. In addition to her household chores, she performs the task of selling and drying the fish and also works as an agricultural labourer. The traditional fishermen communities are socially and economically backward.

Thus, since time immemorial fishing is one of the major occupations of the people in Goa. In fact, fish has become an integral part of life of the people. Fish is a staple food for not only for the fishing communities but also for about 95 per cent of the total population of Goa. It has provided a quality food and sustainable income to thousands of people for centuries. Like agriculture, fishing in Goa was rather a way of life as it was done mainly for consumption purpose. It was not viewed as a business though it was a source of livelihood for many. The traditional fishermen were involved in subsistence and sustainable fishing. The traditional methods like *Rampon*[2] and *Gillnets* were used in fishing. As a tradition, there was a total abstinence from fishing activity during the major part of the monsoon. Thus, traditional fishing was in perfect harmony with the eco-system.

Fishing has not only provided a direct source of employment but it has also induced many other allied activities. The preservation of fish is another traditional household industry. Many are also engaged in net repair (Eco Forum: 1993:82). The members of the traditional fishing community are engaged in making fish pickles, *balcho*[3] and *parra*[4].

Barring few trawlers engaged by the Portuguese Government, fishing activity before liberation was carried out with non-mechanised boats (Angle: 2001:87). However, with the liberation of Goa in 1961 the process of development began in all the sectors including fishing. Since then, the fishing sector has undergone rapid growth and development. It has been subjected to intensive and rapid mechanisation during the last 2-3 decades. With the emergence of new opportunities for export trade and higher profitability on investment, more and more mechanised vessel were added year after year taking advantage of the institutional credit and liberal subsidies, concessions and other facilities extended by the government. This is clear from the fact that the number of mechanised boats has increased from around just 4 in 1961-62 to 1128 in 2001-2002. On the other hand, the number of country crafts has come down from 4125 in 1961-62 to 1963 in 2001-2002 (D' Souza: 2002:17). The deep-sea fishing and aquaculture were the other steps taken by the Government to increase production and export of fish. There are about 47 licensed farms of aquaculture covering an area of 200 hectares (Barbosa and Alexander: 2002:14).

These developments in the fishing sector have created adverse conditions to the traditional fisher folk. *It has led to the entry of non-fishermen into the fishing occupation with the sole motive of making maximum profit. It has given way to the lopsided development of the fisheries as mechanised fishing received priority at the cost of the non-mechanised fishing.* The policies of the government have posed a threat to the fish production of the traditional fishermen. Indiscriminate and over fishing and fishing in rivers and within 5 kms. from the coast and also fishing during monsoon period by the mechanised boats are the other problems faced by the traditional fishermen. As per the recommendation of the Food and Agriculture Organisation of the United Nations, there should be 30 trawlers per 10 kms. of coastline. Considering the 104 kms. length of coastline in Goa, the number of trawlers should be around 315. But today Goa has around 1128 mechanised boats (Barbosa and Alexander: 2002:12). This has endangered the sustainable exploitation of the marine resources. *The pollution of seawater due to effluents from the industries, five star hotels, urban settlements and shrimp farming activities has adversely affected the bio-productivity.* The increase in levels of pollution has reduced the availability of the fish. All these factors have created discontent and unrest among the traditional fisher folk.

Emergence of the GRE and movement of the fishermen in Goa

Though the process of mechanisation of fishing sector in Goa started way back in 1964, it gained real momentum only during the last three decades. The rapid mechanisation process resulted in the massive growth in the number of mechanised boats and there ensued a struggle between traditional fisher folk and the owners of mechanised boats over the control of marine resources. As there was a strong lobby among the politicians owning trawlers, the efforts of the traditional fisher folk to solve their problems through discussion and negotiation with the government failed. This failure to solve the problems democratically created a sense of letdown among the artisan fisher folk. This caught the attention of the enlightened people both among the fishermen community and outside. They felt a need to form an organisation to protect the interests of the traditional fisher folk. Thus, the organisation of the traditional fishermen called in vernacular language, Goenchea Ramponkaracho Ekvott (GRE) came into existence in December 1975.

Organisational structure, membership, ideology and mobilisation pattern of the GRE

The GRE does not have an elaborate organisational structure, which indicates that its founders attached lesser importance to the formal form. The issues of the movement appear to have gained priority over the structure.

At the state level, the GRE consists of a President, Vice- President, Secretary, General Secretary, Treasurer and Members. At the village level there are Vice -Presidents and members. The membership is restricted to the traditional fishermen. It has the members belonging to the traditional fisher folk communities like Ramponkars, Magkars, Cantaikars, Pagelkars and Arrikars[5], etc. Thus, the organisation represents solely the traditional fisher folk communities of Goa.

A membership fee of Rs. 10/- is collected annually from each member. This appears to be the main source of income of the organisation. The meeting of the organisation is held on 5th of every month in the office located at Cansaulim to discuss the issues and problems concerning the traditional fishermen.

The ideological contentions of the GRE are best brought out by an Eco Forum publication entitled, *Fish Curry and Rice* (1993:89) in the following words:

> "The sea is a resource which the Ramponkars are dependent upon and which they exploit in harmony with the environment. Mechanised fishing, on the other hand, relies on ecologically harmful methods of catching fish and will result in depletion of fish resources. Also, in a labour-surplus economy like India, traditional Rampon fishing makes far more sense than capital-intensive mechanised fishing. Finally, it is Rampon fishing, which in the long- run will result in increased catches – the ceiling for trawlers has already been shot through. Thus, one could summarise the GRE's arguments as being based on three sound grounds – ecological, technological and economic'".

As stated by one of the leaders, Mathany Saldanha, the GRE is not against mechanisation but "mechanisation should go where human hands cannot reach". His argument is that whereas the traditional fishing is based on subsistence and sustenance,the mechanised fishing is based on maximum exploitation and money making. Thus, the ideology of the GRE is based on the concept of sustainable development. The rights of the traditional fishermen need to be protected and preserved, as they are dependent on them since time immemorial.

The mobilization pattern is largely based on holding meetings to create awareness among the traditional fishermen about their rights and adverse effects of mechanization. It has also tried to get the support of freedom fighters, MLAs and others sympathizing the cause of the traditional fishermen. It has succeeded also in mobilizing the fisher women mostly involved in the sale of fish by taking up their issues pertaining to marketing.

Major issues

The GRE has tried to address both local and national level issues confronting the traditional fisher folk.

The immediate issue before the GRE was fishing by trawlers and purseiners very close to the shore, which was traditionally the fishing area of the traditional fishermen. This had posed a threat to the livelihood of the traditional fisher folk. The mechanised fishing endangered the century old fishing rights of the traditional fishermen over the coastline. Over fishing, low catch, displacement and ecological disturbance were the other negative consequences of over mechanization. Therefore, the GRE demanded a ban on fishing by the mechanized vessels within 5 kms from the shore and also on night fishing. Their demand was that the traditional fishermen should be given right to fish within zero to five kilometers without the intervention of any mechanized vessel. They wanted a legislation to be enacted in this regard. After a long drawn out struggle in the form of mass hunger strikes, processions and *dharnas,* both at the local and national level, the GRE succeeded in getting the Marine Fishing Regulation Act passed in 1980. The Goa, Daman and Diu Marine Fishing Regulation Act 1980 [Act No. 3 of 1981], though not fully welcomed by the GRE, conceded the long pending demand of regulating fishing by fishing vessels in the sea along the coastline of Union Territory of Goa, Daman and Diu. Clause 4 in the chapter II gave power to regulate, restrict or prohibit certain matters within the specified area. Under chapter 1, 2 [h] "specified area" means such area in the sea along the entire coastline of the Union Territory or such portion of it, but not beyond the territorial waters as may be specified by the Government by the notification in the official Gazette (Government of Goa, Daman and Diu, Law Deapartment Notification LD/6/34, 1981).

In line with the provisions of the Act, the Goa Government issued a notification 2-1-81-FSH [III] barring fishing in an area of 5 kms.

from the coast along the entire coastline of the Union Territory. The GRE took initiative in bringing together the leaders of fisher folk of other coastal states. In 1978, a national level organization called, National Forum for Catamaran and Country Boat Fishermen's Rights and Marine Wealth, which is presently known as National Fish Worker's Forum (NFF), was established to put up united fight to protect the rights and interests of the traditional fishermen. The General Secretary of the GRE, Mathany Saldanha, was the founder chairman of this organization (Souvenir: 1995). In April 1980, there was a major clash between trawler owners and traditional fishermen. Trawler owners burnt about six rampons at different places. Many traditional fishermen along with their leader, Mathany Saldanha, were arrested and jailed. The violent agitation led to police firing, an incident that perturbed the peaceful Goan public. It is these agitations of the GRE that forced the government to pass the Act.

The enactment of the law banning fishing within a range of 0-5 kms from the shore and a total monsoon ban did not end the woes of the traditional fisher folk. The trawler owners challenged the Goa, Daman and Diu Marine Fishing Regulation Act of 1980 in the Supreme Court. The Supreme Court in its interim order reduced the ceiling on fishing area from 5 kms to 2½ kms and imposed a total ban on night fishing. This relaxation on the limit of fishing area was applicable to only those trawlers, which were technologically incapable of fishing beyond 2 kms. This litigation was pending in the Supreme Court for over 12 years. During this period the trawler owners, violating the interim order of the Court, continued to fish in the shallow waters. The traditional fisher folk too continued their nation wide agitation for the implementation of Marine Regulation Act, 1980. Finally, in 1994 after receiving a report from the State Government, which it had asked in its 1993 order, the Supreme Court passed an order banning the mechanized fishing within 5 kms. from the shore. It also empowered the State to make the rules to conserve marine ecology by banning mechanized fishing during monsoon season (GRE Souvenir: 1995).

The order of the Supreme Court also did not bring the much-needed relief to the traditional fisher folk as large-scale violations of the Act continued to occur. This once again became a rallying point for the traditional fishermen to wage a fierce struggle with the trawler owners. The GRE continued its pressure on the Government for the implementation of the laws banning fishing within 5 kms from the shore and also during the monsoon. It demanded the appointment of marine police to enforce the 5 km law (News letter : GRE 2001). The GRE felt that the traditional fishermen are the victims of the Government policies, which led to their impoverishment and loss of employment among the fisher folk. The lack of will on the part of the Government to strictly enforce the laws resulted in the loss of trust of the traditional fisher folk in the Government. This lackadaisical approach of the Government is said to be due to the existing strong lobby within the Government and opposition parties favouring the trawlers and purseiners. Many politicians themselves are the owners of the trawlers. Therefore, the fishermen themselves started apprehending the trawlers violating the laws. A violating trawler was dashed against the rocks causing severe damage in the course of this agitation. Sensing the seriousness of the situation the Government called the meeting of the traditional fisher folk and trawler owners to find a solution. In this meeting, the Government assured the traditional fisher folk of strict enforcement of the ban on trawling and purseining within 5 kms. from the shore and also on mechanised fishing from June to August (Souvenir : GRE : 1995). But a subsequent Government Notification reduced the monsoon ban to 24th July (Government Gazette Series 1, No. 15 dated 18/07/1995). This action of the Government aroused the public suspicion about the sincerity of the Government arbitration. It only confirmed the GRE suspicion that the Government was dancing to the tune of the rich trawler owners. The public apprehension that the Government may further reduce the monsoon ban period invited a public interest litigation (PIL) in the year 2000 in the Panjim bench of the Bombay High Court (Fishing File : Advocate Norma Alvares, Goa Foundation, Mapusa).

The PIL led to a series of developments like the High Court restoring the monsoon ban period from June to August and the angry legislators proposing an amendment to the Goa, Daman and Diu Marine Fishing Regulation Act 1980. The arguments and the counter arguments against this Amendment created such a major controversy that the Governor of Goa refused to give his assent to the amending Bill. In the light of this conflict, the mechanized boat owners made a strong plea for the reduction of the monsoon fishing ban period as the special type of "solar shrimp" was available only during the July month, which brought the much needed revenue to the mechanized boat owners who have been claiming of heavy debt (Herald, 25th July, 2000 Goa). However, the violation of the ban on fishing within territorial waters and fishing at night and during monsoon continues unabated. These issues continue to increase the antagonism between the traditional fisher folk and trawler owners. All these issues made the Government to shed its lethargic approach. It fixed the monsoon ban period from 1st June to 10th August. The Government also assured a strict implementation of the said order.

Besides, the deep-sea fishing policy of the Government of India has also caused resentment among the traditional fisher folk. The GRE has been agitating over this issue on the following grounds:

1. As supported by scientific studies, the commercial fish varieties in our water are very limited.
2. The foreign deep sea fishing vessels having gigantic capacity of halving fish has caused fish famine and destruction of marine ecology in many parts of the world. These sophisticated vessels have destroyed the fishing grounds in whole of Europe, the great parts of North and South America and parts of Asia. They will create the same type of disaster on the Indian waters and in *Indian Exclusive Economic* Zone (IEEZ).
3. The fishermen of Goa are capable of fishing in the deep sea. They almost fish side by side with the foreign fishing vessels in 150-meter depths. If the facilities like echo sounders, G.P.S wireless sets, diesel at international market price, etc are provided, the existing fishing vessels of fisher folk of Goa can provide ten times more foreign exchange than the fishing vessels of the so called foreign joint ventures.
4. The foreign fishing vessels are required to fish beyond 24 kms but quite often they are found fishing in the territorial waters. Many a times, they destroy/damage the nets of traditional and mechanised fisher folk.
5. All the workers from technical to manual labour on these joint venture vessels are foreigners. But in our case all the employees are Indian, which helps to mitigate the ever-growing unemployment problem of our country.

6. The foreign fishing vessels are dumping large amount of commercially uneconomical variety of fish in the high seas, whereas our domestic fishing boats make the same fish available in our domestic market for consumption to our protein deficient people of India. These vessels have no concern to conserve the bio-diversify of marine life.
7. From the time of introduction of foreign fishing vessels, many commercially viable fish species have been reduced by half. We are not able to make fishing economical as the catches are getting reduced day by day.
8. The foreign fishing vessels trade from the high seas on which the Government of India has no control in terms of amount of fish and its value, which is a loss to the nation.
9. The joint venture vessels are supposed to declare the quantity of fish catch which is normally not done leading to loss of foreign exchange in crores of rupees.
10. To help and protect the domestic fisher folk of Goa, both mechanised and traditional, and other ancillary jobs like fish vendors, transporters, freezers, exporters and consumers, the policy of allowing joint venture in fisheries sector needs to be abandoned (GRE Memorandum: 3-1-1996).

With these arguments against the deep-sea fishing by foreign vessels, the GRE along with other fisher folk organisations of the coastal states started agitation for the cancellation of the deep-sea fishing policy. Many *dharnas,* processions and *bandhs* were held to protest against the policy of the Government. It supported and participated in all the activities of the National Fisheries Action Committee against joint ventures. The fisher folk of India were agitating for the implementation of the recommendations of the Sub-Committee of the Review Committee appointed by the Central Government. These Committees have concluded that the deep sea fishing policy of the Government of India is against the interests of Indian fisheries and therefore, needs to be cancelled. Though the Central Government did not cancel its policy totally, it stopped issuing new licenses to the foreign fishing vessels due to the opposition of the fisher folk.

The GRE has also opposed, tooth and nail, the Aquaculture Authority Bill (AAB) 1997. The organisation stated that the Bill intends to restore the industrial shrimp agriculture, which is ecologically harmful. The Bill is a violation of the Coastal Regulation Zone Notification of 1991 and the direction of the Supreme Court judgment dated 11th December 1996. This judgement ordered the closure of destructive aquaculture farms. The GRE characterised the AAB as anti-people, contrary to the Environment Protection Act and to the welfare of the rural population living in the coastal areas. It argued that the industrial shrimp agriculture farm would affect the livelihood of the people of coastal areas adversely. The GRE strongly opposed any change in Coastal Regulation Zone (CRZ) notification of 1991 and also any construction within 200 metres from high tide zone. The GRE stated, "*We do not need any artificial aquaculture in Goa as natural methods used for centuries in cultivating fish are good enough and ecologically sound*" (GRE News letter). Thus, the traditional fisher folk asked the Central Government to withdraw the AAB, 1997 pending before the *Rajya Sabha* and also the 1997 Notification issued by the Ministry of Environment and Forest amending the CRZ Notification of 1991. They also demanded the implementation of the 1996 judgment of the Supreme Court on Aquaculture.

The GRE has also taken up many local issues of the traditional fisher folk. It had demanded the supply of 30 lit. kerosene per day to each motorboat owner at subsidised rate under the special quota (GRE letter to Minister of Civil Supplies, 30.04.97). It had lodged a protest against sand removal from the south coast. Its protest was based on the ground that the sand removal has caused large-scale erosion of land along the coast that may ultimately end up in the loss of beaches (GRE letter to concerned Government Authorities, 17-05-98). The organisation had opposed the establishment of Water Sports Institute at Caranzalem bay. The GRE felt that the opening of Sports Institute would affect the fishing operations of about 2500 traditional fisher folk, thus, denying their source of livelihood. Further, the water sports activities will gradually turn the Caranzalem bay into a docking area for the sports vessels, which means the traditional fisher folk will be unable to carry on their fishing activities (GRE letter to the Chief Minister, 15-09-2001). The issue of marketing place for the fish, shifting of old fish market, high costs of stalls at new market place, etc. were also taken up by the GRE. It has been opposing the Government's decision to allow shacks, umbrellas and resting beds on the sea beach as they block and obstruct the fishing activity.

Thus, the thrust areas of agitation of the GRE are:

1. Mechanised fishing in rivers and within the territorial waters of the State.
2. Pollution of sea water due to industrial aquaculture and mechanised fishing activities resulting in depletion of marine resources and disappearance of some species of fish.
3. Failure of the Government to strictly enforce the laws.
4. Encroachment of tourism on the fishing activities.
5. Fishing during monsoon.
6. Over fishing leading to reduction in fish production over the years (GRE: The Reports and Demands: 27-02-2001).

Fishing issue: A perennial conflict

The conflict between *Ramponkars* and the mechanised fishermen is a fall out of the worldwide conflict between modernization and tradition. However, in Goa this conflict has its own peculiarities and dimensions. The apathy of the Government and the existence of vested interests are perhaps the most significant factors responsible for this long-standing issue. In an interview with one of the authors of this paper, Mathany Saldanha pointed out that the Government's apathy comes from the fact that many of the politicians have become trawler owners directly or in the benami names. The Government failed to ban mechanised fishing within five kms till the GRE pressurised the Central Government to adopt a national law to protect ecology and to ban mechanised fishing within five km. limit, an area in which the artisan fishermen have been traditionally fishing. Fisheries being the State subject, the Central Government was unable to enact a uniform law. It circulated a draft on Marine Regulations Bill to all the states leaving the State Legislative Assemblies to enact their own legislation. The Goa, Daman and Diu Marine Fishing Regulation Act 1980 became a bone of contention between two rival groups. The GRE claims that this was an attempt to satisfy the vested interests of the legislators.

The apathy of the Government was exposed by the confusing notification that went on changing the period of fishing ban. This further strengthened the suspicion of the artisan fishermen that the Government was trying to satisfy the rich trawler owners. The renewal of the conflict in the year 2000 and a series of PILs that came up before the Bombay High Court, Panji Bench have highlighted the fact that the Government had fixed the ban period without proper "application of mind" and without any "scientific data". One of the PILs accused the Government of aligning itself with strong lobby of the mechanised boat owners.

Taking the cognisance of the PIL, the High Court directed the Director of National Institute of Oceanography (NIO) to file an affidavit based on the material available as to the breeding season of the fish. It also directed the Fisheries Department, Government of Goa, Daman and Diu to give information on the ban period imposed by the coastal states of Kerala, Gujarat, Karanatka and Maharashtra. The affidavit submitted by the Director of Fisheries revealed that the ban period varies from state to state and the affidavit submitted by the NIO showed that different fishes have different breeding seasons.

On the basis of this information, the Court ordered that the ban period should be from 1st June to 15th August. However, the trawler owners who feel that it is detrimental to their interests have vehemently contested the ban period of 76 days. They argue that a long wait for the catch is a great loss of income. The solar shrimp, which is the main source of income, is available only during June and July. The trawler owners feel that this is the travesty of justice when the trawler owners from neghbouring states are fishing in Goa waters and going away with a big hawl. The trawler owners contend that the practical experience of sea does not require any scientific data. They also argue that if one goes by the NIO data, fishing in Goa will not be possible at all. They opined that given the pattern of the weather and the early break of monsoon, the High Court ban up to 15th August is irrelevant and had to be rectified. These were the considerations that made the Goa Assembly to propose an amendment to the Goa, Daman and Diu Fish Regulation Act, 1980 which nullified the order of the High Court.

These conflicting interests of the traditional and mechanised fisherman and the Government's failure to act as an impartial arbiter have been responsible for lack of an amicable solution to this knotty problem.

Conclusion

The demands of the traditional fisher folk are genuine from every point of view. They largely constitute the socially and economically backward section of the society. They have meagre resources and employ traditional methods of fishing. They have been fishing in the territorial waters since ancient times. They make their living by catching and selling fish. Their conditions are comparable to the marginalised sections of the Indian society. Given this background, they need the shield of the policy of protective discrimination. It would be ridiculous to ask the traditional fisher folk community to compete with both the Indian and foreign trawlers and purseiners. This is the primary issue dogging the artisan fisher folk.

Another question one needs to answer is whether we want a development that is sustainable or a short-lived development ending in disastrous consequences. The former would certainly be the best option. However, this option requires eco-friendly policies, which are lacking today. Therefore, the GRE is demanding the prohibition of selling of roe (egg) bearing fish from June to 15th August, artificial aquaculture, dumping of industrial and domestic wastes in the sea and netting of small fish. The sea is not infinite pool of living wealth. Food chain must be protected to protect men's needs (GRE letter to the Government of Goa, 17-3-99).

The issues raised by the traditional fishermen's organizations deserve the immediate attention of all the concerned people. The enduring larger good demands the solution of the problems of the traditional fishermen. The natural justice too demands the acceptance of the demands and recommendations of the traditional fisher folk community. Fisheries are bound to doom in the absence of pro-people and eco-friendly policies with emphasis on sustainable development.

Notes

1. *Goenchea Ramponkarncho Ekvott* is a *Konkani* name meaning 'Goa Beach Net-Fisherman's Union'.
2. *Rampon* means beach-seine.
3. *Balcho*-A type of fish pickle made of prawns.
4. *Parra*-A type of fish pickle made of any fish.
5. *Ramponkars, Magkars, Cantaikars, Pagelkars* and *Arrikars* are the names of the traditional communities involved in fishing.

References

Angle, Prabhakar. 2001. Goa: *An economic update,* Mumbai, *The* Goa Hindu Association.

Barbosa, Alexander M. 2002. "Fishing for a high living", *Goa Today,* 37(4): 10-13.

D' Souza, Joe. 2002. "Fishing woes to the fore", *Goa Today,* 37(4): 14-18.

Eco-Forum. 1993. *Fish, curry and rice,* Mapusa , The Other India Press.

GRE. 1995. *Memorandum to the chairman, Murari Sub - Committee on deep-sea fishing,* dated 26-9-95.

Fishing file: Advocate Norma Alvares, Goa Foundation, Mapusa.

Gomantak Times. 2000. July- August.

Herald. 2000. July-August.

GRE. 1996. *Memorandum to Chairman,* Committee on Petitions (Lok Sabha), dated 03-01-96.

GRE. 1997. Demand for supply of kerosene for fishing activities, *Letter to the Minister for Civil Supplies*, dated 30-04-97.

GRE. 1998. Complaint against sand removal from the South Coast, *Letter to the concerned Departments,* dated 17-05-98.

GRE. 1999.*Memorandom to the Governor of Goa* dated 17-03-99.

GRE. 1999. SOS to the Goa Government, *Letter to the Minister of Tourism and Fisheries,* dated 13-13-99.

GRE. 2001. *The reports and demands* dated 27-02-2001.

GRE. 2001. Memorandum to the MLAs and Councilors dated 24-08-2001.

GRE. 2001. The proposed Water Sports Institute at Caranzalem, *Letter to Chief Minister*, dated 15-09-2001.

GRE. *Letter to the Prime Minister regarding aquaculture*, undated.

GRE. 1995. Souvenir.

Editorial. 1994. "Fisher folk fight for survival", *Gomantak Times,* 23-11-94.

Editorial. 1996. "Fish in troubled water". *Gomantak Times,* 25-01-96.

Johnson, Deepak. 2001. 'Wealth and waste: Contrasting legacies of fisheries development since 1950's, *Economic and Political Weekly:* 36(13): 1095-1101.

Mahambre, Umesh. 2001. "Irrepressible voice of Ramponkars". Excerpts of interview with Mathany Saldanha, then General Secretary of GRE, *Navhind Times,* 17-06-01.

Mandal, Hrishikesh. 1993. '*Kharvi/Gabit* (Kshatriya Maratha)', pp. 112-117, in K.S. Singh (ed), *People of India – Goa,* Bombay, Popular Prakashan.

Rao, K.R. 1993. "Catholic Kharvi", pp. 112-117, in K.S. Singh (ed), *People of India* - Goa, Bombay, Popular Prakashan.

Samant, Rupesh. 2002. "Why bother us, we are Hodekars", Excerpts of interview with Ramakant Zuvatkar, leader of Hodekars, *Panorama,* 8-9-2002.

Sehara, D.B.S., et al. 1992. 'Socio-economic aspects of the monsoon fisheries of the west coast of India, *Bulletin of Central Marine Fisheries Research Institute,* Cochin. 4: 242-250.

Other documents referred to

Indian Fisheries Act, 1897 and the Goa Fisheries Rules 1981, Government Printing Press, Panjim Goa - S/121/1000-10/2000.

Government Gazette series 1, No. 15 dated 9-07-19981.

Government Gazette series 1, No. 5 dated 29th April, 1999.

Elementary structure of desire in south Indian kinship: The case of a fishing caste of coastal Andhra Pradesh

Charles W. Nuckolls

The Dravidian kinship system of south India has been characterized as an ideal never realized in practice, and therefore, fundamentally "incomplete" in its own terms (Trawick 1990). Men give up their mothers and sisters, and women give up their fathers and brothers, but the principle of cross-cousin marriage promises a return of the relinquished, if not directly then through substitution in the next generation. It is a very neat symmetrical system, at least in theory. But it can never be achieved, and, thus, the system shapes or gives rise to desires that are incompletely realized. South Indian kinship is not a static form upheld by shared rules, but a process maintained by unrelieved tensions, "its cyclicity that of a hunter following his own tracks" (Trawick: 1990:153).

What is desire in kinship? To seek an answer, we first dispense with the notion that kinship is a set of prescriptive rules or higher-order structural imperatives. Individuals in South India do not marry their cross-cousins simply because these are preferred arrangements, or because (at some higher level of generality) cross-cousin marriages sustain long-term alliances between intermarrying clans or lineages. Most people, in fact, are quite clear on this point: they marry their cross-cousins because they want. While it might be true that a desire of this kind is the consequence of a relational pattern, the one following the other as motivations follow structure, this explanation is far too simple. It assumes that any pattern, if it represents "tradition", naturally and inevitably genetates the desire to fulfil it. But desire is more complex than that-and this we know not just from Freud, but from social psychologists whose vocabulary for discussing the complexities of desire is exceedingly large: "ambivalence", "dissonance", "splitting", "rationalization", and "inner conflict", to name just a few.

The vocabulary of desire is rich in terms which assume the importance of emotional conflict. "Ambivalence" and all the rest refer to experiences of opposition, beginning with the one surely most human beings share: the wanting of things which are in conflict with each other. We cannot have both, yet we want them at the same time. Such a desire is most apparent, perhaps, when the desired objects are other human beings, since their desires are not simply one-sided but reciprocal, and, therefore, very complex. The most obvious case in point is the human infant. He or she desires "attachment", as Bowlby (1969) suggests, but must come to terms with the fact that the desired other (beginning with the mother) is not always available. One response is to construct a memory of the desired other, a "self object" which can be called up during the other's periods of absence. Sometimes, this is called "introjection." Another term used is to "split" the desired other into two parts, one representing the beneficent "good half," who withdraws affection and leaves. Both strategies, if one may call them that, are complex responses to desire, and reveal that desires are often in deep conflict.

But conflicting desires are also dynamically productive, as Obeyesekere(1981) has shown, since introjection and splitting can motivate cultural symbols such as the symbol of the mother goddess in South Asia. The goddess is typically dual, split into two images, one representing the "good mother" and other the "bad mother" (see also Kakar 1981). This is not to reduce the symbol to the workings of the dynamic unconscious, or to replace culture with psyche, but to call attention to the fact that symbols and meanings necessarily implicate desires, and that many deeply felt desires are also in conflict.

Putting "desire" at the centre instead of at the periphery of kinship is anthropologically new, and different from other approaches which, these days, tend to emphasize "power" and define kinship according to the strategies encoded in roles for the acquisition or maintenance of political positions in a field of limited good. Bourdieu (1977:43), for example, considers marriage rules socially disseminated "lies", whose purpose is to conceal the symbolic effects of strategies forced on people by economic and political necessities (see also LiPuma 1983). It is not the purpose of this paper to criticize these approaches, but to consider a crucial missing item: Desire in kinship.

What will this achieve? For one thing, it serves as a much-needed corrective to the tendency to view culture either as a network of finely spun symbolic linements (a view sometimes called "Geertzian") or as an assemblage of discursive strategies which people deploy or resist depending on their positions. Whatever their differences, such views usually end up eliminating or severely restricting the domain of the irrational in everyday life-probably because "the irrational" was claimed by Freud a long time ago, and both the symbol-centric anthropologists of the 1960s and the power-centric anthropologists of the 1990s formally eschew psychoanalysis. However, desire is usually irrational, and requires a different kind of conceptual vocabulary.

More than as a corrective, however, a theory of desire in kinship foregrounds the reality of deeply felt needs and wants. One hesitates to argue for the importance of a phenomenon based on the intuition (assumed to be shared) that it actually exists, yet in this case it would seem to be justified. People do feel strongly about the relationships that bind them together or pull them apart, and to regard these feelings as secondary or epiphenomenal is mistaken. In any case, to set the stage for the discussion that follows, I shall depend on this intuition only in passing. If that is asking too much, then one could imagine the task ahead as an experiment in theoretical understanding: If desire in kinship is central, and not epiphenomenal, then what consequences might follow for ethnographic description? Better still, what does a perspective that puts desire first and foremost tell us about kinship that otherwise we might not know?

As I suggested, the kind of desire I have in mind is of a particular type in which the experience of conflict is foregrounded. In English we have called this experience "ambivalence" ever since Freud coined the term. Of course the experience has been around far longer, and was characterized by Goethe (in the words of Faust) in considerably more poetic language:

> "You are aware of only one unrest; Oh, never learn to know the other! Two souls, alas, are dwelling in my breast, And one is striving to forsake its brother."

Faust struggles between his desires for carnal and spiritual knowledge, and resolves the conflict in favour of the former until he discovers that he has paid too high a price. What appeal would the poem have for us were it not for the ambivalence Faust experiences as he contemplates his choices? If the answer is that it would have less, the reason might be that Faustian choices inspire aesthetic enjoyment. Philosophers at the end of the Eighteenth century even had a word for this kind of enjoyment: they called it the "sublime". My purpose is not to argue a point of aesthetic theory, but to suggest that the poetics of kinship, as it were, might depend on a similar mechanism involving conflicted desires.

Specifically, I will argue that Dravidian kinship is motivated by a desire of a certain kind-call it the desire for "fusion" or "completeness". It is a desire that can never be fulfilled. The reason is in logic of the kinship system, which promises completeness. Brothers hold fast to their unity as members of the same partilineal household, but invariably destroy that unity when they divide, as they must, to form separate sublineages. Brothers and sisters also desire unity, but must separate when they separate-and thereafter their interests regularly diverge, despite their long-term and enduring desire to be united. Men and women want unity, but they also want the things that mjust obstruct the achievement of unity, and the result is more than just "frustration." It is the very dynamics of the kinship system itself, which I will show cannot be understood independently of the ambivalence it provokes.

My main concern is with the paradoxical dynamics of kinship conflict, and the ambivalence it creates. But instead of regarding ambivalence as something extraneous to the system, or even a pathological manifestation, I will show that ambivalence is central to how the system works.[1] In making this argument I will be guided to some extent by Trawick's seminal analysis of Tamil kinship. It pioneered the study in kinship, but for reasons to be considered, it tends to miss important factors-most especially the overwhelming importance of cross-cousin marriage. Also, Trawick does not present her analysis as a theory with implications beyond its application to peninsular India. This can be attributed to the tendency-marked since the unfortunate demise of structuralism as a paradigm-to eschew encompassing social theory in favour of particularistic description and "experience-near" ethnography. This study should be seen as an attempt not only to push the understanding of kinship into new areas, but also to resurrect at least some aspects of the theoretical enterprise once associated with the grand projects of Clyde Kluckhohn and Francis Hsu.

The Jalari of southeastern coastal India

The Jalari are a fishing caste people whose greatest concentration is in the Telugu-speaking areas of coastal Andhra Pradesh state (Nuckolls 1996). Fishing villages dot the northern coast of Andhra, one of the four southern Indian states where Dravidian languages are spoken. Jalaripet, a large fishing village near the large port city of Visakhapatnam, is on a bay that offers a good harbour and ideal protection from rough seas. The village occupies a small piece of coastal land, and the population of the village is around 6,000. Houses are circular and built of compacted earth reinforced with sticks interwoven to provide support up to a height of about six or seven feet. A centre pole supports a roof made of a latticework of toddy trees trunks, split and tied with toddy rope fibre, and overlaid by layers of toddy leaves. Each house (*illu*) is surrounded by a wide porch (*gummam*). Part of the porch is enclosed to make a small room that is accessible through a single door adjacent to the entrance of the main room. The small room is called the *pancotu* or "work-place", a word with a double meaning, since the room is a place both for making things and making love. The floors of the house and the outside porch are made of compressed earth overspread with buffalo dung. The senior woman of the household resurfaces the floor every week and whenever there is a household ritual.

There are two kinds of houses. The *peddillu* or "big house" is the residence of the head of a patrilineage group and the site for the group's rituals. The other kind of house is the *gadillu* or "room house", occupied by adult male lineage members (probably the brothers of the headman) and their families. The *gadillu* may be physically separate from the *pedillu*, but indistinguishable from it except for the absence of a spirit shrine or *sadaru*. Or the *gadillu* may be connected to the big house, as a sort of additional room.

The interior of the big house is divided into two parts separated by a low wall extending across the middle, in front of the entrance, to a point about three quarters of the way toward the opposite wall. The patriline senior and his family sleep and eat in the area in front of this wall, called the *ammavari godi* ("goddess wall"). Behind the wall is the *ammavari gadi*("goddess room") where the spirit shrine or *sadaru* is located. The shrine is a low mound of whitewashed earth in the corner of the goddess room, in an area least accessible to casual observation. Small clay lamps are placed on a series of platforms, each representing one of the several patriline spirits, including goddesses (*ammavarus*) and ancestors (*pedda vallu*). Behind the shrine there are one or more yellow-red circles painted with a combination of turmeric and *kumkum* (lamp black) on the wall. Offerings to the spirits are made by applying a dot of the turmeric-*kumkum* mixture to each circle. There is always a *cupa rayi*, or "seeing stone", a rough hewn rock with a string attached at one end, and a *pasupu kommu* (turmeric root), used with the stone in performing a kind of divination. The seeing stone is the property of the lineage but operated only by the *dasudu*, a medium or *shaman*, who comes on invitation when family members are sick or unable to catch fish.

A room house differs from a big house only in lacking the central dividing wall and the goddess room, which the wall protects. Otherwise, they are identical. Neither it contains much furniture beyond the occasional rope bed, and sometimes a chair or two. Against the far wall, opposite the front door and near the entrance to the goddess room, there may be a wall shelf where precious objects, such as brass cups, are placed on display. Directly below this and in full view of anyone standing at the door are the family's storage vessels (for water and rice,) made of clay, aluminum, or brass. Both the contents of the shelf and the vessels below are visible to visitors and indicative of the family's wealth. The village headman (*kula pedda*) has the largest number of these. These are among the only symbols of prosperity present in the home in a society in which people regard with great suspicion any display of affluence.

The southern and northern borders of Jalaripet are marked by a sudden transition from inhabited to uninhabited space. In the latter area, full of creeping vines and tall grass, the Jalaris perform three vital functions: defecation; burial of the dead; and worship of the village-wide goddesses. Due to encroachment by new housing developments the size of the uninhabited zone is now less than it used to be. Yet, what is left retains, for the Jalari, a forbidding aspect.

Children never go there, and adults are afraid to walk in it after dark or at noon-times when various malignant spirits, including those of suicides and women who died in childbirth, are said to be active.

To the north, toward the Jalari burial ground, are the carved stone images of three village goddesses. Their names are unknown to the majority of villagers. Most of the year they are overgrown by vegetation and surrounded by piles of human waste, making them hard to reach. On their yearly festival days, the village *pujari* builds small palm-leaf huts for them. The huts are then allowed to collapse and the area reverts to its usual desolation. To the south, the land is broken by rolling sand dunes which conceal the only permanent goddess temples built by the goddesses. One is the temple of the goddess Gatilamma, built in 1957 following the last cholera epidemic. The other, a temple to the goddess Ramanamma, was build in 1964 after an outbreak of smallpox. Both were constructed in the traditional South Indian style.

Desire in kinship

Starting from Kakar (1981; 1989; 1990), and Trawick(1990), I shall claim that the desire for fusion, or coalescence, is the goal toward which South Asian kinship structures tend. This goal foregrounds the state of "unity" where otherwise there might be separation, and emphasizes shared dependency over achieved states of independence. As to the reasons why this is so are a matter of debate, but as Trawick notes, "the manifestations of these feelings in Indian superstructure and behaviour are too massive to ignore" (1990:171). Knowledge systems, like kinship, are built up (Weber would say "rationalized") with respect to this goal function to preserve unity where it exsists, and to restore it in circumstances where it has been lost, either directly or by displacement to a substitute.

"Fusion" does not imply that Indians never recognize or seek to elaborate purely individual aspects of personality. Some scholars have taken this view, and argued that Indians lack an abstract sense of the individual as an integrated whole. Some others say that Indians do recognize individuality as an essential feature of ordinary life, and indeed, display a keen awareness of this unique aspects of personality. This awareness, however, is distinct in several respects from Western notions of the individual and of personality.

In the first, place, the desire for fusion is not unproblematic, since the means available for its fulfillment are contradictory. Kakar(1981: 34) notes that:

> "the essential psychological theme of Hindu culture is the polarity of fusion and separation……a dynamic counterpoint between two opposite needs, to merge into and to be differentiated from the 'Other', where the 'Other' is all which is not the self."

But that is only part of the problem, since the means for achieving fusion conflict not only internally, but with each other. In Jalari culture, the problem locates itself in sibling relations, in the choices brothers and sisters are forced to make between different forms of sibling unity and separation. It is in the domain of sibling relations that the work of achieving fusion is supposed to be done, but it cannot be done given the paradoxes embedded in the sibling relationship (Nuckolls: 1996, 1998).

The reason why the goal cannot be reached had to do with the role of sibling relations in South India. According to one set of norms, brothers should remain together as members of the same agnatic group, living in the same house and sharing its resources. But this is impossible. Fraternal interests diverge as brothers establish their own families, and eventually they split up, each to found his own agnatic group. This is the paradox. As brothers fulfil their chief obligation as members of the same patrilineal group, by creating constituent families, they must eventually destroy the group, once their constituent families become established.

According to the other set of norms, brothers and sisters should cooperate with each other as givers and takers of each other's children in cross-cousin marriage. It is a neatly symmetrical system, at least in theory, but the symmetry is disturbed by the exigencies of each family's circumstances. Either there are not enough marriage partners to go around; or the cross-cousins who should marry do not like each other; or there is competition among brothers and sisters for each other's children. One way or another, something is bound to go wrong, imperiling the ideal of cross-sex sibling harmony. This is the other paradox. Although brothers and sisters want to remain tightly linked, they are prevented from doing so by the very nature of the bond that relates them. The fact that South Indians cannot fulfil all normative obligations in their roles as brothers and sisters is the source of a very deep cultural ambivalences, findig expression in a variety of cultural forms, including kinship roles but also mythology and divination.

For example, divination recognizes that all problems have their origin in the paradoxes of the sibling relationship. Divinatory explanation consists of identifying the problem and devising a strategy for setting it right-that is for restoring the unity of these particular relationships, since "unity" is the paramount directive goal. The Jalari recognize two sources of social dispute as prototypic precipitants of spirtitual attack: 1. the agnatic group, composed of male patriline members (prototypically brothers); and 2. the affinal group, composed of married brothers and sisters whose lineages maintain cross-cousin alliance relationships with each other. I use the word "prototypic" to refer to what seem to be core Jalari understandings: While "agnatic" and "affinal" in fact include additional categories, for the Jalari they tend to focus on siblings. Disputes are outcomes of situations which arise predictably and inevitably between relations of these two groups.

In agnatic groups, disputes occur when brothers marry and again, several years later, when their children approach marriageable age. Because each of these two crisis moments intensifies in different ways, each brother's desire to create his own, independent patrlineal group, disputes arise at precisely those points when joint actions are essential, e.g., in offering to the household spirits (*ammavallu*) which represent group solidarity. Between affinal groups, united by cross-cousin marriage, similar crises develop when joint responsibilities arise, as in the exchange of money and in the making of cross-cousin marriage alliances.

Patrilineality and alliance are extensions from fraternal and cross-sex sibling relations and constitute the dialectics of South Indian kinship as well as the determining nexus of the social disputes which culminate in divinatory explanation. Not surprisingly, there are two typical explanatory scenarios which must be evaluated in every divinatory session. Perhaps, they could be called "cultural models" in the fashionable jargon of today. One is the "agnatic" and the other is the "affinal" scenario. They describe the prototypic ways in which the (fraternal) agnatic and (cross-sibling) affinal relations go away leading to attacks by the household goddesses and subsequent distress (usually in the form of illness). There are only two scenarios, and a choice must be made between them in divination. Inevitably, one or the other is found to be the cause. The directive goal is to put the relationship back together, to restore sibling relations in fulfillment of the ideal of fusion of unity. Solutions are always temporary, however, because the contradictions informing the process remain unaltered. That is why crises are bound to recur, ensuring that the social dialetic they constitute continues as long as the unreachable goal of fusion remains culturally salient.

The elementary structures of desire in kinship and the paradoxes of unity and sepatation

If we view Jalari kinship not as a system of rules but as a dynamic of conflicting desires, seven relational sets stand out, each differently configured by the exigencies of cross-cousin marriage. These are the relationships between father and son; mother and son; father and daughter; mother and daughter; brother and brother; brother and sister; and sister and sister. The first four are what I shall term "primary".[2] The last three, between same-sex and cross-sex siblings, are secondary and in some sense derivative. They represent a transformation of the parental relationships which become, through patrilineal corss-cousin marriage, the nexus through which competing desires are represented and, in myth and divination, partially resolved.

Let us consider the four primary relationships, represented in the diagram below as dyads connected by single or double asterix, the latter indicating special prominence.

Father	mother	father	mother
*	**	**	*
Son	son	daughter	daughter

Each dyad is problematic, because each represents in its own way the paradox that centres on the desire both for unity and separation. Between same-sex individuals unity is the desire for continuity, the succession from generation to generation of a connecting identity. The paradox is that although the son or daughter is in some sense the successor to the parent of the same sex, he or she can and must diverge. For sons the inevitable separation occurs when they divide and establish their own lineages, and for daughters at marriage, when they assume the identities of their husbands households. In neither case is the separation complete. It cannot be, given the rules of marriage and residence.

The paradox of unity begins in the parental relationship, but it achieves fullest expression in the relationship between siblings of the same sex. There are many reasons for this. One of the most important, and most obvious, is that siblings know each other longer and more intensely than do parents and children. This is probably true in most places, but only recently has its implications for kinship and family life been recognized (Dunn 1988; Nuckolls 1993; Zukow 1989). In Jalari society, the continuity of a patriline is represented, not by the father, but (mainly) by brothers. The same is true of the continuity between a mother and her daughters. But between sisters the issue of unity does not achieve the same prominence, since lineage membership is reckoned through the male line and groups of descendent daughters possess a status which is informal and, in a sense, optional. When sisters separate, the division does not carry the same structural implications as fraternal division, because the latter puts the integrity of the patriline at risk.

Between cross-sex individuals, unity refers to the desire for attachment which, because of its potentially incestuous nature, must be repressed or displaced. The desire is present but must be denied. According to psychoanalytic theory this incites the development of the Oedipus complex and its resolution in the classic form articulated by Freud. In Jalari culture a similar desire for unity or fusion exists, but because of its configurations it does not have the same outcome. In a pattern described by Kakar (1981), sons respond to the dilemma by identifying with the mother, not the father, and by voluntarily foregoing their masculinity. The maternal-feminine is the superego ideal, as men seek unity through coalescence and fusion. Some even find it in the experience of becoming possession-mediums, in which they achieve absorption in a powerful feminine entity whom they address as "mother" (Nuckolls 1991a, b & c). For most men, however, the paradox relocates itself in the relationship to sisters where it undergoes intensification due to the demands of the cross-sex sibling relationship-demands that are both economic and marriage-related.

Daughters desire unity with their fathers, and in the theory of feminine development proposed by Freud and others (e.g. Chodorow 1978), resolve it by seeking substitutes. In South India the desire is probably stronger, given the fact that daughters stand in as surrogate wives, feeding their fathers and maintaining the paternal household while the mother is at the market selling fish. If there is a substitution, however, it is not only of the father by a husband, but of the father by brothers. Sisters address older brothers as "father" and serve them in much the same way they do the father. Unlike North India, where brothers and sisters are separated by great distances after marriage, cross-siblings in South India usually live close by and see each other every day (Kolenda 1993). They must be close, in fact, since they are each other's principle trading partners in the fish trade and supply each other with marriage for their children.

The dynamics of desire of kinship

Trawick discusses the ambivalence of key relationships, but limits these to only four: Father and son, mother and daughter, brother and sister, and husband and wife. She tries to show how the logic of cross-cousin marriage affects these relationships, but there are problems with this approach. First, there are more than just four relationships to be considered, as I have shown. Second, cross-cousin marriage does much more than merely "affect" them. It plays a determining role in constituting them. Trawick does not take seriously enough the importance of regional differences. In her Tamil ethnography, evidence from North India is presented whenever possible, and without critical comment, to supplement her observations on the South. The purpose of her four primitive relational dyads, consequently, is to constitute a set of primordial relational archetypes, general to most of South Asia, which the dynamics of cross-cousin marriage can play upon or elaborate in culturally distinctive ways.

What, exactly, is the effect of cross-cousin marriage on the relationship between fathers and son, mothers and daughters, brothers and sisters, and husbands and wives that might give to the South a different twist on themes common throughout the subcontinent? The fundamental dynamics of Dravidian kinship is realized in the relationship between siblings as individuals and as groups whose desires must and do diverge. The divergence is central to the kinship system, which necessarily opposes the desires of those related agnatically and affinally.

As soon as brothers marry and bring their wives, vast structural changes begin to occur within the patriline they constitute as prototypic members. New wives are notoriously jealous and (in a scenario familiar from throughout South Asia) quarrel among themselves over the distribution of family resources. At the same time that wives come, sisters leave by marrying out. Married sisters are their brothers' primary trading partners, buying their fish and selling it in the market downtown. They expect favourable trading terms which their brothers, either individually or collectively, find difficult to meet or agree on. Both groups, wives and sisters, complete for the brothers' assistance and support, making the effort to balance their competing needs increasingly difficult.

Because of their sudden juxtaposition as competing expectations, I refer to the co-presence of intense affinal obligations at this point as the first "crisis moment". It may take months or years to develop, as all the brothers and sisters marry, and begin their own families. It comes to an end when brothers can no longer agree on the distribution of resources, including money, food, and fishing equipment, to their dependent affines. Factions develop. Several brothers (usually the yonger ones push for greater individual control and other brothers (usually the older ones) advocate continued collectivization and control of resources by an elder. The result is always the same: dissolutions of the patriline as a residential and coparcenary unit.

Following division of the patriline's property, the brothers leave their joint residence and live apart, in physically separate *gadillus* ("room houses"). But the patriline remains "joint" under the authority of the senior male, usually an elder brother, since by this point the father has died. To be sure, that authority no longer means control over or access to collective property or earnings: it pertains to the group's ritual identity-that is, to its members identification with one "big house" (*peddillu*), where the senior male lives; one "goddess shrine" (*sadaru*), where patriline members worship patriline spirits; and one "goddess money" (*ammavari dabbu*), to which members contribute a portion of their income for the support of rituals. Patriline members remain, both in their own and in the community's eyes, "birds of a single nest".

Agnatic solidarity, represented prototypically in the solidarity between brothers, defines the partilineal ideology that constitutes the ideal of Jalari social life. By "ideology" I refer to what Chasseguet-Smirgel and Grunberger call:

> "the system of thought which claims to be total, (a) historical and political interpretation whose (unconscious) aid is the actualization of an illusion, of illusion *par excellence*, that the ego and its ideal can be reunited by a short-cut, via the pleasure principle"(1986:25-26).

This illusion, with its powerful directive force, is challenged by the fissiparous tendencies of brothers, tendencies which become particularly intense when they marry and start their own families. Eventually, it gives way and brothers divide their residences. The paradox is that not what Jalari men want, or are supposed to want, given the directive goals their culture creates for them. They would prefer to remain united, in multigeneration families, because such families can become powerful in the village both economically and in terms of social prestige. Ironically, the very effort to achieve this ideal results it receding further, until it becomes irretrievably lost.

After the first crisis moment, the deaths of senior males weaken the solidarity of the patriline, leading to changes which now begin primarily on agnatic axis, in the relationship between brothers. Family problems have shifted from the women who marry into and out of the patriline-the cause of the first crisis moment-to the men whom they marry. The shift reflects a change in structural focus, from concern with the incorporation and exodus of members through marriage to a concern with the continuation of the patriline through the bearing and raising of children. The more serious disputes now begin and end among men, and concern the allocation of *ritual identity,* not living expenses.

The reason is that Jalari men become increasingly familo–centric as their children grow up, devoting more and more of their resources to their children's (especially their sons') care and training. Men feel increasingly disinclined to contribute any of their heavily committed funds to the "goddess money", the last collective resource patriline members possess. Serious quarrels between patriline members eventually focus on this money-on how much each member is or is not contributing and on how the collected money should be spent. Since the "goddess money" represents the ritual identity of the patriline, disputes of this kind are really disputes about *patrilineal solidarity*.

The first crisis moment in Jalari family life is succeeded by another, which develops later and whose consequences finally result in the complete breakdown of the agnatic group. In this case, the fault line does not run fraternally, but between brother and sisters, and centres on the issue that concerns adult brothers and sisters most: the marriages of their children in cross-cousin alliance. How can one satisfy the demands of cross-siblings and agnatic kin at the same time, preserving the unity of both groups? The paradox this creates cannot be resolved, except in the temporary accommodations of myth and divination, which we will consider later.

As pressures mount within the patriline, they necessarily affect relations between the patriline and its affinally linked households, especially the households of married sisters. For one thing, brothers and sisters typically find trading with each other less profitable than trading with others. Then, too, brothers may not respond to their sisters' demands for help or, if they do, may respond in ways their sisters do not like. Finally, either a brother or a sister may abrogate an alliance relationship, deciding to marry their children to other related households or (in a growing trend) to households not related at all. Such problems eventually develop, no matter what.

It is easy to see why normal obligations for support and assistance between brothers and sisters add considerably to brother's extra-patrlineal obligations and, thus, diminish the resources they can devote to the maintenances of the patrilineal group. To support affinal relations to the extent normative obligations require means reducing the amount of support allocable to the patriline. And because obligations to the patriline are most intense at this "moment", when brothers are older, that becomes extremely difficult. The opposite is also true. Fulfilling patrilineal obligations means abrogating some or all of the obligations owed to the affines. The patriline is caught in the middle, increasingly unable to hold its ground against the fissiparous pressures exerted by cross-sibling bonds.

Kinship tensions between affinally related patrilines are like tensions within them. They contribute to arguments among patriline members which centre on contributions to the "goddess money". Because of competing obligations, brother stop contributing altogether or demand the return of certain sums to meet personal expenses. Jalaris recognize these acts as symptoms of underlying tension and the *result of competing role expectations.* They invariably signal members' growing disaffection from the group.

The paradox of Jalari kinship is that although brothers must someday separate, the ideology of fraternal solidarity cuts against this, and makes brothers ambivalent about their role in the group and their efforts to divide it. Brothers want to remain together, but cannot, and, in fact, do everything they can to bring about their dissolution as a group. This they then regret. Similarly, brothers and sisters want to remain united, but find this increasingly difficult given their competition among each other and their growing inability to meet each others' needs. Eventually, they go their separate ways, signifying their break in a ritual of chicken sacrifice made at the door of one's sibling. But they always regret it and think that somehow the split might have been prevented.

Kinship as a paradox

This paper suggests that South Indian kinship is much more than a set of norms and rules. It is a dynamic of unfulfillable desires, and this dynamic is fundamental to the working of the system. In the past, anthropologists have considered "desire" a derivative of the system, and, therefore, secondary-something best left to the psychologists. One recalls Leach's dismissal of Spiro thirty years ago on exactly these grounds (Leach 1969). Unfortunately, the "traditional" view tends to represent the people who actually occupy kinship roles as unthinking and unfeeling automatons, blindly implementing cultural programmes. Clearly this is inadequate, but critique does not justify abandonment of the idea of "systems" or worse, the idea that power and position explain everything. The desires people have are essential to their participation in the system, and one that comprehends the dynamic power of conflict, contradiction, and frustration.

This is not the first time that the importance of dynamic conflict has been noticed. In the 1960s, Hsu introduced the concept of dominant kinship relationships to explain how such relationships could have an effect on kin and non-kin behaviour (Hsu: 1965). Hsu's theory is long overdue for reconsideration. According to Hsu's hypotheis, the comparatively few attributes of such relationships provide the frameworks within which a variety of cultural aspects could be understood. It was only a step from this to the view that dominant relationships conflict, and, thus, generate ambivalence which the kinship system both represents and tries to resolve. The anthropologist who first proposed making ambivalence central to the study of kinship was van der Veen (1971). "Of essential importance for every human relationship," he stated, "is the way in which the inherent ambivalence of the relationship is solved"(1971: 379). But van der Veen was concerned mostly with universal conflicts such as he believed in existence between the desire for independence and the need to conform to social norms. One could see cross-cousin marriage in similar terms, perhaps: the patrilineal to be independent against the continuing need to affiliate via the inclusion of affines. van der Veen may be right, but I prefer to adopt a more particularistic frame of reference limiting my description of the conflict to the dynamics of South Indians kinship.

Conclusion

Gregory Bateson (1958) pointed out that there are problems such as alcoholism and the political opposition between Palestinians and Israelis that cannot be solved. What is the nature of these problems? Far from being merely secondary or derivative, such problems might be fundamental to what we call "culture". Where each generation transmits to the next its unresolved problems, there exists continuity between generations that goes by the name *culture*. That is because they are not problems, but *solutions* to problems which are covert and intractable. Such problems are paradoxes, like those I have described as emergent in South Indian kinship. To follow Bateson's insight, what we need is a *theory of paradox in culture.* It has been the purpose of this paper to suggest a strategy for formulating this kind of theory.

Notes

1. Ambivalence of this kind exists among people in conflicting institutions and complex interrelationships such that no single commitment dominates one's life. Related to ambivalence of the psychological type, sociological ambivalence focuses on the ways in which ambivalence comes to be built into the structure of social statues and roles. "It directs us to examine the process in social strcture that affect the probability of ambivalence turning up in particular kinds of role-relations (and) ....it directs us to the social consequences of ambivalence for the workings of social structures. (Merton 1976:5).
2. In agreement with Hsu (1971), and against the argument advanced by Kurtz(1992), this paper will show that the primary relationships are critically important, including the relationship between mother and son.

References

Bateson, G. 1958. *Naven. 2nd edition*. Stanford: Standord University Press.

Bourdieu, P. 1977. *Outline of a Theory of Practice*. Cambridge: Cambridge University Press.

Bowlby, J. 1969. *Attachment and Separation*. London: Hogarth Press.

Chasseguet-Smirgel, J. and B. Grunberger. *1986. Freud or Reich? Psychoanalysis and Illusion*. New Haven: Yale University Press.

Chodorow, N. 1978. *The Reproduction of Mothering: Psychoanalysis and the Sociology of Gender*. Berkeley: University of California Press.

Dunn, J. 1987. *The Beginnings of Social Understanding*. Oxford: Blackwell.

Hsu, F. 1965. "The effect of dominant kinship relationships on kin and non-kin behaviour: a hypothesis," *American Anthropologist* 67: 638-61.

1971 (ed.) *Kinship and Culture*. Chicago: Aldine.

Kakar, S. 1981. *The Inner World: Childhood and Society in India*. Delhi: Oxford University Press.

——1988. "The maternal-feminine in Indian psychoanalysis" *International Review of Psychoanalysis* 19: pp. 355-62.

J. Stigler, R. Shweder and G. herdt. (eds.). 1990. "Stories from Indian psychoanalysis: Context and text", In *Cultural Psychology: Essay on Human Development*. Cambridge: Cambridge University Press.

Kolenda, P. 1993. "Sibling relations and marriage practices: A comparison of North, Central, and South India." In C. Nuckolls.(ed.) *Siblings in South Asia: Brothers and Sisters in Cultural Context*. New York: Guilford Press.

Kurtz, S. 1992. *All the Mothers are One*. New York: Columbia University Press.

Leach, E. 1969. *Genesis as Myth and Other Essays*. London: Jonathan cape.

LiPuma, E. 1982. "On the preference for marriage rules: A Melanesian example", *Man* 18: 766-785.

Merton, R. 1976. *Sociological Ambivalence*. New York: Free Press.

Nuckolls, C. 1991a. "Becoming a possession-mediumship in South India: A psychocultural account", *Medical Anthropology Quarterly* 5: 63-77.

1991b. "Deciding how to decide: Possession-mediumship in South India", in M. Nichter (ed.) special edition, *Recent Trends in Ethnomedicines*, *Medical Anthropology* 13: 57-82

1991c. "Culture and causal thinking: Prediction and diagnosis in a South Indian fishing village", *Ethos:* 17:1: 3-51.

1993 (ed.) *Siblings in South Asia: Brothers and Sisters in Cultural Context.* New York: Guilford Publications.

1996. The Cultural Dialectics of Knowledge and Desire. Madison: University of Wisconsin Press.

1998. *The Culture: A Problem that Cannot Be Solved.* Madison: University of Wisconsin Press.

Obeyesekere, G. 1981. *Medusa's Hair*. Chicago: University of Chicago Press.

Trawick, M. 1990. *Love in a Tamil Family*. Berkeley: University of California Press.

van der Veen, K. 1971. "Ambivalence, social structure, and dominant kinship relationships: A hypothesis", In F.Hsu(ed.) *Kinship and Culture*. Chicago: Aldine.

Zukow, P. (ed.). 1989. *Sibling Interaction Across Cultures: Theoretical and Methodological Issues*. New York: Springer-Verlag.

Ethnographic profile of the Vadabalijas of Andhra Pradesh

S.V. Sudhakar

Introduction

In the state of Andhra Pradesh two types of fishermen communities are in existence. One is marine fishermen community, which lives on the coastal belt of the Bay of Bengal spread over 9 coastal districts starting from Srikakulam to Nellore. The other one is of inland fishermen community, which resides close to rivers, canals, ponds and reservoirs spread over in all the districts of Andhra Pradesh. Both these categories are separately involved in fishing in the marine as well as in the inland water belts. All together 14 sub castes exist in the fishermen population in the state of Andhra Pradesh. They were listed under Backward Classes 'A' group for the reservation purposes by the Government of Andhra Pradesh and in the OBC category by the Government of India. These sub-castes had different nomenclatures. The Vadabalija is one such sub caste of fishermen predominantly inhabiting the north-coastal districts of Andhra Pradesh such as Srikakulam, Vizianagaram, Visakhapatnam and East Godavari.

Meaning and historical traces

Vadabalija is a combination of two words namely Vada and Balija. The word Voda, meaning ship in Telugu has gradually become Vada. The word Balija in Telugu connotes trade. Thus, the people who are engaged in trading by using ships are called as Vadabalijas. Historically speaking, Balijas belong to the generation of King Balichakravarhi of Chandra Vamsam (Chandra dynastry). In other words, Bali (King

Balichakravarhi) and Ja (birth) is explained as the generation of King Balichakravarthi. In later years the generations of King Balichakravarthi got involved in different occupations. As such, it is viewed that Vadabalijas are the descendents of King Balichakravarthi. The other explanation on the emergence of Vadabalija is that its occupation later became a caste name. To mention a few, Vadabalija (fish sellers), Gajulabalija (bangle seller), Pusalabalija (bead seller), etc. Vadabalija as a population thus has become a caste by way of their occupation, namely, ship-building, sailing, fishing, etc. Even today, the Vadabalija caste people are involved in fish catching and fish trading.

Religion

Vadabalijas are pluralists. Their religion consists of many starta. At the top-end, due to *sanskritaization,* they are influenced by the greater theistic cults, relating particularly to the *Avataras* of Vishnu. At the bottom end, the Vadabalijas are ancestor worshippers with a persistent belief in spirits which have to be fended off or propitiated. In between, the divinities with whom they chiefly concern themselves are all designated as female and most of them have names ending in *Amma* – mistress or lady. In this respect they resemble the major religious forms of the Dravidian culture of south India. Accordingly, three main divisions of the pantheon are in existence among the people in this community. It denotes the order of all gods: (1) Male Deities (2) Female Deities and (3) Spirits. However, the principal local deity is Gangammatalli – the sea goddess. The Vadabalijas, particularly womenfolk, are more religious in practice. Besides celebrating Hindu festivals, Vadabalijas attach more importance to their community festivals. During every catching season they perform Gangamma (mother goddess of water) festival and every year they celebrate the event on a large scale. Their dances, dressed in their traditional ways, reveal their traditional culture. Their songs relate to religious parables. Their dramas depict their professional life. All the people worship their ancestors and dead children. They have firm belief in wichcraft and magic. The other significant feature of the community is that each household has a family deity, which is known as *Ilavelpu.* The common word in the usage is that of *Perantalu.* The *Perantalu* is generally a young girl below the age of puberty who dies suddenly and becomes a household deity and is worshiped in the process. The community people believe that the *Perantalu* takes care of the welfare of the entire family. In each of the house a small *goodu* (cupboard) is kept and the family members believe that the *Perantalu* lives there. On a specific day they offer their prayers. During the festival days they offer bangles, turmeric, clothes, sweets, fruits, flowers etc. to the *Perantalu*.

Economic organization

Fishing is the main occupation of the community. They also prepare their traditional boats, nets, ropes and other related requirements. There is a clear-cut division of labour between the sexes. The menfolk go into the sea and catch the fish. The catch is handed over to women who sell it on the seashore itself or take it to local fish market. Women market the household goods and manage the entire household. Thus, the activities of women complement the activities of men. Hence women are given fairly good status in the family. Even the young girls and boys follow the footsteps of their elders and engage in the occupation. The element of chance plays a large part in their occupation and, thus, their income is often very irregular and uncertain due to seasonal variations. The men from Vadabalija community go into the sea in odd hours during nights and they dispose off the catch on the seashore itself wherein the middlemen wait for the catch. The price is fixed as per routine understanding and on the basis of demand and supply. The community, takes advances from the middlemen for various reasons and, hence, is obliged to sell the catch to them. Their catch, if it is to be stored, needs more labour and outlay in equipment for its preservation. Hence, the tendency of a greater involvement of middlemen who take these matters off their hands. Their difficulties are due partly to a lack of acquaintance with modern mechanical equipment, partly due to conservatism and partly to a lack of the capital needed to lift their enterprise to a much higher level of technical efficiency.

Life style

Vadabalijas lead a simple life and the major chunk of the community lives in abject poverty. Education is, to a great extent, a far reaching goal and unfulfilled dream in the community. The food habits in this community are also simple. Mostly they consume sea products and occasionally other non-vegetarian products. The food they consume is generally not balanced in terms of nutritious contents. The men cover half of their bodies and the women still do not use any undergarments. The housing of this community is substandard. Mostly they live in thatched houses. The people quite often are vulnerable to the natural disasters particularly cyclones, *toofans*, tidal waves, etc. This has been creating a perennial problem wherein the community looses it's belongings due to these disasters. This is a community always affected and becomes the victim of the natural disasters. The heavy death toll in the community is a regular phenomenon both on and off the sea. Women are accorded a high place in the Vadabalija community since the whole responsibility of family maintenance rests with them. Women had a predominant role in economic activities. Although illiterate, most of the womenfolk are shrewd in their business activities and are able to provide all the necessary things for the subsistance and survival of the family.

Social organization

Vadabalijas belong to several endogamous groups. Each endogamous group is again subdivided into various patrilineal clans. There are about 100 surnames located and identified among these Vadabalijas. The members of the same intiperu treat each other as siblings. Each such clan consists of members of families, both extended and nuclear. Vadabalijas, as a single caste, is managed by the kula Panchayat (caste council) headed by a *Kulapedda* i.e., caste head. The office is hereditary. The Panchayat performs judicial functions and acts as an agency of social control in all matters of community life. Violators of traditional norms are punished with fines and ex-communication. The organization of the community is based on mutual cooperation and interaction between individuals who are regarded as belonging to the same group or who have intense rights and obligations towards each other. Vadabalijas attach great importance to marriage and affinal alliance. Child marriages are still performed. Marriages are endogamous by caste and exogamous with reference to clan or intiperu. Vadabalijas generally practice monogamy but there is no taboo on polygamy. Cross cousin marriages are preferred. Two kinds of marriages are in practice by Vadabalijas – (1) arranged marriage by elders through negotiation and (2) marriage by elopement. Divorce is permitted and possible on the grounds of adultery, barrenness, prolonged sickness, etc. The man who divorces must pay compensation to the woman. Marriage contract may be terminated through payment by the divorcing party levied by the Kula Panchayat. *Marumanuvu* (remarriage) is also observed in the community. *Nestharikam* (literally meaning friendship) is one peculiar feature of this community wherein one family member may accept the other family member on his choice or by edler's choice, mostly from other caste groups as *Nestham.* It is arranged through a ceremony in which either side of the family members participate and *Nestharikam*-knot is fixed. Though literally *Nestharikam* stands for friendship but in true sense it is accepted and considered as the member of the family. In other words, both the individuals who accept the *Nestharikam* share all the family rituals in either side of the family and it continues from one generation to the an other. Thus, Vadabalijas exhibit various characterstics of a tribe. They practice and perform a number of rituals connected with every phase of the life cycle from birth to death. All the community leaders play important roles in marriages, death ceremonies, religious rituals and festivals. Inspite of modernization taking place at some speed among the Indian masses, these Vadabalijas continue to cling to their traditional occupation of fishing, which incidentally leads to a traditional style of life associated with their occupation. Strong kinship ties, deep religiosity and prevalence of magic are characteristics of these fish folks. In other words, the community represents more or less a cultural island wherein the community members adhere to a way of life inherited from past generations within homogenous, well-knit communities characterized by a simple life and primary relationships. Education seems quite irrelevant to their occupational pursuits and mechanization of their occupational activities is yet to begin.

Surnames (clans – intiperu) among the Vadabalijas

Allipalli
Amara
Ambati
Arjella
Bade
Badrachalam
Barri
Bathula
Behara
Boddu
Bondi
Budda
Bypalli
Chapa
Charapalli
Chavvakula
Chelluri
Chemburi
Chenna
Chepurla
Chidamana
Chikati
Chintakayla
Chippili
Chodipalli
Chokka
Chokkara
Dasari
Doni
Donka
Dooda
Douripalli
Dummu
Erupalli
Ganagalla
Gandha
Garikina
Gokavarapu
Gunti
Guntu
Gurrala
Jogi
Kambala
Kanara
Kanchala
Kare
Karri
Koda
Kola
Komara
Konada
Koviri
Kudathala
Kumpatla
Kundu
Kuppiri
Kurmadasu
Lakili
Landa
Maddu
Marupalli
Matta
Meruva
Moripalli
Mosa
Mugi
Mydi
Mylapalli
Nakka
Padava
Palletti
Para
Peerupalli
Peramburu
Perla
Piradi
Pukkalla
Puvalla
Ragati
Seeram
Senapathi
Setti (Chetty)
Singauluri
Singupalli
Sriram
Surada
Surapathi
Tayya
Thitti
Tholana
Thota
Thummidi
Tikkada
Uddanda
Ummidi
Uppada
Vanka
Varipalli
Vasupalli

Part - IV

Artisan communities

Rural artisans in Bhavnagar district, Gujarat: A study of their socio-economic conditions

C.N. Ray

Rural non-farm sector holds the key to faster economic development of the country. It has the vast potential and an unrealised promise for generating employment and increased incomes. Rural artisans have been an integral part of the traditional socio-economic fabric of rural India. Their crafts are usually characterised as home based activities that use local material, traditional skills and technology and their products have their regional flavour and, market orientation-wise, distinct identities. They are also known as the service providers for the rural communities. However, most of them belong to the lower strata in the social hierarchy and given low social capital have generally failed to capitalise on these advantageous features. Since the attainment of Independence, both the Central and state governments have claimed to have taken a long list of initiatives for the upliftment of the conditions of the rural artisans. However, while the urban-industrial sectors seem to have traveled quite a significant distance nationally and internationally, it remains to be visibly demonstrated how much the artisans, forming the bottom of the socio-economic-political structure of the society, have gained, if at all, during the last 58 years of post-Independence existence.

In Gujarat, the state government frequently flaunts a long list of programmes and projects that it has supposedly undertaken for their benefit. It is also mentioned that many non-government agencies are working for the artisans located in the rural and urban areas of Gujarat. In particular, the official line emphasizes that the cottage and village industries help tackle the endemic problem of unemployment among the local youth without involving too much capital expenditure. The Gujarat government has worked out an Index of Cottage and Rural Industries (INDEX 'C') to provide information about these units and to give financial support, technical guidance, training, marketing assistance and other common facilities through various public sector corporations/Boards.

Sociologically, rural artisans have been an integral part of the Indian villages. Characterised by the home-based enterprises using local material and traditional skills, rural artisans were regarded as rendering services to the village community and were paid in part by share of crop (Gadgil: 1974). *Servitude* was predominant feature of the artisan class and most of them were classified under the lower strata (i.e., *Shudras)* of the social hierarchy (Ghurye: 1969). In Gujarat, artisans are known as *'vasavayas'* that means those associated with the process of settlement or bringing land under the plough (Shah: 2002). Artisans normally belong to specific caste groups, namely weaver, tanner, cobbler, potter, carpenter, and blacksmith, etc. In Gujarat, these caste groups have been classified as socially and educationally backward communities but are variously scheduled as the SCs, STs, and OBCs.

Historically, the artisans (i.e. castes providing services and goods for the rural economy) were linked in a *hierarchical relationship with the agriculturists* who, by virtue of having control over land, were able to keep others *dependent on them.* While the form of relationships varied significantly over space and time, the *exploitative elements were present in most situations* (Breman: 1974). The changes, however, were more significant during the colonial rule, setting the downward trend and the process of de-industrialisation. Nevertheless, at the time of Independence, the economy was still vested with a *fairly large and widespread segment of rural artisans.* The *crucial elements characterising this segment* were as follows:

- Their presence was essential to sustain a self-sufficient rural economy.
- Their growth was mainly dependent on the development of agriculture and allied activities.
- Frequent drought conditions, therefore, exerted disintegrating influence on the artisan sector (Gadgil: 1974).

- Servitude and patronage, on the one hand, and a decentralised production system, on the other, constrained mobilisation of capital and entrepreneurial skills. Moreover, low social status of some of the artisans further aggravated these constrains.
- Traditional arrangements of mutual rights and obligations were undergoing constant changes in the light of overall changes taking place in the economy.
- The process of transformation resulted in gradual shift towards urban centres (Gadgil:op cit) and an advance integration with market economy.

Most of the foregoing characteristics have been closely associated with the early phase of capitalist production. As industrialsation proceeds, eventually the artisan based activities especially those scattered over the countryside would disappear (Singh: 1990). Such transformation also takes place in the less industrialised countries (Stately and Morse: 1965). In their simple form, these changes emerge through transition of artisan industry, replacement of household industry and development of modem small-scale industries along with large-scale production. In the process, the artisan-based production tends to get integrated with the mainstream industrial production by establishing product as well as capital linkages (Shah: 1990). Thus, a shift from home-based to workshop/factory enterprises and from rural to semi-urban/urban locations is a natural phenomenon and perhaps a desirable goal in the process of capitalist development. Moreover, it can pave the way for an upward mobility as well as social integration among the artisan households. Overall, therefore, the changing pattern of artisan-based production can be positive phenomenon.

The crucial questiqn vis-à-vis the foregoing hypothesis is: has this type of transformation been really taking place? If so, has it really proceeded in the same type of sequence as the hypothesis assumes? These questions can be answered only through empirical studies of the artisan groups in different parts of the country.

Objectives of the study

The broad objective of this study was to develop a socio-economic profile of the artisans engaged in the cottage and village industries in Bhavnagar district of Gujarat.

Specific objectives

The specific objectives of the study were:

- To prepare a socio-economic database on the profile of households engaged in cottage and village industries at the village level.
- To look in to their nature of work, level of skills, income and expenditure profile.
- To understand the problems of all such activities for self-sufficiency.

Methodology

The study was conducted in Bhavnagar district of Gujarat. A *preliminary review* of the secondary material, available with the Government of Gujarat, indicated that there were a total of 41 artisan activities being carried out in the selected district. It was decided to carry the field survey using a structured schedule for the interviews conducted with the artisan households in different Talukas of the district.

Artisans in the Bhavnagar District: An empirical profile

Types of artisans

Out of a total of 41 types of artisans found in Bhavanagar, 35 were located at the village level. The largest number of artisans (1702) was involved in *Bharatkam.* The number of artisans in *Motikam* was 854, and 853 in carpentary, followed by 698 in embroidery. The number is much smaller in soft toys making, *Bandhanikam, bamboo* article making, *Zardoshikam, making* of *Shankh* articles, tanning, biba making, *Vajinara, Kalaikam, Jarikam,* packing, mala, pot and paper articles, etc. The profession they are engaged in is traditional for a majority (5925: 78 per cent). Only 1633 artisans (21 per cent) have learnt and adopted a new profession. The percentage of households engaged in traditional artisanal occupations varies in different Talukas of Bhavnagar. It is as high as 90 per cent in Sihor, Umrala and Botad Talukas, more than 80 per cent in Gariadhar, Palitana, Gadhada and Vallabhipur, and more than 70 per cent in Mahua. More than 50 per cent artisans have adopted handlooms and handicraft industry as a traditional occupation in Ghogha and Talaja.In Botad Taluka, just four per cent artisans have taken to a non-traditional occupation whereas 96 per cent are tethered to their traditional occupation only. This pattern is significantly different in Talaja Taluka where as much as 45 per cent artisans have gone over to non-traditional items.

Place of work

About 87 per cent of the artisans in Bhavnagar do not own a shop or workshop and consequently work only at their homes. Since only 13 per cent artisans work at a place other than their own residence, it is clear that the scale at which artifacts are produced is usually quite small. Working at home also means involvement of other family members in the business activities. Due to shortage of capital, women and children of the household also join their men folk in the business activities. The females perform the household duties along with their work in the traditional artisan work. In fact, the children in the family are initiated in to the business activities at a very young age. This is also the compelling reason why many children from the families of the artisans quit school after getting their primary education.

Concentration of artisan households

Concentration of the artisan households in different Talukas of Bhavnagar district is shown in Table l. Mahuva and Talaja, which have 112 and 130 villages respectively, contribute more than 30 per cent artisan families of the entire district. Consequently, they invite special attention of the Gujarat government authorities for this reason alone. Palitana is a quite a large Taluka that has 877 artisan households and contributes as many as 13 per cent of the artisans of the district.

Table 1: Concentration of artisan households in Bhavnagar district

Sl. No.	Talukas	Number of a-tisan households
1.	Mahuva, Talaja	More than 1000
2.	Palitana	Between 800 to 1000
3.	Ghadhada, Sihor, Bhavnagar	Between 600 to 800
4.	Vallabhipur,Botad, Gariadhar, Ghogha,Umrala	Between 400 to 600

On the other hand, Gadhada, Sihor and Bhavnagar Talukas combined contribute only 25 per cent of the artisans. Ghogha and Umrala are the two very small Talukas having only 47 and 41 villages respectively. They contribute only 12 per cent of the total artisans of the district.

Table 2: Main artisan types in Bhavnagar district

Artisan type	Number	Per cent
1. Bharatkam	1702	22.52
2. Motikam	854	11.30
3. Carpentary	853	11.29
4. Embroidery	698	9.24
5. Pottery	595	7.87
6. Cobblers	470	6.22
7. Topala-Supada-making	391	5.17
8. Others	1990	13.89

Gender-wise participation

Looking at the gender-wise distribution of the artisans involved in the handloom and handicrafts at the district level, it is found that 59 per cent of them are male and 41 per cent female. Thus, it is evident that the males contribute the major share of labour force of this line. However, when a Taluka-wise distribution is taken into consideration, the picture undergoes some significant changes. In Bhavnagar, Palitana, and Botad Talukas, where *Bharatkam,* and *Motikam* are dominant artisan lines in which the artisans are engaged in, the proportion of the females is as high as 60 per cent. In the remaining eight Talukas, the proportion of males is more than 60 per cent. If we take female participation in the handloom and handicraft artifacts as a separate category, it is seen that it is highest in Palitana Taluka (645), followed by Bhavnagar (372). On the other hand, male participation is highest in Talaja Taluka (over 83 per cent). It is notable that a majority of the artisans in Talaja Taluka is engaged in embroidery, carpentary, and pottery. Mahuva is another Taluka where the proportion of the males is as high as 66 per cent. *Bharatkam, Motikam,* decorative articles and cotton, wool or, silk items are the traditional artisanal occupations in which more than 70 per cent female artisans are engaged in. This is perhaps more due to the fact that both the household and the occupational responsibilities can be conveniently carried out within the confines of their houses without the necessity of going out to another place of work. In addition, young girls and women have to carry the articles of *Bharatkam and Motekam* to their in-laws' house as a gift as a part of the prevalent local cultural tradition. The situation is somewhat different in so far as the occupations of *Kotaranikam,* cobbler, carpentary, and tools for farming are concerned. Here, hundred per cent males are involved in carrying out occupational duties. In pottery and embroidery more than 85 per cent artisans are males. The high percentage for embroidery is somewhat surprising since in most other parts of the country, this is one area of work that is traditionally dominated by the women. About 25 per cent artisans in *Topala-Supada* making are females while it is 40 per cent in weaving.

Table 3: Gender-wise participation in artisan crafts in Bhavnagar district

(in percentages)

SI. No.	Taluka	Per cent male	Per cent female
1.	Bhavnagar	38.21	61.79
2.	Ghogha	60.17	39.83
3.	Talaja	83.93	16.07
4.	Mahuva	65.81	34.19
5.	Gariadhar	71.84	28.16
6.	Palitana	26.45	73.55
7.	Sihor	68.08	31.92
8.	Umrala	70.07	29.93
9.	Gadhada	60.35	39.65
10.	Botad	39.40	60.60
11.	Vallabhipur	60.74	39.26
	District total	**59.16**	**40.84**

Age-wise distribution of the artisans

An overwhelming majority (81 per cent) of the artisans working in the handloom and handicraft industry is in the age bracket of 21 to 59 years. It is observed that children in the age group 12 to 15 years begin pooling their labour by participating in the artisanal activities of the household. The largest proportion of such adolescent workers (31) is found in Palitana Taluka.As can be seen from Table 4, there are 14 per cent 'workers' below the age group of 20 years. At the other end of the scale, four per cent of the artisans above are 60 years, when people start developing physical weaknesses such as reduced eyesight, pain in the joints, inability to properly maneuver their limbs hindering their work performance quantitatively and qualitatively. However, it is seen that these 'seniors' are engaged in artisanal work such as *Topala-Supada* -making, pottery and cobbler. The largest percentage of such senior workers is located in Garidhar Taluka.

Table 4: Age distribution of the artisans of Bhavnagar

(in percentages)

	Age (in years)		
Taluka	**Up to 20**	**21 to 59**	**60 and above**
Bhavnagar	13.62	82.55	3.83
Ghogha	10.90	88.47	0.63
Talaja	12.97	81.64	5.83
Mahuva	18.10	78.60	3.32
Garidhar	10.73	78.72	10.54
Palitana	31.36	66.37	2.37
Sihor	7.49	90.39	2.12
Umrala	7.48	84.54	7.98
Gadhada	3.33	95.22	1.45
Botad	15.38	78.80	5.82
Vallabhipur	12.08	80.71	7.21
District total	**14.20**	**81.49**	**4.31**

Level of education of the artisans

About 30 per cent of the artisans are totally illiterate. The incidence of illiteracy is highest in Botad Taluka (50 per cent) and lowest in Ghogha Taluka (14 per cent). Even the remaining 70 per cent have had no proper education. Almost two-thirds of the artisans (60 per cent) have studied up to primary school level. This percentage is highest in Ghogha Taluka (68) and lowest in Botad Taluka (44). One tenth of them have progressed up to the secondary level. Secondary education levels are highest in Mahuva (17 per cent) and lowest in Gariadhar Taluka (4 per cent). Compared to the average percentage of 1.44 for higher secondary education for the entire district of Bhavnagar artisans, those in Vallabhipur cross this mark (six per cent) whereas those from Botad are even worse (0.2 per cent). Only negligible part (1.5 per cent) has reached higher levels of education.

Among these fortunate ones, the share of the diploma holders is 0.04 per cent, graduate degree holders 0.15 per cent and PG degree holders just 0.07 per cent. These have profound implications for the workers as well as for their artisanal activities. This means that their mental faculties are more or less closed. They have no knowledge of the fast track changes taking place in their social, economic and political environment and consequently not geared up to change themselves and their businesses according to the changing requirements of the times. Not being aware of the possibile opportunities, they take their children off from schools and instead deploy them in their occupational chores at a very young age.

Table 5: Educational levels of the artisans in Bhavnagar district

(in percentages)

	Levels of Education						
Taluka	**Illiterate**	**Primary**	**Secondary**	**H.Sec**	**Dip**	**Graduate**	**PG**
Bhavnagar	43.52	51.66	4.49	0.33	0.0	0.0	0.0
Ghogha	13.63	80.29	5.87	0.21	0.0	0.0	0.0
Talaja	26.95	61.98	9.28	1.40	0.0	0.20	0.20
Mahuva	19.37	61.10	17.34	1.94	0.24	0.0	0.0
Gariadhar	26.82	67.82	4.41	0.57	0.0	0.0	0.38
Palitana	25.96	62.08	9.37	1.92	0.0	0.68	0.0
Sihor	41.20	44.63	12.38	1.63	0.0	0.16	0.0
Umrala	45.39	49.13	4.74	0.50	0.0	0.0	0.25
Gadhada	25.62	68.60	5.50	0.29	0.0	0.0	0.0
Botad	50.66	43.90	5.25	0.19	0.0	0.0	0.0
Vallabhipur	31.04	51.85	11.24	5.54	0.0	0.34	0.0
District Total	**30.07**	**59.02**	**9.21**	**1.44**	**0.04**	**0.15**	**0.07**

Category-wise distribution of the artisan households

Artisan households can be grouped in to SCs, STs, OBCs, and others. Table 6 presents category-wise distribution of the artisan households in Bhavnagar. Two thirds of the artisans are from the three categories of backward classes, namely the SCs, STs and the OBCs whereas one third of them are from other castes. Among the backward class artisans, the OBCs constitute as much as 53 per cent. Those from the SCs contribute 11 per cent and the STs only 4 per cent. Actually, the proportion of the backwards is still higher since quite a significant percentage of the 32.51 per cent listed as "others" are Muslim artisans who have not been counted as *OBCs. These figures go a long way to demolish the mistaken impression, often seen among many sections of the intelligentsia, that the artisans as a group belong to only the OBC categories.* The distribution of these proportions and numbers, however, varies a great deal in different Talukas of the district. Thus, there is concentration of some particular social categories of the artisans in some places. The maximum percentage of the SC artisans (34) is located in Vallabhipur Taluka followed by Gadhada (29 percent), Talaja (15 per cent) and Gariadhar (12 per cent). The STs are found in good enough numbers only in Ghogha (19 per cent). Although the district percentage of the OBC artisans is 53, they are present in varying percentages in the 11 Talukas.Gariadhar, Palitana and Umrala have more than three fourths of OBC artisans. Ghogha, Mahuva, Sihor also have more than half of their artisans from the ranks of the OBCs. In only two Talukas—Bhavnagar and Botad—are the OBCs less than 20 per cent of the artisans in those places. Bhavnagar has the highest number of the non-backward class artisans (86 per cent), followed by Botad (68 per cent), Talaja (43 per cent) and Sihor (31 per cent). Gariadhar has the lowest number of the non-backward class artisans (just 6 per cent).

Table 6: Category-wise percentage distribution of artisan households in Bhavnagar

(in percentages)

	Categories			
Taluka	**SC**	**ST**	**OBC**	**Others**
Bhavnagar	1.66	0.83	11.63	85.88
Ghogha	4.19	19.08	58.28	18.45
Talaja	14.97	2.59	39.52	42.91
Mahuva	4.02	3.70	66.13	26.15
Gariadhar	12.45	1.72	79.89	5.94
Palitana	0.57	0.68	76.60	23.15
Sihor	0.98	0.33	67.75	30.94
Umrala	6.23	2.99	75.56	12.72
Gadhada	29.09	3.91	47.03	19.97
Botad	9.57	4.50	17.82	68.11
Vallabhipur	34.40	8.56	36.74	20.30
District total	**10.56**	**3.96**	**52.98**	**32.51**

Another important aspect of the social background of the artisans in Bhavnagar is the concentration of some specific sub-category of the backward class artisans in some specific trades. The SC artisans, for example, are engaged in Topala-Supada making, cotton, wool, silk articles, weaving, cobblers, potters, and embroidery. The ST artisans are mostly engaged in Topala-Supada making, weaving and embroidery. Majority of non-backward class 'other artisans' is engaged in Sonikam.

Household size of the artisan families

Household size of the Bhavnagar artisans is shown in Table 7. It is seen that almost two-thirds of the artisans have 5 to 7 members in their households. Those having more than 8 members constitute only 11 per cent. On the other hand, about 20 per cent artisans have less than 4 members in their households. If one were to use the weightage average method, the average size of the artisan families in Bhavnagar works out to 6.

Table 7: Size of the artisan households in Bhavnagar

(in percentages)

	Size of the Households		
Taluka	**Less than 4**	**5 to 7**	**8 and above**
Bhavnagar	22.09	72.59	5.32
Ghogha	11. 95	84.91	3.14
Talaja	27.94	58.58	13.47
Mahuva	21.64	63.15	15.21
Gariadhar	34.10	55.75	10.15
Palitana	11.17	78.79	10.03
Sihor	11.73	68.89	19.38
Umrala	16.96	74.06	8.98
Gadhada	14.47	78.29	7.24
Botad	24.58	63.79	11.63
Vallabhipur	29.87	61.07	9.07
District total	**20.69**	**68.29**	**11.02**

Number of earning members per artisan household

Table 8 provides information about the number of earning members per artisan household in Bhavnagar. *Dependency ratios of the artisan households paint a gruesome picture of their economic status*. About 67 per cent of the households have just one earning member; another 29 per cent have two earning members and about 4 per cent three earning members. Less than half per cent households have more than three earning members. If the figures for different Talukas are taken in to consideration, it is seen that some among them have even *far grimmer picture of dependency*. Botaḍ and Bhavnagar Talukas have 91 and 88 per cent households with only one earning member: Talaja, Mahuva and Umrala have as much as 75 per cent households with a sole earning member and Gariadhar and Palitana have more than 60 per cent households with only one earning member. This raises an important question: are there no other economic avenues available for these families? In case they are, why have the artisan families not taken them up? If indeed these are not available, which appears to be the case, why it has not occurred to the Government of Gujarat to do something about this issue?

Table 8: Number of earning members in the artisan households in Bhavnagar

(in percentages)

	Number of Earning Members						
Taluka	**One**	**Two**	**Three**	**Four**	**Five**	**Six**	**Eight**
Bhavnagar	88.37	10.13	1.00	0.33	0.17	0.00	0.00
Ghogha	49.27	45.70	4.82	0.21	0.00	0.00	0.00
Talaja	75.45	22.16	1.90	0.30	0.10	0.10	0.00
Mahuva	75.22	21.32	2.98	0.08	0.16	0.00	0.24
Gariadhar	67.24	31.23	1.53	0.00	0.00	0.00	0.00
Palitana	60.78	34.55	4.22	4.22	0.46	0.00	0.00
Sihor	49.19	48.86	1.30	0.65	0.00	0.00	0.00
Umrala	74.06	22.94	2.99	0.00	0.00	0.00	0.00
Gadhada	27.35	56.01	16.21	0.00	0.00	0.00	0.00
Botad	90.81	7.50	1.50	0.19	0.00	0.00	0.00
Vallabhipur	75.50	18.79	4.36	1.34	0.00	0.00	0.00
District total	**67.00**	**28.62**	**3.92**	**0.34**	**0.07**	**0.03**	**0.05**

Economic status of the artisan households

The rough economic status of the artisan households is shown in Table 9. It indicates the location of the sampled households into officially designated below the poverty line (BPL) and above the poverty line (APL) categories. The data very clearly establish the fact of very small number of BPL artisan households in Bhavnagar district. The average percentage of APL artisan households in the entire district is 83 although it varies from a very high of 95 in Bhavnagar and Botad, over 80 in Talaja, Mahuva, Palitana, Gadhada and Vallabhipur Talukas and over 75 in Ghogha, Gariadhar, and Umrala Talukas. The lowest percentage of APL artisans is 63 in Sihor Taluka. If one looks at Tables 8 and 9 in tandem, it appears that most of the artisan households may have just crossed the mythical BPL chalk line but are certainly not very well off given their dependency ratios.

Table 9: Economic status of the artisan households in Bhavnagar

(in percentages)

Sl. No.	Taluka	Below poverty line	Above poverty line
1.	Bhavnagar	5.15	94.85
2.	Ghogha	20.34	79.76
3.	Talaja	16.67	83.33
4.	Mahuva	15.29	84.71
5.	Gariadhar	22.22	77.78
6.	Palitana	16.53	83.47
7.	Sihor	36.97	63.03
8.	Umrala	24.94	75.06
9.	Gadhada	18.09	81.91
10.	Botad	5.82	94.18
11.	Vallabhipur	17.11	82.89
	District total	**17.61**	**82.39**

Type of housing

Over half of the artisan households live in *Kuccha* housing units built from local building materials. Given their low incomes, it is quite a difficult proposition to construct a *pucca* house using brick and mortar and steel items. However, this is also equally true that these artisans prefer to live in traditional houses. About one third of the artisans are living in *semi-pucca* housing units and just about 11 per cent of them live in *pucca* houses. The housing position of the artisans is somewhat different in different Talukas. About a quarter of the artisans live in *pucca* houses in Bhavnagar Taluka. The lowest percentages of artisans living in *pucca* houses is found in Talaja (6.89).

Similarly, the highest percentage of artisans living in semi-pucca houses is in Sihor (87.62) while it is lowest in Talaja (8.28). Talaja has the highest percentage of artisans living in *Kuccha* houses whereas the lowest percentage is found in Sihor (5.37).

Table 10: Types of housing of the artisans in Bhavnagar

(in percentages)

		Types of Housing		
Sl. No.	Taluka	Pucca	Semi-pucca	Kuccha
1.	Bhavnagar	24.58	14.45	60.96
2.	Ghogha	12.16	60.38	27.48
3.	Talaja	6.89	8.28	84.83
4.	Mahuva	6.92	26.71	66.37
5.	Gariadhar	10.54	21.84	67.62
6.	Palitana	7.64	15.85	76.51
7.	Sihor	7.00	87.62	5.37
8.	Umrala	9.98	34.91	55.11
9.	Gadhada	9.70	63.24	27.06
10.	Botad	15.75	15.72	62.72
11.	Yallabhipur	12.58	33.22	54.19
	District total	**57.11**	**10.55**	**32.35**

Holding of bank accounts by the Bhavnagar artisans

The findings of the primary survey indicate that even in the Twenty First Century the inclination of the Bhavnagar artisans towards opening saving bank accounts is very low. Just four per cent of the surveyed artisans had a bank account (Table 11). Only in Sihor and Talaja Talukas did the proportion of artisans that had bank accounts reach 18 and 10.

Problems faced by the Bhavnagar artisans in selling the products

Since the artisans have operated on thin margins and a limited range of products, sustainability of their occupations has depended very heavily on the quantities of goods produced and speed of their sales. Between these two, more than the first, traditionally the second aspect has largely settled their existence, viability and earnings. However, during the last 58 years of post-Independence and more particularly after Godhara and post-Godhara physical, social and

Table 11: Holding of bank Accounts by the artisans of Bhavnagar
(in percentages)

		Status on Holding Bank Accounts	
SI.No.	Taluka	Have bank account	Do not have
1.	Bhavnagar	1.16	98.84
2.	Ghogha	2.73	97.27
3.	Talaja	10.38	89.62
4.	Mahuva	2.82	97.18
5.	Gariadhar	1.53	98.47
6.	Palitana	3.88	96.12
7.	Sihor	18.08	81.92
8.	Umrala	0.5 0	99.50
9.	Gadhada	0.87	99.13
10.	Botad	0.10	99.81
11.	Y allabhipur	1.01	98.99
	District total	**95.67**	**4.33**

Table 12: Problems faced by the artisans in procuring the raw materials

Problems	Number of artisans	Percentage
Lack of raw materials	1549	20.49
Quality	413	5.46
High price	2901	38.38
High transportation cost	1781	23.56
Storage requirement	353	4.67
Cost in labour law implementation	8	0.11
Other problems	553	7.32
Total	7558	100.00

Table 13: Problems faced by the artisans in selling their products

Type of problems faced	Number of artisans	Percentage
Not selling	390	5.17
Lack of tools	207	2.74
Not enough demand	4185	55.37
Tough competition	823	10.89
Transportation bottleneck	277	3.66
Storage	181	2.39
Sale at low rate	1341	17.74
Lack of marketing intelligence	6	0.08
Lack of information about the nature of demand	12	0.16
Other	135	1.79

economic cleansing of the minority community, the total environment for their presence, operation, continuation and viability has changed beyond recognition. Prominent social scientists that have keen insight of the Gujarati society, economy and polity have identified specific socio-political context in which the communal carnage had its roots. Among these Sheth (2000) identifies three factors. He states that communal polarization in Gujarat was primarily a post- Independence phenomenon. Several factors contributed to its growth.

- Gujarat underwent *rapid urbanisation* during the last 50 years. The pattern of growth and spread of urbanisation in Gujarat was such that every district, including those falling in the tribal belt, had at least a couple of sizeable cities and a number of small and middle towns. Even the villages are much larger than usual. He added that a large part of Gujarat could in fact be described urban hinterland. Social, cultural, economic and political transactions are close and frequent. In short, it is no longer possible to view the political culture of rural Gujarat as significantly different from that of urban Gujarat.
- Over a period of time, *the Gujarati print and visual media also created a vertically and closely linked system of cultural and political communication that is overtly marked by a majoritarian ethos.* All this transformed the local and rural character of Hindu practices in to some sort of folk Hinduism, giving it strong imprints of anonymity and marketised entertainment. *This, in turn, yielded spaces to the Dalits, OBCs and the tribals and a perceptible decline of Mahajani-Gandhian culture. Political Hinduism also appropriated it.* With the rapid influx of the OBCs, *Dalits* and tribals on the one hand and non-Gujaratis on the other, the demographic composition of the urban centres changed radically. This threw up a new type of leadership among the OBCs, *Dalits* and the tribals.
- This massive infusion of subaltern communities into politics developed a gnawing anxiety and fear of political instability and tensions among the Gujarati elite. Gradually, resentment towards the 'outsiders' took roots in the minds of Gujarati middle class (businessmen, traders, and petty-traders) as well

as among the professionals and intellectuals since the English speaking educated among these new urban entrants found significant positions in the corporate sector and the higher-level government jobs which the Gujaratis felt to be their legitimate preserves. In the Eighties, the *Sangh Parivar* activated the campaign of *Hindu Ekta* in Gujarat to ward off the ethnic conflicts of the type witnessed in Maharashtra. *This was accomplished* by *co-opting the non-Gujarati leadership in BJP and directing the Gujarati ethnic passions towards the religious minorities by portraying them as the villains of the piece.*

- Radhika Desai (2002) identifies a fourth factor. This is *presence of as many as* 44 *Brahmin and over 40 Bania communities in the Gujarati society* which also helped in the consolidation exercise of the *Sangh Parivar.* It played a significant role in the passage of political power from the Congress hands to the BJP. This facilitated easier emergence of a high tide of communalism engineered by the promotion of a political economy that sought to keep the working classes fragmented and in a state of dependency to reduce the price of labour to the lowest levels (Jan Breman: 2003). Once the BJP came to power in Gujarat through this communal polarization, it allowed *the Sangh Parivar* organizations to *Hinduize* the tribals and the *Dalits.As* a consequence, the BJP succeeded in transmuting the ethnic and caste conflicts into communal conflicts.
- Aushutosh Varshney (2000) *identifies a fifth jactor.* This was the *presence of ex-textile mill workers who in the midst of great hardships had got sucked into highly illegal activities as well as becoming mercenaries, available at a price to execute orders from above.* With these advatages, the *Sangh Parivar* had made adequate and elaborate preparations and was only looking for an opportunity to make the minorities a scapegoat and ensure a safe return to power in 2002. Godhra provided this opportunity.

The aftermath of the communal pogram in Gujarat left the Muslim artisans rudderless. Being Muslims, they were targets of communal attacks; post-riots they were isolated; an economic boycott was inflicted on them; quite a large part of their clientele turned hostile. Their traditional occupational trade cycle was disturbed and it affected their economic well-being. Even the non-Muslim artisans got affected very adversely. As a result, the artisans are facing the heat. The artisans are now experiencing several types of problems: these relate to various 'P's of marketing (product, placement, pricing and promotion). The survey responses indicate all these in varying degrees. For example, over 55 per cent felt that there is not good enough demand for their goods. If we add another 18 per cent, who indicated slow rate of off take of their products, to this percentage, the total reaches a staggering 73. There are problems of placement of the products at the marketing destinations due to bottlenecks of transportation and storage. Quite a few of the products, such as *Bharatkam* and *Motikam,* were dependent on the practice of social customs (i.e. part of gifts given to the in-laws of the daughters). Some of these customs continue but certain others have diminished somewhat. There is certainly a need to bring the product range in tune with the changing tastes of the rural and urban Gujarat. As successfully demonstrated by the Khadi and Village Industries Commission for Khadi —cotton, silk, wool—, this can be easily achieved with the inputs from dedicated and innovative NGOs and inputs from institutions such as the Entrepreneurship Development Institute, the IIM, the National Institute of Design, and Centre for Planning and Technology, all located in the capital of the state, Ahmedabad.

Monthly income from the sales of the artifacts

Table 14 provides some telling evidence of the economic hardships that the artisans of Bhavnagar are facing. About 66 per cent of them are realising less than Rs. 1500 per month from the monthly sale of the artifacts that they produce. As already noted, on an average an artisan's family in Bhavnagar has six members and it cannot be supported on this meagre sum. Another 27 per cent of the artisans earn between Rs. 1501 and Rs. 3000 per month. Just two per cent artisans earn above Rs. 3000 per month. Overall, the returns from the artisan related activities are hardly very encouraging. Consequently, it comes as no surprise that many of the interviewed respondents are not engaged in the manufacture of the artifacts whole time these days.

Table 14: Monthly income from the sale of the artifacts of Bhavnagar artisans

(in Rupees)

Sl.No.	Taluka	Range of Income					
		No income	Below 1500	1501 to 3000	3001 to 4000	4001 to 5000	Above 5000
1.	Bhavnagar	1.66	61.30	27.41	5.32	4.32	0.00
2.	Ghogha	2.10	79.66	16.77	1.47	0.00	0.00
3.	Talaja	2.20	40.02	57.29	0.20	0.30	0.00
4.	Mahuva	6.36	57.76	35.08	0.64	0.16	0.00
5.	Gariadhar	13.79	66.86	18.77	0.38	0.19	0.00
6.	Palitana	10.26	78.79	9.92	0.80	0.11	0.11
7.	Sihor	4.72	74.76	16.94	1.30	1.30	0.98
8.	Umrala	1.75	71.57	25.69	1.00	0.00	0.00
9.	Gadhada	1.30	82.20	15.20	1.30	0.00	0.00
10.	Botad	10.32	50.28	33.77	5.25	0.19	0.19
11.	Vallabhipur	1.34	82.05	16.11	0.34	0.17	0.00
	District total	**5.17**	**65.88**	**26.83**	**1.44**	**0.57**	**0.11**

Period of unemployment during last one year

About three-fourth of the artisans (78 per cent) remained employed in the manufacture of the chosen artifacts during the last one year. Among the unemployed ones (about 22 per cent), the period of unemployment varied. About 15 per cent were unemployed for a period ranging between one to three months and about seven per cent for a period ranging between four to six months (Table 15). Some of this 'unemployment' is caused by the specifics of the chosen artisan lines. For example, potters do not get to work during the monsoons and the *Topala-Supada* makers remain idle due to non-availability of raw materials. Gender-wise break-up of the unemployment situation is presented in Table 16. As expected, excepting in a few Talukas, more male remain unemployed than the females. The reason is that the females tend to attend to their domestic chores during the lean periods of occupational engagement.

Table 15: Period artisans remained unemployed during the last year in Bhavnagar

(in percentages)

		Duration of Unemployment			
SI.No.	Taluka	Nil	1 to 3 months	4 to 6 months	7 to 9 months
1.	Bhavnagar	85.38	4.49	9.80	0.33
2.	Ghogha	67.30	30.19	2.52	0.00
3.	Talaja	.96.01	1.30	2.59	0.10
4.	Mahuva	86.16	8.05	5.79	0.00
5.	Gariadhar	87.16	9.58	3.26	0.00
6.	Palitana	52.45	45.04	2.51	0.00
7.	Sihor	83.22	10.26	6.35	0.16
8.	Umrala	92.77	5.99	1.25	0.00
9.	Gadhada	64.11	19.68	16.21	0.00
10.	Botad	78.61	4.32	17.07	0.00
11.	Vallabhipur	59.40	23.83	16.61	0.17
	District total	**77.82**	**14.78**	**7.33**	**0.07**

Table 16: Gender-wise period of unemployment of the artisans of Bhavnagar*

(in percentages)

		Duration of Unemployment					
SI. No.	Taluka	1 to 3 months		4 to 6 months		7 to 9 months	
		Male	Female	Male	Female	Male	Female
1.	Bhavnagar	2.66	1.83	6.81	2.99	0.00	0.33
2.	Ghogha	19.71	10.48	2.10	0.42	0.00	0.00
3.	Talaja	1.10	0.20	2.50	0.10	0.10	0.00
4.	Mahuva	3.22	4.83	5.15	0.64	0.00	0.00
5.	Gariadhar	8.81	0.77	3.07	0.19	0.00	0.00
6.	Palitana	11.29	33.75	2.28	0.23	0.00	0.00
7.	Sihor	10.26	0.00	6.35	‘0.00	0.16	0.00
8.	Umrala	5.74	0.25	1.25	0.00	0.00	0.00
9.	Gadhada	13.60	6.08	13.02	3.18	0.00	0.00
10.	Botad	3.00	1.31	10.88	6.19	0.00	0.00
11.	Vallabhipur	15.77	8.05	8.72	7.89	0.17	0.00
	District total	**7.89**	**6.89**	**5.56**	**1.77**	**0.04**	**0.03**

* Percentages cover only those unemployed.

Self-perceptions about the type of help required from the Government

That the artisans are in dire straights and need immediate help is recognised by both the Central as well as the state governments.

However, the articulation of the nature of help required by the artisans from the government has largely been 'anticipated' by the governments: it has not been seen from the perspectives of the artisans themselves. Of course, it is also true that the artisans have very narrow view of their problems and what is even more precarious is that their own viewpoint on the solutions of their problems may well be clouded by lack of the knowledge about the alternatives that are indeed available. Between these two bipolar ends of the continuum, the fate of the artisans has been largely sealed by the palliatives doled out by the governments on the basis of imagined problems of the artisans that do not attain a good fit with the real ones actually faced by them. Table 17 presents the responses of the artisans themselves indicating the nature of help they would like from the government. The overwhelming demand (about 72 per cent) is for extension of loans to enable them to carry on their lines of business in a more satisfactory manner. About 15 per cent also feel that they need expert guidance to bring their business in tune with the requirements of the changed times. Another eight per cent want setting up of an information centre that provides them comprehensive information about both the forward as well as the backward linkages and a further two per cent want upgradation of their technology. Thus, about 25 per cent artisans are asking for service centre that could cater to their wide ranging needs

Table 17: Perceptions about the type of help required by the artisans of Bhavnagar from the Government

(in percentages)

		Type of Help Required				
SI. N o.	Taluka	Loan	Information Centre	Technology	Guidance	Other
1.	Bhavnagar	40.37	16.61	0.83	42.03	0.17
2.	Ghogha	79.04	7.34	2.31	5.45	5.87
3.	Talaja	98.40	0.90	0.00	0.50	0.20
4.	Mahuva	71.92	6.92	2.33	15.37	3.46
5.	Gariadhar	85.25	8.81	4.60	0.19	1.15
6.	Palitana	27.59	3.88	5.70	47.32	15.51
7.	Sihor	81. 60	10.75	2.12	2.77	2.77
8.	Umrala	80.55	12.72	3.74	1.00	2.00
9.	Gadhada	86.69	9.84	0.43	2.03	1.01
10.	Botad	64.73	8.07	0.00	26.45	0.75
11.	Vallabhipur	81.21	6.71	3.36	6.04	2.68
	District total	**3.55**	**71.96**	**7.65**	**2.25**	**14.59**

of product demand profiles, alternatives in product range, technological choices, and marketing of the products, etc. The responses under the category 'others' included government initiatives in organising handloom and handicraft fairs, gram hats, etc to maximize their sales and advice in marketing. Looking at the perceptions of the solutions indicated by the artisans, it appears that they are hitting the bull's eye in articulating the solutions.

Future-orientation of the Bhavnagar artisans: Willingness to continue in the present lines of artisan professions

The foregoing empirical analysis of the socio-economic conditions of the artisans in Bhavnagar makes it amply clear that they are not at all in a happy position. Their existence is very uncertain; after the communal carnage in Gujarat the market conditions are very unstable; procurement of raw materials is problematic; there is increased competition; products remain unsold for long periods; above all, even continuation in the present lines of business requires financial resources that they clearly lack. In this kind of scenario, one question that assumes crucial significance is whether the artisans would like to continue in their present lines of occupations or, alternately, they would like to seek new pastures for a relatively better and more secure future. From Table 18 it is clear that only less than half of the artisans are inclined

Table 18: Willingness of the Bhavnagar artisans to continue in the profession

(in percentages)

		Willingness to continue in the profession		
SI.N o.	T aluka	Willing	Unwilling	Can't say
1.	Bhavnagar	47.01	16.28	36.71
2.	Ghogha	26.42	42.56	31.03
3.	Talaja	62.67	13.27	24.05
4.	Mahuva	62.19	16.25	21.56
5.	Gariadhar	77.78	5.94	16.28
6.	Palitana	22.92	25.88	51.20
7.	Sihor	34.20	23.29	42.51
8.	Umrala	67.58	3.49	28.93
9.	Gadhada	38.49	22.14	39.36
10.	Botad	50.09	20.45	29.46
11.	Vallabhipur	34.90	14.60	50.50
	District total	**33.33**	**48.15**	**18.52**

to continue in their present lines of business. About 19 per cent are willing to leave the present vocation if they are given an alternative. About one third of the artisans are undecided about their future course of action.

Conclusion

The empirical analysis of the socio-economic status of the artisans of Bhavnagar reveals the fact ofrudderlessness of the rural artisans. Traditionally, their growth was dependent on the development of agricultural and allied activities. However, since the character of the Gujarat economy in general and its agriculture and industry in particular have undergone a significant change, the support that the artisans drew from the rural agricultural economy appears to have declined appreciably. The fact that the rural urban differences themselves narrowed down in Gujarat also affected the demand and supply sides of the artisan trade adversely. The expected gradual shifts of the artisans towards the urban centres on the one hand and advance integration with the market economy that proceed with capitalist development also have not been witnessed. Thus, the artisans find themselves in no man's land: the rural economy is not sustaining them and the urban-industrial one has not integrated them.

As the preceding empirical analysis amply reveals, the artisans know precisely what their problems are but on their own initiative, it appears that the Bhavnagar artisans are hardly in a position to solve them. As Shah (2002) very rightly asks, does this not call for charting a new set of policy initiatives? There is not much hope from the government side since the mid Nineties both the Central as well as the state governments have continued to neglect both the farm and non-farm rural sectors.

References

Basant, Rakesh and R. Parthasarathy. 1991. 'Correlates of inter-regional variations in rural non-agricultural employment in Gujarat'. *Indian Journal of Labour Economics.* 34 (2).

Basant, Rakesh. 1994. 'Economic diversification in rural areas: A review of process with special reference to Gujarat'. *Economic and Political Weekly.* *29* (39).

Breman, Jan. 1974. *Patronage and exploitation: Changing agrarian relations in south Gujarat, India.* Berkley: University of California Press.

Desai, Radhka. 2002. *Slouching towards Ayodhya. New* Delhi: Three Essays Press.

Gadgil, D.R. 1974. *The industrial evolution in India in recent times: 1800-1939. New* Delhi: Oxford University Press.

Ghurye, G.S. *1969. Caste and race in India.Bombay:* Popular Prakashan.

Gohil, Shan~ar.Undated. Rural artisans in Gujarat: A study of their status and role of support agency. Ahmedabad: GIDR (mimeo).

India, Government of. 1977. *Report of the expert committee on small enterprises.* New Delhi: Ministry of Industry.

Shah, Amita.1986. 'Rural industrialisation in Gujarat', *Indian Journal of Regional Science:* 18(1).

Shah, Amita. 2002. 'Changing pattern of rural artisans in Gujarat: Need for a fresh policy?' in Takashi Shinode (ed.). *The other Gujarat: Social transformation among weaker sections.* Mumbai: Popular Prakashan.

Sheth, Dhirubhai L. 2000. 'The politics of communal polarisation; A precursor to Gujarat carnage', *Manushi:* 149.

Stately, E. and *R.* Morse. 1965. *Modern small industry for developing communities.* New York.

Streefkerk, Hein. 1985. *Industrialisation in rural India: Artisans, traders and tribals in south Gujarat.Bombay:* Popular Prakashan.

Varshney, Aushutosh. 2000. *Ethnic conflict and civic life: Hindus and Muslims in India.* New Delhi: Oxford University Press.

Visaria, Pravin. 1994. 'The sectoral distribution of workers in India 1961-1991' in Pravin Visaria and R. Basant (eds.). *Non-agricultural employment in India: Trend and Prospects.* New Delhi: Sage Publications.

Urban settlement patterns of artisans in Karnataka: Geographical expression of thought

Jan Brouwer

Modern town planners and their implementing agencies often find difficulties in resettling slum dwellers and settling of new migrants. According to them, the life-style of those people is one of the main constraints in building a beautiful city. This includes various socio-economic factors.

The studies on urban planning and settlement, whether dealing with ancient, modern or contemporary towns and cities, focus either on the model of planning and/or the practices of those who settle in the towns and cities. The cultural dimension of town settlement itself has hitherto been neglected.

This paper[1] is perhaps the first attempt to gain insight into the settlement dimension of the Indian indigenous knowledge system. I argue that the choice of locale for settlement is neither random nor guided by the principles of efficiency, but follows from indigenous conceptualizations which are informed by categories from various domains simultaneously. From a case study of settlement patterns of one artisan caste, the Visvakarma, a few general conclusions can be drawn.

The data and their analysis refer to the southern, central and northern regions of interior Karnataka. These are presented in three sections. Section one considers the town plan of Mysore city in terms of artisan settlement. Having been the capital of the erstwhile kingdom of Mysore and the later Mysore State, it shows the indigenous model of caste distribution in a more sophisticated form than the other towns of the region. Section two describes the artisans' settlement in towns of central Karnataka and section three considers their settlement in northern Karnataka. Taken together the settlement patterns of the three regions form variations on the same theme guided by the same indigenous categories of segregation and hierarchy. In the concluding section, a few aspects of the indigenous settlement plan are contrasted to those found in Europe and on which India's modern state and its town planning principles are based.

Artisans' settlement in Mysore city

It is only in the city of Mysore, the former capital of the princely State of Mysore, that we find representatives of all Visvakarma sub-castes from southern Karnataka. Here I shall present the distribution of the castes in the city areas of Mysore in some detail, because I have observed a structurally similar pattern in all major towns of this region, e.g., Tumkur, old Bangalore, Nagamangala, Channapatna and Kollegal.

Mysore city used to be the capital of the erstwhile State of Mysore and the residence of the then Maharajas. Today it is a fast growing industrial and cultural center. It is situated on 12.42′ E long on the north-western base of the Chamundi hill. The fort (*Kote*), in which the Palace stands, is situated almost in the geographical center of the city. East of the fort lies the Doddakere tank, now the Exhibition Grounds. Formerly, the tank linked the eastern gate of the Palace with 1000 steps leading to the Chamundi Temple on the hill. To the north of the Fort is the main *bazaar,* called Doddapete, and small *bazaar,* Chikkapete, is found to its western side beside a Brahmin *agrahara*. Another *agrahara* is located to its southern side.

The work on the present Palace was started in 1897 and completed in 1912, after the destruction by fire of the old Palace which stood in the same place since at least 1800. "The archeological records unearthed up to date show that "the city's antiquity goes back to the 10th century, if not earlier"(Rao 1930 :751).

The Mysore Fort area (*Kote*), including the Royal Palace, is commonly referred to as the center of the city. However, if we take the intersection of the main north-south and east-west roads as the real center of the city, the Palace, or the seat of political power, is located slightly to the south-east. A rather neglected temple devoted

Figure 1 : Street plan of Mysore inner city and the localities with a concentration of Visvakarma Sub-castes

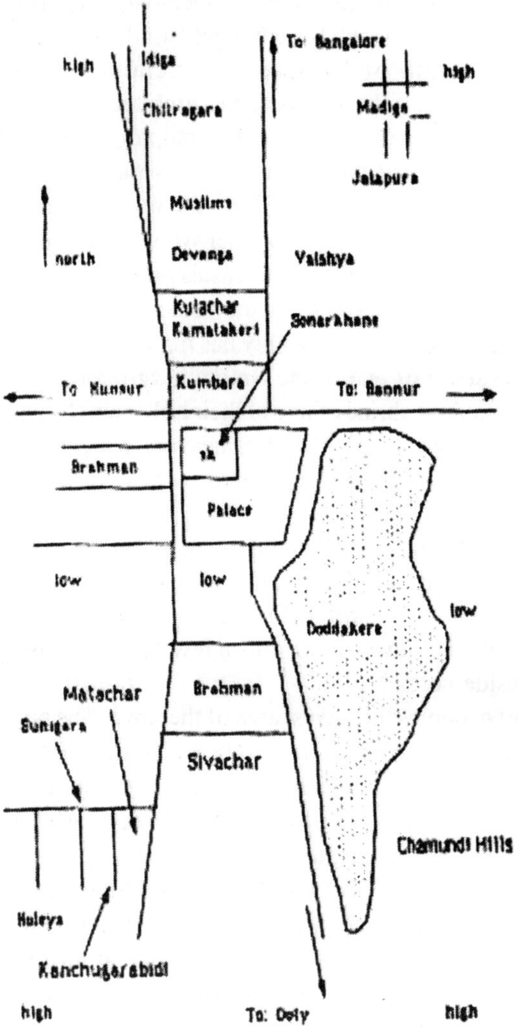

to Siva stands to its north-west. There is a road running diagonally from the north-west to the city center. This road was formerly a path running along the canal that transported drinking water from a hill in the north-west to the Palace.

In those days, the Brahmin residences could all be found within the fort enclosure. The Kulachar and Sivachar gold-smiths' workshops (*sonarkhane*) were to be found in the north-west corner of the Palace ground.[2] Both Kulachar and Sivachar goldsmiths were employed here. The last Maharaja of Mysore could claim master carpenter Yallakappachar (Kulachar) as his chief architect and master sculptor Siddalingachar (Sivachar) as his chief sculptor.

All Kulachars had their houses and workshops in Kamatakere (*kamata* means 'the cultivation which the owner carries on with his own stock, but by the labour of another who is paid for work and *keri* means 'street'). In this locality, three castes predominated: the Kulachar artisans, the Devanga weavers, and the Vokkaliga peasants. Even today, the caste composition of this locality has hardly altered. The Sivachars reside to the south of one of the Brahmin *agraharas* in the south of the town, around the shrine of one of their holy men (Nagalingaswami). The Kulachar own the Kalika Paramesvara temple in Kamatakeri, where the deity is served by an Uttardi, whose residence is close to the temple.

In the south-west corner of the town, adjacent to the Holeyakeri, or locality of untouchables–and serving as main road of the limemakers' locality (*sunigakeri*)–runs the Coppersmiths' Street (*kanchugarabidi*). Now-a-days, only a few Telugu speaking Matachar founders reside here.

The fort occupies the lowest area of the town. The potters' locality (*kumbarakeri*), where the terrain gradually increases in elevation towards the locality of the Idiga (*toddyappers*) and Chitrakaras (painters). The Brahmin localities (*agrahara*), as well as the streets where the Sivachars reside, are on low ground.

The two highest hills of the city area are found in the north-east and south-west. The former area is called Jalapur, because there used to be plenty of drinking water (*jala*), and is the locality, where the Madiga or leather workers–an untouchable caste–live. The latter locality is Holeyakeri.

The settlement of the Visvakarma sub-castes follows a particular pattern. The Sivachar reside on the low terrain and the Kulachar on a slightly elevated terrain. The only other city where all the Visvakarma sub-castes can be found, Channapatna, shows the same distribution of the sub-castes in relation to the terrain.

In Mysore city, as well as in other places of the region, the higher castes such as the Brahmin, Lingayat, Jain, Vaishya, all vegetarian, reside in the least elevated parts of the towns, while lower castes such as the Uppar, Agasa, Hazam, Idiga, Vokkaliga and Muslim, all non-vegetarians, reside on the more elevated terrains.

Regarding settlement, the following consistency has been observed. If there are only Sivachars and Kulachars, the latter reside on high terrain and the former on low ground. If Uttaradis and Kulachars both reside in a town or village, the former reside on low terrain and the latter on high terrain. If Matachars and Kulachars are present, the former live on elevated terrain and the latter on low terrain. If there are only Sivachars, as in Shivarapatna, the founders-cum-sculptors occupy the low terrain and the blacksmith-cum-carpenters the high ground.

In conclusion, the elevated areas are inhabited by the non-Brahmin, or non-vegetarian castes, while the vegetarian, usually Brahmin castes, are settled in the lower wards. Considering the distribution of the Visvakarama sub-castes over the town areas, it may be concluded that the vegetarian Sivachar are generally settled in the lower areas and the non-vegetarian Kulachar in the higher areas.

Artisans' settlement in central Karnataka

In central Karnataka, on the local level, the residences and workshops of the Doddamane and Chikkamane are never found in the same street. The former are settled on streets inhabited by lower castes, such as barbers (hajjam), basketmakers (Medar), washerman (Agasa), masons (Uppar), shepherds (Kuruba), Maratha Kshatriyas and Muslims. These streets are invariably found on the higher ground in towns. The Chikkamane are found in the streets inhabited by Lingayats, Jains or Brahmins, in the lower lying wards in towns. In Shimoga (town), the Doddamane goldsmiths have their shops in the Muslim and oil-maker (Ganiga) locality, on high terrain, and the Chikkamane goldsmiths live on the lower end of the same road, which leads to the Brahmin ward. In Hiriyur and Challekere, the Bayala Akkasaliga have settled in the streets where there were already a few Doddamane goldsmiths. In the places where the Muddekammara are settled, there are no other Visvakarmas.

The Chikkamane chariot makers (rathakara) are settled in two villages–Ajjihalli and Gopinahalli–in Channagiri Taluk. The Chikkamane founder-cum-sculptors are found in two places, in Ajjihalli and in the town of Channagiri, in both cases near the houses of the goldsmiths of the same sub-caste.

Considering the distribution of the Visvakarma throughout the town areas, it may be concluded that the Chikkamane are generally settled in the lower areas and the Doddamane on the higher ground. The Muddekammara are invariably settled in the south-eastern ward near their Kali temple, which is usually built on the highest ground in the place (Hosahatti, Kampli, Kamlapur, K. Gollerahalli). The Bayala Akkasaliga appear not to fit into this pattern. However, since they have begun to give up migration and have started to settle, they appear to be adjusting to the Doddamane pattern.

Artisans' settlement in northern Karnataka

In norther Karnataka, the Visvakarma sub-castes are not regularly distributed over the region. The Madipattar gold-smiths are found in all larger villages, towns and cities. Usually, one to five Madipattar families are settled in one place. Members of the Konnurpanta sub-caste can be found all over the northern region.

A craftwise breakup, however, shows a slightly different picture. The Konnurpanta blacksmith-cum-carpenter are very few in number and are only to be found in places where the Niligundapanta sub-caste is absent, or represented by only a very small number of craftsmen. The Konnurpanta braziers and sculptors are mainly concentrated in Hungund Taluk in Bijapur District, which is very near the Chalukya towns of Aihole and Pattadkal, on the Badami Plateau. The Konnurpanta goldsmiths, however, are found in nearly all parts of this region, and there are usually three to twelve such households in a village or town. A few households of Niligundapanta blacksmiths and carpenters can be found in nearly all places within this region. Vaishnava blacksmiths and carpenters are concentrated in only two towns, namely, Gajendragad in Ron Taluk in Gadag District and in Sandur Taluk in Bellary District, in the central region. The rulers of Gajendragad and Sandur belong to the same royal family and are spoken of by the Vaishnava Visvakarma with respect, as they are considered to be their best patrons. The Vaishnava founders and goldsmiths are concentrated in Yadgir, but only a few of them – all goldsmiths – still practice their craft. A large number of them are settled in Adoni, which is today a large town, just across the present state border in Andhra Pradesh.

To sum up, the members of all four sub-castes can be found throughout the northern region, although there are important variations in the distribution. The Madipattar goldsmiths are settled in the larger towns and cities, but the Konnupanta goldsmiths are also settled in the villages. The Konnurpanta braziers and sculptors are found more or less concentrated on and around the Badami Plateau. The Niligundapanta can all be found in every type of villages and towns. All the Vaishnava are settled in towns with forts. Their blacksmiths and carpenters are to be found close to the forts of the local rulers, while their goldsmiths are located in erstwhile mint towns.

The Madipattar and Konnurpanta goldsmith are mainly to be found in market towns, while the Vaishnava goldsmith – a very small number of whom are actually now craftsmen – are still found in historical mint towns (manufacturing for the market may be distinguished from working for a ruler's mint).

Another difference may be observed in the settlement pattern of the blacksmiths and carpenters. While Niligundapanta, and to a lesser extent Konnurpanta, blacksmiths and carpenters are found in the rural areas, mainly working for the peasants, the Vaishnava blacksmith and carpenter are largely concentrated close to the rulers' forts. They are proud of having been the rulers' weapon makers.

The Konnurpanta braziers and sculptors are still settled in the vicinity of the erstwhile Badami capitals, an area rich in the schist used by the sculptors. Recently, a few of them have migrated to the larger market towns, such as Bagalkot.

In this region, on the local level, one rarely finds all these sub-castes in a place. In those cases in which there is more than one sub-caste in one town or village, the households of these sub-castes are not found together in a single street; a closer inspection of town plans showing the distribution of castes, reveals that such vegetarian castes as Brahmins, Vaishyas, Jains, Jangamas and possibly others, if authochthonous, have their houses in the lower lying wards of the *bazaar* (*pete*). However, all autochthonous non-vegetarian castes, and sometimes the ritually lower sub-castes of the Virasaiva sect, have their houses in the more elevated wards of the *bazaar*.

In the case of a fortified towns, the fort(*kote*) is usually inhabited by the people, who were formerly linked with the court, and by Brahmins. In such cases, the Brahmin ward is situated either to the east or to the south of the palace. The wards of the two major untouchable castes–the Holeya and the Madiga–are never situated inside the fort. If their wards are situated within the larger area of the *bazaar,* they are found on the higher ground.

In other words, the vegetarian, and thus the castes, which are locally considered ritually higher, have settled in the lower lying wards of the towns, and the non-vegetarian, or lower castes, on the higher ground. The lower the ritual status of the caste, the higher the ground on which it lives.

According to this general (unconscious) "rule", one would expect all Smarta[3], and all vegetarian Vaishnava Visvakarmas, to be located in the lower lying wards of towns and the non-vegetarian Vaishnava Visvakarmas on the higher ground of the town. But the distribution of the Visvakarma sub-castes shows a more complicated pattern.

In the case of fortified towns, the Madipattar are always settled inside the fort, but the Niligundapanta are always settled outside it. Apparently, not all Konnurpantas are allowed to live inside the fort. Konnurpanta goldsmiths and specialist carpenters are settled in the lower area inside the fort. In rare cases, the 'mother house" of the village goddesses – the Dayamavva Durgavva Temple – is inside the fort. In such cases, it is the Konnurpanta carpenter who holds this temple's priestly rights. Because this temple is an elevated ward, among the non-vegetarian castes, the house of this Konnurpanta carpenter is found in the elevated area of the fort. However, in all cases the Madipattar are settled in the northern half of the fort and the Konnurpanta in the southern half of the fort.

In non-fortified towns, which are either *bazaar* towns, or larger *bazaars* around a small fort, the Niligundapanta black-smiths and carpenters are invariably settled near the highest area, among the non-vegetarian castes. The Niligundapanta houses are mostly built around the temple of the village goddesses (*gramadevata*), Dayamavva Dugavva, where their carpenters have the priestly rights. Even in places without such a temple, their settlement pattern does not change. The majority of the Madipattar are settled in the higher areas of these towns, and a few of them in the lower areas. The majority of the Konnurpanta are settled in the higher areas and less than half their number in the lower areas.

In relation to the wind-directions, it has been observed that the majority of Visvakarmas, irrespective of craft or sub-caste, are settled in the north-western ward of the towns and a minority of them in the south-eastern wards of the towns.

To sum up, the Madipattar are settled on either high or low terrain and although the Konnurpanta settlement pattern resembles that of the Madipattar, there is one significant difference between them. The Konnurpanta are usually settled on the boundary between the lower and higher ground, and hence also on the 'diet' border. The Niligundapanta are always settled on high ground amidst non-vegetarian castes, close to the temples of the village goddesses. The Vaishnava sub-castes are always settled outside the fort, or on the edge of town or village, and blacksmiths and carpenters are found on high ground and the goldsmiths on low ground.

Considering the distribution of the Visvakarma sub-castes throughout the town areas, it may be concluded that the Konnurpantas are generally settled in the lower and the Niligundapanta in the higher areas. The dichotomous settlement pattern is not observed by the Madipattar, who may be settled in any area of the town, while the Vaishnava are settled outside this town pattern.

Conclusions

In the foregoing sections I have considered the settlement patterns of the Visvakarma artisans in towns of Karnataka. All over Karnataka they are concentrated in the North-west quarter of the town, while a few are settled in the south-east quarter. Thus, in terms of the indigenous compass these artisans control the Vayu-Agni axis of a town. The Scheduled Castes or former untouchable castes, such as the Madiga and the Holeya, control the north-east/south-west axis, while the Brahmin occupied the western and southern ends of a town, and all other castes were distributed over the remaining urban localaities.

The point here is that the settlement in localities was not a random choice, but evolved logically from a commonly shared perception of reality. The concepts underlying the practices of settlement were (are) shared by all.

The conclusions of the analysis of the settlement patterns of a single caste, may be summarized thus:

(i) high (sub-) castes are settled on low terrain;

(ii) low(sub-) castes are settled on high terrain;

(iii) high occupations are settled on low terrain; and

(iv) low occupations are settled on high terrain.

Throughout the history of Karnataka, a general observation of habitation and settlement can be formulated in terms of an opposition between mountains, hills and plains. The mountains and hills are forest areas (often fortified places belonging to local rulers), and mainly inhabited by "tribal" people. The villages and towns of the plains are Brahmin settlements, lying amidst cultivated land.

The distribution of castes in town is, I feel, similar. The elevated areas are inhabited by the non-Brahmin, that is non-vegetarian castes, while the vegetarian, usually Brahmin castes, are settled in the lower wards.

This observation may be contrasted with the indigenous settlement pattern in Europe. Here the highest estates of society inhabited the higher terrains or fortified low and elevated lower areas to occupy literally a high position.

The indigenous knowledge system shows geographical expressions of thought in spatial terms. They are concretized conceptualizations in terms of Indian categories which are often contrasted, if not opposed, to those on which the views of the modern state are based. The town planners and resettlement authorities could benefit from the knowledge of these contrasts.

Notes

1. The data presented in this paper form part of a larger corpus of data collected in Karnataka during field work for different research projects between 1978 and 1996. In my endeavour to understand the working of indigenous knowledge system, the present paper is the third in a series of three. Brouwer (1990) considers tangible expressions of blacksmiths' conceptualizations in their work and life and Brouwer (1998) deals with place names, sub-caste and personal names related to the Visvakarma artisans of Karnataka.
2. The Visvakarma caste of Karnataka comprises blacksmiths, carpenters, coppersmiths, sculptors and goldsmiths. They are distributed into various

sub-castes by region. Thus, in southern Karnataka we find the Sivachar, Kulachar, Mathachar and Uttaradi sub-castes. In central Karnataka, there are the Chikkamane, Doddamane, Bayala Akkasaliga and Muddekammara sub-castes. And in northern Karnataka we find the Madipattar, Konnurpanta, Niligundapanta and the Vaishnava sub-castes.

3. In northern Karnataka, the vegetarian sub-castes called Madipattar, Konnurpanta, and Niligundapanta together form the Smarta Visvakarma category. This category stands in a complementary opposition to the Vaishnava category among whom there are non-vegetarians also.

References

Brouwer, Jan. 1990. 'Material Expression of Thought: Aspects of Ironsmiths in South India', Techniques and Culture, no. 15, Paris: Editions de la Maison des Sciences de l'Homme.

1995. The Makers of the World – Caste, Craft, and Mind of South Indian Artisan. Delhi: Oxford University Press.

Rao, C. Hayavadana (ed.) 1927-29. Mysore Gazetteer, 4 Vols. Bangalore: Government Press.

1998. Nomenclative expressions of thought, place, names and her names related to artisans and their work in Karnataka, *Journal of Social Sciences* 2 (1):

Part - V

Other types

A rural community in the process of modernization: A case study of three Nepalese villages of rural Assam

K.P. Upadhyaya

The process of modernization has influenced rural life in a big way. Every aspect of village life viz. social, economic, political and cultural has experienced a steady transformation. The old structure of village society, and the old pattern of village life have changed appreciably. In this study it is hypothesized that since India attained independence, there has been a perceptible change in the Nepalese individuals, and the social institutions of rural Nepalese community of Assam. The study then proceeds to test this hypothesis through a field study. The universe of the present study is confined to a particular community – the Nepalese with similar traditional and ethnic background. Hence, a generalization can be made about the entire rural Nepalese community of Assam from its findings.

The Nepalese community -people of Nepali origin -has been living in India for a long period of time. It has been participating actively in the socio-economic and political processes in India. Although quite conscious about its identity as Nepalese, it has been going through the process of assimilation within the Indian fold. As we know, even though living in totally different socio-cultural locales, different cultural/linguistic groups have shown a tendency to retain their traditions and maintain the prestige of those traditions throughout the globe. In order to improve their socio-economic status with political power in an alien society, various communities aspire to build their own religion, language and political structures. The Nepalese of Assam are also not an exception in this regard and they have focused on their distinct urge to maintain a separate identity. The Nepalese of Assam have retained their language and culture. After going through a series of movements, the Nepali language was recognized as an Indian language and listed on 20th August 1992 in the Eighth Schedule of the Indian Constitution.

The Nepalese migrated to Assam and some other parts of India from Nepal. The British acquired these areas as a consequence of Gurkha-British War (1814-1816) and the Sugauli Treaty. Even prior to the British rule, the Nepalese came to this part of the country and maintained a cultural relationship with the people of this region.[1] The British, however, accelerated the flow of Nepalese to this region. Thus, in course of time, the Nepalese constituted a sizable section of Assam's total population.

As a result of the Assam Movement (1979-1985), the congenial relations between the native Assamese community and the Nepalese began to deteriorate to a certain extent. The movement commanded a sense of xenophobia among different communities in Assam, which inspired them to retain their culture and traditional way of living. Consequently, they started organizing themselves to assert their unique ethnicity. With the growth of their population and a heightened sense of consciousness of their distinct language and identity, the Nepalese are now able to set up such organizations, under which they may assert their identity within the jurisdiction of Assam as Nepalese of Assam as well as Indian Nepalese and discard their relationship with Nepal in all respects.

The Nepalese of the earlier generations had impressive record of fighting for India's Independence in Assam. Together with the *Assamiyas*, they fought against the notorious grouping scheme.[2]They also fought for the official recognition of *Assamiya* as the medium of instruction at par with English up to the graduate level in the educational institutions. In this modern era, modern Nepalese poets and writers have enriched the Assamese literature. Therefore, for all practical purposes, the Nepalese are an inseparable part of Assamese society.[3] The attitude of the Assamese to the Nepali language is similar to their attitude towards the indigenous tribal languages of Assam.[4]

After independence, the Indo-Nepal Friendship Treaty of 1950, the tripartite Delhi Agreement of 1951, and the revised Indo-Nepal Agreement of 1956 facilitated the Nepalese of Nepal to have equal rights with Indian Nepalese for free movement, employment, agriculture, business, settlement and acquisition of property without hindrance. Though technically Nepal is a foreign country, the Nepalese of Nepal are never treated as foreign nationals in India. This is a serious problem for the Indian Nepalese of the new generation. The Nepalese of Assam are Indians, born and brought up in Assam for generations and possess distinct characteristics of their own.

The sample of the study

With the help of government documents and other available secondary sources and also through discussions with some local people, the researcher prepared a complete list of pre-dominantly Nepalese villages of Assam. A pilot study was then conducted to select the three sample villages where the Nepalese resided in a homogenous way. Many other considerations such as observable infrastructure facilities like literacy, and communication, etc. were also kept in mind while selecting the sample of villages (M.S. Raghuvanshi: 1984 also used a similar technique).[5] The selected villages were categorized as high, medium and low based on their location on the continuum of development. The task of drawing the sample for the present study was accomplished in two stages. Firstly, the villages were selected and secondly, the respondents were selected through the technique of stratified random sampling. Since most of the variables under study were classified into three ordinal categories, it was considered more in the fitness of things to select three villages representing three levels of development. Moreover, our pilot study also convinced us that only three villages could yield us the sample as large as 300 rural Nepalese.

The criteria selected to determine the degree of village development are as follows:

(1) Size of village population

(2) Percentage of literacy in the total population

(3) Percentage of non-agricultural workers in the total population

(4) Distance from the town

(5) Penetration of the means of transport and mass communication

A brief account of the three selected villages follows.

Village Golia

Golia is situated at a distance of about 80 km. from the district headquarters (Tezpur) and 3 km. south from the headquarters of Biswanath Charali sub-division in Sonitpur district. With 596 households and a total population of 3523, it is the biggest Nepalese village of Sonitpur district. It is bounded on the north by the Erabari village grazing reserve. On the eastern boundary lies the Golia *Khola* (stream) and paddy fields, which fulfill the demands of the village agriculturists. The Golia *Khola* is a stream which flows across the paddy fields. Garehagi Gaon is situated on the western boundary of the village. Sogra Tea Estate and Bhirgaon village lie on its southern boundary. There are four big ponds within the village.

Regarding the origin of the name of the village the elderly villagers of the Golia village narrate that there is a *Khola* (stream) on the eastern side of the village known as Golia *Khola*, which flows towards the Brahmaputra and hence, the villagers recognize the village as Golia. Another local story suggests that the earlier inhabitants of the village were compelled to leave the area due to an epidemic and since then the people termed the area as *Erabari* (the abandoned village).

Seventy five per cent people of this village were literate. There were 53 persons who had completed post graduation in various subjects including Nepali. The working population in the village was 1445.The agricultural workers totaled 905 (25.6 per cent and non-agricultural workers number 540 (15.3 per cent) aggregating about 41 per cent of the total population.

Village Udaypur

Udaypur is situated at a distance of about 70 km. from the district headquarters (Tinsukia) and 25 km. east from the headquarters of Margherita sub-division in Tinsukia district. With 572 households and a total population of 3508, it is the biggest Nepalese village of Tinsukia district which is situated at a distance of about 7 kilometers east from the National Highway 38 and Lekhapani town. The Dihing River and Pengree (the famous place for Chitranala plant) bound it on the north. On the western boundary lies the Tirap Gate and National Highway 38. Rampur village, which is totally dominated by the Nepalese community, is situated on the eastern boundary of the village. Tipong colliery and Tirap river are located on the southern boundary. The

Stil-well Road runs 3 km. through the heart of the village. From Lekhapani onward, the road runs in the dale of upper Assam for about 20 km. on Assam-Arunachal boundary.

Regarding the origin of the name of the village the elderly villagers of the Udaypur state that the village is situated in the eastern corner of Assam. *Uday* means rising and *Pur* means place. Udaypur means the land of the rising sun. Hence, the villagers recognize the name of the village as Udaypur.

Out of the population of 3508 persons (1776 males and 1732 females), 2305 (1184 males, 1121 females) were adults and listed in the electoral rolls and 1203 (592 males, 611 females) were below the age of 18 years. 2562 persons (73 per cent approximately) were literate. Of the working population of 1298 in the village, 1043 (29 per cent) were agricultural workers and 255 (8 per cent) were non-agricultural workers together constituting 37 per cent of the total population.

Village Sukuli

Sukuli is situated at a distance of about 60 km. south from the district headquarters (Golaghat) and 20 km. north from the headquarters (Sarupather) of Dhansiri sub-dvision in Golaghat district. With 152 households and a total population of 608, it is the biggest Nepalese village of Dhansiri sub-division, which is situated at a distance of about 10 kilometers north from the Borpather town/railway station. It is bounded on the north by the Naharbari village and Sonali Pather village. On the western boundary lies the village Dubarani and Dhansiri river. The Musar-Bhanga village of Kachamari is situated on the eastern boundary of the village. On the southern boundary there is a Bridge called, Herheri Dalong and a village known as Basapather. The village is connected by a P.W.D. road, which connects the Borpather town.

Regarding the origin of the name of the village the elderly villagers of the Sukuli village stated that the surrounding area of the village is mainly covered by low land area and the *Pavajan* (a small lake) is also not far from the village. The Sukuli village is situated on such a place, which covers the whole high land of the area. In Nepali *Sukulo Thaon* means dry place and *Sukeko Dado* means high land. Therefore, Sukuli means the high land, which always remains dry and the villagers recognize the name of the village as Sukuli.

Since independence, the main produce of the village was sugarcane (*Ukkhu* in Nepali). They started cultivating it from 1956 when the Dergaon sugar mill started to function. Now, they have given up this crop and have started tea plantation and other settled cultivation. Rice, jute, bamboo, betel nut, maize, ginger, and potato, etc. are the main crops of the village.

Out of the total population of 608 persons, 187 males and 119 females (total 306) had the voting rights and 302 (171 males and 131 females) were below the age of 18 years. The village had 426 literate persons (70 per cent approximately). The working population in the village was 182.Among these, 122 (21.2 per cent) were agricultural workers and 60 (9.8 per cent) were non-agricultural workers together constituting 30 per cent of the total population.

Type of families

61 per cent of the respondents belonged to joint families. Only 39 per cent respondents belonged to the nuclear families. Thus, joint family continued to be dominant mode of family organization among the studied respondents. Of the 63 per cent respondents married and living with spouses, 56 per cent had already attained parenthood of either one or two children. While 86 per cent of the respondents fully agreed with the small family norm of two or three children, 12 per cent respondents agreed with it only partially.

Interaction with the opposite sex

The rural people have not been able to break the traditional reluctance to have friendly interaction with the members of the opposite sex for a variety of reasons. Very few of the respondents had the opportunity of an intimate contact with the opposite sex for fear of censure and ridicule. They tend to stand on the doorway, longing for the freedom of an amiable relationship with the opposite sex but were unable to completely cut themselves off from the inherited attitudes of reluctance towards open contacts with the males and the females. The respondents accepted the equality of gender as an emerging principle of new life. They showed little resistance being partners in studies, and sharing household chores. Even at the cognitive level the majority, roughly about 74 per cent of the respondents, completely detached itself from the traditional hold of men over the lives of their wives.

An overwhelming percentage of respondents perceived change in their opinion about the role of the parents, and educational level of their life partner. Still larger was the percentage of respondents who saw change about the age at which marriage should be solemnized. However, they seemed to concede much less change with regard to the caste of the life partner and still lesser in matters of the religion of the spouse. Interestingly, a distinct majority seemed to be at variance with values governing the meeting of boys and girls before marriage in the village.

On arriving at a judgement one must, however, appreciate that there is no uniform baseline for all the respondents against which they have perceived the registered changes. Perceptions of the villagers vary in their change–proneness as also in the degrees of actual change registered. In many of the cases the village as a collectivity itself had changed appreciably and hence the perception of change in the minds of the respondents from such a village would show an altogether different response than the ones who describe changes against the context of a village that has remained largely unchanged.

Selection of the spouse

Two thirds of the respondents declared that the parents should respect the likes and dislikes of the boys and the girls. 85 per cent of the respondents had checked the character of their would be spouses. It was very clear that character was something that the rural people cared for most as in the eyes of the rural people moral virtue was assigned highest importance. In doing so, the rural people demonstrated a good deal of Puritanism. The second important trait, as indicated by the responses, was the temperament of the spouse. More males than females preferred 'good temperament' as an essential quality in their spouses. Education and physical fitness were pushed to third and fourth places respectively though about one-third and one-fourth of the respondents preferred them respectively. Social and economic status of the family of the spouse was given importance more by the male than the female respondents.

Position of women

Regarding the position of women in the family in particular and in the society in general, it appeared that despite the fact that they were the earning members in many families, the males dominated over the females. This was probably because it was a patriarchal society. On the surface of it, one found that the woman enjoyed equal status in day-to-day activities, but as one entered deeper into the lives of the people one discovered that the women had very little power. It was apparent that the Nepalese females of the villages were very hard working. On being acquainted with the daily life of the people, it was discovered that besides child-care and child rearing and performing all the domestic work, the females were also allotted work in the field. While the men relaxed and were engaged in chitchat, the women remained busy in processing food and cooking. During the harvesting and sowing seasons, in addition to her usual domestic preoccupations the female was a regular worker in the farming operations. She sowed and reaped the paddy along with the male members and in the same manner. Thus, it was observed that a woman was an economic asset to the family. However, the hard ground reality was that she was not at par with a man in so as far as her status in the family or society was concerned.

Although the money was kept with the wife in many families, every single *Paisa* was spent with the prior approval of the husband. Of course, this generalization was not applicable in the purchase of foodstuffs. Regarding marriage, divorce, and any other vital decision, it was the male who decided, in fact dictated. Some female 'exceptions' were, of course, also present in the Nepalese community. They married according to their own choice; they also threatened to divorce their husbands because of incompatibility, and the like. Among the young couples, due to recent demands, husband and wife have been found behaving as friends and companions and also as counselors to each other on many personal and/or familial issues.

Modern educated Nepalese women possessed higher position and higher status in the society. But the village women of different backgrounds were not very much aware and conscious of their social and political rights. Most of them were happy if the family was financially solvent and if the relationship between the members of the family remained harmonious. Now, the Nepalese girls have been found to be equally enthusiastic about receiving higher education. It may also be noted here that there was no prostitution in the society.

It was observed that the husband was generally older than the wife among the Nepalese. The wife, though a co-worker in the field or farm or office was loyal and obedient to the husband. The relationship was more or less congenial barring some exceptions. In a joint family, the wife was not subject to that restrictions as are observed in the typical Indian traditional joint family. She can talk to her husband freely in front of other members, but cannot make vulgar jokes.

Among the aged, the husband and wife do not use each other's name. They address each other anonymously and while giving reference, the husband is referred to as *Mero Logne* (my man) and the wife as *Meri Aimai* (my woman). The young and modern couples of today, however, use personal names. Both the husband and wife have equal responsibilities in the welfare of the family and upbringing of the children. Though there is a broad division of labour in the household activities, and most of the chores are allotted to the females, the division is not sharply observed. Occasionally, and in the case of necessity, they share each other's domestic tasks. Very often couples are found going out together for recreation or for visiting others. On the whole, the husband-wife relationship is one of love and shared responsibilities, but there is definite domination of the husband.

Among the rural Nepalese of Assam, the influence of superstition is decreasing due to the interaction with the Assamese and other communities. The influence of modern practices can be observed in many of their socio-religious ceremonies. Moreover, the gradual transition from the traditional religion towards modern practices is also seen. It can be argued that their religious outlook can be viewed along a continuum of traditional Nepalese religion on the one hand and modern influence on the other. So, the religious ideas and practices among them can be viewed according to the modern Hindu religion superimposed with traditional rural practices.

There is a change in the attitude and mentality of the Nepalese community. As aged respondents stated, earlier on marriage outside the caste/community was not even thought of. But today many young men and women are prepared to break through the caste/community barrier if they have fallen in love and situation demands it. The older generation, however, still thinks in terms of old caste/community practices and among the older generation of the surveyed villages the endogamous nature of the caste has remained almost intact. In the villages, they still depend on their castes/communities very largely for help during critical periods of life, like death. Respondents of Golia village reported more liberal views on the issue of inter-caste marriages with different castes and communities of Assam than the respondents of Udaypur and Sukuli. Male respondents showed more rational and progressive attitudes than the female respondents.

In the process of assimilation, the dietary system of the Nepalese community has become similar to that of the neighbouring communities; yet, food items like '*gundruk*' (fermented and dried leafy vegetables), '*sinki*' (fermented and dried radish), '*sel-roti*' or '*ghumaune-roti*'(baked rounded rice powder bread), etc. continue to maintain the distinctive identity of the community.

There are several associations/organizations of the Nepalese community that have been formed with a view to safeguard their identity and interest in Assam. *Assam Gurkha Sammelan* (AGS), *Nepali Sahitya Parishad* (NSP), *Nepali Surksya Parishad* (NSP), *All Assam Nepali Students' Union* (AANSU), *Nepali Sewa Sadan* (NSS), *Special Protected Class Demand Committee* (SPCDC) etc. are the major Nepalese organizations of Assam. Among these, SPCDC is a political organization and others are non-political.

Among the Nepalese of the three sample villages, *Assam Gurkha Sammelan* and *All Assam Nepali Students' Union* are more popular and they think that these organizations are helpful in safeguarding their interest and identity. The organizations viz. *Nepali Surkshya Parishad* and *Nepali Sewa Sadan* are less popular and the organizations vis. *Nepali Sahitya Parishad* (literary organization) and *Special Protected Class Demand Committee* (political organization) have started gaining popularity among the more conscious Nepalese. The consciousness to join ethnic group organizations (stated above) might provide them the chance to become more articulate and organized. Hence, the Nepalese elites want to have a share in the administration of the state so as to safeguard their interests. That is why they have created the political platform of the SPCDC. But the Nepalese of Assam and, particularly, the surveyed villages did not come into conflict with the people of Assam regarding their interests. Most of the time, the Nepalese of Assam, and particularly the surveyed villages, identified themselves with the interests of the Assamese. They thought that the development of the Nepalese would also help in the progress and prosperity of the Assamese society as a whole. Hence, they are interested to contribute their share in the Assamese nation building including a share in the administration of the state. The growth in the numerical strength of the Nepalese community and its growing organizational strength in Assam constitute a strong political force in the state. The Nepalese elite like any other ethnic elite in the state has started bargaining with the ruling elite for an adequate share of the political cake.

They have demanded introduction of visa-passport system in order to make a distinction between Nepalese of Nepal and Nepalese of Indian origin[6], permanent settlement to Nepalese settlers, introduction of Nepali language in all educational institutions, membership of the Nepalese in UPSC and APSC (Assam Public Service Commission) and their inclusion in the Scheduled Tribes/Castes status. The Nepalese of Assam have been sending their representatives to the State Assembly and their numerical strength in some constituencies have enabled them to play an important role in electoral politics.

The Nepalese elite participated in the electoral politics of Assam even in the pre-independence period. Dalbir Singh Lohar, a prominent leader of the Nepalese, was a member of the Assam Legislative Assembly during 1946-52.[7] He was a Congressman and a worker of the '*Chah Mazdoor Sangha*' – a labour wing of the Congress Party.

After independence, under the leadership of emerging educated elite, the Nepalese became increasingly articulate and organized in a bid to maintain their distinct identity in Assam. The growing numerical strength of the Nepalese of the state obviously played a very useful role on this issue. Consequently, the Nepalese became assertive of their rights and acquired a considerable amount of capacity to bargain with the ruling elite for a 'legitimate share' in the administration of the state. The Assamese ruling elite also needed the support of the Nepalese in the game of power politics. Being a permanently settled community, it is the obvious choice of the Nepalese to remain with the ruling party so as to derive benefits for the community. The interests of the Nepalese could be well protected, they thought, if they remained with the party in power. As such, the various socio-cultural organizations of the Nepalese seemed to persuade the party in power to accommodate a considerable number of the Nepalese as their candidates in the elections. The major political parties also gradually realized that due to their organizational capability, the Nepalese emerged as a significant political force in Assam. Therefore, different political parties (ruling and non-ruling) preferred to put the Nepalese candidates in those constituencies where they constituted a sizeable number of the voting population in order to gain the support of the Nepalese voters. Thus, the Nepalese of Assam started getting involved in the electoral politics of the state. They gradually realized that their socio-economic development would not be possible if they remained under-represented in the state legislature.

Despite the fact that they find city people less congenial and trustworthy, the rural Nepalese prefer city to the village for the opportunities offered by the former. This is particularly due to their preference of the city for employment, education, and to some extent, building a house for themselves.

The Nepalese respondents showed greater openness of mind where traditional morality was not at stake. They were prepared to change the occupation or places, adopt machine to increase productivity and need for efficiency as a prelude to progress. Sixty five per cent of the respondents fully concurred and 23 per cent partially agreed with the statement, "We should not hesitate to change our occupation or place of occupation, if we are to profit from it". "One should attain proficiency day after day in whatever work is done or else on would lag behind" was fully agreed to by 80 per cent and partially by 14 per cent respondents.

In the field of family planning, there was a world of difference among the three villages. In Golia, people were anxious to know details about contraceptives. There was no shyness in talking about family planning. In Udaypur, there was a great deal of awareness about family planning but only five vasectomy operations had been undertaken. In Sukuli, however, only a few respondents knew about contraceptives and they claimed that they got the ideas from the TV. In all the three villages people appreciated the message of the small family norm.

Nepali language and literature is rich and some of the Nepali litterateurs have won *Sahitya Akademy* awards for their creative work. The major Nepali literary organizations that exist in Assam are *Nepali Sahitya Parishad, Nepali Sahitya Sabha, Navadhwani Sangathan, Hari Bhatkta Katuwal Samiti, Hamro Sayapatri Privar, Neapli Sahitya Sammelan, Bhetghat Mitra Mandali, Kilaj Parivar, and Nepali Sahitya*

Sewa Sadan, etc. These literary organizations have contributed towards the development of Nepali literature in Assam. In addition to the literary contribution, a section of the Nepalese elite took active interest in spreading education in the remotest corner of the state. In fact, a number of educational institutions were established at their initiative.

Among the older section, males are more liberal and progressive than the females because females are basically dependent on males and they have stereotyped ideology. The group seems to concede much less change in regard to caste of the partner and still lesser in matter of religion of the partner. However, the younger generation of both the genders analyzed showed liberal attitude in social relations, and inter-personal relationships. The age at marriage has been rising; respondents supported nuclear family type and small family norms and in assuming reasonable autonomy for themselves. They are independent in the selection of marriage partner; they give importance to the education of the spouse and economic independence as a prelude to marriage. They believe in gender equality, free mixing of man-woman, and women excelling men in different spheres of activity. They are prepared to accept the gender equality as a principle of emerging life.

Golia village is highly developed as a large percentage of the respondents have perceived change in themselves regarding their role as parents, in assuming reasonable autonomy for themselves and the educational level of their life partner; still larger is the percentage of respondents who see change about the age at which marriage should be solemnized and they support the nuclear family and small family norms. Udaypur village is medium developed; this village is changing moderately and the respondents are not in a position to change themselves drastically. But the respondents have shown eagerness towards change. Sukuli village is least developed owing to the fact that villagers of different backgrounds are not aware and conscious about the various facets of emerging modern life and social positions. Most of them are happy if the relationship between the members of the family remains harmonious. By their nature of organization, joint families are a source of social and economic security. They discourage the growth of individuality, initiative, and enterprise – a set of attributes encouraged in the urban way of life as key to success. The respondents with joint family background face difficulty in assuming reasonable autonomy for themselves.

From the data presented, it is found that the social institutions like family, religion, polity, economy and education among the Nepalese community are passing through the modernization process. All the social institutions in the respective villages have been influencing the Nepalese community as far as possible within the village social structure vis-à-vis the level of village development (low, medium or high). We started with a hypothesis that 'there has been a perceptible change in the rural Nepalese community of Assam with reference to their social institutions and individuals respectively since independence of India'. Our empirical evidence generally proved this hypothesis. However, it is felt that further research is necessary to make a broader generalization about the nature of changes registered by the Nepalese community in Assam.

Notes and References

1. Sarmah, Tirthanath. 1976. 'Asomot Nepali' (in Assamese), *Souvenir*, Assam Gurkha Sammelan, Guwahati: The 16th Annual Conference.
2. Bhuyan, A.C. and S.P. De. 1980. (ed.) "*Political History of Assam: 1940-1947*", Vol. III, Guwahati: Govt. of Assam
3. Neog, Maheswar. 1974. Presidential Address, *Assam Sahitya Sabha*, Jorhat :Mongaldoi Session.
4. Borgohain, Homen. 2001. Presidential Address, *66th Conference of Assam Sahitya Sabha*, Dibrugarh Session,
5. Raghuvanshi, M.S. 1984. *Modernizing Rural Youth*. Delhi: Ajanta Publications.
6. The Assam Tribune. 1999. 'Introduction of Passport system between India and Nepal demanded'. May.
7. Talukdar, Dibakar(ed.) 1998. *The Journal of Assam Legislative Assembly*: 1(1): April 1998.

Influence of Gulf migration on identity assertion patterns: Denominational contestations and the emerging public-sphere among Muslims of Kerala

Shareena Banu C.P.

Introduction

The identity of a community is not only a conscious construct of the group members but is perpetually influenced and redefined through the mediation of various historical and socio-political circumstances.[1]Contemporary social-identity studies have broadened the scope of the concept of identity from individual role-conflict to a larger socio-political issue. Thus, identity is seen as constantly in the process of construction rather than a static entity. Communities are today understood as constantly redefining their boundaries along with the dynamics of socio-political forces. To be regarded as an ethnic community of distinct identity, the members should have a sense of being distinct from the rest of the society and institutionalized boundary marking mechanisms through which they maintain social and cultural differences. Any community with a shared cultural history and traditions tends to create a 'we feeling' among its members. Though the cultural traits of ethnic groups change over time, the sense of distinctness, of belonging to an ethnic group persists through the maintenance of cultural and symbolic boundaries. Frederic Barth (1969) emphasized the importance of boundary marking mechanism in the process of identity formation and maintenance. He makes a very crucial observation that the cultural content enclosed by boundaries can vary from setting to setting and across time.

For the Muslims in India, religious beliefs and practices are an important part of their ethnicity. These beliefs and practices are in turn shaped by history and socio-economic events as well as the regional culture. It is generally acknowledged by the scholars on Muslims in India that the religious culture undergoes change responding to the challenges of modern society. However, these religious/cultural changes are, generally speaking, not a consequence of any particular enthusiasm towards emulation of the western value system (see Metcalf, 2002). Various socio-religious reforms taking place within the community are generally not rotted in any comprehensive attempt towards incorporation of modern/western lifestyles and values–the basic religious principles followed by the group define the contours of religious and cultural reform, if any. The motivation for reform is derived from a reaction to the western modernization agenda. The orientation towards religious/cultural reforms remains more or less ethnocentric, except a few attempts like the Aligarh movement for the Muslims in India.[2]

This has particularly been so in the case of Muslims in contemporary Kerala also where they are categorized among the backward communities. The community is experiencing tremendous strain in order to come to grips with the rapid social change. There are various endogenous and exogenous factors contributing towards this tension. Some of the anxiety or challenges in front of the community are the Islamic values and discrepancy with modern education, fast changing society and changing value systems, globalization or homogenization of western culture, international politics, clash of civilization discourse, terrorism, etc. Alongside these endemic concerns of all Muslims, the Muslims in Kerala are also wedged up in the debate on the legitimacy and authenticity of the local cultural influence on the religious practices of the community. In recent times, they have been engaged in serious religious polemic concerning the community's response towards many social challenges. These pressures, in fact, have expedited the process of initiating innovating strategies to comprehend these complexities. There exist different voices within the community in response to the challenges of local and global social situations. Deciphering the unsettled discourse and counter-discourse on religious practices and customs is an interesting exercise for the local scholars and intellectuals. Kerala has been able to provide an amiable secular atmosphere conducive to such dialogue. This has not been possible for the members of Muslim community in other parts of India on account of the psychic insecurity and perception of discrimination.[3]

To put it differently, the community is witnessing internal differences, as various groups and denominations following alternative religious ideologies and worldviews are increasingly critical of the socio-religious traditions followed by the members of other denominations. Each group offers a different interpretation of various religious issues, such as theological matters, religious legitimacy of many of the local customs and practices such as the *nerccha* festivals, marriage rituals, dress pattern, issues regarding modernization of education and education of women along with other ethical issues. These contestations had been there in the past also to some extent, especially during the British rule, as a reaction to colonial rule and cultural domination (see Pannikar, 2001). Another instance was during the period of active involvement of some of the socio-religious reformers and leaders of the community. These reformers had attempted to encourage the common mass to actively participate in the debate on issues regarding the community, especially modernization and social-cultural reform. Though these efforts had a historical impact on the socio-cultural life of the community, they were confined to the social sphere. What distinguishes the previous engagement and the present one is the dynamic participation and mobilization of the community members in these dialogues leading to fractures in the community on the basis of contesting religious ideas. The manifestations of these contestations are present equally in public and private life of the members.

This article maintains that the rising activism towards cultural and religious dialogue is part of the change in socio-economic structure of the Muslim community in Kerala in the recent decade brought about by the Gulf migration. A large section of the Muslim population has been continuously migrating to the Gulf countries since the 1960s. The resultant economic prosperity and the emergence of 'neo-rich' within the community had a deep impact on their socio-economic culture, affecting the class composition and religious orientation of the community.[4] The article argues that Gulf migration is an important factor shaping the reformulation of religious identity and engagement of the community members. Similarly, in relation to the capacity to initiate dialogue on the existing religious observance and practices, Gulf migration is one of the crucial factors behind it.

International migration is in no way confined to the economic influence as its effect is all-encompassing: it has latent potential for inducing new meanings to socio-cultural practices. Among other things, this article argues against the hitherto practiced uni-dimensional analyses confined to the consequences of Gulf remittance on the material culture of Muslims or the sweeping generalizations related to the pan-Arabic influence. This article brings forth the need to look into these dimensions with a fresh perspective. It advocates for a multilevel exploration essential for delineating the gamut of contemporary social change among Kerala Muslims. The 'Gulf connection' and the emerging intra-community dialogue/conflict contribute towards redefinition of the social identity of the Muslim in Kerala. It is argued that this contestation is latently favourable, contributing towards the formation of new social space. It is initiating a process towards formation of a fragmented 'public sphere' with accommodative ethos enabling a re-orientation of socio-cultural aspects of life. It is expected to infuse Muslim religious identity with new enthusiasm while providing room for accommodating multiple or alternative worldviews. Thus, this intra-community contestation/conflict is a process of adjustment and preparation of a 'community in transition'.

This paper is an attempt to delineate some of the recent trends emerging among the Muslims in Kerala. It explores the process of construction and reconstruction of identity of the community in the changing socio-political scenario. It raises the question of community identity – what is to be a Muslim in Kerala in contemporary times – and how their consciousness of being a member of Muslim community is being asserted. It also looks at the role played by some of endogenous and exogenous factors, which influence the nature and character of Muslim social life. The Muslim 'community' in Kerala today faces manifests and latent challenges from various socio-political aspects in relation to the modernization process while it is attempting to maintain and negotiate cultural and symbolic boundaries.[5]

Rather than looking at identity as a static entity, the study proposes to look into the dynamic nature of identity construction. The religious and cultural identity is negotiated and asserted through an engagement of various socio-historical forces. The study takes into consideration how in the changing scenario, new meanings are attributed to a range of symbolic religious activities associated to community life. In this process the agents are initiating innovative strategies to make a requisite array of meaningful association with the changing social world, where new identities are being forged and existing orders either challenged or in some way reasserted.

Revisiting collective memory: A brief survey of social history

Historical events and conjectures provide a basis for a community's disposition towards social life. A sense of historical roots is essential for the formation of a collective consciousness and cultural continuity. The community constantly relates with its cultural past to legitimize its socio-religious practices and traditions. Collective history is embedded in the narratives of folklore, myths and memories of collective living. To a large extent, local cultural symbols, language and local metaphors and folklore, along with the socio-political events of Kerala shape the cultural and religious experiences of the Muslim community. Religious culture is symbolized through local experiences of the community. Nevertheless, the customs and traditions have an Islamic quality.[6] The Muslims in Kerala share a common socio-political history with other communities; they have always been able to maintain their distinct religious and cultural identity (see Miller: 1992).

The origin or spread of Islam in Kerala[7] is generally traced to the peaceful and extensive economic and social relationships between the early Arab traders and the native Keralites. Alongwith economic relations, the Arab traders established conjugal ties with the native women, which led to the spread of Islam in Kerala. Arnold (1896) in his study, *Preaching of Islam*, provides an elaborate picture of the missionary preaching in Kerala. He gives a detailed historical account of the spread of Islam in the Malabar coast. Instead of coercive force, peaceful preaching of Islam by Muslim missionaries and *Sufis* was responsible for large-scale conversion. Many *Sufi* saints and theologians have contributed towards establishing a strong religious base in Kerala. Though there is scanty information on the early missionary tradition, the local folk traditions narrate the accounts of various *Sheikhs* and saints for whom people still have high esteem. The folklore and Muslim songs, extensively sung, and the *nercca* festivals, extol the activities and miracles of these saints (see Kunju: 1989).

The tradition of Malik-ibn-Dinar and his disciples has played a major role in spreading the religion. The tradition suggests that Chereman Perumal, the last Perumal ruler of Kerala embraced Islam. On his return journey from Arabia, he was accompanied by the family and friends of Malik-ibn-Dinar. When the king died at Zufar on the Arabian coast, he instructed his friends to proceed to Kerala and spread the new faith. They landed at Kodunnallur, visited different parts of Kerala and established several cathedral mosques in different parts of the state.[8] In one of the earliest travel accounts about Muslims in India, Ibn-Batuta, describes the extent of religious activity in the Kerala coastal region. He visited Kerala around AD 1342. He mentions that many distinguished theologians and saints from the Middle East, for instance from Baghdad, visited the place. The theologians were honoured by the local rulers and people from different parts, including the Chinese, sent offerings to them. He visited some of the famous hermitages in Khozhikode (Calicut). The Arabi-Malayalam linguistic form, which is Malayalam written in the Arabic script had developed. Innumerable Mappila folk songs, written in this linguistic form, are a rich resource on the saint tradition among the Muslims.

There are different explanations about the spread of Muslims in the interiors of Kerala coast. Extensive trade and economic links existed between Kerala and the Middle East in the first century AD. The Arabs controlled the trade in the Arabian Sea. Arab merchants had managed to establish a monopoly of the import and export trade of the Zamourins. The long-distance voyage in the Arabian Sea and the changing climate, made it necessary for the Arabs to stay in the western coastal areas for longer durations, sometimes even for months. Trade relations provided opportunity for Arabs to get married to the native lower-caste women with the permission of the Zamourin. The alliance of lower-caste women with the Arab traders led to the improved status of the castes, as the Arab traders were attributed an equal status to that of the upper caste Nayars. Changed social status enabled these women to enjoy freedom hitherto not possible in the restrictive caste structure. This might have attracted many low castes to encourage this type of alliance. Thus, the Muslims of Kerala are the descendents of the offspring of the Arab traders and the lower-caste women. However, in later days, many lower caste Hindus also converted and embraced Islam.

The Muslims in Kerala also witnessed many socio-religious reforms and modernization movements during the colonial period and after independence. Response to reforms was not in consonance with the expectation of the leaders as the community was deeply rooted in traditional local practices and dogmatic beliefs. Logan (1951) recorded that the only education received was religious in content. Curriculum included the Holy *Quran*, *Hadith*, Arabic and jurisprudence. Education was confined mostly to the *Madrasa* attached to the mosques. The study of Malayalam, especially by females is opposed on the grounds that it was an *Aryan* language.[9] Similarly, the reason for indifference towards English education was antagonism towards the British with whom the Mappilas had historic hatred.

Modernisation among the Muslims in Kerala started during the late Nineteenth century under the able leadership of socio-religious reformers such as Makthi Tangal (1847-1912) and Vakkam Maulavi (1873-1932). The early movement they initiated is known as the *Islahi* movement, which was later on known as the Aykya Sangam Movement. The *Islahi* movement advocated modern educational and social reforms among the Muslims in different parts of Kerala (see Sethi: 2000). It also attempted to disseminate Islamic knowledge through printing and publications and opening up of numerous educational institutions. Most popular among the later leaders were Vakkam Maulavi, both a nationalist and a socio-religious reformer, who started newspapers like *Deepika* and *Swadeshabhmani*. The Maulavi spread a rational outlook towards the world, criticized religious fanaticism, superstition, and all kinds of un-Islamic practices. To propagate modern education and overcome backwardness of the community they started numerous educational institutions and banks. The Aligarh movement initiated by Sir Sayed Ahmad Khan and the ensuing educational reform had its influence on the early Islamic socio-religious reformers like the Maulavi in Kerala. The Maulavi and others emphasized the need for modernization of religious education and incorporation of modern secular education in the curriculum. He organized the Muslim youth under various cultural committees. The

'Muhamaddeya Sabha' is one among the several cultural groups which initiated educational activity among the Muslims. Efforts were also made to translate Arabic religious texts into Malayalam. The old syllabus and curriculum was criticized as it hardly left any scope for the youth to gain the relevance of contents in Islamic texts or to inculcate critical literary ability. The new syllabus gave emphasis upon both the religious and non-religious education (see Samad: 1998 and Sethi: 2000).

The reformists were later on called by the more conservative Sunni section as *Mujahids*. The *Mujahid* group generally criticized superstitious practices and was engaged in puritanical reforms. They were critical of the native Muslim practices like *Nerccha*, *Mulid*, *Malappattu*, which were conducted anticipating the intercession by the dead saints and prophets. The Sunnis were in favour of practices like *Nercca, urus, Chanandankkudam, Maulid, Malas,* and *Ratib*, which are prayers done in the name of saints as an act of piety and valid in Islam. The *Mujahids* consider all kinds of worship other than of *Allah* as un-Islamic and equivalent to idol worship. This counter-argument about religious practices and local tradition is contested among the community members on religious grounds. Gulf migration has augmented this trend, discussed in detail in the following sections.

Gulf migration and Kerala Muslims

Geographic relocation through international migration forces the imagination and articulation of personal and group identity, especially in cultural terms (Appadurai, 1996). As mentioned earlier, the relation of Muslims of Kerala with the Persian Gulf has a history of centuries, when the native Keralaites from the coast had peaceful and extensive economic and social relationships with the early Arab traders and settlers. After a long gap, the old relationship to the Persian Gulf was renewed in the mid-Twentieth century, i.e., around the 1930s. There were migrants from Kerala in the Persian Gulf region as early as the 1930s when the oil industry in the region began to develop. But large-scale migration began only during the oil boom of the early 1970s. In the last few decades there has been large-scale migration, particularly of Muslims from Kerala to the Middle East.[10] This migration to the Gulf countries for around three decades has deeply influenced the economic behaviour, religious culture and tradition of native Muslims in Kerala. It has resulted in the emergence of neo-rich in the community. This group is playing a principal role in the social transformation of the community members, in terms of setting standards and influencing social behaviour, attitude and aspirations. Before analyzing this dimension an exploration of the nature of migration is attempted here.

Till today, Kerala, a small state in India has been a major labour exporter to the Middle East countries. Although the state's population of around 30 million comprises only 3.43 per cent of the population of the country, around 35 to 50 per cent of the migrants from India have been from this state. The influence of Gulf migration is much larger among the Muslims in north Kerala as compared to other parts, in spite of the fact that they account for only one-fifth of the total population of the state. Statistically, they constitute as much as 78 per cent of the migrant population. Hindus and Christians account for only about 12 and 10 per cent of the outflow. Reports show that at least one male member of every Muslim household is working in the Middle East at this point of time. A survey conducted in 1998 estimated that there were 33 international migrants for every 100 households. Entire village populations sometimes migrate affecting the very social structure and composition of the village. Researches show that economically and culturally, there are distinct characteristics of these villages which distinguish them from the non-migrant villages.[11]

Social scientists, especially economists, have been interested in the emerging trends and characteristics of this international migration, especially nature of the migrant labour. Various studies in this area substantiate the fact that more or less, all the migrants are unmarried males[12] in the age group of 20-30, with low levels of education. It is neither the traditional rich nor the extremely poor who migrate. Most of the migrant labour in the Gulf belongs to lower middle-class consisting of unskilled and semi-skilled workers, relatively less qualified population in the region.[13] They also come from poor, rural families engaged in low productivity, traditional activities such as fishing, agricultural labour, cottage industry, and service sector jobs such as helpers in tea shops and salesmen in grocery stores. Only a few migrants come from well-to-do families of plantation owners or professionals such as engineers, doctors and college teachers and middle-level industrialists and businessmen. Mostly, the migrant labourers are engaged as construction workers, employees in private firms, employees in government and public sector institutions, traders and businessmen and domestic servants.[14] Professional or technical education initially was not an important prerequisite for migration. In majority of the cases, vocational training played a more important role than higher technical education.[15]

The migrants' return to the country is inevitable due to emigration policy of the Gulf countries, which put variety of restrictions regarding Asian expatriate labour, the length of their stay and the admittance of dependants. As the labour importing Gulf countries allow only a few years of stay till the contract period ends, the migrants live frugally so that they can remit a large portion of their incomes to their families. Consequently, due to the fear of repatriation migrants are perpetually oriented toward their home communities, visiting them frequently. Thus, the domicile continues to influence all aspects of the migrant's social life in the Gulf countries.[16]

The economic condition of the home state influences the magnitude of migration to the Gulf countries, and correspondingly the return migration also. Economic opportunities in the state determine the factors contributing towards large-scale migration and the nature of remittance investment of the returning migrants.[17] In contemporary Kerala, tardy growth of employment opportunities in the agricultural or industrial sector continues despite mass internal and international migration from the state. Thus, financial crisis is attributed to the inhospitable investment climate and also to the non-productive investment habits of the Malayali people. Future migration is greatly dependent on the generation of employment and investment opportunities within the state and also migration policies of the Arab countries. In recent times, the Middle East countries have promoted *Arabisation* policies and the legal control on labour import has tightened. Alongside this, the migrants face competition from others with better technical skills in the competitive market. Zachariah (2002) and others underline the need for immediate steps to be taken by the state government to improve the technical skill of the migrant workers. They warn that Kerala workers are going to lose out in the international competition for jobs in the Gulf market. The new immigration policy of the Gulf countries deter unskilled Asian workers and the future demand will be for skilled workers, technicians, and computer operators, professional categories such as doctors, nurses, engineers, and teachers. The Keralite workers are increasingly finding themselves incapable to compete with other South Asian countries. The solution lies in equipping the workers with better education and technical skills. The future emigrants should be equipped to meet the changes and development of labour market in the Gulf countries. As a major section of migrants are from the Muslim community and lacking proper higher education and technical skills, they will be seriously affected. This issue needs to be addressed immediately and measures should be taken to improve the labour standards of the migrant workers.[18]

In spite of this dismal picture, Gulf migration has been able to enhance the economic condition of the individual migrant family by increasing the overall income level of the family, especially in the last two decades. The impact of migration can be observed in terms of the socio-economic status, attitudes and behaviour, values and religious practices of migrants and their family structure and gender roles,[19] the very nature of investment, and cultural influence.[20]

In comparison to other communities, Muslims in Kerala have witnessed rapid enrichment of the lower classes by Gulf remittances. A change in life-style, increased demand for consumer goods such as vehicles, ornaments, jewellery, gadgets like TV, refrigerators and other electrical appliances, increased spending in marriage and other ceremonial functions, land purchase and construction are most visible signs of the accumulating wealth. In fact, a large proportion of Gulf remittance is being used by the newly rich Muslims in showing off affluence by buying real estate, palatial houses, school and hospital construction, *salkkaaram* (feasting relatives and neighbours on special occasions), and religious philanthropy. Wealth has become a claim for higher social status. Besides enhanced status brings about privileged positions in the local power structures.

However, it need not be emphasized that this zeal about material wealth and ostentatious spending is in no way an indication of change in the core values and attitude.[21] In fact, in many quarters, profligate exhibition of wealth is observed as a sign of the acceptance of western values and a manifest challenge on the way to the sacred life. However, quite contrarily, there is also an augmentation of religiosity among the returning migrants and their families. This is partly explained in terms of cultural contact of the migrants with the Islamic state and society in their workplace. In a Mappila Muslim village, a great deal of importance is attached to distribution of wealth in a large circle of people within the community and support of religious activities. Migrant's families flaunt their wealth for religious rituals, donation for construction of religious institutions like mosques, *Madrasas* and religious-cultural organizations and charitable activities. In this sense, economic prosperity and outside exposure has not led to a decline in religious faith and practice; religious attitude and feeling remain unchanged in the community (see Nair: 1986).

However, what is interesting is the way Gulf money is being used for redefining religious identity. The middle classes are in a process of status assertion to gain better social position and recognition in the community. The Gulf tradition provides a new legitimacy to their religious existence. Their attempt to gain space within the community is reflected in their increasing criticism of the religion followed by native Muslims. There is an attempt of re-conceptualization of meaning and significance of their identity, concretely manifested through modifications in ritual practices to attribute Islamic quality and religious sanction to many of the practices. One important trend is the increasing attention towards proper etiquette in both private and public life.[22]

Increased status in society is appropriated through renewed interest in religious etiquette.[23] Religious etiquette here can be understood as the set of moral values and standard for guiding Muslims in all aspects of life such as eating, drinking, dressing, sleeping, talking, family life, and marriage, etc. The mastery of etiquette helps to discipline and train and endows Muslims with the qualities to follow an exemplary life. The theory of etiquette ensures that all Muslims become capable of spiritual discipline and self-realization. Believers whether saint, teacher, craftsmen, family head and women all have equal potential to be blessed. The behaviour of every Muslim should be shaped in accordance with the moral values exemplified by the Prophet Mohammed through his life. His life and commandments are compiled in the form of *Hadith*. This was compiled after the death of Prophet by his associates and eye witnesses. There are various narrations and interpretations among which the compilation of Malik, Bukhari, Tirmidhi, and Ibn Majah are considered to be the most authentic.

Etiquette governs the interpersonal conduct between relatives, family members, and strangers in public forums.[24] Etiquette determines status in society and position in the social hierarchy. The neo-rich enhance their prestige through imitating the normative patterns of the traditional elite. The traditional elite attempt to de-legitimise these efforts by attributing innovative symbolic meanings to etiquette and ritual practice. The traditional elite assert their identity through the historical legitimacy of the family to maintain their superior status in the local hierarchies.

The influence of migration on etiquette in the case of Kerala Muslims has started redefining well-mannered behaviour for Muslim women. The increase in number of women wearing *Parda* compared to earlier periods is an illustration of this phenomenon.[25] Etiquette has evolved as a form of the value of social capital through which the dedication towards religious life is demonstrated. Manners are symbols of one's higher status manifested through modifications in ritual practices which have religious connotations.

Muslim community in transition: Denominational contestations and emerging public sphere

Though in Kerala there is already a relatively well-established public sphere, there are many discourses which have not found their appropriate place. Among the different communities such as Nayars, Dalits and Christians there has been much dialogue and engagement with regard to problems and prospects within their community. The Muslim community is generally considered as passive in its reaction and response to various socio-political changes it faces. Except during the British period, the discourse of conflictual interpretation has not gained much attention in the public sphere. With the emergence of a newly rich class trying to assert its status and the increasing assertion of multiple identities within the community, a large section of the community is today stimulated to participate in religious contestations in the social sphere. The diverse voices within the community along with emergent new faces among the leadership augments this process.

At this moment, there is a strong tendency towards branding oneself as the authentic representative of Islamic values and consequent marginalization of oppositional groups. The various revivalist and reform movements have lead to more and more intra-community division on the issue of tehological matters, jurisprudence and modernization. It is not possible to talk about a monolithic Muslim community in Kerala in its real sense as differential identities are emerging from conflicting ideologies. In recent times, there exists an intensified and open expression of differences. Here we try to understand the intra-community relations, looking into some of the socio-religious movements and ambiguities involved in the diverse religious ideologies and worldviews discussed within the community.

The differences between various sections became more and more visible and open. Miller calls the period 1976-1991 as a history of struggle (Miller: 1992). Muslims in Kerala developed many approaches on theology and law, etc. During this period the Sunni majority experienced a division into two groups: A.P. Sunnis and the E.K. Sunnis, the major cause being the Gulf money. The A.P. or the Kandapuram group is lead by A.P. Abu Bakr Musaliar, known for his strong Gulf connection which enabled him to accumulate large amounts of donation through charity boxes in the Gulf and in Kerala to establish his group in Kerala. They established, as cultural complexes, a large number of educational institutions for the propagation of Islamic values. This group opposes political involvement of Muslims, which is a departure from the Sunni leadership, which maintains faith in the political involvement with the Muslim League for the transformation of the Muslim life. The group is popular among the youth having their own organization called the Sunni Students Federation (SSF).

The E.K. group is the other section of Sunni group with the leadership of E.K. Abu Bekr Musaliar. They support the theological tradition and the legitimacy of Muslim saints saying the saints do posses special powers and grace. Praying at the shrine is both permissible and helpful. They provide support to the political party, Muslim League, and actively engage in political issues. They are critical of the *Mujahid* argument, and favour *Itjihad* or the private interpretation of *Quran*. Their youth organization is called the Samasta Kerala Sunni Students Federation. Both A.P. and E.K. groups differ in political and financial matters but otherwise share the same theological positions. Their main fight is with the Mujahs and Jamaat-Islam group spread Islamic principles with the goal of creating an Islamic society. They also give much emphasis to character building like other groups, the major difference being that they do not allow the members to engage in government service or government grants, or any kind of political involvement. They have their own student wing called the Students Islamic Organisation (SIO). They also started a newspaper named '*Madhyamum*'.

There are also other less significant sections such as the Tabiligh Jammat group, Islamists, the Ahamadiyas, and the Chekannur Maulavi group working with differential perspectives on religion trying to spread religious values among the community members. The differences between various groups become evident, as the hardcore followers strictly follow the commandment of their *Ulama.* Different sections have also started their own educational institutions such as *Kerala Nadvattul Mujahindin, Jammat-I-Islami of Kerala,* and *Samastha Kerala Jamiyyathul Ulama* to propagate their own theology (see Samad: 1998).

Here, Habermas's concept of 'public sphere' is important to apprehend the recent transformation of the Muslim community in Kerala. The denominational rivalry among Kerala Muslims over the issue of the authentic religious behaviour provides an interesting case of multiple validity claims to legitimize their understanding of Islam as authentic. Though there were differences during the colonial and post-colonial periods, what characterizes the recent period, especially after 1991, is the *expansion of the public sphere.* Increased awareness due to the earlier religious and political discourse and the newly achieved self-confidence of the neo-rich provides opportunities for engagement in serious polemic in everyday interaction within the community.

It is widely accepted that the traditional intellectuals (*Ulama, Musaliar, Quazis*) had a crucial role in the Kerala Muslims' social life. The leadership had strong linkages with the community and is involved in various aspects of socio-political life. They provide socio-political, religious leadership and guidance to the community. In shaping the outlook of the rural Mappillas, they played a dominant role. Their influence was not limited to ecclesiastical matters, but also extended to everyday life issues (Pannikar: 2001). Though there are many religious and political leaders who still have authority over the community, their influence is being contested now. In recent years the domination of the traditional religious authority is weakening, as new leadership has come up, which is a challenge to the traditional leadership. The factionalism within the Sunni community is an illustration of this fact. This challenging and questioning may lead to a collapse of the earlier hierarchical notions of religious authority. The religious interpretation of social life today is not a monopoly of any particular leadership. Earlier, the situation was of a general acceptance of the prescriptions of political-religious leaders without much debate. Now, there exist differential 'validity claims' by various denominations projecting their ideologies as authentic and their interpretation of religious life and community activity as proper.

These developments form the core of contestation in everyday life. Within one family it is possible today to find different members following different interpretation of theological matters. The meaning of religion is being contested in the public and private life. Legitimacy of the local is in contestation with the so-called universal aspects of Islam. Local Islam is challenged in the process of the inclusion and exclusion of social life. The universal tenets of Islam are being underlined as the basic principles in which any kind of local innovation is to be put into the array of serious polemic and contestations. Any native innovation is facing a threat from the puritans. This is not only a specific feature of Kerala Muslims but a similar phenomenon is being observed in other South Asian countries, for instance in Sri Lanka.

Migration may also lead to change in socio-religious identity and status to the migrants in society and even spiritual relationship with God may be reformulated in the process. As Gardner and Osella (2003) point out in several cases the '..... migrant move away from Islam based on the local shrines, saints and hierarchies, and engage in a new global form of Islamic purism and brotherhood. Here the "tradition" assumes a central role in the struggle not only over status and power, but also in the peoples' attempts to reformulate their relationship with god' (p.xxiii). The historically evolved cultural life is redefined to suite to the changing orientation towards religious life. The contestation is not confined to the linguistic polemics only as they are engaged in serious observance and practice of their religious ideology. The youth is also actively involved in this contestation as members of the youth wings of various groups and denominations. Active participation, thus, necessitates the sharpening of views and critical outlook and a boost to mass education.

Ordinary people now have unprecedented access to information about religion and other aspects of their society. Mass media, especially print and audio-visual media, is playing an important role. Sensitisation and acceptance of the possibility of multiple interpretations of Islam and Islamic values may be one of the outcomes of the expansion of media's reach and importance (Eickelman, 1999). Forums like newspapers, journals, pamphlets, new television channels and marketing of religious and political sermons through audio-cassettes are important sites of dialogue and debate. The marketing of religious sermon through audiotapes especially during religious occasions has an important role in this dialogue process. It is pertinent to look at Hirsch Kind's study (2000) which provides an anthropological analysis of role of audio tape-recorded sermons in the Egyptian revivalist movement. Tapes are considered as an extension of religious sermon in the mosque. These sermons are used to reinforce moral values and self-discipline, especially among women. The Friday prayer (*kuttuba*) and cassette sermons have an important role not only for promotion of religious values but also for educating people of various interpretations of social issues. These kinds of denominational polemics through mass media lead to 'spiritualization' of every day life. Thus, conflict is an expression of creating legitimate space for itself in public domain.

Concluding comments

In the process of social life, the community is experiencing a tremendous exertion to comprehend and interpret the rapid form of social change in all spheres of life. These socio-psychological pressures, in fact, augment the process of initiating innovative strategies and imagination to handle the complexities. In recent times, the community is engaged in serious religious polemic and self-introspection on the community's response towards various social and cultural challenges. Deciphering this state of interpretive ambivalence is indeed a challenge for scholars and intellectuals.

Difference of opinion can be seen as an indication of the intellectual and religious vibrancy of the community. With the community actively engaged in dialogue, it is expected that this 'density' of interaction will multiply the possibilities of dissolving prior barriers of space and opening new grounds for interaction and mutual recognition. The existing discourse enables to create spaces for the inclusive process, where the alternative approaches towards

Muslim way of life attains recognition and legitimacy among a larger population. If not so, the domination of any one interpretation can no more have an uncritical acceptance within the community. The creation of a 'new space' will lead to accelerated possibility of creating a more vibrant public sphere effectively addressing contemporary problems.

These contestations need to be channelled to a particular direction so as to initiate among the members a more effective and productive dialogue, which will help the community in the long run. Efforts are needed to canalize the debate on some of the practical issues of the community, which need immediate attention. For instance, the recent CDS study (see Zachariah, 2002) shows that if the Gulf labour migrants – mostly consisting of Muslims – are not equipped to meet the developments of Gulf labour markets, it will seriously affect their economic and developmental prospects. As mentioned earlier, lack of higher technical education skills will be the greatest hurdle for the migrants in coming times.[26]

As mentioned earlier, material prosperity has not led to inculcation of motivation towards higher education or professional qualifications. Thus, it is noted that the economic achievement of the community is not conducive to the social-cultural development of the community. For instance, the Mujahid group within the community, which started the reformatory measures long back and in the areas of their presence have had a strong impact on the educational development. They are making use of the Gulf money for developmental activities. This can be seen in contrast to other sections, which even after improvement in the economic conditions have not made sufficient efforts to invest in education. In fact, they use large amounts of funds in religious and other socio-cultural activities. However, the Mujahid group lacks support from the larger community because of lack of free and open public space. The moderate section has been unable to create an environment suited for proper intervention on the internal dynamics of the society. As a matter of fact, it is noted by scholars that the Muslims have been only able to achieve basic literacy and lag behind in higher education. The governmental and the private efforts have not helped the community in any substantial manner (see Salim: 1998). Thus, within the community there is less enthusiasm towards engaging in serious dialogue on non-religious issues. It must be understood that an expanding public sphere is no guarantee for better prospects of the community. However, *possible creation of a vibrant pubic sphere is necessary for creating a new path for cultural changes in everyday life.* It can be expected that in near future, with evolution of an open social sphere congenial for innovative strategies, there will be more enthusiasm towards facing the challenges of the community successfully without compromising the socio-religious identity of the community. However, it should be mentioned here though there has not yet been any real rapproachment for the common interest, the community has been able to unite especially in political terms.

To conclude, there are two major reminders for any kind of future research in the community. First, the modernization process will continue to play a key role in stimulating and influencing the social attitude and behaviour of the community. Global reaction to western cultural domination and hegemonisation has its manifest and latent impact on attributing cultural meanings to their practices and beliefs. The reaction to this hegemonic redefinition of cultural life may vary from time to time. The assertion of religiosity in recent time is a manifestation of the reaction of the community within the social milieu they are located. Various exogenous and endogenous factors have dialectic interaction determining the basic nature of strategies evolved. At present, these factors contribute unconsciously towards the intensification of cultural and religious contestations. The theory that consciousness of the community did not move outside basic tenets and principles of Islam is asserted. International migration has led to economic transformation and in turn resulted in changing the attitude and expectations of the community affecting the entire socio-cultural milieu. However, it should be mentioned that this phenomenon needs more attention for a better understanding of the cultural impact of Gulf migration on the community.

Notes

1. See Nagel, J. 1994. 'Constructing Ethnicity: Creating and Recreating Ethnic identity and Culture': *In Social Problems*, 41:152-176, p. 152.
2. The modernists generally regard that the modernization process would lead to disappearance of the traditional loyalties like religion, racism and caste system, etc. There has been an upsurge in ethnic awareness in multicultural societies and groups are trying to rediscover their cultural roots. The recent ethnic conflicts show that the ethnicity asserts itself in even more concrete forms. Numerous studies have pointed out that

economic and social development do not replace ethnocentric and communal feelings. For a detailed study on the response of Muslims to colonial dominance, see the work of Metcalf (2002) on Deobandi movement.

3. It is pertinent to note here that scholars engaged in studying community relationships, especially the study of communalism, hardly appreciate the relevance of studying peaceful societies and how people of different communities there relate themselves with the 'other' and engage in the process of constructing identity boundaries. In fact, analysis of the conflict and contestations within the community in a relatively peaceful society is equally important to gain a better understanding of the process of pressure group creation and negotiations related to socio-political issues concerning the community. The intra-community contestation is a manifestation of the active and critical self-analysis by the community in the process of construction and reconstruction of identity in religious terms. Other exogenous factors only play the role of ameliorating and intensifying the process. Also, in the era of globalization it is difficult to maintain that the south Indian states (like Kerala) are unaffected by socio-political tensions. Studies on communal/ethnic/sectarian conflict suggest that the scope for conflict has expanded from local to national and international dimensions due to the expansion of communication technology and information revolution. This immunity has never been complete though it is true that communal political issues of north India have had relatively lesser impact on the Kerala society. Evidence of this fact is the sectarian debate on puritan and revivalist tendencies and the increasing relationship of Muslim leadership with the Arab World; increasing adherence to Arabic-Islamic symbolic culture and religious obligations.

   Gulf migration has influenced all aspects of Kerala's socio-economic life. It has contributed immensely towards rearranging of the social strcture of the Muslim community. Changing class composition and growth of the neo-rich, lack of psychic security, emerging leadership patterns along with the changing religious experiences and reorientation are crucial for understanding the emerging trends within the community. Many studies ignore this phenomenon which remains a characteristic impact on the social and cultural life of the Muslim community.

4. The author attempts to deal with the influence of Gulf migration on the migrant and their social life. The paper addresses the following questions: Has Gulf migration influenced the understanding of socio-religious life in any manner? Does it in any way contribute towards new trends within the community? How do the Kerala Muslims come to terms with their association with the Gulf countries in terms of cultural meanings?

5. The existing studies among Kerala Muslims are based on the textual understanding of religion which brings out the fundamental principles of Islam that do not reveal much about the actual influence of Islam in everyday life practices. There are lots of gaps in the study of the change in the Muslim community in Kerala. There are hardly any sociological works looking into the trends and dynamics of recent changes among Muslims in Kerala. Also, these studies fail to provide a comprehensive analytical understanding of the process of construction, and reconstruction of boundaries of the community in the changing socio-political scenario. Similarly, there are few studies which attempt to comprehend the changing trends in the cultural traditions of Kerala Muslims.
6. The early historical mosque architecture and the structure of house buildings is an excellent example of the cultural milieu of harmonious blending of Arab and indigenous tradition. For further details, see K.J.John, 'The Muslim-Arabs and Mosque Architecture in Malabar': In Asghar Ali Engineer (ed) *Kerala Muslims: A Historical Perspective,* 1995, New Delhi, Ajanta Publications. Ahmad (1980) also observes that a dynamic society constantly engages in the process of dialectic interaction with the native cultural tradition and shared experience along with the blending of Islamic belief and practice.
7. According to the 1991 Census the religious constitution of Indian population was: Hindus 82 per cent, Muslims 12.12 per cent and Christians 2.34 per cent, Sikhs 1.94 per cent, Buddhists 0.76 per cent, and Jains 0.40 per cent. Numerically, the Muslims constitute the most predominant minority in India. In 1961 Census, Kerala stood as the fourth largest state in India with the largest number of Muslim population following Kashmir, Assam, and West Bengal. In the 1991 Census, the district wise population of Muslims of Kerala is as follows: Malappuram 63.93 per cent, Calicut 30.62 per cent, Cannanore 24.3 per cent, Palghat 21.27 per cent, Quilon 21.27 per cent, Trichur 12.83 per cent, Ernakulam 13.69 per cent, Trivandram 12.33 per cent, Aleepey 12.01 per cent, Waynad 6.85 per cent, Idukki 6.06 per cent and Kottayam 3.48 per cent. Two-thirds of the Muslims are concentrated in northern Kerala that is around 67 per cent of the total population. In 1981, the population composition of north Kerala was as follows: Hindus 56.3 per cent Muslims 34.3 per cent and Christians 9 per cent respectively as compared to south Kerala, that is 57.5 per cent, 10.5 per cent and 32.0 per cent respectively. In north Kerala, only Malappuram district Muslims outnumber both Hindus and Christians. Other than Kashmir and Lakshadeep only Malappuram has the highest percentage of Muslim population among districts in India.

8. See Kunju 1989, also Zaynud-Din and Shaykh, 1942, 'Tuhfat Ul-Mujahidin', Translated by Muhamed Husayn Nainar. Madras: University of Madras.

9. See, S.M. Mohamed Koya, 'Educational and Social Progress of the Mappilas', Symposium on History Conference, Mysore, 1985.

10. Gulf countries undertook a massive infrastructural reconstruction and in a relatively short period of time were able to transform into most technologically advanced nations of the world. Foreign labour was central to this transformation. Since 1970s there has been a large-scale out-migration from Asian countries, particularly India and Pakistan to the Middle East. By 1980, 69.8 per cent of the workforce in the region consisted of foreigners. Among these, Asians constituted around one-third of the foreign workforce in the Gulf countries. Indians and Pakistanis account for more than 18 per cent. According to B.A.Praksh (1998), in the same year there were 2.8 million Indians in Middle East and in 1990-1991 the figure was 1.5 to 1.7 million. 95 per cent of the emigrant's countries of destination were Saudi Arabia, United Arab Emirates (consisting of Abu Dhabi, Dubai, The Small Emirate of Sharja and The Village States of Ras-Al-Khaimah, Umma-Al-Quaiwain, Ajman, Fujairah), Baharin, Kuwait, Qatar and Oman. A large section has immigrated especially to Saudi Arabia and U.A.E. Emigration from India to Gulf countries took place mainly from seven states: Kerala, Andhra Pradesh, Gujarat, Goa, Maharashtra, and Tamil Nadu.

11. Within Kerala, Mallapuram district has the highest rate of emigration, which is followed by Pathanamthita, Trissure and Kozhikode in the year 1998. For a detailed account of the economic profile of migration along with the effects on the sending country, see the following:

    Gulati I.S., and A. Modi, 1983. "Remittance of Indian Migrants to the Middle East: An Assessment with Special Reference to Migrants from Kerala State." Working Paper 182, Centre For Development Studies, Trivandrum, Kerala, p. 58.

    Gopinathan Nair P.R. 1986, "India", in Godfrey Guntilleke(ed), 'Migration of the Asian Workers to the Arab World, Japan, The United Nations University. Gopinathan Nair, 1989. "Incidence, Impact and Implications of Migration to the Middle East from Kerala." In Amjad Rashid, (ed.), To the Gulf and Back, New Delhi: ILO(ARTEP) 343. Gopinathan Nair P.R. 1991, 'Asian Migration to the Arab World: Kerala (India)' in Godfrey Guntilleke (ed.), *Migration to the Arab World: Experience of Return Migrants,* The United Nations University, Hong Kong. Sekhar, T.V., 1997, Migration and Social Change, New Delhi, Rawat Publications. Prakash B.A., (ed) 1998, "Gulf Migration and its

Economic Impact: The Kerala Experience." *Economic and Political Weekly,* Dec. 12. Zacharia K.C., B.A. Prakash, S. Irudaya Rajan, 2001, 'Kerala Emigrants in the UAE: Issues, Problems and Prospects,' CDS, Kerala University and Govt. of Kerala.

12. Women are going to the Gulf countries in very small numbers, as many incidents of misuse have been reported by the various foreign departments.

13. For statistics and further details, see Sekher, 1997. See also Zacharia, Mathew, and Rajan, 1999.

14. See Myron Weiner, "International Migration and Development' in *Population and Development Review* 8, March 1982, p. 13.

15. Thus, they are in no way a brain drain to the sending country. As the migration of the unskilled human labour in turn brings remittance, it is an added advantage rather than a human resource loss. From the national point of view, migration of a few million persons does not perceptibly affect the labour situation in India since unemployment is severe and the population growth rate is high.

16. It is to be noted that there is hardly any study on the socio-political influence of the large number of the immigrants from the Asian countries on the Gulf society. The understanding of the behaviour and change in the nature of the returning migrants is incomplete without studies in this dimension. There is serious complaint of Arab countries discriminating against Indians on the ground of nationality. There also exist wage differences between East Asian and South Asian migrants (for details see Nair, 1986). Nair observes that Indians face distress and contempt from the host-country nationals. Indians are known to be the "ABCs" of the Gulf- i.e., Ayahs, Barbers, and Cooks".

17. The Kerala state is not able to provide equal salary to the returning migrants. In the Gulf even the menial job is accepted owing to the distance from the home place and the five digit salary for a menial job is unthinkable for a low educated semi-skilled labourer working in Kerala. The war between Iraq and Kuwait had a strong impact on the small state in India. The entire state was facing economic crisis as it was difficult to rehabilitate the huge number of returning migrants. The Gulf crisis of 1990 created a havoc in the state. The massive inflow of the returning migrants gave an opportunity for the state to actually witness the real state of the economy and how deeply it was dependent on the Gulf economy. The domestic income of the state was affected. The migration and the remittance has not changed the economy as a whole though it has contributed towards economic growth through the inflow of foreign exchange, and reducing unemployment.

18. The interesting issue is that there is little effort on part of the natives to create their own civil society organizations to support their cause in any substantial way. There is a lack of such organization which can function as a pressure group and influence the foreign policies of the state.

19. Gulf migration being a male phenomenon, the women folk spend the better part of their family life in the absence of their husband. Separation from family for long periods affect the social structure, especially family system. In case of joint and extended family the elder male member is the main decision-maker. In most families, it is the elder male members who plays the social role in the absence of the husband. The women are passive members whose only engagement is their presence at the site of decision-making. Female folk in general have a low status in the social life and it is difficult to maintain that the male folk have faith on their wives was to give the full responsibility in the hands of the female folk. The women also feel more convenient to take decision after discussing it with the male members as they themselves are not confident of their capacity to understand the dealings of the outside world.

    But in most cases, the wife in the family takes responsibility for shopping, looking after children's education, which can be seen as a temporary structural adjustment. The acting head of the family reattributes all the responsibility to the male member the moment he returns. The females, in fact, do not feel empowered and free to take decisions. Every member will have their own bias and interpretation imbued with their own interest. Even in the physical absence of the male migrant he is very much the head. The mother-in-law has the claim that she knows her son best and she knows the best way he would have liked to take a certain course of action.

20. Most of the literature on international migrants and immigrants focuses on the impact of immigration on receiving societies, particularly to the developed countries. Since short-term migration is generally undertaken for economic reasons, most studies have tended to focus on the economic aspects of short term-migration. The studies focus primarily on the economic consequences of the migration that are framed within the neo-classical tradition. According to this perspective, the economy is an autonomous realm largely unaffected by the social and cultural context.

21. In the general diaspora studies the scholars observe that the migrant settlers have an imaginative and nostalgic narrative of their home, which most of the time is outdated or unrealistic. But in case of the Kerala migrants to Middle East the case is different as the migrants though physically are in a different territory, they are imaginarily still in their hometown. Their close interaction is being reinforced by the constant

interaction with close relatives and friends through various means of communication. There are increased number of STD/ISD phone-booths, newspapers and magazines. Big budget entertainment and cultural programmes are also organized by the well-known TV channels and cinema artists in the Malayali populated areas of the Gulf countries. And most importantly, the influence of media especially the TV channels (like Asianet, Kilari, Surya, India Vision) with vide inter-action viewership is widely linking Malayalies globally. A migrant Malyali is equally aware of all the socio political events of his native place. So the effect of migration on the religious attitude is not formed by the non-presence of the migrants in their homes.

22. See Gardner, Katy and Filippo Osella, A, 2003, 'Migration Modernity and Social Transformation in South Asia: An Overview', In *Contribution to Indian Sociology,* N.S. 37, 1&2 pp. v-xviii.
23. In recent years, scholars such as Geertz, Metcalf and Robinson have tried to analyse this trend from more flexible categorization. Metcalf in her book "*Moral Conduct and Authority: The Place of Adab in South Asian Islam*" (1984), attempts to put forward a new approach towards the understanding of Muslim culture.
24. In Islam, realization of human being comes through the cultivation of *Aqal* and the consequent disciplining of the *Nafs*. This process of controlling the Nafs through the mediation of *Aqal* is considered as the 'greater jihad', as it tries to win upon one's own life through a constant every day spiritual battle targeted against the evil thoughts inside human beings, see Metcalf (1984).
25. It has been noticed in Islamic history that when the religion or cultural tradition was in trouble, there is an increased degree of focus on the dissemination of etiquettes. Robinson's essay "Ulama of Farangi Mahal" (1984) and Metcalf writing on Behisti. Zewer (2002) shows that religions and political leaders use etiquettes as text of right conduct and disseminate on the basis of guarding the tradition and Muslim identity. Women are considered as the main carriers of the moral value and social role and responsibility is determined by the socio-political situation. Metcalf's book "*Perfecting Women*" (2002) provides a detailed account of the obligation of the women in both private and public life. Any attempt to combat with the observance of un-Islamic practice has tendency of focusing on women. Since women were the prime practitioners of the host of the rituals and customs, *Deobandi Ulama* started taking interest in the Islamic education of women. Thus, emphasis on the changing value orientation and motivation towards etiquettes will reflect upon the mental make up of the Muslims.

26. In terms of the educational level of the community, the low level of aspiration towards education can be attributed towards this Gulf phenomenon. Though the performance of the community cannot be addressed in isolation with the historical and political issues of the community, the aversion towards English education has led to the low esteem towards higher or professional education.

References

Ahmad, Imtiaz. 1981. *Modernization and Social Change among Muslims in India*, New Delhi, Manohar Publication.

Ali, Mohammed. 1985. *The Development of Education among the Mappilas of Malabar 1800 to 1965*, New Delhi: Nunes Publishers.

Appadurai, Arujun. 1996. *Modernity at Large: Cultural Dimensions of Globalization*, Minneapolis: University of Minneapolis Press.

Barth, Fredrik. (ed.), 1996. '*Ethnic Groups and Boundaries: The Social Organization of Cultural Difference*', George Allen and Lonwin, London: Oslo Universities Forlaget.

Bourdeu, Pierre. 1987. 'Legitimization and Structured Interests in Weber's Sociology of Religion', in Samwhimster and Scott Lash, (ed.) *From Max Weber. Rationality and Modernity* (ed.) Allen and Unwin London: Allen (translated by Chris Tumer).

Eickelman, Dale. 1999. 'The Coming Transformation of the Muslim World' *Middle East Review of International Affairs* 3 (3), Sept.

Gardner, Katy and Filippo Osella. 2003. 'Migration, Modernity and Social Transformation in South Asia: An overview', *Contribution to Indian Sociology*, N.S. 37, 1&2: V-XXVIII.

Geertz, Clifford. 1960. 'Religion of Java', Glencoe: Illinois.

Gulati, Leela. 1983. '*In the Absence of their Men: Impact of Male Migration on Women*', New Delhi: Sage Publications.

Habermas, Jurgen. 1989. *The Structural Transformation of the Public Sphere: An Inquiry into a Category of Bourgeois Society*, Trans by Tomas Burger with the Assistance of Frederic Lawrence. Cambridge: Massachusets.

Hasting, Donnan. 2002. '*Interpreting Islam*', New Delhi: Vistaar Publications.

Hirschkind, Charles. 2000. 'Passionate Preaching Aural Sensibility and the Islamic Revival in Cairo', in Michael Lambek (ed.), *A. Reader in the Anthropology of Religion*, Polity Press.

Koya, Mohamed S.M.. 1983. '*Mappilas of Malabar*', Kerala, Sandhya Publication.

Kunji, Muhammad P.K. 1982. '*Muslimigalum Kerala Sanskaravum*', Trishur: Kerala Sahitya Akadami.

Kunju, Abrahim A.P. 1989. '*Mappila Muslims of Kerala: Their History and Culture*', Sandhya Publication.

Kurien, A. Prema. 2002. '*Kaleidoscopic Ethnicity: International Immigration and the Reconstruction of Community Identities in India*', New Brunswick: Rutgers University Press.

Metcalf, Babra Daly. 2002. *Islamic Revival in British India: Deoband, 1860-1900*, New Delhi: Oxford University Press.

Miller, Roland. E. 1976. *Mappila Muslims of Kerala: A Study in Islamic Trends*, Madras: Orient Longman.

Pandey, Gyanendra. (ed.), 1993. *Hindus and Others: Question of Identity in India Today*, New Delhi: Viking Publication.

Panikkar, K.N. 2001. *Against Lord and State: Religion and Pesant Uprisings in Malabar 1836-1921*, New Delhi: Oxford University Press.

Salim, Abdul. A. 1999. *Educational development at micro level: Case study of two villages in Kerala*. Tiruvanantapuram: CDS Publication.

Samad, M. Abdul. 1998. *Islam in Kerala: Group and Movements in 20th Century*, Kottayam: Laurel Publications.

Schneider D.M. and Kathleen Gough. (ed), 1962. *Matrilineal Kinship, Berkly* and Los Angeles: University of California.

Singh, Yogendra. 1999 (Reprint). *Modernization of Indian Tradition*, New Delhi: Rawat Publications.

Wilson, Brayan, R. 1996. *Religion in Secular Society*, Wonder: C.A. Walts and Company.

Zachariah, K.C., et al. (eds.), 2002. *Kerala's Gulf Connection*, Kerala: Centre for Development Studies.

Social isolation and backwardness of an ethnic community: A case study

Monirul I. Khan

This paper is derived from a larger study on the economic issues of the tea plantation workers.[1] In course of the study the focus extended into the life of the tea plantation workers, particularly the static character and backwardness in their condition. The static scenario could be understood in terms of a set of indicators, such as literacy, housing, occupational mobility, income, social interaction or the health condition among the tea plantation workers. To pursue this goal, additional information was gathered to probe the issues further to link with the causal background and the consequences thereof. What is called static is related to social isolation and a large difference with the relevant national estimates. However, social isolation is also accompanied by their backwardness on the social front. In a way each reinforces the other and the end of one may trigger changes in the other.

The social isolation of an ethnic community could be an outcome of their own choice. Some of the ideas in this regard were developed by Chatterjee (1999) in the course of the explanation offered about Indian nationalism. In his polemics with a different view, Chatterjee argues that Indian nationalism was not simply an uncritical replication of a model developed in the West. At the level of culture, ideas and outlook the ingenuity of the Indian people lent the necessary uniqueness. His argument implies that a community borrowing institutions from others leans primarily towards the material component leaving behind mostly the essence of the 'inner world'. In other words, the borrowing community preserves its sovereignty or uniqueness protecting its own ideas and values.

In the interacting relationship between an ethnic community and the mainstream the former may preserve its cultural purity at the cost of isolation. It means social isolation is directed to the attainment of a cultural goal of a small community. Although the tribal and ethnic communities may opt for isolation or limited interaction to protect their cultural and economic uniqueness they may not be benefiting in the long run. The finding of this paper has an indication of a similar kind.[2]

On the other hand, social backwardness is a developmental as well as structural issue. It is developmental in a comparative sense and its lack of certain standards makes it conceptually meaningful. While backwardness may be interpreted as something relative, it may also carry some absolute sense. In the definition of poverty this has been clarified to some extent. For example, a slum dweller may be ranked as backward in comparison with a person from a middle class. In the recent formulation of the concept of human well being (or the Human Development Index) the relevant standards and social goals of development have been given further precision. When backwardness is an outcome of a particular type of relationship it is indicative of structural factors. It is more likely that a person without any access to resource or labour market will remain backward in terms of different social parameters.

Although the point has not been pursued well in literature, it is possible that a class in the driving seat of surplus exploitation may encourage the isolation and backwardness of the dependent class. Even the ideology that promotes segregation among the dependent classes would be patronized by the dominant class. In colonial India, it was believed that the Hindu-Muslim divide was encouraged by the colonial power to weaken the anit-colonial movement.

Colonialism has special significance in relation to the establishment of tea gardens in Bangladesh.[3] Capitalism commenced its journey in India with colonialism. On the economic front, the colonial forces were busy with implanting capitalism fast to extract surplus value. Colonial capital was merciless, as indicated by the infamous chopping of hands of the weavers' producing the famous *Dhaka Mosleen* that used to be exported into Europe.

Tea was an important cash crop in the new colonial venture. In the districts of Sylhet and Chittagong tea gardens were founded in the parts constituting the present day Bangladesh. At present there are about one hundred tea gardens in Bangladesh and a few thousand people are engaged in tea leaf plucking, processing, packaging and other related tasks. However, interestingly enough, instead of employing the local people the colonial owners hired the tea plantation workers from what is now India. The labour came from Orissa, Bihar, West Bengal, Andhra Pradesh and Tamil Nadu. Several reasons could be presumed why the workers were brought from the states far away from the gardens. One could be their longer association with the techniques of work such as tea plucking and their caste background. Most of them were from low castes, economically and socially backward, easy to be controlled by the colonial masters. The caste titles of the tea plantation workers were found to be the following: Tanti, Chasa, Bunarji, Das, Rabidas, Madrazi, Chatri, Sinchatri, Uria, Singh, Roy, Goala, Kurmi, Kaloar, Mura, Mridha and others.[4] After the partition of India, most of them stayed back and continued under new employers when the ownership of the gardens changed. Gradually, the linkage between tea plantation workers and their ancestral homes disappeared. It was not possible for them to complete the official formalities of getting passport, and visa to visit their ancestral homes. Following the independence of Bangladesh, the formalities to visit India became easier to some extent but did not encourage them to make such visits. One possible reason could be their economic limitation to undertake such visits. Moreover, many of them lost the address of their ancestral homes over the years.

Both quantitative and qualitative techniques were employed to collect data. Among purposively chosen households, questionnaire survey was conducted. Six tea gardens at Srimangal of Maulavibazar district were chosen first. The ownership of the selected gardens was in the hands of foreign nationals and private groups. The names of the workers of the sampled gardens were listed comprehensively. Then, the sample size of two hundred was proportionately divided in six gardens corresponding to their proportion among the total. Several cases were also studied in addition to focus group discussions.

As we have mentioned earlier, the tea workers had been engaged in tea plucking. Only a few of them could remember vaguely how many generations ago they migrated to the gardens. For example, Anila saw her grandfather and heard that only one generation ago they came to the tea garden. But Rabi Das could not correctly remember when her forefathers first migrated. Anila and her predecessors have been working in the same garden. She has also been married in the same place. But Surbala came from another garden following marriage. She replaced her mother-in-law who was a regular worker. Replacement is seen as a great favour by the poor tea workers. Anila works as a *ifaltui* or temporary worker. The difference between temporary and permanent workers is notable. Uncertainty of an extraordinary nature always haunts the temporary workers as they may lose the job any time.

The tea workers exclusively remain stuck to the garden. Employers provide them with a small plot of land where they manage to build a small hut. These are of poor quality, such as thatched houses in a shabby condition. Only the regular workers are fortunate enough to get the allotment of land. However, the temporary workers somehow manage to find a shelter for themselves through their kin or close neighbours (i.e., taking the advantage of social capital), but there is always uncertainty in it. The slums where they live are also characterized by poor sanitation and congested conditions.

Illiteracy prevails widely to the scale of 86 per cent among the women and 53 per cent among the men. Others attended primary schools but failed to complete even Primary education. The number of schools is extremely inadequate. It is a common scenario that the Primary Schools are managed by a few teachers. Drop out is common and the children join their mothers in tea plucking very early and share the household chores. Many are engaged in shepherding cattle, a lucrative economic source. About 40 per cent women were married off before they were fifteen years old, indicating the traditional condition of the women. Monthly average incomes stand around TK 2300. Remember that the poverty level (per day per person 212 kilo Calorie) income is about TK 500 in Bangladesh. Average household size among the tea workers is 3.32. It implies that an average size family will require minimum TK 1700 to afford poverty level food intake. It will be difficult for them to afford expenditures for other purposes like health, education, clothes or recreation. The economic situation of the temporary workers is further worsened as they pass through stretches of unemployment at frequent intervals.

Spatial mobility among the tea workers is extremely limited. For example, Anila is now thirty-seven years old and has never visited even the Srimangal town only eight kilometers from the tea garden where she has been living since her childhood. Once she traveled to a distant tea garden to visit relations. The temporary workers travel a long distance to get work in different gardens. However, the travel remains confined to different tea gardens. Moreover, there is distrust among them about the town and the mainstream community. Considerable ignorance about the town and the people living there prevails in them. Although many tea workers have learnt Bangla their differences with the members of the mainstream community are still very deep. Such differences will be evident not only in terms of language, but also in terms of religious practices, festivals and other social events. Routine social interaction of the workers is confined within the tea gardens. A brief profile of their daily life indicates the scale of confinement. Coming back from work in the evening they quickly finish household chores such as cooking. If there is leisure time they might visit their neighbour's house. Male members start taking country liquor after dusk. Sometimes they gather at the house of panchayat to engage in gossiping.

For shopping, the tea workers depend on periodic *mela* or fairs. Itinerant traders assemble in the tea gardens to sell their goods which include clothes, and toiletries, etc. Extensive sale on credit is present and payment is made in instalments.

Another instance that they live in as a closed community isolated from the others is revealed in the form of existing marital practices. The principle of endogamy is still followed restricting the matrimonial engagement with the same caste. Instances of leaving tea garden through marriage are not common. It could be another garden from where the bride or groom is selected but not from a place or distant town outside the community and culture of the tea workers. It indicates not only their strong adherence to preserving ethnic uniqueness by the tea workers but also their reluctance to beak their isolation. Perpetuation of the closeness/isolation or other forms of disadvantages is related more to establishing community identity than to derive any material benefit. Actually, the perception of disadvantage is completely different among the tea workers. What may appear disadvantageous to others, is a necessary strategy to preserve their ethnic uniqueness.

A few of them have come out of this mindset, but the majority is firmly attached to it.

In the observance of religious festival also one may notice the phenomenon of isolation. *Durga puja* is the most important religious festival observed by the tea plantation workers. It takes place completely within them. All events remain confined within the garden. Outsiders are hardly welcome to take part in it.

Occupational mobility is almost absent among the tea plantation workers giving an impression that they continue with the caste obsession (e.g., not to abandon the occupation pursued by the forefathers). Several of them inherited the jobs from their fathers. Sometimes it is a daughter inheriting from an ailing mother while in other cases daughter-in-law from a mother-in-law. This replacement takes place with the approval of the employers. Job transfer along descent line is more noticeable among the plucking workers while others, such as the factory workers, would not enjoy this privilege. It was found that 90 per cent women workers joined plucking as their first job. Tea plantation work is extremely valuable to the tea workers. Many of them nurture the dream of getting a permanent position some day. There is routine unemployment, hence the rush for a permanent job. The job of a clerk (*babu*) is greatly valuable to them. Many male workers also harbour the dream of becoming a *sardar* (or labour leader) one day. Among the women more than 50 per cent joined plucking before they were fifteen years old. Male members who are physically active are mostly engaged within the garden. The absence of occupational mobility further reinforces the isolation among the tea workers. Perpetual attachment to the same form of work weakens the spirit of innovation and the urge for looking outside.

Patriachy is still strongly present. Often it was heard that the male members of the households spend their earnings on country liquor whereas the women keep on organizing the livelihood for the families. Isolation has further consolidated the hold of patriarchy. There is violence against women reported by the community members leading to physical abuse from time to time. We have found in the village studies in Bangladesh that mobility of the women has contributed to their empowerment and the weakening of patriarchal control. This is absent in the tea garden.

Political awareness is poor among the tea garden workers. The male is obsessed with country liquor and hardly expresses any interest to discuss about their condition or how to change it. In the process, fatalism grips their mind. Trade unionism is present but its activities are confined to revising wages, providing benefits, and securing employment. Only in 1999 a memorandum of understanding (MOU) has been signed fixing minimum wage, health benefits, employment security and other matters. Only the regular workers fall within the purview of the MOU, not the temporary workers. There is no radical movement undertaken by the tea workers. The trade union contributed very little to break the age long isolation and the poor standard of living. A large number of workers are engaged on a temporary contract, as we have mentioned earlier. For the temporary workers, functionally there is no minimum wage rate. The presence of a large number of temporary workers reduces the bargaining capacity of the permanent workers. Further, irony in the role of the trade union is reflected in the fact that many of their leaders maintain a living standard, which could hardly be comparable with that of the poor tea workers. On the other hand, the tea workers are so polite that one may mistake this attitude for timidity. Protest is hardly noticeable. They are traditionally known as simple and not used to employ trickery to increase their advantages. However, sometimes they turn violent particularly if they feel that they have been cheated.[5] Violence surfaced in the past when they confronted the management. But they conform to the rules and regulations of the garden by and large without making any deviations. However, the activists of the national political parties do not visit the place to engage these people with their organization unlike the rest of the country.

Tea gardens are located in places, which are far from the urban areas. This has contributed to the perpetuation of isolation. However, with the present improved communication in the country geographic distances should not have mattered as much except locations in a very remote area, such as an inaccessible valley. Thus, the isolation that has been reported does not result from mere geographical distance. At a preliminary stage in the development of plantation this could have been an important factor to bring isolation but it should not be so at present. There should be a few sociological factors accounting for the isolation. I would like to suggest the following that may have contributed further to the phenomenon of isolation.

Firstly, the inward-looking mentality of the tea workers. They feel protected in maintaining a distance from the mainstream community. Perhaps, they are skeptical that frequent interactions with the members of the local community will weaken their separate identity. They can easily identify their separateness in language, religion and other norms. It is part of their cultural uniqueness that has constituted their identity. Losing that uniqueness could be considered as losing their self (actually this is now recognized as the minority complex). Secondly, the lack of educational opportunities for a long period. Whatever the reason, the tea workers have been allowed to go to school only recently. Previously, schools were absent. This has accentuated their isolation along with lack of mobility. Because of the above, they have been deprived of valuable information which could be useful in their migrating from the gardens. Thirdly, the absence of alternative job opportunities intensified their link with the tea gardens. Over the years, a fear has grown in them about the outside world. The lack of confidence overshadows their mind keeping them away from a new job. They also did not have the skill to expand their choice of jobs. Fourthly, the absence of any intervention programmes from the outside world may be another factor to prolong the isolation. It is difficult to get access to the community of tea workers. As they are suspicious of the outsiders, the employers are also reluctant to allow the outsiders to interact with them closely.

The price of isolation is considerable. Tea workers have not only lost their linkage with their ancestral homes but have failed to change their living standards and seize the opportunities that could be found outside. Had they been mobile enough, certainly that would have left positive impact on their bargaining capacity.

Although we made a few observations on the role of employers it may be elaborated further. Did the isolation of the tea workers from the outside world benefit the employers? Yes, it has. Readily, we can identify two benefits. Greater isolation means limited mobility. With the demand increasing very slowly a larger supply pushes the wage rate down. Any employer will be happy to see the wage level low provided it does not affect the skill level.

Keeping the awareness level low is another precondition to imposing strong control over the tea workers. Interaction with the outside world would allow them to learn about the wage level prevalent outside as well as establish linkage with other workers. This may increase bargaining power and also allow them to learn about workers' rights as enunciated in the national labour codes. It may also give them opportunity to organise protest against their exploitation with the help of the workers in other parts of the country. Actually, one can list many more implications in this respect. The exploitation of the tea workers has been largely possible through keeping them isolated.

There are two consequences. On the one hand, there is a choice of the tea workers not to change the phenomenon of isolation in the name of preserving the so-called ethnic uniqueness. On the other, there is a benefit for the employers if the workers remain isolated particularly from the larger union movements of the country. Politically diffused tea workers contribute to a smooth process of surplus generation in the tea plantations. Therefore, their isolation and backwardness should not be perceived as a cultural phenomenon only. It is very much linked to the political economy that operates in the tea plantation's surplus generation process.

Despite the fact that the majority of the tea workers now live without any past and history, a few families could come out of this general trend. They could find out their ancestral homes. By receiving education from outside some families have also switched over to new occupations. Recently, some non-governmental organisations have come forward with skill development and non-formal educational programmes. One can only hope that these and other interventions will break the isolation lasting through several generations soon, with positive implications for reductions in backwardness also.

Notes

1. There is a dispute on calling the Hindu low castes an ethnic tribal group which the tea workers are: There are views both in favour and against it as reflected in the following comment, "Anthropologists concerned with India have for some time debated the problem of distinction between autochthonous tribal groups and Hindu castes. Those speaking of a tribe-caste continuum hold the view that it is impractical to draw a sharp line between tribes and castes, whereas others feel confident of their ability to decide in concrete cases whether a given community should be classified as a tribe or a caste' (Furer-Haimendorf: 1985:32).
2. The advocates of the globalisation thesis would take a strong position against maintaining social isolation as an effective way of promoting self-interest.

3. About this context a relevant account includes the following observation, 'plantations tended to be the preferred area of investment and operation of European capital, the tea plantations of the northern districts of Darjeeling and Jalpaiguri using large-scale migrant labour being the most prominent example.' (Bose 1993:41).
4. It is interesting to note that the tea workers received very little attention from the researchers dealing with the issue of ethnicity/tribe in Bangladesh. As we saw that the migrant tea workers were mostly Hindu low-caste, attention was not paid to them in the writings on the Hindu low-caste. For example, Maloney (1984:20-22) discussed about different Hindu low castes but did not touch those engaged in tea leaf plucking. Sattar (1983) also did not include the tea workers as a particular tribe in his book on the tribes of Bangladesh.
5. It reminds us what has been underlined by the subaltern theorists. The people in the margin of the society possess potential to rise spontaneously without the assistance of any external organization (Guha: 1986).

References

Bose, Sugata. 1993. *The New Cambridge History of India: Peasant Labour and Colonial Capital, Rural Bengal Since 1770*. Delhi: Cambridge University Press.

Chatterjee, Partha. 1999. *The Nation and its Fragments: Colonial and Postcolonial Histories*. Delhi: Oxford University Press.

Furer-Haimendorf, Christoph von. 1985. *Tribes of India: The Struggle for Survival*. Delhi: Oxford University Press.

Guha, R. 1986. *Elementary Aspects of Peasant Insurgency in Colonial India*. Delhi: Oxford university Press.

Maloney, Clearance T. 1984. "Tribes of Bangladesh and synthesis of Bengali culture in tribal cultures". In Mahmud Shah Qureshi (ed.) *Bangladesh Institute of Bangladesh Studies*, Rajshahi University.

Sattar, Abdus. 1971. *In the Sylvan Shadow*. Dhaka: Bangla Academy.

Annexures

Landmark documents on the OBC problematic

A: Findings/Recommendations of Commissions/action taken on their reports

D-1: The First Backward Classes Commission, 1956 and the view of the Mandal Commission on the treatment of its report

1.1 The First Backward Classes Commission was set up by a President Order under Article 340 of the Constitution of India on January 29th, 1953 and it submitted its report on March 30th, 1955.

1.2 The Commission issued a Questionnaire comprising 182 questions for eliciting the views of the State Governments and the general public on various aspects of its inquiry. It also undertook extensive touring of the country to collect on the spot evidence.

1.3 After sifting and sorting the facts collected as above the Commission formulated the following criteria for identifying socially and educationally backward classes:

(i) Low social position in the traditional caste hierarchy of Hindu society.

(ii) Lack of general educational advancement among the major section of a caste or community.

(iii) Inadequate or no representation in Government service.

(iv) Inadequate representation in the field of trade, commerce and industry.

It also prepared a list of 2399 backward castes or communities for the entire country, and 837 of these were classified as 'most backward'. The Registrar General and Census Commissioner of India assisted the Commission in making population projections of 930 backward castes or communities.

1.4 The recommendations of the Commission for the upliftment of the backward classes are extremely wide-ranging and comprehensive. They cover such diverse fields as Extensive Land Reforms, Reorganisation of Village Economy, Bhoodan Movement, Development of Livestock, Dairy Farming, Cattle Insurance, Bee-keeping, Piggery, Fisheries,

Development of Rural and Cottage Industries, Rural Housing, Public Health and Rural Water Supply, Adult Literacy, University Education, Representation of Backward Classes in Government service, etc. Some of the most noteworthy recommendations of the Commission were:

(i) Undertaking caste-wise enumeration of population in the Census of 1961;

(ii) Relating social backwardness of a class to its low position in the traditional caste hierarchy of Hindu society.

(iii) Treating all women as a class as "backward";

(iv) Reservation of 70 per cent seats in all technical and professional institutions for qualified students of backward classes;

(v) Minimum reservation of vacancies in all Government services and local bodies for other Backward Classes on the following scale:-

Class I	..	25 per cent
Class II	..	33-1/3 per cent
Class III & IV	..	40 per cent

1.5 It is pertinent to note that the Commission could not present an unanimous report. In fact, five of its Members recorded minutes of dissent. Dr. Anup Singh, Shri Arunangshu De and Shri P.G. Shah were opposed to the view of linking caste with backwardness. They were also opposed to the reservation of posts on the basis of caste. On the other hand, Shri S.D.S. Chaurasia strongly advocated the acceptance of caste as the criterion for backwardness in his 67-page minute of dissent. Shri T. Mariappa's minute of dissent was concerned only with the inclusion of a couple of castes in the list of Other Backward Classes.

1.6 Shri Kaka Kalelkar, the Chairman, took a rather equivocal stand on this issue. Though he did not record a formal minute of dissent in his forwarding letter to the President, he opposed the acceptance of caste as the basis for backwardness. He also expressed his reservations regarding several other important recommendations made by the Commission.

Government action on Kaka Kalelkar commission report

1.7 After a detailed examination of the Commission's Report, the Government laid its copy together with a Memorandum of Action Taken before each House of the Parliament on September 3rd, 1956 in compliance with Article 340(3) of the Constitution. In this Memorandum it was observed, "For the purpose of the enquiry specifically contemplated in Article 340 of the Constitution it was necessary to consider whether these other backward sections could be properly classified, and the Commission had to find objective tests and criteria by which such classifications were to be made; they had to find indisputable yardsticks by which social and educational backwardness could be measured. The report of the Commission has not been unanimous on this point. In fact, it reveals considerable divergence of opinion." It was further stated, "The Commission's list contains as many as 2399 communities out of which 930 alone account for an estimated population of 11.5 crores; Scheduled Castes and Tribes will make up another 7 crores" (on the basis of 1951 Census). Regarding the acceptance of caste as criteria for backwardness, it was stated, "It cannot be denied that the caste system is the greatest hindrance in the way of our progress towards an egalitarian society, and the recognition of the specified castes as backward may serve to maintain and even perpetuate the existing distinctions on the basis of caste."

1.8 Regarding the recognition of a large number of castes and communities as backward, it was pointed out, "If the entire community, barring a few exceptions has thus to be regarded as backward, the really needy would be swamped by the multitude and hardly receive any special attention or adequate assistance, nor would such dispensation fulfil the conditions laid down in Article 340 of the Constitution."

1.9 In view of the above, the Government considered it necessary that "some positive and workable criteria should be devised for the specification of the socially and educationally backward classes" and to undertake further investigations "so that deficiencies that have been noticed in the findings of the Commission are made good...." It was also pointed out in the Memorandum that the Planning Commission had already formulated the development programmes for the removal of backwardness and "the main point to be stressed was whether the special needs of the backward classes could be intensively and effectively served by appropriate shifts of emphasis or by rearrangement of priorities within the framework of the existing programmes or whether additional programmes needed to be drawn up".

Incidentally, the Commission's Report was not discussed by the Parliament.

1.10 After presenting the Memorandum to the Parliament, the Government made efforts "to discover some criteria other than caste which could be of practical application in determining the backward classes." The Deputy Registrar General was asked to conduct a pilot survey to see if backwardness could be linked to occupational communities instead of caste. Such a survey was undertaken but it failed to throw up the desired criteria. The matter was also discussed at a conference of State representatives on 7-4-1959 and subsequently reviewed at a meeting of State members convened by the Ministry of Home Affairs, but no consensus emerged as a result of these efforts.

1.11 The Central Government ultimately took a decision that no all India lists of backward classes should be drawn up, nor any reservation made in the Central Government service for any group of backward classes other than the Scheduled Castes and Scheduled Tribes. Consequently, on August 14th 1961, the Ministry of Home Affairs addressed all the State Governments stating, "While the State Governments have the discretion to choose their own criteria for defining backwardness, in the view of the Government of India it would be better to apply economic tests than to go by caste." Regarding the preparation of lists of backward classes it was observed, "Even if the Central Government were to specify under article 338(3) certain groups of people as belonging to 'other backward classes', it will still be open to every State Government to draw up its own lists for the purposes of Articles 15 and 16. As therefore, the State Governments may adhere to their own lists, any all-India list drawn up by the Central Government would have no practical utility".

Some observations on Kaka Kalelkar Commission Report

1.12 It is well worth remembering that Kaka Kalelkar Commission Report was the first national level inquiry of its kind after the adoption of the Constitution. Since then ten States have set up fifteen Commissions and their reports provide a wealth of material on this subject. Further, the present Commission has the additional benefit of a plethora of judicial pronouncements by the Supreme Court and several High Courts on the question of extending various types of benefits to backward classes other than the Scheduled Castes and Scheduled Tribes.

1.13 But despite making due allowance for its handicaps, it cannot be denied that Kaka Kalelkar Commission Report suffers from grave flaws of methodology and serious internal contradictions. For instance, the Commission was required to determine the criteria for identifying socially and educationally backward classes and, in accordance with such criteria, to prepare a list of such classes. The criteria evolved by the Commission is given in para 1.3. The list of 2399 backward classes identified by the Commission is contained in Volume II of Kaka Kalelkar Commission Report. But it is not clear from the Report as to how the lists of backward classes were derived by the application of that criteria. The Commission's State-wise lists are based on the lists prepared by the Ministry of Education for the grant of scholarships, etc. to 'Other Educationally Backward Classes' in 1949. The Ministry of Education, in its turn, had compiled these lists on the basis of the recommendations received from the respective State Governments.

1.14 It is seen that Ministry of Education had prepared its list not only without undertaking any special survey for the identification of the backward classes, it was meant only for 'Other Educationally Backward Classes' and not for 'Socially and Educationally Backward Classes' as contemplated in Article 340 of the Constitution.

1.15 Of course, Kaka Kalelkar Commission modified the Education Ministry's original lists in the light of the evidence collected by it. But the fact remains that it broadly adopted the lists of Other Educationally Backward Classes prepared by another Government agency for an entirely different purpose, and treated it as the list of socially and educationally backward classes of India. This was done without undertaking any field survey to check their validity for the purpose of the Commission. Nor were they tested against criteria evolved by the Commission for identifying socially and educationally backward classes.

1.16 As stated in para 1.4, Kaka Kalelkar Commission recommended different percentages of reservation of seats/vacancies in educational institutions, Government services, etc. for other Backward Classes (OBCs). For instance, it recommended reservation of 40 per cent posts in Class III and Class IV categories, 25 per cent in Class I category and 70 per cent of the seats in professional and technical institutions. But in the absence of any explanation of the rationale for fixing different percentages for different groups of posts etc. the approach appears somewhat arbitrary.

1.17 Though the above failings are serious, yet the real weakness of the Report lies in its internal contradictions. As stated in para 1.5, three of the Members were opposed to one of the most crucial recommendations of the Report, that is, the acceptance of caste as a criterion for social backwardness and the reservation of posts in Government services on that basis. The degree of dissidence greatly compromised the force of the Commission's recommendations. But it was the 30-page forwarding letter of Shri Kaka Kalelkar to the President which demolished the very basis of the Report. The following extracts from this letter speak for themselves:

"Beside convinced that the upper castes among the Hindus have to atone for the neglect of which they were guilty towards the 'lower' classes, I was prepared to recommend to Government that all special help should be given only to the backward classes and even the poor and the deserving among the upper classes may be safely kept out from the benefit of this special help. My eyes were however opened to the dangers of suggesting remedies on the caste basis when I discovered that it is going to have a most unhealthy effect on the Muslim and Christian sections of the nation....."

"This was a rude shock and it drove me to the conclusion that the remedies we suggested were worse than the evil we were out to combat."

"This painful realization came to me almost towards the end of our labours. I could not stem the current of opinion without the Commission itself and ultimately decided, though reluctantly, to side with the majority with whom I had cooperated throughout in formulating remedies on caste basis. It is only when the Report was being finalized that I started thinking a new and found that backwardness could be tackled on a basis or a number of bases other than that of caste. I only succeeded in raising the suspicion of the majority of my colleagues that I was trying to torpedo the recommendations of the Commission. This was another reason why I signed the Report. Without even a minute of dissent...."

".......... If such communities have neglected education it is because they had no use for it. Now that they have discovered their mistake it is for them to make the necessary efforts for making up the leeway."

"Till recently, good many communities were organizing caste conferences and collecting funds for granting scholarships to boys and girls of their own community. That was a good lesson in self help and a good number of communities have thus come forward in material well-being. But now all burdens is sought to be thrown on the common exchequer and those who have thoughtlessly neglected education in the past are now seeking preferential treatment in Government services. This is anything but fair....."

"I am definitely against reservation in Government services for any community for the simple reason that the services are not meant for the servants but they are meant for the service of society as a whole...."

"I believe that in Class I and Class II services, the backward classes will stand to gain, both morally and materially, if they do not demand a reservation percentage in the vacancies and simply rely on the fair-mindedness of the administration to use their preference in favour of the backward classes......"

1.18 The above extracts form an eloquent testament of Shri Kalelkar's views on backwardness and social justice. It must have caused this gentle Gandhian no end of anguish to refrain from recording a formal note of dissent to a Report which recommended caste as one of the main criteria for determining social backwardness. Despite giving such clear expression to his views, he observed in a latter para of this letter, "Following the analogy of the proverb, viz., 'Use the thorn to remove a thorn', we held that the evils of caste could be removed by measures which could be considered in terms of caste alone". Here, the strain of squaring the circle becomes so palpable that one can only sympathise with Kaka Sahib in his predicament.

1.19 A Report so fragmented in its conceptual design carried within itself the logic for its rejection.

Some observations on Government Action

1.20 Whereas Kaka Kalelkar Commission Report received the closest attention of the Government right upto the highest level, there is one aspect of its examination which merits special attention. Despite referring to various constitutional provisions and accepting the need to give special relief to socially and educationally backward classes, in the overall context the Government thinking was mainly conditioned by the national imperative of reducing economic disparities between different classes of society. This approach is clearly summed up in the letter that Home Ministry addressed to all the State Governments after full examination of the Report. The concluding sentence of this letter reads, "They (Government of India) also consider that while the State Governments have the discretion to choose their own criteria for defining backwardness, in the view of the Government of India *it would be better to apply economic tests than to go by caste*." (Emphasis added).

1.21 As the main thrust of Government's development programmes has always been the removal of mass poverty, this pre-occupation with economic criteria in determining backwardness is quite understandable. But howsoever laudable the objective may be, it is not in consonance with the spirit of Article 340 of the Constitution, under which the Commission was set up: Both Article 15(4) and 340(1) make a pointed reference to "socially and educationally backward classes". Any reference to "economic backwardness" has been advisedly left out of these Articles. Whereas we shall have more to say on this subject in a subsequent Chapter, it may be pertinent to point out that in giving primacy to 'economic tests' in determining the type of backwardness referred to in Article 340(1) of the Constitution, the Government has, perhaps inadvertently, paid less than adequate attention to the constitutional requirements in this matter. It may be possible to make out a very plausible case for not accepting caste as a criteria for defining 'social and educational backwardness'. But the substitution of caste by economic test will amount to ignoring the genesis of social backwardness in the Indian society.

D-2: The Memorandum of Action Taken on the First Backward Classes Commission Report, 1956

(Prepared by G.B. Pant), Government of India,
Ministry of Home Affairs

Subject : *Report of the Backward Classes Commission-Memorandum Explaining the Action Taken Thereon*

The President, under Article 340 of the Constitution appointed the Backward Classes Commission on January 29, 1953, with the following terms of reference :

(a) to determine the criteria to be adopted in considering whether any sections of the people in the territory of India (in addition to the Scheduled Castes and Scheduled Tribes specified by notifications issued under Article 341 and 342 of the Constitution) should be treated as socially and educationally backward classes; and in accordance with such criteria, prepare a list of such classes setting out also their approximate numbers and their territorial distribution;

(b) to investigate the conditions of all such socially and educationally backward classes and the difficulties under which they labour; and make recommendations

   (i) as to the steps that should be taken by the Union or any State to remove such difficulties or to improve their condition; and

   (ii) as to the grants that should be made for the purpose by the Union or any State and the conditions subject to which such grants should be made;

(c) to investigate such other matters as the President may thereafter refer to them; and

(d) to present to the President a report setting out the facts as found by them and making such recommendations as they think proper.

2. The Government has given careful thought to the report submitted by the Commisson. The task that had been entrusted to the Commission was of great complexity, specially in respect of the first term of refernce. There is a well-defined easily ascertained criterion, namely that of untouchability, in the case of the scheduled castes, and similarly such a criterion is available in the case of the scheduled tribes. But no such simple and clear-cut line of distinction is available regarding other castes and classes whose members may be backward. For the purpose of the enquiry specifically contemplated in Article 340 of the Constitution, it was necessary to consider whether these other backward sections could be properly classified; and the Commission had to find objective tests and criteria by which such classifications were to be made; they had to find indisputable yardsticks by which social and educational backwarndess could be measured. The report of the Commission has not been unanimous on this point; in fact, it reveals considerable divergence of opinion.

3. A plethora of claims were pressed before the Commission for acceptance as distinct and separate categories of backward classes, which for lack of trained staff to help them, the Commission found it

difficult to analyse. They have further included in their list even communities about whom no other information was available except the names, and abandoned their first idea of preparing a complete glossary of communities. The result of the adoption of such a procedure has been obvious and has led the recommendations of the Commission into difficult straits. The Commission's list contains as many as 2399 communities out of which 913 alone account for an estimated population of 11.51 crores! Scheduled Castes and tribes will make up another 7 crores. Women as a class have also been regarded by them as backward, though they have not listed them among the backward classes since they do not form a separate community. In this way, the bulk of the country's millions could be counted as coming within the category of backward, and no useful purpose would obviously be served by an enqiry conducted by a special Commission of this nature. In one sense, however, these figures serve a very useful purpose. They remind us of the general backwardness, social, educational and economic of our country as a whole, and also of the fact that the difficulties and handicaps from which the backward classes suffer differ only in intensity and not in kind from the general problem which applies to the country in its entirety.

4. It is nevertheless necessary to recognize that there are some really backward sections in the community, and it is the duty of all of us to do all we can for their uplift. Under foreign rule, they were neglected, and equal opportunities for advancement were not available to them. This fortunately is now a thing of the past. The constitution guarantees euqlity of opportunities for all citizens, irrespective of religion, race, caste, etc. and this fundamental principle of State policy has already been in force for some years. Large sums of money have been spent by Governments both at the Centre and in the States on the work of reconstruction and development during the period of the First Plan, resulting in an expansion of employment opportunities in the public services and elsewhere, and in the raising of the per capita income. The benefits of this nationwide endeavour have been shared by all citizens. The old conditions under which people suffered and backwardness thrived no longer find approbation in our land. With the establishment of our society on the socialist pattern to which we all are pledged social and other distinctions will disappear as we advance towards that goal.

5. So, while looking into the problem of the backward classes, it is necessary not to lose sight of its true perspective. The majority of the members of the Commission hold the position of the individual in the social hierarchy based on caste as determining the degree and extent of backwardness. The emphasis on caste has further been highlighted by

some of the minutes of dissent. The tone and temper displayed therein bring into prominence the dangers of separatism inherent in this kind of approach. It cannot be denied that the caste system is the greatest hindrance in the way of our progress towards an egalitarian society, and the recognition of the specified castes as backward may serve to maintain and even perpetuate the existing distinctions on the basis of caste. Besides, there may be castes a large number of whose members may be classed as backward educationally and economically, but still there may be others among them who cannot be so classified. Similarly, among the so-called upper and advanced classes there may be, as in fact there are, large numbers of those who are not less backward educationally and economically, and even among the backward classes some castes are more backward than others. Then there are differences in conditions between States and States, regions and regions, etc.

The Commission have also suggested certain other certeria such as "lack of general educational advancement among the major sections of a caste or community," "inadequate or no representation in Government service" and "inadequate representation in the field of trade, commerce and industry", "communities consisting largely of tenants without occupancy rights and those with insecure land tenure", and "communities consisting of a large percentage of small land-owners with uneconomic holding". But these are obviously vague tests, more or less of an individual character, and even if they are accepted, they would encompass a large majority of the country's population. If the entire community, barring a few exceptions, has thus to be regarded as backward, the really needy would be swamped by the multitude and hardly receive any special attention or adequate assistance, nor would such dispensation fulfil the conditions laid down in Article 340 of the constitution.

6. It has, therefore, become necessary that some positive and workable criteria should be devised for the specification of the socially and educationally backward classes of the people so that they may be given adequate assistance and relief in all suitable ways to make up for the leaway of the past to acquire the normal standards of life prevalent in the country. There are certain distinct groups to whom disabilities are attached by reasons of environments and occupations which are considered low, and in their case, even in the absence of such criteria, there need be no difficulty in providing special relief. There will be, besides, other classes who, adjudged in the light of reasonable standards, might well be regaqrded as socially and educationally backward. But action on a systematic and elaborate basis can be proceeded with only after the necessay postivie tests and criteria have been laid down for determining which classes or sections are really entitled to get special relief and assistance. To that end, further investigations will have to be undertaken so that the deficiencies that have been noticed in the findings

of the Commission are made good and the problem is solved with due regard to the requirements of Article 340 of the Constitution. Simultaneously, it is desirable to hold ad hoc surveys to determine the numbers that sould come within the category of such classes. The State Governments have been addressed accordingly.

7. The bulk of the other recommendations made by the Commission in their report which are of a general nature have been duly examined, and the ameliorative measures suggested by the Commission have been brought to the notice of Planning Commission, the Central Ministries and the State Governments for being taken into consideration in the formulation of their programmes of development. Many of the factors which contribute towards backwardness have been tackled by the Planning Commission under the appropriate schemes outlined by them, and in their case, the main point to be stressed was whether the special needs of the backward classes could be intensively and effectively served by appropriate shifts of emphasis or by rearrangement of priorities within the framework of the existing programmes or whether additional programmes needed to be drawn up. Instructions have further been issued to the state Governments requesting them to render every possible assistance and to give all reasonable facilities to the people who come within the category of backward classes in accordance with their existing lists and also to such others who in their opinion deserve to be considered as socially and educationally backward in the existing circumstances.

8. The President thanks the Chairman and Members of the Commission who bestowed so much time and labour upon the difficult task that was entrusted to them, and expresses his appreciation of the pains they have taken in the preparation of their report which involved extensive touring in different parts of the country and discussions with numerous organizations and individuals.

(Sd.) G.B. Pant

D-3: Criteria adopted by the Second Backward Classes Commission to identify the SEBCs

11.23 As a result of the above exercise, the Commission evolved eleven 'Indicators' or 'criteria' for determining social and educational backwardness. These 11 'Indicators' were grouped under three broad heads, i.e., Social, Educational and Economic. They are :

A. Social

(i) Castes/Classes considered as socially backward by others.

(ii) Castes/Classes which mainly depend on manual labour for their livelihood.

(iii) Castes/Classes where at least 25 per cent females and 10 per cent males above the State average get married at an age below 17 years in rural areas and at least 10 per cent females and 5 per cent males do so in urban areas.

(iv) Castes/Classes where participation of females in work is at least 25 per cent above the State average.

B. Educational

(v) Castes/Classes where the number of children in the ave group of 5-15 years who never attended school is at least 25 per cent above the State average.

(vi) Castes/Classes where the rate of student drop-out in the age group of 5-15 years is at least 25 per cent above the State average.

(vii) Castes/Classes amongst whom the proportion of matriculates is at least 25 per cent below the State average.

C. Economic

(viii) Castes/Classes where the average value of family assets is at least 25 per cent below the State average.

(ix) Castes/Classes where the number of families living in Kuccha houses is at least 25 per cent above the State average.

(x) Castes/Classes where the source of drinking water is beyond half a kilometer for more than 50 per cent of the households.

(xi) Castes/Classes where the number of households having taken consumption loan is at least 25 per cent above State average.

11.24 As the above three groups are not of equal importance for our purpose, separate weightage was given to 'Indicators' in each group. All the Social Indicators were given a weightage of 3 point each, Educational 'Indicators' a weightage of 2 points each and Economic 'Indicators' a weightage of one point each. Economic, in addition to Social and Educational Indicators, were considered important as they directly flowed from social and educational backwardness. This also helped to highlight the fact that socially and educationally backward classes are economically backward also.

11.25 It will be seen that from the values given to each Indicator, the total score adds upto 32. All these 11 Indicators were applied to all the castes covered by the survey for a particular State. As a result of this application, all castes which had a score of 50 per cent (i.e., 11 points) or above were listed as socially and educationally backward and the rest were treated as 'advanced'. (It is a sheer coincidence that the number of indicators and minimum point score for backwardness, both happen to be eleven). Further, in case the number of households covered by the survey for any particular caste were below 20, it was left out of consideration, as the sample was considered too small for any dependable inference.

11.26 The above system of listing castes as socially and educationally backward on the basis of their score may appear somewhat arbitrary. On the face of it, this is a tenable viewpoint. On the other hand, the points scored by a particular caste under the above system actually reflect the number of indicators of backwardness.

D-4: Recommendations of the Mandal Commission

Recommendations

13.11 It may appear that the upliftment of other Backward Classes is part of the larger national problem of the removal of mass poverty. This is only partially correct. The deprivation of OBCs is a very special case of the larger national issue: here the basic question is that of social and educational backwardness and poverty is only a direct consequence of these two crippling caste-based handicaps. As these handicaps are embedded in our social structure, their removal will require far-reaching structural changes. No less important will be changes in the perception of the problems of OBCs by the ruling classes of the country.

Reservations

13.2 One such change in the attitude of the ruling elite pertains to the provision of reservation in Government services and educational institutions for the candidates of Other Backward Classes. It is generally argued that looking to the large population of OBCs (52 per cent), recruitment of a few thousand OBCs every year against reserved vacancies is not going to produce any perceptible impact on their general condition. On the other hand, the induction of a large proportion of employees against reserved vacancies will considerably impair the quality and efficiency of the Government services. It is also stated that the benefits of such reservations will be skimmed off by those sections of OBCs which are already well off and the really backward sections will be left high and dry. Another argument advanced against this approach is that the policy of large scale reservations will cause great heart burning to those meritorious candidates whose entry into services will be barred as a result thereof.

13.3 All the above arguments are based on fairly sound reasoning. But these are also the arguments advanced by the ruling elite which is keen on preserving its privileges. Therefore, like all such reasoning, it is based on partisan approach. By the same token, while illuminating some immediate areas of concern it tends to ignore much larger issues of national importance.

13.4 It is not at all our contention that by offering a few thousand jobs to OBC candidates we shall be able to make 52 per cent of the Indian population as forward. But we must recognize that an essential part of the battle against social backwardness is to be fought in the minds of the backward people. In India Government service has always been looked upon as a symbol of prestige and power. By increasing the representation of OBCs in Government services, we give them an immediate feeling of participation in the governance of this country. When a backward class candidate becomes a Collector or a Superintendent of Police, the material benefits accruing from his position are limited to the members of his family only. But the psychological spin off of this phenomenon is tremendous; the entire community of that backward class candidate feels socially elevated. Even when no tangible benefits flow to the community at large, the feeling that now it has its "own man" in the "corridors of power" acts as morale booster.

13.5 In a democratic set-up every individual and community has a legitimate right and aspiration to participate in ruling this country. Any situation which results in a near-denial of this right to nearly 52 per cent of the country's population need to be urgently rectified.

13.6 Apprehensions regarding drop in the quality of Government services owing to large scale induction of S.C./S.T. and O.B.C. candidates against reserved posts may be justified only up to a point. But is it possible to maintain that all candidates selected on merit turn out to be honest efficient, hard-working and dedicated? At present, top echelons of all the Government services are manned predominantly by open competition candidates and if the performance of our bureaucracy is any indication, it has not exactly covered itself with glory. Of course, this does not imply that candidates selected against reserved posts will do better. Chances are that owing to their social and cultural handicaps they may be generally a shade less competent. But, on the other hand, they will have the great advantage of possessing first hand knowledge of the sufferings and problems of the backward sections of society. This is not a small asset for field workers and policy makers even at the highest level.

13.7 It is not doubt true that the major benefits of reservation and other welfare measures for Other Backward Classes will be cornered by the more advanced sections of the backward communities. But is not this a universal phenomenon? All reformist remedies have to contend with a slow recovery along the hierarchical gradient; there are no quantum jumps in social reform. Moreover, human nature being what it is, a "new class" ultimately does emerge even in classless societies. The chief merit of reservation is not that it will introduce egalitarianism amongst OBCs when the rest of the Indian society is seized by all sorts of inequalities. But reservation will certainly erode the hold of higher castes on the services and enable OBCs in general to have a sense of participation in running the affairs of their country.

13.8 It is certainly true that reservation for OBCs will cause a lot of heart burning to others. But should the mere fact of this heart burning be allowed to operate as a moral veto against social reform. A lot of heart burning was caused to the British when they left India. It burns the hearts of all whites when the black protest against apartheid in South Africa. When the higher castes constituting less than 20 per cent of the country's population subjected the rest to all manner of social injustice, it must have caused a lot of heart burning to the lower castes. But now that the lower castes are asking for a modest share of the national cake of power and prestige, a chorus of alarm is being raised on the plea that this will cause heart burning to the ruling elite. Of all the spacious arguments advanced against reservation for backward classes, there is none which beats this one about 'heart burning' in sheer sophistry.

13.9 In fact the Hindu society has always operated a very rigorous scheme of reservation, which was internalized through caste system. Eklavya lost his thumb and Shambhuk his neck for their breach of caste rules of reservation. The present forces against reservations for OBCs is not aimed at the principle itself, but against the new class of beneficiaries, as they are now clamouring for a share of the opportunities which were all along monopolized by the higher castes.

Quantum and scheme of reservations

13.10 Scheduled Castes and Scheduled Tribes constitute 22.5 per cent of the country's population. According, a pro-rata reservation of 22.5 per cent has been made for them in all services and public sector undertakings under the Central Government. In the States also, reservation for SCs and STs is directly proportional to their population each State.

13.11 As stated in para 12.22, the population of OBCs, both Hindu and non-Hindu, is around 52 per cent of the total population of India. Accordingly, 52 per cent of all posts under the Central Government should be reserved for them. But this provision may go against the law laid down in a number of Supreme Court judgements wherein it has been held that the total quantum of reservation under Articles 15(4) and 16(4) of the Constitution should be below 50 per cent. In view of this the proposed reservation for OBCs would have to be pegged at a figure which, when added to 22.5 per cent for SCs and STs, remains below 50 per cent. In view of this legal constraint, the Commission is obliged to recommend a reservation of 27 per cent only, even though their population is almost twice this figure.

13.12 States which have already introduced reservation for OBCs exceeding 27 per cent, will remain unaffected by this recommendation.

13.13 With the above general recommendation regarding the quantum of reservation, the Commission proposes the following over-all scheme of reservation for OBCs:

1. Candidates belonging to OBCs recruited on the basis of merit in an open competition should not be adjusted against their reservation quoto of 27 per cent.
2. The above reservation would also be made applicable to promotion quota at all levels,
3. Reserved quota remaining unfilled should be carried forward for a period of three years and dereserved thereafter.
4. Relaxation in the upper age limit for direct recruitment should be extended to the candidates of OBCs in the same manner as is being done in the case of SCs and STs.
5. A roster system for each category of posts should be adopted by the concerned authorities in the same manner as presently done in respect of SC and ST candidates.

13.14 The above scheme of reservation in its toto should also be made applicable to all recruitment to public sector undertakings both under the Central and State Governments, as also to nationalized banks.

13.15 All private sector undertakings which have received financial assistance from the Government in one form or the other should also be obliged to recruit personnel on the aforesaid basis.

13.16 All universities and affiliated colleges should also be covered by the above scheme of reservation.

13.17 To give proper effect to these recommendations, it is imperative that adequate statutory provisions are made by the Government to amend the existing enactments, rules, procedures, etc. to the extent they are not in consonance with the same.

Educational concessions

13.18 Our educational system is elitist in character, results in a high degree of wastage and is least suited to the requirements of an over-populated and developing country. It is a legacy of the British rule which was severely criticisised during the independence struggle, and yet, it has not undergone any structural changes. Though it is least suited to the needs of backward classes, yet, they are forced to run the rat-race with others as no options are available to them. As 'educational reform' was not within the terms of reference of this Commission, we are also forced to trend the beaten track and suggest only the palliative measure within the existing framework.

13.19 Various State Governments are giving a number of educational concessions to Other Backward Class students (Chapter IX, paras 9.30 – 9.33) like exemption of tution fees, free supply of books and clothes, mid-day meals, special hostel facilities, stipends, etc. These concessions are all right as far as they go. But they do not go far enough. What is required is, perhaps, not so much the provision of additional funds as the *framing of integrated schemes for creating the proper environment and incentives for serious and purposeful studies* (emphasis contributed).

13.20 It is well known that most backward class children are irregular and indifferent students and their drop-out rate is very high. There are two main reasons for this. First, these children are brought up in a climate of extreme social and cultural deprivation and, consequently, a proper motivation for schooling is generally lacking. Secondly, most of these children come from very poor homes and their parents are forced to press them into doing small chores from a very young age.

13.21 Upgrading the cultural environment is a very slow process. Transferring these children to an artificially upgraded environment is beyond the present resources of the country. In view of this it is recommended that this problem may be tackled on a limited and selective basis on two fronts.

13.22 First, an intensive and time bound programme for adult education should be launched in selected pockets with high concentration of OBC population. This is a basic *motivational approach,* as only properly motivated parents will take serious interest in educating their children. Secondly, *residential schools* should be set up in these areas for backward class students to provide a climate especially conducive to serious studies. All facilities in these schools including board and lodging, will have to be provided free of cost to attract students from poor and backward homes. *Separate Government Hostels* for OBC students with the above facilities will be another step in the right direction.

13.23 A beginning on both these fronts will have to be made on a *limited scale* and *selective basis*. But the scope of these activities should be expanded as fast as the resources permit. Adult education programme and residential schools started on a selective basis will operate as growing-points of conciousness for the entire community and their multiplier effect is bound to be substantial. Whereas several States have extended a number of ad hoc concessions to backward class students, few serious attempts have been made to integrate these facilities into a comprehensive scheme for a *qualitiative upgradation of educational environment available to OBC students.*

13.24 Aft all, education is the best catalyst of change and educating the backward classes is the surest way to improve their self image and raise their social status. As OBCs cannot afford the high wastage rates of our educational system, it is very important that their education is *highly biased in favour of vocational training.* After all reservation in services will absorb only a very small percentage of the educated backward classes and the rest should be suitably equipped with vocational skills to enable them to get a return on having invested several years in education.

13.25 It is also obvious that even if all the above facilities are given to OBC students, they will not be able to compete on an equal footing with others in securing admission to technical and professional institutions. In view of this it is recommended *that seats should be reserved for OBC students in all scientific, technical and professional institutions run by the Central as well as State Governments.* This reservation will fall under Article 15(4) of the Constitution and the quantum of reservation should be the same as in the Government services, i.e., 27 per cent. Those States which have already reserved more than 27 per cent seats for OBC students will remain unaffected by this recommendation.

13.26 While implementing the provision for reservation it should also be ensured that the candidates who are admitted against the rserved quota are enabled to derive full benefit of higher studies. It has been generally noticed that these OBC students coming from an impoverished cultural background, are not able to keep abreast with other students. It is, therefore, very essential that *special coaching facilities are arranged for all such students in our technical and professional institutions.* The concerned authorities should clearly appreciate that their job is not finished once candidates against reserved quota have been admitted to various instiutitons. In fact the real task starts only after that. Unless adequate follow-up action is taken to give *special coaching assistance* to these students, not only these young people will feel frustrated and humiliated but the country will also be landed with ill-equipped and sub-standard engineers, doctors and other professionals.

Financial assistance

13.27 Vocational communities following hereditary occupations have suffered heavily as a result of industrializations. Mechanical production and introduction of synthetic materials has robbed the village potter, oil crusher, black-smith, carpenter, etc. of their traditional means of livelihood and the *pauperization of these classes is a well known phenomenon in the country-side.*

13.28 It has, therefore, become very necessary that suitable *institutional finance* and *technical assistance* is made available to such members of village vocational communities who want to set up small scale industries on their own. Similar assistance should also be provided to those promising oBC candidates who have obtained special vocational training.

13.29 Of course, most State Governments have created various financial and technical agencies for the promotion of small and medium scale industries. But it is well known that only the more influential members of the community are able to derive benefits from these agencies. In view of this, it is very essential that *separate financial institutions for providing financial and technical assistance are establishe for the backward classes.* Some State Governments like Karnataka and Andhra Pradesh have already set up separate financial corporations etc. for OBCs.

13.30 Cooperative Societies of occupational groups will also help a lot. But due care should be taken that all the office-bearers and members of such societies belong to the *concerned hereditary occupational groups* and outsiders are not allowed to exploit them by infliltrating into such cooperatives.

13.31 The share of OBCs in the industrial and business life of the country is negligible and this partly explains their extremely low income levels. As a part of its overall strategy to uplift the backward classes, it is imperative that all State Governments are suitably advised and encouraged to *create a separate network of financial and technical institutions to foster business and industrial enterprise among OBCs.*

Structural changes

13.32 Reservations in Government employment and educational institutions, as also all possible financial assistance will remain mere palliatives unless the problem of backwardness is tackled at its root. Bulk of the small land-holders, tenants, agricultural labour, impoverished village artisans, unskilled workers, etc. belong to Scheduled Castes, Scheduled Tribes and Other Backward Classes. "Apart from social traditions, the *dominance by the top peasantry is exercised through recourse to informal bondage* which arises mainly through money-lending, leasing out of small bits of land and providing house-sites and dwelling space to poor peasants. As most of the functionaries of Government are drawn from the top peasantry, the *class and caste linkage between the functionaries of Government and the top peasantry remain firm.* This also tilts the socio-political balance in favour of the top peasantry and helps it in having its dominance over others."

13.33 The net outcome of the above situation is that notwithstanding their numerical preponderance, backward classes continue to remain in *mental and material bondage of the higher castes and rich peasantry.* Consequently, despite constituting nearly 3/4th of the country's population, Scheduled Castes, Scheduled Tribes and Other Backward Classes have been able to acquire a *very limited political clout,* even though adult franchise was introduced more than three decades back. Through their literal monopoly of means of production of higher castes are able to manipulate and coerce the backward classes into acting against their own interests. In view of this, *until the stranglehold of the existing production relations is broken through radical land reforms, the abject dependence of under privileged classes of the dominant higher castes will continue indefinitely.* In fact there is already a sizeable volume of legislation on the statute books to abolish Zamindari, place ceilings on land holding and distribute land to the landless. But in actual practice its *implementation has been halting, half-hearted and superficial.* The States like Karnataka, Kerala and West Bengal which have gone about the job more earnestly have not only succeeded in materially helping the Backward Classes, but also reaped rich political dividends into the bargain.

13.34 It is the Commission's firm conviction that a radical *transformation of the existing production relations is the most important single step that can be taken for the welfare and upliftment of all backward classes.* Even if this is not possible in the industrial sector for various reasons, in the agricultural sector a change of this nature is both feasible and overdue.

13.35 The Commission, therefore, strongly recommends that all the State Government should be directed to enact and implement progressive land legislation so as to effect basic structural changes in the existing production relations in the countryside.

13.36 At present surplus land is being allotted to SCs and STs. A part of the surplus land becoming available in future as a result of the operation of land ceiling laws etc. should also be allotted to be *OBC landless labour*.

Miscellaneous

13.37 (1) Certain sections of some occupational communities like Fishermen, Banjaras, Bansforas, Khatwas, etc. still suffer from the stigma of untouchablity in some parts of the country. They have been listed as OBCs by the Commission, but their inclusion in the lists of Scheduled castes/Scheduled Tribes may be considered by the Government.

(2) Backward Classes Development Corporations should be set up both at the Central and State levels and in implement various socio-educational and economic measures for their advancement.

(3) A separate Ministry/Department for OBCs at the centre and the States should be created to safeguard their interests.

(4) With a view to giving better representation to certain very backward sections of OBCs like the Gaddis in Himachal Pradesh, Neo-Buddhists in Maharasthra, Fishermen in the Coastal areas, Gujjars in J&K, it is recommended that areas of their concentration may be carved out into separate constituencies at the time of delimitation.

Central assistance

13.38 At present no central assistance is available to any State Government for implementing any welfare measures for Other Backward Classes. The 18 States and Union Territories which have undertaken such measures have to provide funds from their own resources. During the Commission's tours practically every State Governmnt pointed out that unless the Centre is prepared to liberally finance all special schemes for the upliftment of OBCs, it will be beyond the available resources of the states to undertake any worthwhile programme for the benefit of Other Backward Classes.

13.39 The Commission fully shares the views of the State Governments in this matter and strongly recommends that all development programmes specially designed for Other Backward Classes should be financed by the Central Government in the same manner and to the same extent as done in the case of Scheduled Castes and Scheduled Tribes.

13.40 Regarding the period of operation of the Commission's recommendations, the entire scheme should be reviewed after twenty years. We have advisedly suggested this span of one generation, as the *raising of social consciousness is a generational progress.* Any review at a shorter interval would be rather arbitrary and will not give a fair indication of the impact of our recommendations on the prevailing status and life-styles of OBCs.

D-5: The adequacy or otherwise of representation of the Backward classes in public services of Kerala: Important findings of the K.K. Narendran Commission

Composition of the Commission: Justice K.K. Narendran: Chairperson: K.V. Ravindran (former Chief Secretary, Government of Kerala), and T.M. Savankutty (former Chairperson of the Kerala Public Service Commission), Members. The three members represented three different backward communities.

Terms of Reference: The Commission was asked to study the adequacy or otherwise of representation of the backward class communities in four categories of public services (state government departments, the judiciary, public sector undertakings and universities and other autonomous institutions under the government) in the state of Kerala.

Appointment: February 2000: *Submission of Report:* November 2001

Present reservation percentage in vogue in Kerala: 50 per cent: *OBCs:* 40 per cent (Ezhavas: 14; Muslims; 12: Latin Catholics; 4; Nadirs: 2; Christian converts from SCs: 1; Dheevaras: 1; other OBCs: 3; *SCs and STs:* 10 per cent.

Political context of constitution of the Commission

The Narendran Commission was appointed by the Left Democratic Front (LDF) government as a multi-pronged strategy to satisfy such conflicting demands of political and community organizations following the introduction of the creamy layer norm in the state in 2000 (roughly eight years after the historic Indra Sawhney judgment that directed identification of the creamy layer among the OBCs first before designating them as the OBCs in 1992). While most of the states and Union Territories had either adopted the creamy layer criteria fixed by the Central government (following the recommendations of the Ram Nandan Prasad Committee Report) or, as in the cases of Uttar Pradesh and Bihar, had decided their own creamy layer criteria for implementing the reservations under Article 16(4), Kerala was caught between the conflicting demands of two politically powerful forces-one, led by the Nair Service Society (NSS), insisting that the existing system in Kerala had proved to be baneful to the interests of the forward casters, especially the poor among them, and hence needed to be changed; and the other claiming that it had not yet achieved the desired results for the improvement of the lot of the backward classes, and hence needed to be continued without change and certainly without implementing the creamy layer norm. Kerala is a state where political parties – including the Left parties – supported by different religious and caste groups have been an integral part of the ruling coalitions and where an objective assessment of the real nature of backwardness of Kerala society had remained beyond the courage of successive state governments.

This peculiarity was also the cause of the very bland nature of its terms of references. The Commission was merely asked to study and report whether the representation of the backward classes in public services was 'adequate' or not: although the strident nature of several organisations after submission of its report emphasized 'implement the recommendations of the report', in reality it was not at all asked to recommend 'remedial measures'. Similarly, the subsequent demand that the United Democratic Front (UDF) implement the special recruitment drive for the backward classes based on the Commission's report, supposedly promised in its election manifesto, was not exactly included in that document. What the UDF manifesto had in fact stated was that it would take steps to fill the backlog in reservation posts in the government services on the basis of the recommendations of an Assembly Committee.

Similarly, claims of organisations such as the NSS that the very constitution of the Narendran Commission was illegal and hence unacceptable and that they had challenged it and the validity of its recommendations before the Supreme Court too was deliberately off the mark, as the pending petition of the NSS before the Court is with regard to an earlier one – man Commission, headed by the same retired judge of the Kerala High Court, K.K.Narendran, and appointed by the LDF government to identify the creamy layer among the backward classes in the state and to recommend norms for its exclusion from reservation benefits. The one-man creamy layer Commission, using the norms approximating the Uttar Pradesh expert Committee on creamy layer (Umesh Chandra Committee: 1993) had earned the wrath of the forward castes since it recommended a higher annual income limit of Rs.3.5 lakhs as against the Rs. 1.5 lakhs fixed by the Joseph Commission appointed by the Kerala High Court at the behest of the Supreme Court when the ruling and opposition parties, except the CPM, unanimously decided to override the verdict of the court and passed a law declaring that there was no creamy layer among the backward classes in the state. In sharp contrast to the Joseph Commission, but much in tune with the Ram Nandan Prasad Committee of the Government of India, the Narendran Commission on creamy layer had also recommended that salary and income from agriculture should not be considered while deciding the ceiling limit of Rs. 3.5 lakhs, a ceiling that allowed a vast section of the backward classes to continue to enjoy the benefits of reservation. A final decision of the Supreme Court on the creamy layer question in Kerala is still awaited. The LDF government appointed the three-member Narendran Commission to deal with the conflicts that arose following the implementation of the new creamy layer norm.

Methodology Adopted by the Commission: The practical method adopted by the Commission to determine the adequacy of or otherwise of representation of the backward classes was to study how the representation of each group compared with its reservation quota. The Commission considered data for 11 years (but only up to August 2000, and not since the implementation of the creamy layer norms) of nearly five lakh government employees belonging to the 78 backward castes, Scheduled Castes and Scheduled Tribes and the forward castes in the state. Anticipating a possible controversy on its findings, the Commission forestalled any criticism by stating that 'adequacy' in the context of representation of the backward classes in public services was essentially a 'matter of opinion' and that their main task was only to collect appropriate data and make them available so that 'different individuals and organisations may, according to their varied perceptions, come to different conclusions from the same data'. It also stated that 'observations of the Commission on adequacy of representation too should not be taken as the only authentic conclusion that can be arrived at from the data'.

Important/Findings of the Commission: The following are important findings of the Report of the Commission:

- Almost all BC communities in Kerala improved or were improving their presence in the public services through the system of reservation, and some have even managed to get jobs in excess of their reservation quota. The Commission, however, felt that they still were not in a position to reach 'adequacy of representation' without the continuance of reservation.
- The representation of the forward castes in public services is of much less proportion, ranging between 36 per cent and 51 per cent of total employees in the four categories of public services. The backward classes obtained a bigger share of the posts, their representation ranging from 41 per cent to 48 per cent. As such, in all the four categories, the backward classes as a group secured employment in excess of their combined reservation quota. Taken individually, there are instances where backward class communities hold posts substantially fewer in number than their individual reservation quota, or where they have obtained posts in excess of the reservation quota marginally, or where they have got substantially in excess of their quota (though this is not the general pattern).
- There is clear inadequacy of backward communities in public services, though the extent of inadequacy varies from one community to another. If some backward communities have been able to get jobs in excess of their reservation quota, 'it only meant that the policy of reservation is helping them to move towards adequacy of representation in public services'.

- The Ezhavas, the most socially and educationally backward community among the OBCs, have universally secured better representation by securing posts in the merit quota over and above the reservation quota. In comparison, the Muslims, another backward class community, have not fared well. The Commission argues that this is due to the educational backwardness of the Muslims and advises the Muslim as well as other backward communities to emulate the Ezhavas.
- An approach of reservation that ensures a minimum level of representation for the backward classes – a level certainly not too low compared to their population – in public services and at the same time encouraging them to increase their share in open competition is giving encouraging results. However, there are instances where the representation of the most backward among the backward classes continues to be unsatisfactory. This calls for intelligent and imaginative corrective action on the part of the government. In the interest of fairness to all, the corrective action should not trample on the legitimate and reasonable prospects for promotion and career advancement of those outside the reservation umbrella and those who, eligible for reservation, are recruited earlier on merit, or in the reservation quota. This corrective action should be taken in such a way as to avoid any unintended benefit accruing to certain communities coming under the backward classes category.
- On the backlog in the representation of the major backward class communities as on August 1, 2000 when against their respective reservation quota, the deficiency in the number of posts actually held (in reservation and open merit competition together) compared to their entitlement in reservation quota for the various communities was as follows: Muslims: 7,383 (reservation quota: 12 per cent); Latin Catholics: 4,370 (9.4 per cent); Nadirs: 2,614(2 per cent); SCs converted to Christianity: 2,290 (1 per cent); Dheevara: 256(1 per cent); other OBC communities: 460 (3 per cent); Vishwakarmas: 147 (3 per cent). Significantly enough, the backlog for the Ezhavas, eligible for the highest reservation quota of 14 per cent, was only five posts.
- Without the benefit of reservation, no community among the backward classes can have adequate representation in public services and that even with reservation most communities are not getting adequate representation in all the categories of posts.
- Reservation is only a means to an end, not an end in itself. It cannot be a permanent feature.

Political turmoil since the submission of the report in November 2001

It is the IUML, which has been sharing power with the Congress for the last four years, which is at the forefront of the raging agitation of the backward class organisations demanding special recruitment to fill the backlog of posts due to them. The UDF government, in the throes of a financial crisis, is trying to cut costs and that also involves cutting jobs. The alienation of the IUML was one of major considerations in the ouster of the former Congress Chief Minister. Not successful in securing its demand, the IUML paid its political price by losing the Muslim dominated stronghold of Manjeri in the Lok Sabha elections in 2004. The issue is likely to be a major factor in the ensuing Panchayati Raj elections. The NSS too is very aggressively campaigning against continued reservation policy and with the expulsion of Murlidharan, son of former Chief Minister and Congress strongman Karunakaran, from the Congress party, there is a live possibility of emergence of a third political front in Kerala in which the Nairs would play a significant role.

B. GOs on reservations for the OBCs

D-6: Communal GOs

First communal G.O., 1921

(M.R.O. Public G.O.613, dated 16th September 1921)

In order to increase the proportion of posts in Government offices held by non-Brahmins, the Government direct that the principle prescribed for the Revenue Department in Board's Standing Order No. 128(2), on the subject of the distribution of appointments among various castes and communities, should be extended to appointments of all grades in the several departments of Government. All heads of departments and other officers empowered to make appointments are requested to adhere strictly to this principle in filling up vacancies in future.

2. Heads of departments, Collectors and District Judges are requested to submit to Government half-yearly returns showing, in respect to their own offices and the subordinate offices under their control, the number of men newly entertained in the permanent service during the half-year and classifying them under the following heads:

1. Brahmins
2. Non-Brahmin Hindus
3. Indian Christians
4. Mohammadans
5. Europeans and Anglo Indians
6. Others

The returns should be submitted not later than the 15th January and 15th of July of each year. The first return should be for the half-year ending 31st December 1921.

(by order of the Governor in Council)

N.E. Marjobibanks
Acting Chief Secretary

Second gommunal G.O., 1922

(M.R.O. Public G.O. 658, dated 15th August 1922)

In a resolution passed at their meeting held in August, 1921, the Legislative Council made a recommendation to the Government to the effect that, with a view to increasing the proportion of posts in Government offices held by non-Brahmin communities, the principles prescribed for the Revenue Department in Board's Standing Order No.128(2) be at once extended to all departments of the Government and be made applicable, not only to the principal appointments, but to posts of all grades, and that the Government should issue orders accordingly and insist on their being enforced, and that to this end, half-yearly returns showing the progress made should be made available to the members of the Legislative Council.

2. In giving effect to this resolution in G.O.613, Public, dated the 16th September 1921, the Government called for a return showing the number of men newly entertained in the permanent service of Government during each half-year's returns compiled under this order have now been received and a copy is attached to the present proceedings (Appendix 1). It will be seen that the general percentage of new appointments from the several communities in the half-year ending 31st Dece. 1921 is; Brahns 22 per cent; non-Brahmin Hindus 48; Indian Christians 10; Mohammadans 15; Europeans and Anglo-Indians 2; others 3.

3. In circulating these returns, the Government are not unaware that some dissatisfaction has been expressed with the fact that they are confined to persons newly entertained, and a resolution was tabled for the substitution for them of returns of all appointments whether permanent, temporary, or acting and whether the officers appointed were appointed for the first time or promoted from subordinate grades. The Government have examined the question of extending the scope of the returns in the sense suggested and are disposed to agree that some amplification is necessary if the returns are to show the progress made in the carrying out of the policy in the matter of the representation of various communities in the public service which is expressed in the Board's Standing Order, namely, that endeavours should always be made to do justice to the several castes. The Government recognize that, if the principal appointments are to be divided among the several communities, the lower appointments from which recruitment is made to them must be likewise divided, and are quite prepared to agree that, in order to give effect to this policy, other things being equal, the principle specified in the Board's Standing Order should be given effect to both at the time of the initial recruitment and at every point at which men are promoted

wholly by election or by seniority. At the same time they have been unable to devise any form of return which would illustrate satisfactorily the progressive enforcement of such a policy as regards all the stages at which promotions, whether permanent, acting or temporary, are made, and his Excellency the Governor in Council, with the concurrence of his Ministers, has come to the conclusion, after careful consideration of that question, that the only way in which to secure satisfactory information as to the representation of the various communities in the different branches of the public service is, to have a return made out once a year showing the extent to which each of the six main subdivisions is represented in each department. A comparison of any year's return with that for the previous year will then show the extent of the progress made in any particular department. The return will be confined to non-gazetted officer and will be divided into two sections one for officers drawing Rs.100 and over and the other for officers drawing from Rs. 35 to Rs.100. All heads of departments will be requested to secure from the officers subordinated to them a view of all the officers in the non-gazetted service who held permanent appointments of Rs. 35 and upwards on Ist April 1922. These returns should be submitted in time for publication by Ist Oct. A fresh return for the year ending 31st March 1923 should be submitted not later than August 1923.

4. In the case of officers in the gazetted service, the Government propose to accept the suggestion made in another resolution which was moved in the course of the last session to the effect that a column indicating the community to which each officer belongs should be added to the quarterly Civil List. For the purpose of this entry, all heads of departments will be requested to call upon the officers whose names appear in the Civil List to declare to which of the six main divisions they belong and to send the return to the Superintendent. Government Press. The Superintendent, Government Press, will be requested to suggest a set of simple symbols which can be inserted after the names of officers so as to indicate to which ot the six communities they belong.

5. Further, in pursuance of the desire, which has been repeatedly, expressed in the Legislative Council, and with which the Government has every sympathy, that the public officers in each language should be posted to those language areas, all heads of officers in language areas should be manned, as far as possible, by persons belonging to those language areas, all heads of officers in Telugu districts and in Oriya tracts will be instructed to keep a record of all persons not belonging by origin to those districts or tracts respectively, and to take steps so far as possible to reduce the proportion whenever

opportunity offers. For the purpose of this order, the Telugu districts and the Oriya tracts will be defined in Appendix II.

6. The Government hope that the instructions given will suffice to meet the desires of members of the Legislative Council and others who have been interested themselves in this matter and that the policy of Government being thus clearly declared, the demand for further statistics in regard to the representation of communities, castes or sub-castes in the public services generally or in particular offices will cease.

(by order of the Governor in Council)

R.A. Graham
Chief Secretary

Third communal G.O. 128

(G.O.No.1129 Public, dated 15th December 1928)

The Government direct that future initial recruitment to the service shall be made in the following proportion and order:

(a) If qualified and suitable candidates are available in each community, Officers shall be appointed, so that the proportion of appointments made from each community may, out of every 12 posts be as follows:

Non-Brahmins (Hindu)	5
Brahmins	2
Muhammadans	2
Anglo-Indians and Christians (including Europeans)	2
Others (including Depressed Class)	1

(b) Such appointment shall be made in the following order:

1. Non-Brahmin (Hindu)
2. Muhammadan
3. Non-Brahmin (Hindu)
4. Anglo-Indian or Christian
5. Brahmin
6. Non-Brahmin (Hindu)
7. Others
8. Non-Brahmin (Hindu)
9. Muhammadan
10. Non-Brahmin (Hindu)
11. Anglo-Indian or Christian
12. Brahmin

(c) If a qualified and suitable candidate of a particular community is not forthcoming in the turn allotted to that community, the appointment shall be made of a candidate belonging to the next community specified in clause (b) above if he is otherwise qualified and suitable, for appointment, and qualified and suitable candidate belonging to the former community will have a preferential claim to appointment on the next occasion when it is made.

D-7: GO on Backward Classes by the GOI

Social Welfare Department. G.O.M. No.73, dated 1.2.1980

In the G.O. M.No.695, Social Welfare Department, dated 7.6.1971 the Government inter alia fixed reservation for Backward Classes at 31 per cent. The need for enhancing this percentage has been carefully considered by the Government with a view to providing the Backward Classes adequate opportunities for employment and admissions into educational institutions commensurate with their population. The Government now direct that with effect from 24.1.1980, reservation of seats be made at 50 per cent for Backward Classes and at 18 per cent for Scheduled Castes and Scheduled Tribes in respect of all courses in all kinds of educational institutions under all kinds of managements (like Government, local body and Aided Managments) where reservation is provided by the State Government for the above classes. The reservation of seats as per the above orders shall be a condition for the payment of any grant-in-aid from the funds of this Government to any private management or Local Body or to the Universities (in respect of courses conducted and institutions run directly by them).

2. The claims of members of the Backward Classes, Scheduled Castes and Scheduled Tribes should also be considered for the remaining 32 per cent of seats which are filled on the basis of merit. Where a candidate belonging to Backward Classes or Scheduled Castes or Scheduled Tribes is selected on the basis of merit against any of the seats reserved for Backward Classes, Scheduled Castes and Scheduled Tribes, as the case may be, reserved quota should not in any way be affected.

3. Necessary amendments to Rule 22 of the General Rules will be issued separately by the Government in Personel and Administrative Reforms Department.

4. The Expression "Backward Classes" wherever it occurs in this order shall be deemed to include Most Backward Classes and Denotified Communities also.

5. This order takes effect from 24.1.1980 in supersession of the orders issued in G.M. Ms No.695, Social Welfare dt.7.6.1971 and all subsequent orders issued on the subject.

A.S. Ahluwalia

Commissioner and Secretary to Government

D-8: Statement of the then Prime Minister and Office Memorandum dated August 13, 1990

No action was, however, taken on the basis of the Mandal Commission Report until the issuance of the Office Memorandum on August 13, 1990. On that day, the then Prime Minister, Shri V.P. Singh made a statement in the Parliament in which he stated inter alia as follows:

"After all, if you take the strength of the whole of the government employees as a propotion of the population, it will be 1 per cent or 1½. I do not know exactly, it may be less than 1 per cent. We are under no illusion that this 1 per cent of the population, or a fraction of it will resolve the economic problems of the whole section of 52 per cent. No. We consciously want to give them a position in the decision-making of the country, a share in the power structure. We talk about merit. What is the merit of the system itself. That the section which has 52 per cent of the population gets 12.55 per cent in government employment. What is the merit of the system. That in Class I employees of the government it gets only 4.69 per cent, for 52 per cent of the population in decision-making at the top echelons it is not even one-tenth of the population of the country; in the power structure it is hardly 4.69 per cent. I want to challenge first the merit of the system itself before we come and question on the merit, whether on merit to reject this individual or that. And we want to change the structure basically, consciously, with open eyes. And I know when changing the structures comes, there will be resistance........

What I want to convey is that treating unequals as equals is the greatest injustice.

And, correction of this injustice is very important and that is what I want to convey. Here, the National Front Government's commitment for not only change of government, but also change of the social order, is something of great significance to all of us; it is a matter of great significance. Merely making programes of economic benefit to various sections of the society will not do......

There is a very big force in the argument to involve the poorest in the power structure. For a lot of time we have acted on behalf of the poor. We represent the poor......

Let us forget that the poor are begging for some crumbs. They have suffered it for thousands of years. Now they are fighting for their honour as a human being......

A point was made by Mahajanji that if there are different lists in different States how will the Union list harmonise? It is so today in the case of the Scheduled Castes and the Scheduled tribes. That has not caused a problem. On the same pattern, this will be there and there will be no problem."

The Office Memorandum dated August 13, 1990 reads as follows:

Office Memorandum dated August 13, 1990

Subject: *Recommendations of the Second Backward Classes Commission(Mandal Report) – Reservation for socially and educationally Backward Classes in services under the Government of India*

In a multiple undulating society like ours, early achievement of the objective of social justice as enshrined in the Constitution is a must. The Second Backward Classes Commission called the Mandal Commission was established by the then Government with this purpose in view, which submitted its report to the Government of India on December 31, 1980.

2. Government have carefully considered the report and the recommendations of the Commission in the present context regarding the benefits to be extended to the socially and educationally backward classes as opined by the Commission and are of the clear view that at the outset certain weightage has to be provided to such classes in the services of the Union and their public undertakings. Accordingly orders are issued as follows:

   (i) 27 per cent of the vacancies in civil posts and services under the Government of India shall be reserved for SEBC.

   (ii) The aforesaid reservation shall apply to vacancies to be filled by direct recruitment. Detailed instructions relating to the procedures to be followed for enforcing reservation will be issued separately.

   (iii) Candidates belonging to SEBC recruited on the basis of merit in an open competition on the same standards prescribed for the general candidates shall not be adjusted against the reservation quota of 27 per cent.

   (iv) The SEBC would comprise in the first phase the castes and communities which are common to both the lists in the report of the Mandal Commission and the State Governments' lists. A list of such castes/communities is being issued separately.

   (v) The aforesaid reservation shall take effect from 7-8-1990. However, this will not apply to vacancies where the recruitment process has already been initiated prior to the issue of these orders.

3. Similar instructions in respect of public sector undertakings and financial institutions including public sector banks will be issued by the Department of Public Enterprises and Ministry of Finance respectively.

Sd/-

(Smt. Krishna Singh)

Joint Secretary to the Govt. of India.

D-9: The Office Memorandum dated September 25, 1991 (issued by the P.V. Narsimha Rao Government)

After the change of the government at the Centre following the general election held in the first-half of 1991, another Office Memorandum was issued on September 25, 1991 modifying the earlier Memorandum dated August 13, 1990. The later memorandum reads as follows:

Office Memorandum

Subject: *Recommendations of the Second Backward Classes Commission (Mandal Report)–Reservation for socially and educationally Backward Classes in services under the Government of India.*

The undersigned is directed to invite the attention to O.M. of even number dated the 13th August 1990, on the above mentioned subject and to say that in order to enable the poorer sections of the SEBCs to receive the benefits of reservation on a preferential basis and to provide reservation for other economically backward sections of the people not covered by any of the existing schemes of reservation, Government have decided to amend the said memorandum with immediate effect as follows:

(i) Within the 27 per cent of the vacancies in civil posts and services under the Government of India reserved for SEBCs, preference shall be given to candidates belonging to the poorer sections of SEBCs. In case sufficient number of such candidates are not available, unfilled vacancies shall be filled by the other SEBC candidates.

(ii) 10 per cent of the vacancies in civil posts and services under the Government of India shall be reserved for other economically backward sections of the people who are not covered by any of the existing schemes of reservations.

(iii) The criteria for determining the poorer sections of the SEBCs or the other economically backward sections of the people who are not covered by any of the existing schemes of reservations are being issued separately.

The O.M. of even number dated the 13th August 1990, shall be deemed to have been amended to the extent specified above.

Sd/-

(A.K. Harit)

Ey. Secretary to the Government of India"

C. Authoritative judicial verdict on reservations

D-10: Indra Sawhney: an Epoch-making judgment in its essence

Neeta Verma

That Indra Sawhney was not an ordinary case was known and realized: what was clearly glossed over by even not so uninformed was the fact that it was a bunch of a large number of writ petitions, transferred cases and interventions. The enormity of the specifics raised should not be lost sight of. It consisted of 38 writ petitions of 1991 and one of 1992; it also included 10 transferred cases of 1990 and one of 1992. Seventeen states/UTs were respondents to different writ petitions and there were six independent respondents as well. A large number of legal brains represented the various viewpoints and the case itself took many twists and turns, and, of course, an inordinately long time to get decided.

Facts of the case

Very briefly summarized, the facts of the case are set out in the next few paras.

Whereas the Congress government had been stonewalling, some other political parties had been agitating for the acceptance and implementation of recommendations of the Mandal Commission. Only the Janata Dal had put it as the main poll campaign issue in the Lok Sabha elections of 1989. V.P. Singh had put himself as the principal proponent of the Mandal Commission in the Janata Dal. When, however, his government came to assume power, true to his diabolical character he was not inclined to implement the recommendations of the Mandal Commission straightway. It was only when he had to ease out Choudhary Devi Lal from his government and feared trouble from all other quarters as well as his own Janata Dal that he ferreted out the moth-eaten Mandal Commission recommendations and issued an OM without operational logistics and adequate preparations.

The OM issued on 13 August 1990 purported to extend 27 per cent reservations to the SEBCs in government services with effect from August 7,

1990. Reservation was to be given in direct recruitment. Such SEBCs as obtained entry in the open competition on merit were not to be counted in the 27 per cent reservations earmarked for them. The list of the SEBCs to be used was to be made of communities common in the state-wise lists of the Mandal Commission and the existing lists of the state governments. The reservation envisaged included reservation also in the public sector undertakings and financial institutions.

Widespread instigated protests, 'self-immolations' and extensive damage to the public property in Delhi, and some areas in north India, followed the issuance of the OM. Public interest writ petitions were filed before the Supreme Court. A three-judges bench consisting of Rangnath Misra, acting CJ and K.N.Singh and M.H.Kania, JJ heard the same. By its order of September 21, 1990, it refused to intervene on the ground that the matter was a political one. The Court, considering the gathering storm and turmoil, issued an appeal to the nation that the matter was being adjudicated upon and everybody's rights would be protected. A five-member Constitution bench of the Supreme Court stayed the operation of the OM on October 1, 1990 when the societal turbulence did not subside. To carve a constituency for itself, the BJP detached itself from the V.P.Singh government and embarked on *Mandir Rath* and the V.P. Singh government collapsed in its aftermath.

The new government which assumed office following the general elections in the first half of 1991 was asked by a five-member Constitution Bench to make its stand clear on the issue. The government indicated its intention to implement the OM of August 13, 1990 with certain modifications. It issued another OM on September 25, 1991 modifying the earlier OM of August 13, 1990 by introducing the economic criterion in grant of reservations by giving preference to the poorer sections of the SEBCs in the 27 per cent quota, and (ii) reserving another 10 per cent of the vacancies for 'Other Economically Backward Sections' not covered by any of the existing schemes of reservation, which was explained to extend to the poorest among the higher castes and other religions also. It was indicated that the economic criteria was to be specified separately.

The constitutional validity of the second OM was also challenged and since by now it had emerged in the arguments before the apex court that the major issues concerning the reservation law required an authoritative delineation, a nine-member Special Constitution bench was constituted to hear the entire gamut of framed issues. The government was given time through more than one adjournment to indicate economic criteria but displaying Narsimha Rao's principal characteristic of sleeping over important issues and not deciding them, never submitted the same before the Court. The Court declined to vacate the stay of the OM.

The various contending parties to the case themselves raised several issues. The Court itself also added some of its own. Eventually, 14 major questions were finalized for adjudication. The matters were heard by the nine-judges Bench and by a 6:3 ratio the constitutionality, validity and enforceability of the impugned OM issued on August 13, 1990, subject to the specific conditionalties and requirements indicated in the judgments(s), was upheld.

Six separate judgments, totaling 866 paragraphs and about 500 printed pages in foolscape size, were handed down. The leading judgment was written by B.P. Jeevan Reddy, J for M.H. Kania, C.J. and M.N. Venkatachaliah, A.M. Ahmadi, JJ and himself), with R.S.Pandian and P.B. Sawant, JJ concurring by their separate judgments. The dissenting minority was comprised of Dr. T.K. Thommen, Kuldip Singh, and R.M. Sahai, JJ, each one delivering his separate judgment. The minority also pronounced a combined order on their behalf.

The judges ranged on the side of majority and minority took independent positions on different issues. At some places, the judges of minority side individually agreed with the leading judgment while on certain others the judges on the majority side individually disagreed with the leading judgement. All the judgments also did not necessarily answer all the posed questions.

Given the foregoing backdrop, the Indra Sawhney judgment has been analyzed question-wise. As far as possible, an earnest attempt has been made to highlight the distinctive character of the opinions offered. The directions given by the minority common judgment are not detailed since they are not enforceable.

The judgment in its essence

Question 1(a): Whether the 'provision' in Article 16(4) must necessarily be made by the Parliament/Legislature?

Reddy, J: Apart from Parliament/Legislature, the executive can also make such a provision. Local bodies, statutory corporations and other instrumentalities of the state falling under Article 12 are themselves competent to make such a provision, if so advised (part III, paras 735-737).

Pandian, J (paras 170-172, 243) and Singh, J (para 392) concurred with the majority view of the Court whereas Dr. Thommen, J did not offer any specific views on the question. Sawant, J also concurred with the majority adding that an executive order was no less law under Articles (13(3) and 309 (paras 526, 552).

Sahai, J held that reservation by an executive order was not invalid but the present one having been made for the first time, it should have been laid before the Parliament (para 636).

Question 1(b): Whether an executive order making a 'provision' is enforceable forthwith?

Reddy, J: Yes (para 738-740). The government issued orders where the rules were silent (para 739).

Sawant, J concurred with the majority (para 527) whereas Pandian, J did not offer any specific opinion on the question. Sahai, J having offered the opinion under question 1(a) making it conditional to be laid before the Parliament before being enforced.

Singh, J held that executive instructions under Articles 16(4), 73 or 162 providing reservations but contrary to the statutory rules under Article 309 or other statutory rules should not be operative to the extent contrary to the statutory provisions (para 392).

Question 2(a): Whether clause (4) of Article 16 was an exception to clause (1)?

Reddy, J: No. It was an instance and illustration of classification inherent in clause (1) (paras 741-742). Reservation can also be given under Article 16(1) (para 741). Article 16(4) must be read along with and in harmony with Article 16(1) (para 741). Article 16(1) conferred benefits to the individual citizens whereas Article 16(4) did so for the socially disadvantaged classes (para 814).

Pandian, J and Sawant, J concurred with the majority but they offered their additional views. Pandian, J held that Article 16(4) was neither an exception nor a provision to Article 16(1) (paras 167-168, 243). He also held that Article 16(4) over-ridded Article 16(1) (para 243(1), 92)). Similarly, Sawant, J held that Article 16(4) merely explicitly said what was implied in Article 16(1) (paras 428-429, 522). Article 16(4) specified a special class for reservations (para 430).

On the other hand, Singh, Sahai and Dr. Thommen, J J held the dissenting viewpoint. Among them, Singh, J held that Article 16(4) was another facet of Article 16(1). Article 16(4) took away special classification from the purview of Article 16(1) (para 382). Sahai, J held that Articles 16(1) and 16(4) operated in the same field. Article 16(1) applied to 'all' citizens whereas Article 16(4) applied to 'any' class of backward citizens. Article 16(1) was substantive equality and Article 16(4) was protective euqlity. Article 16(1) was fundamental right of citizens whereas Article 16(4) was an obligation of the state. Article 16(1) was enforceable in a court of law, whereas Article 16(4) was an enabling provision (para 563, 566). Continuing in the same vein, Dr. Thommen, J held that Article 16(4) was in the nature of an exception to the general rule of equality. The Supreme Court had generally treated it as an exception to Article 16(1) (paras 284, 288).

Question 2(b): Whether Article 16(4) was exhaustive of concept of reservations in favour of the backward classes?

Reddy, J: Yes. It included all supplemental and ancillary provisions as also lesser special provisions (paras 743, 859, 860(1)).

All other judges of the Special Constitution Bench concurred with the viewpoint of the leading judgment and yet, they offered varying shades of reasoning. Thus, Pandian, J held that Article 16(4) was indeed exhaustive of reservations for the BCs but, at the same time, held that no reservation can be made under Article 16(4) for classes other than the BCs [paras 168. 243(1), (2)]. Sawant, J held that Article 16(4) was exahaustive of all reservations for the BCs but not of reservations under Article 16(1) (paras 169, 430). While answering the question in affirmative, Singh, J held that no reservation of any kind was permissible under Article 16(1) (paras 382-383). Sahai, J also endorsed the opinion of Singh, J (paras 566, 6350. Dr. Thommen, J too affirmed the view that reservation under Article 16 was exhaustively for the BCs who were not adequately represented in the services under the state [para 323 (3)].

Question 2(c): Whether Article 16(4) was exhaustive of the very concept of reservations?

Reddy, J: No. Reservation can also be provided under clause (1) of Article 16. It was not confined to extending preference, concessions, or exemptions alone. Reservations under Article 16(1) had to be adjusted and implemented as not to exceed the level of representation prescribed for 'backward classes of citizens' (paras 744-745). He, however, added a caveat that reservations under Article 16(1) should be provided under very exceptional situations, necessary to redress a specific situation [paras 859-860(1), 733]. Sawant, J agreed with the leading judgment (paras 431–2, 552). Pandian, J too agreed but in an altogether different refrain. According to him, Article 16(4) was not exception to Artlce 16(1) and Article 16(2) and it overrode Articles 16(1) and (2). Reservations under article 16(1) can be made for classes not covered under Article 16(4) [paras 168, 243(2)].

The dissenting trio of Singh, Sahai and Dr. Thommen, JJ, however, felt otherwise. Among them, Singh, J held that Article 16(1) permitted protective discrimination short of reservation (para 382). Sahai, J held that Article 16(4) was exhaustive of the very concept of reservations. Accordingly, he held that no reservation could be provided under Article 16(1) (paras 610, 612, 617). Perferential treatment may be given in very limited cases (paras 617, 619) Dr. Thommen, J held that preference without reservation can be provided to the chosen class of citizens (para 293).

Question 3(a): Meaning of 'backward class of citizens' in Article 16(4).

Reddy, J: A caste can be and quite often was a socially homogenous class in india. If it was a class backward socially, it would be backward class for the purposes of Article 16(4). Among non-Hindus, there were several occupational groups, sects and denominations that, for historical reasons, were socially backward. They too represented backward social collectivities for purposes of Article 1694) [part IV, paras 746, 779, 859(3)].

The other two members of the Special Constitution bench concurring with the leading judgment, while generally agreeing, elaborated their views. Thus, Pandian, J held that 'backward' had a very wide meaning covering different types of backwardness. The batteries of tests recognized by the courts in determining the SEBCs were caste, lack of education and also standard of education (paras 44-45). The SEBCs were a group of persons having common traits or attributes coupled with retarded social, material (economic) and intellectual (educational) development (para 58). Sawant, J held that the SEBCs referred to in the OMs were BCs under Article 16(4) and this had been contested (para 433). Significantly, he held that the backward class of citizens under article 16(4) were socially backward class of citizens whose educational and economic backwardness was on account of their social backwardness (para 552). According to him, the term 'BCCs" was wider and included SEBC, SCs and STs(para 441). Backward class of citizens referred to those classes which could not advance socially and educationally because of taboos and handicaps created by the society in the past or on account of geographical or other factors (para 446).

The dissenting members of the bench held a diametrically opposite view. Singh, J held that caste and class were different. Class under Article 16(4) cannot, therefore, be read as caste (para 350). Sahai, J held that differentiation had to be made between 'backward classes' and 'citizens' (para 567-5680. According to him citizens included people irrespective of race, religion or caste. All backward and not adequately represented citizens in the services were BCs under Article 16(4) (para 568). 'Backward' had to be understood in relation to opportunity of employment (para 570). It referred to class backwardness (para 571). Picking among the BCs was to be discretionary. The state was not bound to grant reservations to all BCs (paras 579-580). BC in Article 16(4) was not backward class. They were not confined to erstwhile *Shudras* or depressed classes or intermediate backward classes among the Hindus only. The width of the expression included in its fold any community (para 594).

Dr. Thommen, J held that the SEBCs or BCs were only those who were socially and educationally backward due to identified prior discrimination and its continuing effects as to be comparable to the SCs/STs [para 323(4)]. Burden was on the state to show past discrimination [para 323(4)]. These BCs were constitutionally intended beneficiaries of reservation not because of their castes or occupations but because of their backwardness and disabilities stemming from identified past or continuing inequalities and discrimination [para 323(4)]. Converted to Sikh, Buddhist, or any other religions, SCs continued to receive benefits of reservation [para 323(5)].

Question 3(b): Identification of 'backward class of citizens'

Reddy, J: The SCs and the STs were admittedly BCs under Article 16(4) (paras 780-781). BCs under Article 16(4) did comprise some castes (para

782). These were, however, not confined to caste among the Hindus (para 782). The Constitution and the law did not prescribe the procedure or method of identification of backward classes. The Court left the question of identification to a specified authority (National/State Commission of Backward Classes) to decide conventiently. All that the Court prescribed was some kind of overriding guideline: *that the survey for identification purposes must cover the entire population (para 782). The survey itself can begin with caste but one cannot wind up the process of identification with castes (para 782). Identification can certainly be done with reference to castes among Hindus and along with other occupational groups, classes and sections of people among other religious denominations* (paras 782, 783). One can start with occupational groups or with castes or with some other groups, apply the evolved criteria on them and find out whether they satisfy the criteria. Similar procedure had to be followed with other groups. *The exercise of identification must cover all available groups, sections and classes in society (paras 780-785* embhasis contributed*)*. Lingering effects test was not valid. What was important was whether at present they were backward and inadequately represented (para 785). Reservation under Article 16(4) was being made in favour of the caste but a backward class. Once a caste satisfied the criteria of backwardness, it became a BC for Article 16(4)(para 784).

The two concurring judgment did make significant departure on methodology of identification. Significantly, Sawant, J held that *equality measures would have to use the same tools by which inequality was introduced and perpetuated (para 415). Pandian, J similarly held that caste was a dominating/primary criterion in determining backwardness of a class of citizens in Hindu society but it must satisfy the primary tests of social and educational backwardness* (para 82 emphasis contributed). He also held that caste was also important among other religions and, therefore, it cannot be divested from other established or agreed criteria in ascertaining and identifying the BCs (paras 83-84). However, he too qualified its use not at the end point of the identification process (para 108). Sawant, J elaborated another dimension of caste. *Caste had all attributes of class and can form a separate class* (paras 452-453 emphasis contributed). When members of an entire caste were backward and on that account were treated as a backward class, the expressions 'backward castes' and 'backward class' became synonymous (para 462). He emphasized the fact that emphasis in Article 16(4) was on class of citizens and not on citizens (para 435). According to him, the term 'backward class of citizens' in Article 16(4) has been used to accommodate non-Hindus as well (paras 474, 477, 477-478). Pandian, J deprecated the tendency to criticize the Mandal Commission Report and called it uncharitable (paras 130-131). Critics, he felt, had no legitimate ground to ask the Supreme Court to throw the Mandal Commission Report out (paras 132-139). He held that the recommendations of the Mandal Commission were supportive of affirmative action (para 140).

Among the dissenting judgments, Singh, J held that class in Article 16(4) cannot be read as caste (para 351). He also held that reservation in Article 16(4) was only for the class and not individuals (para 376). Similarly, Sahai, J held that class had a wider meaning than caste (paras 572, 576, 580). The term 'backward class of citizens' did not warrant reading of the expression as 'backward castes' (para 574, 579, 594). Identification of BCs cannot be based on caste and economic consideration (para 603). Ideal and wise method of identification, according to him, among the Hindus, would be to mark out various occupations, find out their social acceptability and educational standard, and weigh them in the balance of economic conditions. The result would be backward class of citizens (para 605). Sahai, J significantly enough, wanted identification of the BCCs at the national level also and, therefore, felt the need of evolving some principles of universal application as he was of the opinion that giving them benefit of Article 16(4) solely on the basis of state lists may not be valid (paras 601, 635). Dr. Thommen, J held that religion, race, caste, sex, descent, place of birth, residence or any of them was not the sole or dominant or indispensable criterion to identify backwardness. Each of them was, in conjunction with, factors such as poverty, illiteracy, demeaning occupation, malnutrition, physical and intellectual deformity and like disadvantages were relevant criteria [para 323(2)]. Identification of backwardness must be with reference to their social and educational backwardness (paras 270, 272).

Question 3(c): Whether backwardness in Article 16(4) should be both social and educational?

Reddy, J: BCs contemplated in Article 16(4) were not the same as the SEBCs of Article 15(4): they were much wider (para 787). However, he clarified that the SEBCs referred to by the Government of India OMs were undoubtedly BCs within the menaing of Article 16(4) (para 789). Similarly, he clarified that the SEBCs referred to in Article 340 were for only categories for which Article 16(4) was enacted (para 787). The accent in Article 16(4) was on social backwardness. Social, educational and economic backwardness were closely interwined in the Indian context [paras 788, 859(b), (c)]. He found no objection to validity and relevancy of the criteria adopted by the Mandal Commission (para 788). He also held that it was not correct to say that backwardness under Article 16(4) should be both social and educational (para 788).

The two concurring judgments by Pandian, J and Sawant, J also reaffirmed the primacy of social backwardness in the identification of the backward class of citizens. Thus, Pandian, J held that the primary consideration in identifying BCs under Article 16(4) was social backwardness. The degree of importance attached to social backwardness was much more than to educational backwardness and economic backwardness (paras 116-117). Similarly, Sawnat, J held that the BCs under Article 16(4) were socially backward whose educational and economic backwardness was on account of social backwardness. A class that was not socially and educationally backward though economically or even educationally backward was not a backward class for the purposes of Article 16(4) (para 492).

The dissenting judgments took a totally different position on this point. Singh, J, for example, held that what was to be identified under Article 16(4) was not 'backward class' but a 'class of citizens' which was inadequately represented in the services under the state (paras 355, 358, 389). BCs under Article 15(4) were BCs (paras 355, 358, 389). The two classes were different (para 357). Importantly, he held that social backwardness was not essential characteristic of BCs under Article 16(4)(paras 389, 352, 371). Sahai, J similarly held that the SEBCs might be BCs but not vice versa (para 583). While determining social backwardness, one cannot lose sight of the type of society, social mobility, economic condition and the political power (para 581). He also felt that backwardness should be both social and educational (para 607). Unlike his two dissenting colleagues, Dr. Thommen, J held that the BC mentioned in Article 16(4) was synonym for the class mentioned in Article 15(4)(para 267). He also endorsed the view that the BCs under Article 16(4) were composed of persons whose backwardness was comparable to the SCs and the STs (para 267).

Question 3(d): 'Means test' and 'creamy layer'

Reddy, J: In conferring benefits of Article 16(4), the 'creamy layer' can be and must be excluded (paras 790-793). Basis of exclusion should not be mere economic advancement but it should be social advancement (para 792). Sawant, J provided most elaborate opinion on the creamy layer issue. According to him, creamy layer should be measured in terms of forwardness of forwards and not forwardness of the backward sections of the said class (para 520). It should be judged on the basis of social capacities gained by the BCs to compete with the forward classes (paras 520-522). Social capacities themselves should be determined on the basis of their capacities for higher-level posts also (paras 520-522).

The issue was where the similarity of two sets of judgments ended since all three dissenting judgments mandated application of 'means test' uniformly. All three advocated usage of economic criteria for defining the 'creamy layer'. Singh, J held that economic ceiling shall be used to skim off the affluent sections (para 385). Sahai, J similarly held that annual income should be the criterion of 'creamy layer'[paras 629, 635(8)]. Dr. Thommen, J felt that economic level should be the guiding consideration to decide the creamy layer [para 323(6)].

Pandian, J was the only member of the Bench who held that the application of 'means test' was invalid. He also held application of 'means test' impractical [para 207(1)-(8)].

Question 3(e): Whether a class should be situated similarly to the SCs/STs?

Reddy, J: No (paras 794-797). Pandian, J held that it was not necessary for the BCs to be similarly situated to the SCs/STs to be treated as BCCs for Article 16(4) (para 126). Sawant, J not only felt that the BCs and the SCs/STs need not be similar but, significantly enough, also argued that if the BCs were similar to the SCs/STs, they should be treated as SCs/STs(para 447).

From the dissenting side, only Dr. Thommen, J held that the BCs should be comparable to the SCs/STs (paras 264-284).

Question 3(f): Adequacy of representation in the services under the state.

Reddy, J: Whether the representation of the BCs in the services under the state was adequate or otherwise was a matter within the subjective satisfaction of the appropriate government. The judicial scrutiny in that behalf was the same as in matters within the subjective satisfaction of an authority as stated in Barium Chemicals vs. Company Law Board(para 798). Pandian, J was a little more forthcoming on this issue. Whereas he too held that the matter was within the subjective satisfaction of the state, he added that it could not be challenged on the grounds of propriety, reasonableness and sufficiency (para 174). However, he too felt that existence of circumstances relevant to formation of opinion was a sine qua non (para 174). Sawant, J linked the issue of representation to giving due share of power to the BCs in matters of state. What was important in deciding the issue was backwardness of the whole class and not of some individuals (para 482).

Among the dissenting judgments, Singh, J held that only backward section of the class was meant to be represented in the services under the state (para 363). Not adequately represented was the test (paras 364-365). Sahai, J held that reservation cannot be on extraneous considerations and it should be objectively done (para 564).

Question 4(a): Whether BCs can be identified only and exclusively with reference to economic criterion?

Reddy, J: No (para 799). Both concurring judgments of Pandian and Sawant, JJ also answered the question in the negative. Pandian, J, however, held that the 'means test' was not practical (paras 207-208). Sawant, J too provided a very convincing reason for answering the question in the negative. According to him, reservation under Article 16(4) was not for economic upliftment (paras 482, 484, 492).

On the dissenting side, Singh, J held that the BCs can be identified solely on the basis of economic criterion (paras 386, 391). Sahai, J had already expressed himself on the issue while answering question 3(b) above. Dr. Thommen, J held that poverty by itself was no test of backwarndess (para 281).

Question 4(b): Whether a backward class can be identified on the basis of occupation-cum-income without reference to caste?

Reddy J: Yes (para 800). Others did not offer their explicit opinions on the issue.

Question 5: Whether BCs can be further sub-divided into backward and more backward categories?

The dividing lines among the members of the Bench on this issue changed significantly as Sahai, J disagreed with the idea. Sawan, J did not offer any specific opinion on the matter. The remaining judgments were agreed on the issue. Reddy, J held that there was no bar in sub-dividing the BCs (paras 801-803). He went on to give the illustration of AP where the BCs had been sub-divided into four sub-groups (paras 802). Pandian, J not only agreed with the idea but also felt that it was imperative to make sub-divisions (paras 524-525). He wanted the sub-classification to be made based on degrees of backwardness and not on economic criterion alone (para 552).

Question 6(a): Whether the 50 per cent rule enunciated in Balaji was binding rule or only a rule of caution or a rule of prudence?

Question 6(b): Whether the 50 percent rule, if any, was confined to reservations under Article 16(4) or whether it took in all types of reservations that can be provided under Article 16?

Question 6(c): While applying 50 per cent rule, if any, whether a year should be taken as a unit or whether total strength of the cadre should be looked into?

Question 6(d): Was Devadasan correctly decided?

Reddy, J: Reservations under Article 16(4) should not exceed 50 per cent (part V, para 809). Adequate representation did not mean proportional representation (para 807). While 50 per cent was a rule, it was necessary not to put out of consideration certain extraordinary situations in the great diversity of this country and people. Some relaxation in the strict rule may become imperative in far-flung areas where the population, being out of the mainstream of national life and in view of the considerations peculiar to and characteristic of them need to be treated in a different way was present (para 810). This type of relaxation must be done with extreme exercise of caution and a special case must be made out (para 810). If reserved category candidates get selected in the open competition field on the basis of their own merit, they would not be counted against quota reserved for the reserved categories: they would be treated as open competition candidates (para 811). *The rule of 50 per cent should apply for each year. It cannot be related to the total strength of the class, category, service, or cadre as the case may be* (para 814). Devadasan was wrongly decided and was, accordingly, overruled to the extent inconsistent with this judgment (paras 815-818 emphasis added).

Between the two concurring judgments, Pandian, J held that Balaji, a case under Article 15(4), was only obiter dicta and there should be no limit of 50 per cent on reservations (paras 178-179). He, however, did indicate that reservations under Articles 16(4) and 15(4) could not be extended to the totality of 100 per cent (para 182). The position of other learned members of the Bench on this issue was also noteworthy. Whereas the leading judgment held that adequate representation did not mean proportional representation, Sawant, J held that adequacy of representation shall have to be proportional to the population (para 495). In addition, he also held that adequacy shall have to be determined at all levels (paras 496, 505). Reservation percentage had to be adjusted to meet the needs of the forward and backward sections of the BCs. Forwards of the BCs cannot compete with the forwards (para 506). *He also allowed the state to vary percentage of reservation at different levels and fields (para 507). According to him, reservation can be made under Article 16(1) and total percentage of reservations under articles 16(1) and 16(4) can exceed 50 per cent but this would depend on the facts of each case (para 518, emphasis added).*

Among the dissenting judgments, Singh, J held that the reservation had to remain below 50 per cent (para 384). Reservation above 50 per cent would be unconstitutional. There could be carry forward of reservations but the percentage cannot exceed 50 per cent (para 3840. Sahai, J held that reservation could be given only in initial appointments [paras 859(7), 860(8)]. Consequently, reservation in promotions already provided shall continue only for five years [paras 831, 859(7)]. Minimum lower standard of qualifying for resefation was a must (para 837). Dr. Thoomen, J held that reservations must remain well below 50 per cent [para 323(8)].

Question 8: Whether reservations were anti-meritarian?

On this question, four members comprising the team that authored the leading judgment plus the two concurring judgments and Dr. Thommen, J from the dissenting side offered one opinion: the remaining two members from the dissenting side did not provide any explicit opinion. Reddy, J held that while the rule of reservation cannot be called anti-meritarian, there were certain services and posts to which it may not be advisable to apply the rule of reservation (paras 832-841). Sawant, J provided a very telling reply to those who argued that reservation was anti-meritarian per se by holding that minimum qualifying marks/conditions were there and there was fierce competition among the BCs (paras 403, 408). Dr. Thommen, J held that concessions in specialized institutions must not lower efficiency (para 298).

Question 9: Would the extent of judicial review be limited or restricted in regard to the identification of the BCs and the percentage of reservation made for such classes to a demonstrably perverse identification or demonstrably unreasonable percentage?

Eight out of the nine members of the Bench held that reservations were open to judicial review. Only Singh, J did not offer any specific view on the question. Reddy, J held that there was no particular or special standard of judicial scrutiny applicable to matters arising under Article 16(4)(para 842). Judgments of Pandian, Sahai, and Dr. Thommen, JJ were all agreed on this view. However, there were certain conditionalities attached by different judgments that need to be made explicit. Thus, Pandian, J held that there should be periodic review by the government itself. However, the general area itself was open to well-settled principles of judicial review (para 229). He also held that formation of opinion by the state was purely a subjective process. It cannot be challenged in a court on grounds of propriety, reasonableness and sufficiency. *But for drawing such requisite satisfaction, the existence of circumstances relevant to formation of opinion was a sine qua non. If the opinion suffered from the vice of non-application of mind or formation on collateral grounds or beyond the scope of the statute, or irrelevant and extraneous material, then the opinion was challengeable* (para 174 emphasis added). Dr. Thommen, J, similarly, held that reservations must stand the test of judicial review [para 323(ii)]. Regarding the subjective satisfaction of the state, he held that the state's opinion had to be based on reason and facts must be objectively considered and also competing claims must be suitably weighed in before making up its mind (para 286).

Sawant, J, however, took a different line on the nature of judicial review. Although he too felt that there was no special law for judicial review of Article 16(4) issues, it should be made only in demonstrably perverse identification of the BCs and unreasonable percentage of reservations (para 552). He also considered judicial scrutiny desirable if inconsistent criteria were applied for identification or wrong inclusion/exclusion or when the percentage of reservation was disproportionate or unreasonable (paras 529-531, 537).

Question 10: Whether the distinction made in the second OM between 'poorer sections' of the BCs and others was permissible?

The second OM, brought by the Narsimha Rao governament without as much as defining the economic criterion, had inserted the provision that would have enabled it to practice what the Court eventually overruled. The method employed was to use very laudable principle whereas the real intention was to deny the benefits of reservations to a large segment of the BCs, especially the one which took the leadership of its struggles against injustices. The other important objective was to make them quarrel among themselves. The Court did not like the dilly-dallying tactics employed by the Narsimha Rao government nor its double dealing and deceptive methodology. The ruling handed down by the leading judgment was, therefore, quite significant not only in its content but also by the route it eventually took. Thus, Reddy, J held that the distinction (between 'poorer sections' and 'others' among the BCs) was not invalid if the classification was understood and operated as based upon relative backwardness among several sub-categories (viz., backward and more backward) identified as OBCs (paras 843-844). This knocked the very rationale and the not so hidden objective behind this provision.

Among the majority-concurring separate judgments, Sawant, J held that benefits of entitlements under Article 16(4) would accrue only for the backward sections of the BCs. If sub-classification was made, separate percentage of reservations had to be kept [para 553(2)]. However, Pandian J, in a very elaborate and erudite delineation of the issue, held that this distinction was invalid and benefits of reservations should be available to all the BCs without application of the creamy layer test [paras 207-208, 211, 218, 243(8)].

The dissenting judgments upheld the distinction.

Question 11: Whether the reservation of 10 per cent of the posts in favour of 'other economically backward sections' of the people who were not covered by any of the existing schemes of reservations made in the OM of September 25, 1991 was permissible?

Eight out of nine members of the Bench gave their opinion on this question: only Dr. Thommen, J did not offer any specific opinion on the issue. Of the eight offering their opinion, seven (for giving the leading judgment, the two writing concurring separate judgments and Sahai, J from the dissenting side) held that such a stipulated reservation for the 10 per cent of the people was constitutionally invalid and was, therefore, accordingly struck down (para 845). Only Singh, J held it valid (para 394).

Question 12: The concept of positive action and positive discrimination

Four out of the nine members of the bench did not offer any specific opinion on this issue; the five who did, held that programmes under Article 15 (4) cannot be confined to programmes of positive action alone (para 846). Whereas the majority concurring judgments had earlier on held that Article 16 (4) was wider than Article 16 (4) in as much as several kinds of positive action programmes can also be evolved and implemented there under to improve the condition of the SEBCs, SCs and STs, on this point they stated that Article 16 (4) spoke of only remedial measure, namely reservations of appointments/posts (para 846).

Question 13: Desirability of a permanent statutory body to examine complaints of over-inclusion/under-inclusion

The Court directed that the Government of India and the state governments have the power and ought to create a permanent mechanism, in the nature of a Commission, for examining requests of inclusion and complaints of over-inclusion or non-inclusion in the lists of the OBCs and to advise the government which advice shall ordinarily be binding upon the government. Where, however, the government did not accept the advice, it must record its reasons there for (para 847).

Question 14: Should the matter go back to the Constitution Bench to go into the defects of the Mandal Commission Report?

Reddy, J: The Mandal Commission Report did not automatically vitiate the OMs and it had to be shown further that particular defect crept in to the OM as well (para 851). The Government of India had not accepted the Mandal Commission Report in its fullness, nor had the government accepted the list of the OBCs prepared by it in its entirety. What was at issue was not the validity of the Mandal Commission Report but the validity of the OMs issued on the basis of Mandal Commission Report. What the OM of August 13, 1990 did in effect was to enforce the respective state lists (para 851). The state lists were prepared both for the purposes of Article 15(4) as well as Article 16(4). Particulars served by the Union of India did establish that these state lists had been prepared after due scrutiny and investigation and stood the test of time and judicial scrutiny (para 851). Even if in one or two cases, the list was not prepared without appointing a Commission, it cannot be said to be bad on that account. The government, which drew the list, must be presumed to be aware of the conditions obtaining in their states/areas. Unless so held by any competent court or the permanent mechanism (in the nature of a Commission) directed to be created herewith, holds otherwise, the lists must be deemed to be valid and enforceable (para 852).

Due to the aforesaid reasons, it was not necessary to express any opinion on the correctness and adequacy of the exercise done by the Mandal Commission nor was it necessary to send it back to the Constitution Bench of five judges (para 851). Criteria adopted by the Mandal Commission for identifying the OBCs cannot be said to be irrelevant. Perhaps, there were errors in the actual exercise of identification, in the nature of over-inclusion or under-inclusion. These errors cannot be made basis for rejecting either the relevance of the criteria evolved by the Mandal Commission or the entire exercise of identification (para 854). The government could have, even without appointing a Commission, specified the OBCs on the basis of such material as it may have had before it (i.e., lists prepared by various state governments) and appointed the Commission to investigate their conditions and to make appropriate recommendations (para 855).

The directions made herein for constitution of a permanent Commission to examine complaints of over-inclusion or under-inclusion obviated the need of any such scrutiny by this Court. Perhaps, aggrieved can always approach them for appropriate redress. Such Commission, which would have powers to receive evidence and enquire into disputed questions of facts, can more appropriately decide such complaints than this Court under Article 32 (para 855).

Identification of the Mandal Commission Report with the OM of August 13, 1990 was basically erroneous. The OM did not incorporate the Mandal Commission lists of the OBCs as such. In truth and in effect, it incorporated the state lists. In social measures, the Court must give due regard to the judgment of the executive, a co-equal wing of the state and approach the measure in the spirit in which it was conceived(para 857).

Among the concurring judgments, Pandian, J held that the Mandal Commission lists approved by the government should be given benefit of 27 per cent reservation (para 235). Endorsing the line followed by Reddy, J, Sawant, J held that the government OM was not based on Mandal Commission lists only. The list, even if incorrect somewhat, may be implemented and a new Commission may be appointed to correct the list (para 551).

Among the dissenting judgments, Dr. Thommen and Sahai, JJ held both the OMs unenforceable (paras 325 and 635 respectively). Singh, J held Mandal Commission lists wholly unconstitutional and invalid (para 393-394).

Directions given by the majority-concurring judgments

The following directions were given by the majority-concurring judgments:

1. **Establishment, empowerment, equipping the National and state Commissions for Backward Classes to an operational position**

   1.1 There ought to be a permanent body in the nature of a Commission or Tribunal to which complaints of wrong inclusion or non-inclusion of groups, classes and sections in the lists of the OBCs can be made (para 847).

   1.2 Even if any new class/group was proposed to be included among the OBCs, such matter must be referred to the said body in the first instance and action taken on the basis of its recommendation (para 847).

   1.3 The body so created can also be consulted in the matter of periodic revision of lists of OBCs. As suggested by Chandrachud, CJ in Vasanth Kumar, there should be periodic revision of these lists to exclude those who have ceased to be backward or for inclusion of new classes, as the case may be (para 847).

   1.4 Such a body must be constituted both at the central and at the level of states within four months from the date of judgment (i.e., November 16, 1992) (para 847).

1.5 Such a body must be empowered to examine requests/complaints of the said nature and pass appropriate orders. Its advice/opinion should ordinarily be binding upon the government. Where, however, the government did not agree with its recommendations, it must record its reasons (para 847).

1.6 The body must be composed of experts in the field, both official and non-official, and must be vested with necessary powers to make a proper and effective inquiry (para 847).

1.7 It was equally desirable that each state constituted such a body which step should go a long way in redressing genuine grievance. Such a body can be created under Article 16(4) – as a concomitant of the power to identify and specify backward class of citizens, in whose favour reservations were to be made (para 847).

1.8 Strictly speaking, appointment of a Commission under article 340 was not necessary to identify the OBCs. Article 340 does not say so. According to it, the Commission was to investigate the condition of the SEBCs and difficulties under which they laboured and to make recommendations as to the steps that should be taken by the Union or any state to remove such difficulties (para 847).

1.9 They should become immediately operational and be in a position to entertain and examine forthwith complaints and matters of the nature aforementioned, if any (para 847).

1.10 It should be open to the Government of India and the respective state governments to devise procedures to be followed by such a body (para 847).

2. Correction and updating of the OBCs lists

The Government of India adopted the state lists as on August 13, 1990 for its own purposes but that did not mean that those lists were sacrosanct and unalterable. There might be cases where the Commissions appointed by the state government might have, in their reports, recommended modification of such lists by deletion or addition of certain castes, communities and classes. Wherever such Commission reports were available, the state government was bound to look into them and take action on that basis with reasonable promptitude. If the state government effected any modification or alteration by way of deletions or additions, the same shall be intimated to the Government of India forthwith which shall take appropriate action on that basis and make necessary changes in its own list relating to the state. Further, it shall be equally open – indeed the duty of – the Government of India to look into the reports of such Commissions, if any, and pass its own orders, independent of any action taken by the state government, thereon with reasonable promptitude by way of modification or alteration. It shall be open to Government of India to make such a modification/alteration in the lists adopted by way of additions or deletions, as it thought appropriate on the basis of reports of the Commission(s). This direction, in the opinion of the Court, safeguarded against perpetuation of any errors in the state lists and ensured rectification of these lists with reasonable promptitude on the basis of reports of Commissions already submitted, if any. This course may be adopted de horse, the reference to or advice of permanent mechanism (by way of Commission), which the Court had directed to be created at both central and state levels and with respect to which it had made appropriate direction elsewhere (para 853).

3. Specification of the bases of the creamy layer

Within four months of the date of the judgment, the Government of India shall specify the bases, applying the relevant and requisite socio-economic criteria to exclude socially advanced persons/sections ('creamy layer') from the 'Other backward Classes". The implementation of impugned OM of August 13, 1990 shall be subject to exclusion of such socially advanced persons ('creamy layer'). This direction shall not, however, apply to the states where reservations in favour of the backward classes were already in operation. They can continue to operate them. Such states shall, however, evolve the said criteria within six months from the date of the judgment and apply the same to exclude the socially advanced persons/sections from designated OBCs[para 861(B)].

4. Litigation regarding classification among the backward classes, creamy layer and implementation of the OMs only before the Supreme Court.

Any and all objections to the criteria that might be evolved by the Government of India and the state governments in pursuance of the direction contained in clause (B) of para 861 as well as to the classification among the backward classes and equitable distribution of benefits of reservations among them that may be made in terms of and as contemplated by clause (i) of the OM of September 25, 1991, as explained herein, shall be preferred only before the Supreme Court and not before any other High Court or other court or tribunal, similarly, any petition or proceeding questioning the validity, operation or implementation of the two OMs, on any ground whatsoever, shall be filed or instituted only before the Supreme Court and not before any High Court or other court or tribunal[para 861(c)].

5. Implementation of two OMs

The OM of August 13, 1990 impugned in these writ petitions was accordingly held valid and enforceable subject to the exclusion of the socially and advanced members/sections from the notified OBCs as explained in para 861(B)(para 862). Clause (i) of the OM of September 25, 1991 required to uphold its validity – to be read, interpreted and understood as intending a distinction between backward and more forward classes on the basis of degrees of backwardness and rational and equitable distribution of benefits among them to be valid, the said clause would have to be read, understood and implemented accordingly (para 863).

Conclusion

Whereas the declared objective of Indra Sawhney verdict was to delineate the law on specified issues authoritatively, the foregoing analysis makes it clear that at least on some of the issues it had failed to do so. Second, as pointed out in relevant sections of this analysis, it contained a few contradictions that could cause major consequential damage to the BCs. Third, a few observations of the Court – forming part of the obiter dicta – could well be taken as mandatory directions. Subsequent events have proved that all of these three have worked to the distinct disadvantage of the OBCs.

D. Creamy layer

D-11: Report of the Expert Committee for specifying the criteria for identification of socially advanced persons among the socially and educationally Backward Classes

Justice Ram Nandan Prasad — *New Delhi-110001*
Former Judge, — *Dated 10th March, 1993*
Patna High Court,
CHAIRMAN

Dear Hon'ble Minister,

I have the privilege of presenting the Report of the Expert Committee constituted under Resolution No.12011/16/93-BCC(C), dated 22nd February, 1993, of the Ministry of Welfare, Government of India. I and other Members of the Committee, namely, Dr. M.L.Sahare, Shri P.S. Krishnan and Shri R.J. Majithia, assumed charge on 23rd February, 1993 and from day one, we got down to serious work, as all of us were fully conscious that the Report has to be completed and presented by the 10th March,1993.

2. Needless to say, all of us had to work very hard to complete the Report and in this difficult and daunting task, we received full cooperation from you as well as all the officers and staff of the Ministry of Welfare. We justifiably feel happy that we have completed the work within the targeted time.

3. We hope that our labour will serve the purpose and our report will enable the Government to commence implementation of the policy of reservation for Socially & Educationally Backward Classes at the earliest, fulfilling the directions of the Supreme Court.

With regards,

Yours sincerely,
Sd/-
(Ram Nandan Prasad)

Shri Sitaram Kesari,
Minister of Welfare,
Government of India,
New Delhi-110001.

No. 12011/16/93-BCC(C)
Government of India
Ministry of Welfare
News Delhi, the 22nd February, 1993

Resolution

The Supreme Court, in its majority judgment in Writ Petition (Civil) No. 930 of 1990, Indra Sawhney and Others etc. Vs. Union of India and Others etc., delivered on 16th November, 1992 has, interalia, directed that "within four months from today the Government of India shall specify the bases, applying the relevant and requisite socio-economic criteria to exclude socially advanced persons/sections ('creamy layer') from 'Other Backward Classes' and further that the implementation of the impugned O M dated 13th August, 1990 shall be subject to exclusion of such socially advanced persons ('creamy layer)".

2. Having regard to the fact that a lot of specialized inputs would be needed to determine the bases viz., socio-economic criteria for identification of the 'creamy layer', it has been decided to set up an Expert Committee consisting of:

1.	Justice Ram Nandan Prasad (Retd.) High Court, Patna	Chairman
2.	Shri M.L.Sahare (Social Scientist) Former Chairman, U.P.S.C.	Member
3.	Shri P.S. Krishnan, Former Secretary (Welfare), Govt. of India	Member
4.	Shri R.L. Majithia, former Chairman Revenue Board, Government of Rajasthan	Member Secretary

to make recommendations to the Govt. of India in regard to the said socio-economic criteria. The Committee will also give recommendations on such other matters relating to the implementation of the judgement of the Supreme Court as the Government of India may consider necessary.

3. The Headquarters of the Committee will be located at Delhi.

4. The Committee will devise its own procedures in the Discharge of its functions. All the Ministries and Departments of the Government of India will furnish such information and documents and provide such assistance as may be required by the Committee. It is hoped that the

State Governments and Territory Administrations and others concerned will extend their fullest cooperation and assistance to the committee.

5. The committee shall submit its Report on the socio-economic criteria for exclusion of the 'creamy layer' from Other Backward Classes latest by 10th March, 1993.

Sd/-
(M.S. Pandit)
Jt. Secy. (M&BC)

ORDER

Ordered that a copy of the resolution be communicated to all Ministries/ Departments of the Government of India/State Government and U.T. Adminstrations.

Ordered also that the resolution be published in the Gazette of India for general information.

Sd/-
(M.S.Pandit)
Jt. Secy. (M&BC)

Report

The 9-Member Constitution Bench of the Supreme Court of India delivered its historic judgment in the reservation case relating to Socially and Educationally Backward Classes (Indra Sawhney and Others vs. the Union of India and Others) on the 16th November, 1992. The case arose out of several Writ Petitions filed to challenge the Office Memorandum dated 13th August, 1990 and the Office Memorandum dated 25th September, 1991 issued by the Government of India for implementing, according to the respective modes prescribed in the two office Memoranda, the recommendations for reservation for Socially and Educationally Backward Classes (SEBCs) in public employment, made by the Second Backward Classes Commission appointed under Article 340 of the Constitution, popularly known as the Mandal Commission.

2. The Supreme Court while upholding by majority the basic principle of reservation for the SEBCs have at the same time, directed that the socially advanced persons of the SEBCs category ought not to be given the benefit of reservation. In order to carry out this directive and specifying and determining as to who from amongst the SEBCs would be liable to be excluded from the benefit of reservation, the Government has appointed the Expert Committee as per Resolution No.12011/16/93-BCC(C), dated the 22nd February, 1993 of the Ministry of Welfare, Government of India. The Court has also directed that the reservation shall not become operative till the criteria to exclude the socially advanced persons are ascertained and specified.

3. Four Hon'ble Judges who were members of the Special Bench, namely, the then Hon'ble Chief Justice Shri M.H. Kania, Hon'ble Justice M.N. Venkatachaliah (now Chief Justice), Hon'ble Justice A.M.Ahmadi and Hon'ble Justice B.P. Jeevan Reddy delivered a common judgment written out by Hon'ble Justice B.P. Jeevan Reddy, and this is known as the majority judgment and we shall refer to it as such in our report. Hon'ble Justice S.R. Pandian and Hon'ble Justice P.B. Sawant have, no doubt, written out separate judgments of their own, but they have in substance supported most of the conclusions of the majority judgment and we will refer to the judgment of these two Hon'ble Judges by their respective names. The dissenting judgments separately written out by Hon'ble Judges T..Thommen, Hon'ble Justice Kuldip Singh and Hon'ble Justice R.M.Sahai have a common operative order and this is known as the dissenting judgment and we shall refer, if need be, to the same in the above terminology. When we refer to the ratio decidendi of the entire judgment we will be referring to it as the judgment of the Court.

4. It is necessary to bear in mind that the Court has accepted the principle of reservation on the reasoning that the SEBCs on account of their social and eductational backwardness are truly in need of reservation. In other words, the dominant consideration for upholding the reservation is the social and educational backwardness and not the income test, although in actual life it mostly happens that economic backwardness is a natural consequence of the social and educational backwardness. It logically follows, therefore, that for determining who from amongst the SEBCs shall be denied the benefit of reservation, the basis again would be the social and educational factors and only when a person's social and educational advancement is such as to put that person at par with the forward classes that he may be placed in the excluded category. In the majority judgment, it has been observed that only when a person's social and educational advancement is such that it totally snaps the connecting link of backwardness between him and other members of his community, he can then be said to be a misfit in his own class and so ought to be taken out from there and placed in the "Creamy Layer" category. The following passage in the judgment of Hon'ble Justice Sawant (paragraph 522 Judgments Today Vol.VI, No.9, 30th November, 1992) elaborates the point more succinctly:

> *The correct criterion for judging the forwardness of the forwards among the Backward classes is to measure their capacity not in terms of the capacity of others in their class, but in terms of the capacity of the members of the Forward Classes, as stated earlier. If they cross the Rubicon of backwardness, they should be taken out from the Backward Classes and should be made disentitled to the provisions meant for the said classes.*

Hence, while determining the criteria of exclusion we have kept in mind the guiding principle laid down by the Hon'ble Court as mentioned above.

However if economic betterment flows from social and educational advancement, then this also has to be taken note of.

5. Before specification of the actual determinants is taken up, it will be useful, nay necessary, to indicate and explain what exactly the term "Creamy Layer" on the rule of exclusion in actual application would imply. When a person has been able to shed off the attributes of social and educational backwardness and has secured employment or has engaged himself in some trade/profession of high status, as categorized by us below, he, at that stage is normally no longer in need of reservation for himself. For example, if a person gets appointed as a Class I Officer either on open competition basis or reservation basis, the question of excluding him on the ground that he forms part of the 'Creamy Layer' does not at all arise. But since he himself has come into the socially advanced category he will be in a position to provide the means, the equipments and the opportunities which are necessary for the uplift of his offspring form the level of social and educational backwardness. As such, the question of applying the Rule of Exclusion will arise only in the case of his offspring. In the present social set-up, when the joint family system, particularly among the upper strata of society, has been breaking up, we are regarding the family to constitute husband, wife and children and on that basis applying the exclusion principle. In other words, even if a person, say Mr. "X", has become a Class I Officer, this will not deprive his brother and sister of the benefit of reservation on the basis that Mr. "X" will or will not get the benefit of reservation shall depend upon the status of their parents.

6. Now we proceed to indicate and define the criteria for application of the Rule of Exclusion. The rise in social and educational status may result from different kinds of positions and placements in life and we shall deal with them one by one as noted below. To the categories listed below, the Rule of Exclusion will apply unless exceptions are specifically indicated.

I. Constitutional Posts

7. President, Vice-President, Judges of the Supreme Court and High Courts, Chairman/Members of the Union Public Service Commission and State Public Commissions, Chief Election Commissioner, Comptroller and Auditor General of India and persons holding Constitutional positions of like nature.

The Constitutional posts of Governor, Minister, and Membership of Legislatures, are, in the very nature of things, temporary and often transitory. Further, in most cases such persons would be covered in one or the other categories which have been enumerated in this report. Hence such persons have not been separately categorized.

II. Service Category

A. Group A/Class I Officers of the All-India, Central and state Services (Direct Recruits)

8. If either of the spouses is a Class I officer rule of exclusion will apply. Where both spouses are Class I officer and one of them dies the situation remains unchanged and the rule of exclusion will apply. However, if both of them die then obviously, the offspring are not only left to suffer mental agony and hardship in different ways but they are also denied the benefits and status resulting from the posts of their parents, and due to this disadvantage thrust upon them, the children shall not be denied the benefits of reservation, i.e., the rule of exclusion will not apply to them. It may be noted that if permanent incapacitation occurs which results in putting an officer out of service, then it shall be treated as equivalent to death so far as the application of rule of exclusion to the offspring is concerned. Hereafter, wherever death has been mentioned it shall include permanent incapacitation as stated above. To the unfortunate situation of death or permanent incapacitation of the only spouse who is in this category of service, or of both spouses who are in this category of service, an exception has to be recorded. If before the unfortunate event of death of either of both such spouses occurs, either of the spouses has had the benefit of employment in any international organization like the UN, IMF, World Bank, etc., for a period of not less than five years then exclusion from the benefit of reservation will continue to apply to the offspring.

9. It sometimes may happen that a lady who has got married to a Class I officer may herself like to apply for a job. If she belongs to SEBC category, she will not be disentitled by the rule of exclusion. The reason for saying so is that originally having been a member of SEBC, she carries with her the attributes of backwardness even after she is married to a Class I officer and though she may economically be in a better position, the initial attributes of social backwardness continue to linger on and will not get shaken of during the short period (in view of the age limit) which will be available to her for getting into any service employment. Therefore, we consider that such a person, more so because she is a lady (which in our society may be generally regarded as a weaker class) should not be denied the benefit of reservation. Therefore, to such a lady rule of exclusion will not apply.

B. Group B/Class II – Central Services and State Services (Direct Recruitment)

10. If both spouses are Class II officers then rule of exclusion will apply to their offspring. If only one of the spouses is a Class II officer it will not apply, but if a male officer from Class II category gets into Class I category at the age of forty or earlier, then the rule of exclusion will apply to his offspring. Where both spouses are class II Officers and one of them dies, it is better to

let the children have the benefit of reservation which means rule of exclusion will not apply; however, if either of the spouses has had the benefit of employment in any international organization, as indicated above, for a period of not less than five years, then even in the event of death the application of the rule of exclusion will not be taken away. But if by great misfortune both the spouses die, then the rule of exclusion will not apply to the offspring even in one of the spouses has had the benefit of employment in an international organization.

11. Where the husband is a Class I officer (Direct Recruit or pre-forty promoted) and the wife is a Class II Officer and the husband dies, the rule of exclusion will not apply. Also when the wife is a Class I Officer (i.e., Direct Recruit or pre-forty promoted) and the husband is a Class I officer and the wife dies the rule of exclusion will not apply but if the husband dies the rule of exclusion will apply on the principle that one of the parents, namely, the mother continues to be a Class I officer.

C. Employment in Public Sector Undertakings, etc.

12. The service category is not confined to employment under the Government only, whether at the Union or at the State level. The criteria enumerated above will apply mutatis mutandis to officers holding equivalent or comparable posts in public sector undertakings, banks, insurance organizations, universities, etc. and also to equivalent comparable posts and positions under private employment.

13. The evaluation of the posts on equivalent or comparable basis is bound to take some time. In order that this may not become a ground for postponing the implementation of reservation in respect of persons under this category, it is made clear that so long as the evaluation process is not completed and made operative, the income/wealth test under item VI will govern the persons under this category. In other words, even during the interim period, the employees under this category will get the benefit of reservation, and if any exclusion is to be made it shall be on the basis of the criterion under Item Vi.

III. Armed Forces Including Para Military Forces (this will not include persons holding civil posts)

14. The exclusion rule will apply at the level of Colonel and above in the Army and to equivalent posts in the Navy and the Air Force and the Para Military Forces. If the wife of an Armed Forces Officer is herself in the Armed Forces (i.e. the category under consideration) the rule of exclusion will apply only when she herself has reached the rank of Colonel; the service ranks below Colonel of husband and wife shall not be clubbed together. Even if the wife of an officer in the Armed Forces is in civil employment, this will not be taken into account for applying the rule of exclusion, unless she falls in the service category under Item No.II in which case the criteria and conditions

enumerated therein will apply to her independently. In making these recommendations, we have borne in mind the peculiar nature of the service and hardships faced by the members of the Armed Froces and the Para Military Forces. It has also to be remembered that there is no reservation in recruitment to the Armed Forces, which means that a person at the stage of recruitment in these services is denied the benefit of reservation even though it may otherwise be entitled to it.

IV. Professional class and those engaged in trade, business and industry

15. This will include persons not in service employment either Government or private, but those who are engaged in profession as a doctor, lawyer, chartered accountant, income-tax consultant, financial or management consultant, dental surgeon, engineer, architect, computer specialist, film artist and other film professional, author, play-wright, sports person, sports professional, media professional, or any other vocations of like status. All these persons for the purpose of determining whether they will fall in the disentitlement category or not will be governed by the income/wealth criterion as noted in Item No.VI. Likewise, persons engaged in trade, business and industry will be governed by the income/wealth criterion.

16. In a situation where the husband is in some profession and the wife is in a Class II or lower grade employment, the income/wealth test will apply only on the basis of the husband's income; in other words, the wife's employment will not be taken into account. If the wife is in any profession and the husband is in employment in a Class II or a lower rank post, then the income/wealth criterion will apply only on the basis of the wife's income and the husband's income will not be clubbed with it. The rationale is to avoid discouragement of women entering service or professions in a gender-discriminating society such as ours.

V. Property owners

A. Agricultural landholdings

17. It may not only be difficult but hazardous to prescribe any criteria on the basis of income from agricultural land holdings and this is borne out by the following observations in paragraph 809 of the majority judgment (Judgments Today):-

> "Further, income from agriculture may be difficult to assess and, therefore, in the case of agriculturists, the line may have to be drawn with reference to the extent of holding. While the income of a person can be taken as a measure of his social advancement, the limit to be prescribed should not be such as to result in taking away with one hand what is given with the other".

So we proceed to indicate the criteria on the basis of the extent of landholding.

18. If a person belongs to a family (father, mother and minor children) which owns only irrigated land, and the extent of irrigated land is equal to or more than 65 per cent of the statutory ceiling area, then the disentitlement will occur. It generally happens that a person holds different types of irrigated land. In such a situation, the different types of lands should, on the basis of the conversion formula existing, be brought into a single type of irrigated land as a common denominator and on the basis of such denominator, the above cut-off point of 65 per cent will have to be determined.

19. The rule of exclusion will not disentitle persons belonging to families owning only unirrigated land irrespective of the area of such land. This is on account of the constraints imposed on the risks implicit in unirrigated cultivation.

20. In the case of members of a family owning both irrigated and unirrigated land, the exclusion rule will apply where the pre-condition exists that the irrigated area (having been brought to a single type under a common denominator) is 40 per cent or more of the statutory ceiling limit for irrigated land (this being calculated by excluding the unirrigated portion). If this pre-condition of not less than 40 per cent exists, then only the area under unirrigated land will be taken into account. This will be done by converting the unirrigated land on the basis of the conversion formula existing into the irrigated type. The irrigated area so computed from unirrigated land shall be added to the actual area of irrigated land, and if after such clubbing together the total area in terms of irrigated land is 65 per cent or more of the statutory ceiling limit for irrigated land, then the rule of exclusion will apply and disentilement will occur.

21. On the basis of data supplied to us, we find that there is no ceiling law in the States of Nagaland, Mizoram, Meghalaya, Arunachal Pradesh and Goa and in the Union Territories of Andaman & Nicobar Islands, Lakshadweep, Daman & Diu. Apparently this is on account of the peculiar situation prevailing in these areas including topography, climatic conditions, etc. Under the circumstances the exclusion rule on the basis of land holding will not be applicable here. However, if at a future date ceiling law is enacted for any of such States or Union Territories, it would then have to be considered and determined if the rule of exclusion on the basis of land holding criterion will be made applicable or not and if so, in what manner.

B. Plantations

22. The plantations like coffee, tea, rubber, etc. which are not regarded as agricultural holdings will come under this category. Since they are not regarded as agricultural holdings, they are not covered by ceiling laws. Therefore, the criterion at "A" above cannot apply to them and there is no alternative but to apply the criterion of income/wealth under Item No. VI.

23. From the data supplied to us, it appears that mango, citrus, apple plantations, etc., are regarded as agricultural holdings and they will be covered by the criterion at 'A' above.

C. Vacant land and/or buildings in urban areas or urban agglomeration

24. To identify those who come under this category the criterion of income/wealth under item No.VI will apply. When we refer to a building it is made clear that the building may be used for residential, industrial or commercial purposes and the like, or two or more such purposes.

VI. Income/Wealth Test

25. This criterion is on the basis of income or wealth. We are conscious of the fact that in the Majority judgement and the judgements of Pandian and Sawant, JJ it has been clearly emphasized that when placing a person in the excluded category, it should be unmistakably evident that social backwardness has come to an end. Their Lordships have emphasized that unless there is social advancement to such a degree as to bring a member of the SEBC more or less at par with the members of the forward classes, he should not be denied the benefit of reservation.

26. Since the people of this country are engaged in innumerable types of vocations and callings, it is simply not possible to assess the degree of social backwardness or advancement by specifying each one of such vocations or callings and under these circumstances, we have to take recourse to the only discernible criterion available, namely the criterion of income or wealth. As such, this category may be said to be the residuary category. However, while prescribing the limit for this category, it has been kept in view that improvement in economic condition is so marked as to necessarily imply social advancement. Thus, here the rise in social status is presumption based indicating that it has followed necessarily from the economic betterment. This aspect of treating social advancement on the basis of presumption has been kept in mind in prescribing the limit of gross income. In this connection, the following passage occurring in paragraph 809 of the majority judgment may be usefully quoted:

> "The basis of exclusion should not merely be economic, unless of course the economic advancement is so high that it necessarily means social advancement."

(Vide Judgment Today, Vol.VI, No.9, Nov. 30, 1992)

Hence, persons having gross annual income of Rs.1 lakh or above or possessing wealth above the exemption limit as prescribed in the Wealth Tax Act will be excluded from the benefit of reservation. Only when such level of income or wealth has a consistency for a reasonable period will it be justifiable to regard a person as socially advanced on the basis of income. We consider a period of three consecutive years to be a reasonable period for the purpose of the application of the criteria under consideration.

27. In addition to the above, we have to say that the income/wealth test governs categories IV, V(B) and V(C) as stated earlier. For the remaining categories, namely, I, II, III and V(A), specific criteria have been laid down; however, if in these categories, any person, who is not disentitled to the benefit of reservation, has income from other sources or wealth, which will bring him within the criterion under item No.VI, then he shall be disentitled to reservation, in case his income–without clubbing his income from salaries or agricultural land–or his wealth is in excess of cut-off point prescribed under the income/wealth criteria.

28. Since the rupee value is bound to undergo change the income criterion in terms of the rupees as stated above will *accordingly stand modified with change in the value.* The modification exercise may, normally speaking, be undertaken every three years but if the situation so demands the interregnum may be less.

29. Persons working as artisans or engaged in the hereditary occupations, callings, etc., like potters, washermen, barbers, etc., are exempted from application of the rule of exclusion.

30. The Supreme Court judgment indicates that classifying the socially and educationally backward classes into two or more categories (backward, more backward, most backward and if necessary, further sub-categorisation) is not only desirable but perhaps actually necessary. As and when such categorization is done we feel that for those who fall in the two lowest strata at the bottom, i.e., the strata having the maximum backwardness, the application of the rule of exclusion may be kept in abeyance on the reasoning that the process of "creamy layer" formation will take more time in their case. While doing so the Government may examine its legal permissibility in terms of the Supreme Court Judgment.

31. We are aware of the strain imposed on candidates who seek certificates of caste, etc. The strain for them and the existing administrative machinery will be all the more where certification is required not only of caste but that the candidate is or is not affected by any of the criteria of exclusion. In order that SEBC candidates are not put to any harassment in this regard, we recommend that Government may make smooth and satisfactory arrangements for the issue of such certificates without delay and without any difficulty. Government have created a single window system for entrepreneurs applying for certificates and facilities for setting up new industries. Similarly, an appropriate single window system needs to be created at State/District level and necessary guidelines to be issued to see that correct certificates are issued promptly, and without harassment to the applicants.

32. We are also aware of the fact that in some cases false certificates of caste are issued to candidates who do not belong to the reserved categories.

In order to prevent this and to ensure that certificates of caste as well as exclusion/non exclusion criteria are factually correct, innovative arrangements such as transparency through steps like publication in the village/mohalla/ Panchayat raj offices, etc., may be considered.

Conclusion

33. In specifying the determinants and prescribing the different formulations therein, we have adopted a pragmatic approach and we have considered it prudent as well as desirable to err on the right side. In other words, it appeared while defining the criteria that a more strict formulation would have the possible effect of excluding more than it ought to, we have chosen not to adopt such a course. And for this approach of ours we find support from observations in different judgments of the Special Bench as well as from other sources.

34. Reservation has been adopted as a remedy for curing the historical discrimination and its continuing ill-effects in public employment. That being the object in view, the denial of reservation to any member of a socially and educationally backward class is, and has to be, treated as an exception. In identifying such an exception, i.e., applying the rule of exclusion, it has to be ensured that the ill-effects have been fully and finally eliminated and no grey zone is discernible. The nature of such an exercise itself makes the rule of caution inherent.

35. Hon'bie Mr. Justice Pandian does not subscribe to the "creamy layer" theory. Dealing with the off repeated criticism that the reserved posts are lapped up by the socially advanced ("creamy layer") among the socially and educationally backward classess, Pandian J. has quoted with approval the observation of Chinnappa Reddy J. in the case of Vasant Kumar. The relevant passage is given below:

> ".....That a few of the seats and posts reserved for backward classes are snatched away by the more fortunate among them is not to say that reservation is not necessary. This is bound to happen in a competitive society such as ours. Are not the unreserved seats and posts snatched away, in the same way, by the top creamy layers amongst them on the same principle of merit on which the non-reserved seats are taken away by the top layers of society. How can it be bad if rserved seats and posts are snatched away by the creamy layer of backward classes, if such snatching away of unreaserved posts by the top creamy layer of society itself is not bad?"

Pandian J. says "The above observation, in my view is an apt reply to such a criticism with which I am in full agreement."

(Paragraph 229 and 230 Judgments Today)

36. Another passage from the judgment of Hon'ble Mr. Justice Pandian justifies the rule of caution and of erring on the right side adopted by us. The passage is as below:

> "It is after 42 years since the advent of our Constitution, the Government is taking the first step to implement this scheme of reservation for OBCs under Article 16(4). In fact, some of the States have not even introduced policy of reservation in the matters of public employment in favour of OBCs."
>
> *(Paragraph 225 Judgments Today)*

37. In the above context would it not be proper, nay desireable to let there be acceleration and let some distance be covered before we apply the brakes?

38. What the Supreme Court has directed is identification of the "Creamy layer". This obviously means that we have not to take note of sprinklings of cream or the mere appearance of cream at the surface. Only when the 'creamy layer' is substantial and stable, formed after crossing the Rubicon of social backwardness, then and then alone can it be made the basis for disentitlement. In such a situation, can it be said that adopting a rule of caution and erring on the right side is not justified? Apprehension has been expressed, and rightly, that applying the rule of exclusion on the ground of social advancement may be counter-productive, in as much as by excluding those who have become capable of facing the fierce competition for appointment in the services what will remain are those of the socially backward who are simply not equipped and ready to face the competition and this will have the effect of many of the reserved seats being left vacant. The well-known writer and columnist. Mr. S.Sahay is one among many who have expressed such an apprehension. In an article entitled "A Moment of Truth" published in the Hindustan Times, Patna Edition dated 26.11.1992, this is what he has to say:

> ".....Approval in principle of the concept of backward and more backward is rational and so is the exclusion of the creamy layer. However, the consequences in the immediate future of the exclusion of the creamy layer, even though desirable and necessary, are not going to be happy.....The poor remain both poor and uneducated. Count the cost of education today and realize for yourself whether the boy or girl from the *chaupal* has ever the chance of getting higher appointment under the Central Government. Even now the reserved jobs for the Scheduled Castes and Tribes are not fully filled. Would the lot of the OBCs be any better, especially after excluding the creamy layer?'

39. We can cite many more such quotations and also give more reasons in support of the approach which we have adopted, but in our opinion what we have said above is sufficient to highlight the point under consideration.

40. We are happy to say that all the Members of this Expert Committee have worked day and night in a spirit of cooperation and understanding with each other. There has been free and frank exchange of views on almost every point dealt with in this Report and thereafter the Committee has arrived at a consensus on the basis of which the criteria have been laid down.

41. For its deliberations, the Committee had to gather and examine a large volume of literature and documents including the judgment under consideration (Indra Sawhney & Others), various other related judgments on the subjects, report of the Mandal Commission, report of the Chinnappa Reddy Commission, reports of the various State Commissions of OBCs/SEBCs. We have had also to look into a large amount of data furnished by the Ministry of Welfare itself or by other Ministries/Departments through the Ministry of Welfare which had relevance or threw light on the points under consideration.

42. It is not out of place to mention that formulation of the criteria for ascertainment of the socially advanced among the SEBC (termed Creamy Layer by the Supreme Court) in the manner it required to be done for practical application, is unique in the sense that to our knowledge, such an exercise has been taken up in this country for the first time. Though we find that in the Report of the Third Backward Classes Commission for Karnataka 1990 there is mention at page 174 Vol.I, of categories among socially and educationally backward classes who should be entitled to reservation, but we have undertaken an elaborate exercise to make the formulations as far reaching and comprehensive as possible. Of course, it may be desirable, perhaps even necessary at a future date, to give a second look to the criteria evolved by us and make suitable changes on the basis of experience of implementation and other relevant factors.

43. We are happy to place on record our gratitude for the unstinted cooperation extended to the Committee in the discharge of its work by the Hon'ble Minister of Welfare, Government of India, Shri Sitaram Kesari and by the Secretary and all other officers and staff of the Ministry of Welfare, and it is because of this, we have been able to complete this difficult task within the allotted short time.

Sd/-	*Sd/-*
(Ram Nandan Prasad)	**(M.L. Sahare)**
Chairman	*Member*
10.3.1993	10.3.1993
Sd/-	*Sd/-*
(P.S. Krishnan)	**(R.J. Majithia)**
Member	*Member*
10.3.1992	10.3.1992

D-12: Criteria adopted by the Government of India for the identification of creamy layer among the OBCs

Description of category	To whom rule of exclusion will apply
I. Constitutional posts	Son(s) and daughter(s) of: (a) President of India (b) Vice-President of India (c) Judges of the Supreme Court and High Courts (d) Chairperson and members of UPSC and State Public Service Commissions, Chief Election Commissioner, Controller & Auditor General of India (e) Persons holding constitutional positions of like nature.
II. Service Category A. Group A/Class I Officers of All India Central and State Services (Direct Recruits)	Son (s) and daughter (s) of: (a) Parents, both of whom are class I officers (b) Parents, either of whom is a Class I officers. (c) Parents, both of whom are Class I officers, but one of them dies or suffers permanent incapacitation. (d) Parents, either of whom is a Class I officer and such parents die or suffer permanent incapacitation and had the benefit of employment in any international organizations like UN, IMF, World Bank, etc., for a period of not less than five years. (e) Parents, both of whom are Class I officers, die or suffer permanent incapacitation and before such death or such incapacitation of the both, either of them has had the benefit of employment in any international organizations like UN, IMF, World Bank, etc., for a period of not less than 5 years. Provided that the rule of exclusion shall not apply in the following cases: (i) Sons and daughters of parents either of whom or both of whom are Class I officers and such

parent(s) die(s) or suffer(s) permanent incapacitation.

(ii) A lady belonging to OBC category has married to a Class I officer, and may herself like to apply for a job.

B. Group B/Class II officers of the Central and State Services (Direct Recruitment)

Son(s) and daughter(s) of:

(a) Parents both of whom are Class I officers.

(b) Parents of whom only the husband is a the Class II officer and he gets into Class I at the age of 40 or earlier.

(c) Parents, both of whom are Class II officers and one of them dies or suffers permanent incapaciation and either of them has the benefit of employment in any international organizations like UN, IMF, World Bank, etc., for a period of not less than five years before such death or permanent incapacitation.

(d) Parents, of whom the husband is a Class I officer (direct recruit or pre-forty promoted) and the wife dies or suffers permanent incapacitation.

(e) Parents, of whom the wife is a Class I officer (direct recruit or pre-forty promoted) and the husband dies or suffers permanent incapacitation.

Provided that the rule of exclusion shall not apply in the following cases:

Son(s) and daughter(s) of:

(a) parents, both of whom are Class II officers and one of them dies or suffers permanent incapacitation.

(b) Parents, both of whom are Class II officers and one of them dies or suffers permanent incapacitation, even though either of them has had the benefit of employment in any international organizations like UN, IMF, World bank, etc., for a period of not less than five years before their death or permanent incapacitation.

C. Employees in public Sector Undertakings etc.	The criteria enumerated in 'A' and 'B' above in this category will apply mutates mutandis to officers holding equivalent or comparable posts in PSUs, banks, insurance companies, universities, etc., and also to equivalent or comparable posts and positions under private employment, pending the evaluation of the posts on equivalent or comparable basis in these institutions, the criteria specified in category VI below will apply to the officers in institutions.
III. Armed Forces including Para-military Forces (persons holding civil posts are not included)	Son(s) and daughter(s) of parents either or both are in the rank of Colonel and above in the army and to equivalent posts in the Navy and the Air Force and the para-military forces. Provided that (i) If the wife of an Armed Forces officer herself is in the Armed Forces (i.e., the category under consideration), the rule of exclusion will apply only when she herself has reached the rank of Colonel. (ii) The services rank below Colonel of husband and wife shall not be clubbed together. (iii) If the wife of an officer in the Armed Forces is in civil employment, this will not be taken into account for applying to the rule of exclusion unless she falls in the service category III in which case the criteria and conditions enumerated therein will apply to her independently.
IV. Professional Class and those Engaged in Trade and Industry (i) Persons engaged in professions such as a doctor, lawyer, chartered accountant, IT consultant, dental surgeon, engineer, architect, computer specialist, film artist and other film professional, author,	Criteria specified in category VI will apply.

	playwriter, sports person, sports professional or any other vocations of like status.	
(ii)	**Persons engaged is trade business and industry**	Criteria specified in category VI will apply. Explanations: (i) Where the husband is in some profession and the wife is in a Class II or lower grade employment, the income/ wealth test will apply only on the basis of the husband's income. (ii) If the wife is in any profession and the husband is in employment in a Class II or lower rank post, then the income/ wealth criterion will apply only on the basis of the wife's income and the husband's income will not be clubbed with it.
V.	**Property Owners**	Son(s) and daughter(s) of persons belonging to a family (father, mother and minor children) which owns:
(a)	**Agricultural holdings**	(a) Only irrigated land which is equal to or more than 85 per cent of the statutory area, or (Prasad Committee recommended 65 per cent area). (b) Both irrigated and un-irrigated land, as follows: (i) The rule of exclusion will apply where the pre-condition exists that the irrigated area (having been brought to a single type under a common denominator) 40 per cent or more of the statutory ceiling limit for irrigated land (this being calculated by excluding the un-irrigated portion). If this pre-condition of not less than 40 per cent exists, then only the area of un irrigated land will be taken into un irrigated land on the basis of the conversion formula existing into the irrigated type. The irrigated area so computed from unirrigated land shall be added to the actual area of

	irrigated land and if after such clubbing together the total area in terms of irrigated land is 80 per cent or more of the statutory ceiling limit for irrigated land, then the rule of exclusion will apply and disentitlement will occur.
	(ii) The rule of exclusion will not apply if the land holding of a family is exclusively unirrigated.
(b) Plantations	
(i) Coffe, tea, rubber etc.	Criteria specified in category VI will apply.
(ii) Mango, citrus, apple plantations etc.	Deemed as agricultural holding and hence criteria at 'a' above under this category will apply.
(c) Vacant land and/or buildings in urban areas or urban agglomerations.	Criteria specified in category VI will apply. Explanation: building may be used for residential, industrial or commercial purpose and the like two or more such purposes.
VI. Income/Wealth Test	Sons(s) and daughter(s) of: (a) Persons having gross annual income of Rs.1 lakh or above or possessing wealth above the exemption limit as prescribed in the Wealth Tax Act for a period of three consecutive years. (b) Persons in categories I, II, III and V(a), who are not disentitled to the benefit of reservation but have income from other sources of wealth which will bring them within the income/wealth criteria mentioned in (a) above. Explanation: Income from salaries or agricultural land shall not be clubbed. The Income criteria in terms of rupee will be modified taking into account the change in its value every three years. If the situation however, so demands, the interregnum may be less.

Explanation: Wherever the expression 'permanent incapacitation' occurs in this schedule, it shall mean incapacitation, which results in putting an officer out of service.

D-13: Comparative analysis of creamy layer criteria recommended by the Uttar Pradesh Expert Committee and provisions made in Schedule II of Uttar Pradesh Lok Sewa Adhiniyam

Sl.No.	Categories or persons	Criteria of exclusion fixed by U.P. Act	Criteria of exclusion recommended by Expert Committee
(A)	Single Criteria Categories **I. Constitutional Posts**		
(1)	President, Vice-President, Judges of Supreme Court and High Courts, Chairman and Members of UPSC/UPPSC, Chief Election Commissioner, CAG	Not covered	Covered
(2)	Ministers in Central/State Governments, MPs, MLAs/MLCs	Not covered	Covered
(B)	Two or More Criteria Categories **I. Service Category**		
(a)	Sons and daughters of IAS, IFS, Indian Forest Service, other central services (direct or promotes)	(i) Income from salary of such members of service is Rs. 10,000 p.m.	Same
(b)	Group 'A'/Class I officers of any department (institute of Govt. of India or educational, research institutions, directly recruited	(ii) Spouse is at least graduate (iii) He or his/her spouse owns a house in an urban area	

	through UPSC/ other sources and not cover by (a).		
(c)	Officers of Defence/ Paramilitary Forces		
Forces not below the rank of Colonel or equivalent:			
(a)	U.P. Civil Services (direct recruites)		-do-
(b)	Group 'A'/ Class I officers of any state governament department (direct recruits and not covered under (d)		-do
	II. Professions Son(s) and Daughter(s) of:		
(a)	**Self-employed occupations** (doctors, surgeons, engineers; lawyers, architects, chartered accountants, other consultants, media and information professionals, share/stock brokers, film artists, professionals, running coaching institutions, etc.)	(i) Average income from all sources should not be less than Rs. 10 lakh per year in three consecutive years (ii) Spouse at least a graduate (iii) His family property (immoveable) should be worth Rs. 20 lakh	(i) Rs. 2 Lakh (ii)Rs. 10 lakh
(b)	**Business**	(i) Provided whose average income for 3 consecutive financial years	(i) Rs. 2 Lakh

		is not less than Rs. 10 lakh	
		(ii) Spouse is at least graduate	(ii) Same
		(iii) Immovable property worth at least Rs. 20 lakh	(iii) Rs. 10 lakh
(c)	**Industrialists**	(i) Whose level of investment in running units is over Rs. 10 crore and such units are engaged in production for at least five years	(i) Rs. 5 crore
		(ii) Spouse is at least graduate	(ii) Same
(d)	**Farmers, farmers-lanters etc., whose holdings are within the limits fixed under U.P. Imposition of Ceiling on Land Holding Act, 1960**	(i) whose income is Rs. 10 lakh in a year from sources other than agriculture	(i) Rs. 5 lakh
		(ii) Spouse is at least a graduate	(ii) Same
(e)	**Persons not covered in aforementioned categories**	(i) Whose income from all sources for three consecutive financial years is not less than Rs. 10 lakh per year	(i) Rs. 2 lakh

E. Listing of the OBC communities by the Central and State Governments

D-14: Number of castes/communities appearing in the Mandal, State and Central lists

S. No.	State/ Union Territory	Mandal list	State list	Central list: Common list as per NCBCs Advice	Central list: Included	Total (cols 5+6)
1	2	3	4	5	6	
1.	Andhra Pradesh	292	95	11	104	2
2.	Arunachal Pradesh	-	-	-	-	-
3.	Assam	135	126	123	-	122*
4.	Bihar	168	138	122	6	128
5.	Delhi	82	54	51	2	53
6.	Goa	18**	9	3	12	15
7.	Gujarat	105	127	79	18	97
8.	Haryana	76	72	60	14	74
9.	Himachal Pradesh	57	57	48	2	50
10.	Jammu & Kashmir	63	20	20	1	21**
11.	Karnataka	333	202	170	14	184
12.	Kerala	209	76	73	9	82
13.	Madhya Pradesh	279	112	78	13	91
14.	Maharashtra	272	355	207	7	214
15.	Manipur	49	4	4	-	4
16.	Meghalaya	37	-	-	-	-
17.	Mizoram	5	-	-	-	-
18.	Nagaland	-	-	-	-	-
19.	Orissa	224	202	175	18	193
20.	Punjab	83	68	62	4	66

contd.

S. No.	State/ Union Territory	Mandal list	State list	Central list Common list as per NCBCs Advice	Included	Total (cols 5+6)
1	2	3	4	5	6	
21.	Rajasthan	140	74	52	12	64
22.	Sikkim	10	7	7	3	10
23.	Tamil Nadu	288	252	170	9	179
24.	Tripura	136	42	35	8	43
25.	Uttar Pradesh	116	79	53	21	74
26.	West Bengal	177	60	14	40	54
Union Territories						
1.	A&N Islands	17	-	-	-	-
2.	Chandigarh	93	60	54	5	59
3.	Daman & Diu	-	-	19	-	19
4.	Dadra & Nagar Haveli	-	-	10	-	10
5.	Lakshadweep	-	-	-	-	-
6.	Pondicherry	260	260	259	2	261
	Total	3742	2551	2041	231	2271

* Rajbangshi Koch has been deleted from the list.

** Lohar, Tarkhan included by the GoI on its own.

F. Consequential proposals on empowerment of the OBCs in Plan documents

D-15: Development and empowerment of the OBCs as viewed by the Working Group of the Tenth Five Year Plan

In many respects, the Working Group Report (February-April 20010 is a qualitative departure in viewing the OBC problematic. It stated that the development of the OBCs cannot merely mean some alterations here and there or some humanistic ameliorations. It considered it necessary to start with an integrated vision of Indian society and within that frame the future of the OBCs in Indian society and with a clear understanding to where the OBCs have reached after centuries of India's socio-economic history, five decades of independent existence and nine plans of development. In so far as the attitude of the Central Government towards the OBCs was concerned, it termed this period of history as '*eight Plans of non-development and one Plan of marginal development*'. The Working Group undertook the exercise of framing a vision for the development and empowerment of the OBCs. Keeping both the constitutional and egalitarian human traditions in view, it felt that *the OBCs represent still, as in the past, the 'unfreedom' of Indian society in different forms.* In the economy, they substantially include a large number of castes and communities who were required to produce a variety of goods and provide a variety of services on terms unfair to them, thus *constituting different forms and degrees of exploitation.* They were – and still are – engaged in a very wide and rich variety of economic activities, and possessed considerable traditional technical skills pertaining to their spheres of economic activities. Different sub-strata of the OBCs face different types of threats and the *development and empowerment strategy for them has to follow differentiated approach, which is sensitive to different economic and social needs of communities placed at different levels of social and educational backwardness.* As indicated earlier, the Working Group categorized them into five sub-categories. The Working Group felt that the OBCs should secure economic self-reliance in their traditional activitites or in other diverse activities according to their choice, given full benefit of modern technology, access to finance, control over raw material resources, marketing facilities, etc., on terms which are fair to them, facilities for education, health, housing so that they cease to be placed at a disadvantage in the process of development.

Objectives and elements of development and empowerment of the OBCs indicated by the Working Group

(1) Removal of social backwardness.

(2) Creation of educational parity at each stage, phase, course of education.

(3) Removal of economic underdevelopment, dependency, inadequacy and exploitation by (a) strengthening the OBCs in their traditional occupations and securing for them control and mastery over their respective traditional fields of economy, (b) training and helping the OBCs to shift from stigmatized occupations, (c) to help the OBCs to diversity into a variety of modern occupations in proportion to their population, and (d) creating conditions in which the OBCs occupy due proportion in all types of occupations including those of social prestige.

Process and approach of empowerment advocated by the Working Group

Empowerment, according to the Working Group, has two aspects, viz., the *outcome* and the *process.* The outcome would consist of the realization of the foregoing objectives, listed earlier. The *process consists of the role to be accorded to the groups of the OBC communities in conceptualizing, formulating, planning, designing, implementing, supervising, monitoring and, where required, timely course-corrections of the schemes for and programmes of their own development.* What this requires is that the agencies of the state like the National backward Classes Finance and Development Corporation (NBCFDC) and its counterparts in the states should take up groups of communities instead of individual applicants and *dialogically evolve schemes appropriate to each of them.* In turn, this requires association of the concerned OBC groups in the entire decision-making process of problem identification, formulating areas of intervention including strategy and instrumentalities as equal and active participants in a democratic and transparent manner. Genuine and democratic occupational associations of the OBC communities should be associated in this dialogical process by all levels of state agencies. Quite a few of these associations require training and capacity building to delineate their natural and expected role. In actualizing this process, *the services of the national and state level commissions for the OBCs and the competent and professionally endowed citizens from amongst the OBCs, who would only want functional facilitation, functional empowerment and functional equipment, should be used.* The governments at the center and in the states can divest themselves of inappropriate work like processing and sanctioning individual applications of NGOs for funds and transfer this function to existing or new bodies.

Different OBC communities are at different stages and levels of backwardness in different socio-cultural-geographical locales. At one end of this continuum are the *vimukta jatis,* nomadic, semi-nomadic and non-SC *safai karmcharis*. Small in numbers, these have been ignored in terms of empowerment measures. At the other end are peasant communities having land resource base and skills. The traditional economy kept them at a disadvantage but they do retain certain amount of local initiative and freedom. Irrigation and power have enabled them to make greater progress than the other sub-categories of the OBCs but they remain distinctively backward – socially and educationally. Within this category one sub-group consists of regionally/locally populous and possessing relatively more of land resources whereas the other does not possess the advantage of numbers and whose command over land resources is meagre. The latter also includes tenant peasants.

The artisan castes/communities of artisanal or artisan-like producers are located between the *vimukta jatis* and nomadic/semi-nomadics and the peasant sub-categories of the OBCs. They provide various traditional services to the general community. This sub-category has no resources but possesses only the skills. This category has two sub-categories; artisans like goldsmith, silversmith and other metal smiths, etc. A peculiar form of occupational nomadism characterizes some of them (like the stone-cutters and marine fisherfolks). Even the water-related and riverbank communities like Nishads, though not occupationally nomadic, also represent the socially less esteemed and educationally more backward.

Since even the most advanced category of the OBCs is still backward, there is need for state support for their further advancement to reach the level of socially advanced sections of the Indian society. To the extent financial resources are a limitation, the Working Group recommended first preference total coverage (or as close to total coverage as possible) for the most backward sub-categhories of *vimukta jatis* and nomadic/semi-nomadics, followed by the middle or more backward sub-category of artisan, artisanal and service providing castes. The Working Group also recommended consideration of empowerment measures subject to the priority justified for the most and more backward sub-categories. It did not indicate that the peasant communities constituted in some states as much as 70-80 percent of the OBCs and left their empowerment subject to availability of scarce funds. This amounted practically to no viable empowerment measures at all. This is the technique that has been used against them by the Indian ruling classes in the post-independence period.

INDEX

A

Acquaculture Authority Bill, 1997; 10, 221

Adi Gram Samiti, 141

Aligarh Movement, 313

Aligarh Muslim University, 137

All Assam Nepali Students Union, 302

Anti-Brahmin Movement, 60

Artifacts of Bhavnagar Artisans, 272, 273

Artisan Families, 265

Artisan Households, 263, 265-267

Artisans in Bhavanagar, 258, 259, 268, 272, 274, 275

Arya Samaj, 136

Assam Gurukha Sammelan, 302

Assam Movement, 294

Aykya Sangam Movement, 313

B

Babar, 126

Backward Classes (Backward Castes), 60, 61, 64, 66, 246, 348-351, 354, 370, 371, 377, 386-394

Backward Classes Commission-
First, 349, 353-357
Second, 357, 379, 380
Third, 413

Backward Classes Movement, 64

Bahadur Nahar, 125

Bakshi Commission, 46, 60

Balban, 125

Balichakravarhi, King, 246, 247

Baluchistan, 186

Bangladesh, 335, 336

Bank A/c of Bhavnagar Artisans, 268, 269

Bhetghat Mitra Mandali, 304

Bikaner, 188, 191, 193

Birth Pollution, 163

Brahmins, 2, 23, 24, 27, 28, 48, 67

C

Caste System, 26, 28, 41

Central Karnataka, 284

Cherur, 28, 29, 32

Cherur Region (Cherur Area), 38-40

Chinappa Reddy Commission
Report, 166
Recommendations of, 167

Christians, 23

Coastal Regulation Zone
Notification, 221

Constitution of India, 348-351, 353, 354

D

Dalits, 3, 270

Dewasi, 184

Dowry System, 158

Dravidian Kinship System of South India, 227, 230, 238

E

Endogamy, 157

Entrepreneurship Development Institute, 272

Europe, 335

Ezhavas, 23, 26-31, 38, 40, 41

F

Firoz Shah, 126

Fishing in Goa, 211

Five Year Plans:
 Eighth, 17
 Tenth, 17, 423

Food & Agriculture Organisation of UN, 214

G

Gabit Community, 211

Gandhi, Mahatma, 65

Ghori, Muhammad, 126

GOs on Reservations for OBCs, 373

Goa, 212

Goa, Daman & Diu Marine Fishing Regulation Act, 1980; 10, 222, 223

Goenchea Ramponkarancho Ekvott (GRE), 9, 10, 214-217, 220-224

Golia Village, 296, 305

Gollas, 146-151, 168

Gulf Labour Market, 324

H

Handloom & Handicraft Industry, 261

Harijans, 39, 40

Hindus, 5, 27, 40, 122, 125, 129, 136

Hypergamous Marriages in Kerala, 34

Hypergamy, 193

I

IIM, 272

Illiteracy, 337

India, 138, 293

Indian Caste System, 22

Indian Council of Medical Research, 199, 200

Indian Nepalese, 295

Indo-Nepalese Friendship Treaty of 1950; 294

Inter-caste/Inter-religion Marriages, 158

Islahi Movement, 313

Islam, 126, 129, 130, 195, 311, 313, 322

Islamization, 122, 135

J

Jaisalmer, 188, 191

Jalari, 231-234

Jalari Kinship, 236, 241

Jamia Millia Islamia, 136

Jaswant Singh, Maharaja, 188

Jats, 124, 131

Joseph Commission, 369

K

KHAM Group (KHAM Alliance), 66

KK Narendran Commission, 16, 368, 369
  Report of 369, 370

Kakakalekar Commission, 16, 348-351
  Report, 348-351

Karnataka Backward Class Commission Report, 147

Kayasthas, 22

Khadi & Village Industries Commission, 272

Kiloj Parivar, 304

Kolis, 6, 45-55, 60-67

Kshatriya Sabha, 6, 58, 59, 67

Kshatriyas, 6, 23, 57, 58

Kurmis, 7

Kutch, 186, 187, 191, 194

L

Lanka (Sri Lanka), 189, 196, 322

Level of Education of Artisans, 262

M

Malaysia, 28, 25

Mandal Commission, 16, 46, 60, 201, 381, 395, 402
  Report of, 378, 387, 395, 396
  Recommendations of, 359, 379, 387

Marriage among Gollas, 154
  Rules of, 156

Marwar, 178, 186, 189, 191

Maulana Muhammad Ilyas of Nizamuddin, 137

Meo Community of Mewat, 8, 121, 122

Meo Panchayats, 137

Meo Women, 131, 133, 141

Meos, 122-143

Mewar, 186

Mewat, 121-126, 130-135, 138-141, 143

Muhammad daya Sabha, 314

Muslim Artisans, 263

Muslim Law, 128

Muslim League, 137

Muslim Rulers, 148

Muslims in India, 14, 23, 122, 135-139, 141, 143, 271, 308, 312, 324

Muslims in Kerala, 308-315, 317, 319-322

N

NGOs, 272, 426

NSS Organisation, 4

Nair Service Society (NSS) 368, 369, 372

Nambudris, 24, 26, 37, 40

National Backward Classes Finance and Development Corpn., 425

National Disaster Management Authority, 25

National Fish Workers' Forum, 217

National Forum for Catamaran, 217

National Instt. of Design Centre for Planning & Technology, 272

National Missile Test Range Centre, 7

National Research Centre on Camel, 198, 199
National & State Commission for Backward Classes, 396
Nayars, 23, 24, 30, 31, 36-41
Nepal, 296
Nepalese of Assam (Nepalese Community of Assam), 293-295, 301, 306
Nepalese of Nepal, 294, 295
Nepali Sahitya Parishad, 302, 304;
 Sabha, 304
 Sammelan, 304
Nepali Sewa Sadan, 302, 304
Nepali Surksya Parishad, 302
Non-Muslim Artisans, 272
North India, 238

O

OBC Artisans, 264
OBCs, 1, 2, 4, 7, 16, 17, 60, 62, 122, 167, 201, 246, 256, 263, 270, 359-362, 364-368, 371, 394-397, 412-414, 424-426

P

Pakistan, 137
Persian Gulf Countries, 21
Planning Commission, 17, 349
Polygamy, 155
Polyandry, 155
Primary Schools, 337
Problems of Bhavnagar Artisans, 268, 269, 275

R

Rabari, 184, 186-191, 195, 196
Raika, 172, 173-184, 186-201
Raika Women, 190
Raj Marwar Census, 180-182, 184, 193, 195
Rajasthan Canal Project, 173
Rajput Clans, 125
Rajputanization, 6, 191
Rajputs, 6, 7, 50, 52-55, 60, 65, 122
Raika of Rajasthan, 172, 174-183
Ram Nandan Pd. Committee, 369
Rane Commission, 61
Reservation for OBCs, 361, 362
Reservation for SCs/STs, 361, 362

S

SC Artisans, 264, 265
Salar Masud, 125
Samast Koli Samaj, 59
Samast Talpada Koli Samaj, 59
Sanskritization, 22, 25, 37, 38, 41, 47, 52
Saurashtra, 191
Scheduled Castes & Scheduled Tribes (SCs & STs), 2, 256, 263, 349, 350, 361, 362, 366, 367, 370, 377, 390, 394
Shudra Varna (Shudras SCs), 2, 4
Singapore, 28, 29
Sir Sayed Ahmad Khan, 313
Socially & Educationally Backward Classes (SEBCs), 381, 382, 386-389, 394, 397, 400, 402, 403, 405, 413
South Africa, 361
South Asian Kinship, 233
South India, 247
South Indian Kinship, 242

South Indians, 234
Special Protected Class Demand Committee (SPCDC), 302, 303
Sudras, 23
Sukuli Village, 296, 305

T

Tea Gardens, 335, 340
Third Karnataka Backward Classes Commission, 166, 167
  Report of, 147
Tribals, 270
Tuglaq Firozeshah, 125
Types of Housing Kaccha, 267, 268
  Pucca, 267

U

Udaypur Village, 296, 305

V

Vadabalijas, 248-250
Vaisyas, 23
Vijaya Rao (Maharaja of Jaisalmer) 188
Visvakarma Artisans in Karnataka, 289

W

Western Ghats, 146
World War II, 28

Y

Yadavas, 124, 148, 151